# ISLAM AND THE POST-REVOLUTIONARY STATE IN IRAN

# Islam and the Post-Revolutionary State in Iran

Homa Omid

**St. Martin's Press**

First published in Great Britain 1994 by
THE MACMILLAN PRESS LTD
Houndmills, Basingstoke, Hampshire RG21 2XS
and London
Companies and representatives
throughout the world

A catalogue record for this book is available
from the British Library.

ISBN 0–333–48446–0

Printed in Great Britain by
Antony Rowe Ltd
Chippenham, Wiltshire

---

First published in the United States of America 1994 by
Scholarly and Reference Division,
ST. MARTIN'S PRESS, INC.,
175 Fifth Avenue,
New York, N.Y. 10010

ISBN 0–312–10737–4

Library of Congress Cataloging-in-Publication Data
Omid, Homa.
Islam and the post-revolutionary state in Iran / Homa Omid.
p.    cm.
Includes bibliographical references and index.
ISBN 0–312–10737–4
1. Islam and politics—Iran.    2.    Iran—Politics and
government—1979–    I. Title.
DS318.825.O46    1994
306.6'97'0955—dc20                          93–31444
                                            CIP

This book is dedicated to my beloved mother, who set me an example which was hard to follow and impossible to forget, and to my adored father, who remained philosophical about my indiscretions and tolerant of our different views, politics and interpretations. Despite his constant fear for my life, he always retained his sense of humour and continued to be supportive, patient and loving throughout his life. This book is a small token of my immense love and gratitude to them both.

# Contents

# Acknowledgements

I am most grateful to RAWR for his encouragement and for cheerfully reading through the earlier draft of this book and finding out more than he ever wished about Iranian politics – a kindness well beyond the call of duty. His prompt and incisive comments have been invaluable. I should also like to thank PK for his detailed and extensive comments on Chapter 3, I very much appreciate his help and advice. Similarly many thanks to VP for information concerning the Iranian government's debt and foreign currency loans. Of course all mistakes, and misrepresentations remain entirely my responsibility.

I would also like to thank T.F. who accepted the very first book that I ever did and has remained optimistic and kind ever since; he continued to believe in the arrival of this book, despite the numerous delays and never-ending shifts of deadline. Now I will not need the special room for delinquent authors that he had reserved for me in the Tower of London!

Last but not least I would like to thank my children for giving me the time to work and MMD for holding the fort throughout. Without his constant help this work would not have been completed.

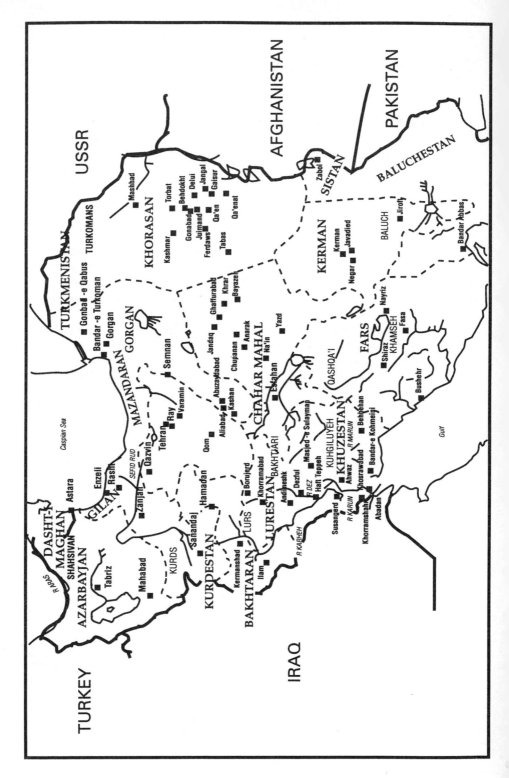

# Introduction

The 1979 revolution in Iran is a landmark in the implementation of revivalist Islamic policy. It enabled the Iranian religious institution, *ulema*, to set up the Islamic Republic and to claim to be the first truly populist *Shia* rule since the death of the first *Imam*, Ali ibn Abu Taleb.

The *Shia ulema* who have through the centuries proclaimed themselves to be the defenders of the poor and dispossessed, have traditionally contested secular rule in Iran and twice in the twentieth century have joined forces with the intelligentsia to form a revolutionary force. But the diffuse political aims of the revolutionaries – and the religious institution itself – have resulted in a political and economic flux which has continued throughout the decade.

The diffuse polity is a reflection of the hierarchy and the ambivalent approach of the *ulema* to the twentieth-century state formation in Iran. It is in part the result of the rejection of temporal power by the twelver *Shia*. In principle the doctrine accepts only the legitimacy of the rule of the Prophet and the twelve imams that followed and reject all other rulers as usurpers. The true believers should await the rule of the twelfth imam who will return from occultation to bring justice to the world. But such rejection has had to coexist with the reality of tacit collaboration of the *ulema* with dynasties of rulers in Iran.

The post-revolutionary State in Iran has been characterised by a profusion of administrative and theocratic institutions working, not always harmoniously, with the newly emerging revolutionary organisations, which occasionally duplicate, often compete with, or even work against, the older established bureaucracy. At the level of government there is a similar development of pre- and post-revolutionary decision-making bodies and command structures coexisting uncomfortably. In the first decade of the revolution, the inherent conflicts that arose were often resolved by the personal intervention of the Ayatollah Rouhollah Khomeini, whose directives were to be obeyed to the letter. With the demise of the leader of the revolution, the political containment of these differing chains of command is becoming more difficult. Such bureaucratic pluralism is rooted in the character of the religious establishment in Iran and therefore difficult to alter in the context of the current theocracy. The post-revolutionary political structure is the product of the fragmented, competitive and sometimes contradictory attempts of the *ulema* at curbing and controlling the process of secularisation.

It is the contention of this author that the form of conservative, theocratic, government that has emerged in Iran, does not only counter the vision of the revolutionaries, but also goes against the very core of Shiism. The conservatism of the religious institution has stripped Shiism of its embattled, egalitarian and progressive impetus. As a result, what has emerged over the past decade and a half is a stumbling, self-serving administration, that has failed its people and has chosen to forget the high-minded aims and ideals that Islam and Shiism had set.

After a long revolution, an eight-years war and untold bloodshed, Iranians – men and women – find themselves poorer, less educated, more numerous and, in the case of women, considerably more oppressed than before. This was a revolution that betrayed its cause and its people.

# 1 Ulema and Secularisation: Conflict or Coincidence of Interest?

The Iranian revolution of 1979 had considerable similarities to the constitutional revolution of 1906–9. Both reflected, in part, the continuing historical oppositional claims to legitimate ruling authority by the state and the *Shia* religious establishment, *ulema*. Devout Muslims agree that Islam provides both a political and an ideological framework. All that rulers can do is understand and implement the laws of Islam, as formulated by the Prophet, and recorded in the Muslims' holy book, the Quran, or as practised by the Prophet himself, *Sunna*. Since its inception, after the death of the Prophet of Islam, *Shias* have contested the right of caliphs and subsequently secular rulers to govern over the Muslim community, *umma*. The *Shias* claim that only the Prophet's cousin and son-in-law, Ali ibn Abu Taleb, and his direct descendent the Shiite *imams* have had the divine ability to understand Islamic law and implement it. Therefore they alone have had the right to rule over Muslims – a view that is contested by the Sunni majority who accepted the rule of the caliphs who were selected and supported by the consensus, *ijma*, of the Islamic community. The *Shias* contested the caliphate, and followed the teaching of the *imams*. After the occultation of the twelfth *imam*, in the ninth century, their *ulema* gradually acquired the mantle of the Prophet.[1] They extended the laws through interpretation and collected taxes, *khoms* and *zakat* from the believers. Over the centuries they managed to amass both wealth and authority and came to act as an alternative government, regulating the daily lives of the *Shias*.

Shiism was born of protest: the first *Imam*, Ali and his two sons Hassan and Hosein took up arms against the caliphs. The third Imam, Hosein, in particular, chose to sacrifice himself and almost his entire family on the battlefield in Karbala, in 680 AD, rather than accept the rule of the caliph, whom he denounced as a usurper. Ever since, the *imams* and subsequently the *ulema* have been seen as the guardians of justice and the protectors of the needy.

The *Shias* remained a minority sect until the sixteenth century, when the Safavid adopted the religion as the official religion of Iran. The Safavid, who claimed to be *seyed*, descendants of the Prophet, secured the support of the religious institution for their rule and stayed in power until the eighteenth century. In the nineteenth century the Qajar dynasty came to power and maintained a more or less cooperative relation with the *ulema* till the twentieth century. Throughout this period, however, the *ulema* remained, at least at the level of theoretical analysis, in opposition to the secular government.

In the late nineteenth century, the *ulema* chose to follow the more assertive *Usuli* school of thought which bestowed considerable power and authority on individual religious leaders, *alem*, as a source of emulation, *marja' taqlid*, and demanded obedience from his followers. The weakness of the Qajar bureaucratic structure, which depended very much on the grace and favour of the Shah and the ability of his appointees to extract taxes and impose laws,[2] and the widespread support the *ulema* enjoyed, particularly among the influential and wealthy merchant classes, enabled the religious institution to operate as an alternative source of power.

The Qajars ruled over a country which was divided along tribal groupings and allegiances, with the well-armed tribes protecting the borders. The rudimentary state bureaucracy was largely directed towards collection of taxes by appointed tax collectors, *tuyuldar*, to fund the royal household and to pay for the secular, *urf*, law courts, and the enforcement of their judgements. The king, shah, was an absolute ruler, but, as Abrahamian notes:

> although the contemporary visitor was struck by the extensive powers of the Qajars, the modern observer is struck by the intriguing fact that they had no effective instrument for enforcing their power.[3]

Thus, whereas in theory the shah had absolute power, in practice he was unable to ensure the enforcement of his wishes.[4] He governed, assisted by a Prime Minister who acted as the intermediary between the shah and the implementation of his will. Towards the end of the century a number of reformist Prime Ministers attempted to initiate a ministerial decision-making body and establish a degree of central control. Parallel to the secular structures, the religious establishment had its own legal, financial and educational institutions. They ran the religious, *sharia*, courts and carried out social and charitable services.

This chapter addresses the ideological development of the *ulema's* oppositional position under the Qajar and finally their active participation in the constitutional revolution of 1906–9 which paved the way for the establishment of a secular monarchy in Iran.

## ULEMA AND THE STATE

Within Islamic discourse, the *Shias* may be singled out as representing the most ardent opponents of secularism. Islam, itself envisaged as a political framework with God as the sole legislator, would always find any transfer of legislative power to civil institutions difficult. The state exists only to protect and apply the law as stated by God, through his Prophet Mohamad and recorded either in the Quran or in *Sunna*, the customs and practices of the Prophet, which form the basis of *Sharia*, which is the correct Islamic path for Muslims to follow. But, whereas the majority of Sunni Muslims have, since the death of the Prophet, found a *modus vivendi* with the rule of a succession of caliphs,[5] the *Shias* have always contested the legitimacy of all subsequent temporal rulers. The only exception is the fourth caliph, Ali ibn Abu Taleb, who was Mohamad's cousin and son-in-law and became the first Imam of the *Shias*. The imams are divinely inspired and, like Mohamad and his daughter Fatima, are *masoum*, protected against sin. They are able to delineate the clear path of Islam; to them belongs all legitimate rule. So long as they were alive, they were able to interpret the laws of Islam and create new precedence and practices in accordance with the *Sharia*. Thus even though, other than the first Ali ibn Abu Taleb, no imam ever held the reins of government, the imamate provided an alternative, heaven-inspired government for the *Shias*. But the line of succession of the *Imams* came to an abrupt end in 874 AD with the occultation of the 12th *Imam*, Mohamad al-Mahdi. With him disappeared all possibility of the legitimate exercise of power in this world. The theory of imamate deprives a temporal ruler of ultimate legitimacy, since universal authority rests with the *Imam* and no government could claim to be anything other than, at best, the protector of the land of Muslims.

Yet, despite its opposition, and the absence of any mechanism to legitimise temporal power, *Shias* have both tacitly and expressly accepted the rule of a long line of caliphs. They have chosen to obey the commandment of the *Quran* that believers must obey God, the Prophet and 'those in power'.[6] They have accepted government as a social necessity and obedience to those who govern as a means of securing the protection and execution of the *Sharia*.[7] But although the caliph was the absolute master of Muslim society he did not have the right to legislate. He could only issue decrees, within the limits of the *Sharia*, and hence Islamic law, to meet administrative and judicial needs of the day. So long as his rule protected Islam, and was not perverted to serve the personal interest of the ruler, the believers were to obey. There have been repeated attempts by Islamic scholars to reconcile the ideological opposition of the *Shias* with the reality of the existence of the State. They have had to accept the rule of a temporal power to secure order and prosperity even though they may continue to deny its ultimate legitimacy. 'And, in an apparent paradox, this leads to *de facto* support for the temporal ruler because he is the guarantor of the commonweal.'[8] A caliph may well need to use coercion. So long as the coercive power is used to sustain Islamic dictum, then the justice and righteousness of society could well depend on the presence of a powerful ruler.[9] Hence the recommendation of leading *ulema*, religious leaders, 'to pay allegiance to a type of ruler who is called "righteous, just ruler" (as *sultan al-haqq al-adil*) who is evidently not the same person as the *Imam*'.[10] Such acquiescence, however, has always been conditional on the essential need for justice to be seen as an integral part of the exercise of power.

Thus in essence Shiism has contained the kernel of resistance and rebellion against injustice and oppression. Yet in practice this revolutionary potential had been rarely realised, and it was by its quietism that Shiism was best recognised. The reality of *Shias'* history, where they had for the most part formed a threatened minority, has contributed to the creation of such acquiescence. They chose the acceptable option of not revealing their opposition to the rule in order to survive. Thus, they combined 'a denial of legitimacy with a quietist pattern and abstention from action'[11] and remained 'unyielding to *de facto* authority'.[12] Accordingly, their religious leaders, the *Shia ulema*, have on the whole retained a degree of separation from the state. But their emergence as an alternative source of political power and the protectors of the people against *zolm*, injustice, is very much a nineteenth-century experience and one that places them in a difficult position *vis-à-vis* secularism and constitutionalism. The difficulty is in part caused by the success of the Usuli school of thought which placed the *ulema*, religious leaders, in a powerful place as unquestioned authorities delineating the clear path of virtue for true believers to follow. In part it is the result of the *ulema's*, religious leaders, decision to question openly the legitimacy of the state and the Qajar dynasty's rule in Iran.

## USULI AND AKBARI SCHOOLS

Islam does not bestow sanctity on the rulers, nor for that matter on the *ulema*: the religious establishment. They are respected for their learning, but are not regarded as having any spiritual power or worldly authority. They are not permitted to administer sacraments, pardon sins or pronounce communion.[13] Nevertheless as the *ulema* acquired the mantle of protection of the unprotected and began emerging as an alternative government, so, to some, they acquired some of the charisma and authority of the *imam*. This development was caused by the leading part they played in delineating the correct path for Muslims to follow and by their ability to interpret the *Quran* and the rulings of their religion according to the needs of the time. In practice, the ensuing status contradicted the denial of worldly authority to all but the imams so that Iran found itself with:

> something like an official clergy, exclusively concerned with legality and jurisprudence, to such a point that original Shiism, in its essence gnostic and theosophic, has, so to speak, to hide itself.[14]

But this official and legal attitude was very much a characteristic of late Shiism,[15] and associated with the success of the Usuli school which demanded firm allegiance to the *mujtahed*, leading *alem*, religious leader, whose teachings the faithful were to follow. The gnostic character of Shiism was more evident in the Akbari school of thought which was primarily literalist, emphasising transmission of knowledge, *naql*, rather than the use of interpretive reason, *aql*.[16] They saw the sacred texts as sufficiently explicit, thus denying the need for the exercise of independent judgement by the *ulema*, clergy. Even though the *imams* had not prepared the way for such a role to emerge,[17] gradually the *ulema*, assumed among their own ranks the role of deputies of the imam. As history moved on and the process of interpretation evolved, so did the importance of *ejtehad*, 'the search for a correct opinion... deducing... the specific provisions of religious law, *fru'*, from its principle, *usul*, according to logical proof'.[18] Eventually the *ulema* came to act as if *ex-ante* they had been appointed by the *imam*.[19] In so doing they were helped by Aqa Mohamad Baqer Behbahani (1705–1803) who reorganised the more aggressive *Usuli* position.[20] In particular, the school affirmed the need for the faithful to follow the teachings of a *mujtahed*, a leading clergy man who exercised *ejtehad*. Although such a religious leader was not thought to be infallible, the believers should nevertheless follow his teaching Since those who have not attained high levels of religious education are not permitted to engage in religious discourse and interpretation, they must of necessity follow the teachings of a living *mujtahed*, religious leader, of their choice. This duty was defined, by leading *mujtahedin* such as Morteza Ansari, as unavoidable for all *Shias*.[21]

In accordance with the collective character of the religious institution, and its informal nature, there is no clear institutional ladder of promotion for emerging as a *mujtahed*. Access is relatively easy and open and based on merit. A good student of religion can, on the recommendation of his teacher move on from provincial schools to higher institutes of religious learning, *maddares*, in centres such as Qom, Isfahan or Najaf. Women, however, were not allowed to follow this route and very few have been allowed to become learned religious figures. What is required is for a student of religion, *talabeh*, to excel at learning and to gain the support of his teacher who would be an established *mujtahed*. On the recommendation of his tutor, such a student may be able to continue, to write a thesis, to get involved to a greater degree in the discussions and scholarly activities at a centre of learning and gradually emerge as a *mujtahed* in his own right. The *mujtahedin*, religious leaders, in turn accord respect to a leading member, the *marja' taqlid* who emerges as a supreme source for emulation. Once more there is no obvious mechanism for reaching this position and at times there is no single, universally recognised *marja*, but rather a fluid hierarchy which is neither elected, nor appointed,[22] but which derives its status from piety and learning. However, the emphasis on the necessity for believers to follow a living *mujtahed*, does allow the possibility of the eldest and most respected of *mujtahedin* to emerge as the *marja*. There have been times, when an eminent *mujtahed*, such as Sheikh Morteza Ansari in the mid-nineteenth century, has emerged as the undisputed *marja*, for all *Shias*. But the precedents set by him have not always been followed, and frequently there has not been such an obvious leader uniting Iranian, Turkish, Arab and Indian *Shias*.[23]

The success of the *Usuli* school provided the *ulema*, with a basis to demand that the ruler should follow the dictate of the *alem*, clergyman, and not *vice versa*. The ability of the religious institution to exploit this power, however, was linked directly with the inability of the central State to impose its will.

With the decline of the authority of the Qajar, the *ulema* began exercising their authority and claiming the *Usuli* position which gave a greater authority to the legal and political ruling of a *mujtahed* than to that of any temporal ruling by the State. The *ulema* contrasted their own power, confirmed by their 'constant presence before God', with the temporary rule and the ranks bestowed by mere monarchs.[24] In particular the religious establishment continued to hold the judicial reins. They presided over the religious (*Sharia*) courts which dealt primarily with disputes or litigations of a personal or commercial nature. Gradually, however, they extended their ruling to include aspects of common law, *urf*, normally dealt with by the State. The State held the means of enforcement of its laws, through municipal or village leaders; the *ulema* enforced their decisions with the help of their own private armies, *lutis*. These were devout followers who benefited from the alms that the *ulema* could disburse, or exchanged their strong arms for the religious establishment's protection in times of need.[25] In addition the *ulema* could enforce their ruling by public denouncement of the guilty party as an 'infidel' and mobilisation of social opinion against such a person. Or they could issue a decree, *fatwa*, which had to be obeyed by the *Shia* believers. The combination of moral and legal authority enabled the *ulema* to shoulder the mantle of power and they began acting as political leaders.[26] Gradually the government came to depend on the religious establishment to provide it with an 'effective ideological underpinning'.[27] Thus by the end of the nineteenth century the *ulema* emerged as 'a central force, which could be allied with, manipulated, combated, but never ignored'.[28]

## ULEMA, WEALTH AND POWER

By the end of the nineteenth century the *ulema* were involved at every stage of a Muslim's life in Iran:

> Matters of personal law were decided by them, title deeds were written by them, and attested before them; disputes were often settled by them; commercial affairs which required the witnessing of documents were referred to them; and education was largely in their hands. Functions connected with birth, marriage and death all required the assistance of the *ulema*.[29]

In addition, they were entrusted with deposits, the estates of minors, guardianship of orphans and the administration of private and religious endowments, *oqaf*.[30]

The religious institution itself remained diffuse and multidimensional in its opinions and activities and in the extent of power that it could exercise. The success and prosperity of members of the religious institution varied considerably. The hierarchy was flexible and extensive and ranged from the very rich to extremely poor individuals. The more respected an *alem*, the greater his access to wealth and power. The believers pay the *mujtahed* religious dues, *zakat*, amounting to about one-fourth of his or her surplus material goods and *khoms*, one-fifth of the yearly income, surplus to expenditure. A part of these dues could legitimately be claimed by those collecting and disbursing them. Half of *khoms*, religious tax, must be paid by the *mujtahed* to the descendant of the Prophet and the rest spent at his discretion. The greater his assets, the better would be his school, the more generous his payment to the needy and therefore the higher his status in society. So long as the *ulema* retained their spiritual and ideological supremacy, they remained well-placed for the accumulation of wealth.

Each of these sources could bring a substantial income for a well-placed religious leader. It has been estimated that by the end of the nineteenth century *oqaf* for example was worth 4 million *tumans*, (about £1 million)[31] which was about half the total state revenue.[32] Fees from legal transactions and government religious law, *shar*, business provided important sources of wealth for the eminent *mujtahedin*. Thus they were able to maintain both economic and political independence from the State, without fear of impoverishment. Morteza Ansari, for example, is reported as having received and disbursed 200 000 tumans (about £50 000) in alms and voluntary contributions.[33] In addition some of the *ulema* invested in land and in trade or accepted a stipend from the state. A few became extremely wealthy and powerful. One of the richest ever is Sheikh Mohamad Baqer Shafei who lived in Isfahan during the first half of the nineteenth century. He owned more than 400 caravanserais, and about 2000 shops in Isfahan, Burujerd, Yazd and Shiraz. In his time he condemned some 80–100 people to death for offences against *Sharia* laws.[34] Though exceptional, Sheikh Mohamad was not alone. By 1900 there were one or two *alem* among the 134 leading creditors of the Tehran branch of the Discount Loan Bank with assets of 5000 *tumans* (about £250) or more.[35]

It was not so much wealth, but influence and power that characterised the *ulema* during the late eighteenth and nineteenth century in Iran. Wealth enabled a *mujtahed* to pay for a large group of supporters. These were either his students, *tolab*, or his popular followers or gangs, *lutis*. The students, who subsequently became *ulema* in their own right, transmitted the teachings of a *mujtahed* from the pulpits. The larger the numbers of students, the more important a *mujtahed*. The *lutis* represented his executive and coercive powers. They were able to ensure that his rulings in the religious courts were enforced and when necessary helped in the collection of religious dues.[36]

By the end of the nineteenth century the *mujtahedin* were by and large financially independent of the government, and politically powerful. Nevertheless for most of the lesser known *ulema* the financial basis was less than secure; some engaged in trade and money-lending, others accepted pensions, funds or even government stipends.[37] Although many did not accept direct government appointment, they did accept government funds and endowments, *vaqf*. A number had hereditary pensions and many were fief-holders, *tuyuldar*; that is the entitlement to collect taxes in a given area, or to the revenue from a post or crown lands.[38] Furthermore the State appointed a religious leader, *Sheikh al Islam*, to supervise religious courts in each town and another religious leader, *Emam Jomeh*, to lead the Friday prayers and pronounce the Friday sermons. Although acceptance of such posts did not necessarily undermine the respect accorded to these religious leaders or diminish their independence, it may have contributed to their quietism.

But perhaps the most important power-base for the *ulema* has always been their close connections with the merchants and the *bazaar*. The Prophet Mohamad began his career as a representative of a wealthy merchant, Khadija, who subsequently married him. Much of the early Islamic dictum was formulated during her lifetime and merchants were given a respect, that they have continued to enjoy, among Muslims. Merchants formed the most important source of religious taxes, endowments and financial security for the *ulema*. Most of the *ulema* had close ties with the merchants.

Up to the turn of the century, the merchant classes had formed an important part of the Iranian economy, and were central to the process of accumulation of capital and funding of growth:[39]

> In the traditional economy the bazaar was more than a market-place; it was the granary, the workshop, the bank and the religious centre for the whole society. It was there that landowners sold their crops, craftsmen manufactured their wares, traders marketed their goods, those in need of money raised loans, and it was there that businessmen built and financed mosques and schools.[40]

At the same time, the merchants' commercial and daily lives were regulated and facilitated by the *ulema*. This symbiotic relation, often enforced by intermarriage, ensured the support of the *ulema* for the merchants when the latter's interest began to be threatened by penetration of foreign capital. This was all the more critical since European firms were allowed to have a preferential tariff for their imports, which automatically gave them an advantage over Iranian merchants.[41]

Foreign powers, particularly Russia and England, had for some time sought to extend their control over the country and had gradually come to dominate certain aspects of political life. Their authority was extensive and so was their animosity to each other. So much so that Naser a Din Shah is reported to have remarked:

> should I wish to go out for an exertion or a shooting expedition in the north, east and west of my country, [which were under Russian influence], I must consult the English, and should I intend to go south [under British influence], I must consult the Russians.[42]

Each sought greater economic and political influence and both backed their own nationals or governmental projects for 'developing' the Iranian economy. This was achieved through concessions granted by the shah.

Interaction with Western capitalism, on unequal terms, gradually eroded traditional craft-based production of textiles, silks and woollens in Iran, though increased demands for carpets had encouraged the growth of this industry with both Iranians and foreign merchants involved in its export. But the development of this sector did not compensate for the deterioration of traditional craft-based industries. Iranian currency, which was based on silver, took a tumble with the dramatic fall of silver prices after 1870. This fall, combined with the debasement of the coinage by the Iranian government, resulted in an estimated 410 per cent fall in the external value of the currency in the nineteenth century.[43] At the same time increasing exports and decreasing imports led to a growing trade deficit.

To counter the ever-worsening terms of trade, and to pay for the foreign travels on which he had embarked, the Qajar king, Nasseredin Shah, began granting generous concessions to foreign nationals. In 1872 a wide-ranging economic concession to Baron Julius de Reuter gave him the right to all mineral extraction for a modest payment to the Iranian crown. But the agreement met with resistance from local entrepreneurs and the clergy and from Anis el Doleh, the powerful wife of the Shah, who was instrumental in engineering an excuse for Nasseredin shah to revoke the concession.

A number of smaller concessions were granted to Russia and British interests and in 1890 the shah gave a tobacco monopoly to British. This meet with violent protests throughout the country. Tobacco was a local product, and a mainstay of some merchants' and land owners' income. The old clergy/merchant alliance came once more to the fore and a *fatwa*, religious command, was issued against the use of tobacco. The boycott was total: even in the shah's harem his wives broke their water pipes and refused to smoke. Mass demonstration and protests eventually obliged the government to cancel the concession. But the Iranians had to pay exorbitant compensations to the British which resulted in £500 000 foreign debt. Iranians's first successful attempt at negotiating politics at the street level and through mass demonstrations resulted in Iran's first foreign debt.[44]

By the end of the nineteenth century, the country was in the grip of economic difficulties, with an ever-increasing debt burden, rising inflation and devaluation of currency. To deal with the problems the state embarked on a slow but steady process of modernisation and centralisation of trade and finance. At the same time they agreed to hand over more and more of the national resources to the British, Russian and Belgian interests under various concessions.

The merchants feared the transfer of the economic affairs of the country to the foreigners. This view was shared by the clergy who saw a threat to its hold on education, law and social control.[45] They effectively opposed the Reuter concession in 1873, and the tobacco concession in 1891.[46] But they failed to counter the oil concession of 1901 which entitled a British subject, William Knox D'Arcy, to explore for oil in all of Iran, except the northern provinces. As it became evident that the shah was no longer able to defend the interest of the nation the merchants and the clergy joined forces with the intelligentsia to initiate the constitutional revolution of 1906 which eventually undermined the absolute power of the shah.[47]

## ULEMA AND THE CONSTITUTIONAL REVOLUTION

The leading role played by the *ulema* in opposing foreign intervention placed the political discourse in Iran within a clearly Islamic framework. The religious establishment protecting the poor, collaborating with the wealthy and reflecting the emotional and ritualistic aspects of Shiism, came to represent the national consciousness and defend it against encroachment by the ungodly. The *ulema* appealed to the population at large through their own religious learning, and demanding that the masses to follow *ejtehad*. This demand was combined with the emotional appeal of Shiism expressed in religious ceremonies of mourning the dead martyrs of Karbala with plays, *taazieh*, and recitals *rozeh*. The plays provided a forum for public expression of faith and the recitals, *rozeh* conducted in the homes brought religious devotion, and advice, to the very core of the homes. The call to rebel in the name of God was thus carried by the religious establishment using the language and medium of Shiism. This practice continued with varying degrees of success throughout the twentieth-century political life of Iran.

The Qajar monarch's economic concessions to Westerners alarmed merchant and clerical powers about the consequences of the absolute power of the shah and they joined the revolutionary forces demanding the establishment of a constitutional monarchy, controlled by a democratically elected parliament, *Majlis*. From the early years of the constitutional movement, it was very much the defence of the realm against foreign intervention that fuelled the *ulema's* anger, rather than a positive desire to usher in a new form of government. The justification, however, has always been in the name of Islam. The prime loyalty of the people has always been towards the religion rather than nationalism and the *ulema* were perceived as leaders who provided both religious and political directives.[48] Their function as the symbol and embodiment of national aspirations secured almost unconditional support for their calls.[49] In the event the 1906–9 revolution which ensued served the merchants' interest, rather than national or religious interests.[50]

Given the first and basic Islamic assumption that the sole legitimate lawmaker is God, it is difficult to see how the religious institution could in the first instance justify constitutionalism in the name of Islam. Undoubtedly the *ulema*, clergy, were divided on this issue, and even their close ties with the bazaar and the mass of the population did not make them into unquestioning devotees of constitutionalism. After the success of the tobacco boycott some of the leading *mutjahedin* were:

> assimilated in the structure of corruption and oppression. Titles and allowances were lavished upon them, and their recommendation became essential for the success of any petition or request to the government... Now it seemed that the *ulema* were to become partners of the state in oppression.[51]

Although this alliance was to prove temporary, at least some of the *ulema* had an interest in securing the continuity of the Qajar dynasty. Others, though independent of the State, heeded the views of their financial backers, the merchants.[52] The State's introduction of Belgian-run custom and excise duties posed an immediate threat to the merchants' interests and the 10 per cent tax on government salaries alienated those members of the religious establishment who were employed by the State. Furthermore, since the pensions of the *ulema* were, by 1905, three years in arrears,[53] many did not have the means to deliver these dues to the state.

The delicate balance of power between the *ulema* and the State finally snapped in 1905 with direct attempts by the government to bring the merchants in line. Two leading sugar-merchants refused to lower the price of sugar, which they had raised as a result of the new taxes; the government responded by bastinadoing them. The baazar went on strike and a group of religious leaders took sanctuary, *bast*, in the shrine of Abdul Azim. *Bast*, was a symbol of the function fulfilled by the *ulema* mediating between the State and the people. It enabled those who were persecuted by the illegitimate tyranny of the state to take refuge with the representative of the only legitimate authority. It is worth noting that one of the sugar-merchants had built three mosques and the *bast* in Abdul Azim was financed by a wholesale dealer and a number of merchants.[54] But it would be wrong to assume that economic interests alone were at the root of the *ulema*'s support for the merchants. At the heart of their resistance was the belief on the part of the *ulema*, that the interests of Islam and Muslims were threatened by foreign penetration and secularism.[55] What they sought was a halt to Westernisation and innovation, not the creation of a new system of government.

Those who supported the constitution, did so on the assumption that the prevailing injustice, *zolm*, would be replaced by fairness and justice. Thus in the first instance the religious establishment did not demand a constitution, but rather a house of justice, *edaltkhaneh*, which would enable them to implement Islamic laws, *Sharia* in its entirety.[56] In this they were encouraged by the intelligentsia, who chose to couch its demands for a constitution in largely Islamic terms.[57]

Some of the leading religious figures backed the movement because they felt it would improve the lives of people. Tabatabayi, for example is quoted as saying:

> We ourselves had not seen a constitutional regime. But we had heard about it, and those who had seen the constitutional countries had told us that a constitutional regime will bring security and prosperity to this country, so we strove to establish a constitutional regime.[58]

Others were well aware that constitutionalism would not necessarily bring about a legitimate rule to the nation. However, they argued that whereas tyrannical rule was unjust to God, to the *Imam* and to the people, constitutionalism would be unjust to the Imam, and therefore preferable.[59] A major proponent of such views, Sheikh Mohamad Hosein Naini, envisaged a constitutional State that would curtail the excesses of the ruler through an assembly of the 'intelligent and wise well-wishers of the people'.[60] Such an assembly would gain legitimacy for its measures by securing the approval of a number of leading *mujtahedin* for its laws. Naini went further than most of the *ulema* in endorsing constitutionalism. He even argued that innovation, seen as anathema to Islamic dictum, could be acceptable,

> If one does not associate the non-Islamic provision with *Sharia* then there would be no innovation.[61]

Similarly representative elections were recommended:

> under the principle of *nahi as monker*, demanding [that] people [to] avoid
> wrongdoing, which is an obligatory duty of all Muslims.[62]

Thus in the early stages of constitutional revolution, a new uneasy alliance was
formed between the modernists and intellectuals, who underplayed their Western orientation, and the *ulema*, who opposed internal tyranny and foreign
intervention.

There was a conscious wooing of the *ulema*, by modernists such as Malkum
Khan and Mirza Aqa Khan Kermani. Openly cynical, Kermani was not above
using them:

> If we ask for very limited assistance from this half-alive horde of *mullas* [a
> derogatory term meaning uneducated religious preachers] maybe we should
> reach our aims faster.[63]

All too aware of the power of the religious institution over the hearts and minds
of men and women, Malkum Khan stated:

> We found that ideas which were by no means accepted when coming from...
> Europe, were accepted at once with the greatest delight when it was proved
> that they were latent in Islam.[64]

So, diplomatically, he sought to marry modernism with Islam stating that with
the exception of polygamy:

> there is not a single point in which Islam is really in contradiction with your
> civilising principles.[65]

This view was shared by the women of the aristocracy and upper middle
classes who joined forces with the modernist to support the revolutionary movement. Women were well-represented and active on the first committee of the
constitutionalists. Of its fifty-four members, twenty were women,[66] including
Nasseredin Shah's own daughters: Tajelsaltaneh and Malekeyeh Iran who were
actively involved in setting up secret societies to secure a constitutional
government.[67] They shared the view that the only civilised way forward was
through the overthrow of the autocracy. So, for example Tajelsaltaneh wrote:

> Constitutionalism is to fulfil the conditions of freedom and progress for a
> nation without ulterior motives and treachery.[68]

Eventually it was the arrest of a number of preachers and religious leaders in
1906 that threw the masses on to the street. Most remarkable was the role of the
women who attacked the shah's carriage, stopped the royal procession in protest
against the arrest of the religious leader and said:

> We are Muslims and owe absolute obedience to their *ulema*'s commands!
> They have ratified our marriage contracts. They are the ones who act on our
> behalf to rent our houses. In short, all our worldly goods and other-wordly

affairs are in the hands of these gentlemen. How could we allow anyone to banish or exile our *ulema*? O shah of the Muslims, respect the leaders of Islam. O shah of the Muslims, do not denigrate or undermine the leaders of Islam! O shah of Islam, should Russia or England invade, these leaders could order sixty thousand Iranians to fight a *jehad*, holy war, against them.[69]

The religious tone was set and the movement orchestrated by the *ulema*. These women echoed the religious establishment's fear of foreign intervention, as well as their concern to save Muslims from oppression and arbitrary rule. Characteristically, different religious figures participated in the revolution for different reasons. Some, such as Behbahani, may well have been motivated by personal gain. Others, such as Tabatabai, did so in the full knowledge that the establishment of a house of justice and National Assembly would lead to loss of clerical priveliges.[70]

The revolution gained momentum with the encouragement of preachers who took to their pulpits, *manbar*, and the merchants who in July 1906 left Tehran *en masse* to take refuge, *bast*, in Qom. Economic activities came to a halt in Tehran and the shah agreed to the establisment of constitutional assembly.

The first parliament, *Majlis*, reflected the importance of the *baazar* and the elections were conducted by a six-class division which enabled the guilds to have a substantial representation. But subsequent parliaments, *Majlis*, were elected by a one-class system which permitted the dominance of the landed gentry, the rich and the clergy. The first parliament, *Majlis*, elected in 1906, set about writing the constitution.[71]

The schism in the religious establishment widened after the new constitution came into force in 1909. As the modernist demanded ever-greater degrees of secularism, so more religious leaders deserted the cause. Many were reluctant to engage in politics on a long-term basis; they saw themselves as acting only in critical circumstances. Of those who did remain with the constitutionalists, some may not have realised the insecure position of religion in a democratic institution. But others, such as Naini remained steadfast and wrote extensively to prove the legitimacy of a constitutional government and the illegitimacy of tyranny.[72] Some of the *ulema* such as Seyed Mohamad Tabatabayi, and Abdolah Behbahani were of the view that it was essential to institute constitutional checks to prevent excesses by the ruler.

Those who broke rank, feared the consequences of the modernists' demands for equality of all citizens, irrespective of their gender and religion. They feared that human legislation would replace God given laws as interpreted by the *mujtahed*. Led by Sheikh Fazl Allah Nuri, they rejected the view that sovereignty should ultimately be held by the nation. He stated the view, that was to be echoed across the century by Khomeini in years to come, that God alone is the law-maker in Islam. His laws were announced by the Prophet Mohamad and interpreted by the imams and were finally to be understood and disseminated by the learned clergy. There was no room for the masses to exercise their will. In an attempt to accommodate these views, the constitutionalists formulated article 35 of the Supplementary Fundamental Laws to state:

Sovereignty is a trust confided (as a divine gift) by the people to the king.[73]

Nuri also denounced the representative system of the government, *vekalat*, as a poor substitute for *valayat*, the supervisorship of the *ulema*. They saw the demands for equality as a first step towards anarchism and socialism.[74] Sheikh Fazl Allah Nuri argued that:

in Islam there is no equality between the mature and the immature, the sane and the insane, the healthy and the ill, the slave and the free, wife and husband, the learned and the ignorant, the Muslim and the non-Muslim and so on.[75]

Nuri's objections were met by article 18 of the constitution which stated that religious minorities did not have an equal status to Muslims in Iran. Nuri had sought justice, but not secularism. He was of the view that any constitutional government in Iran should be conditioned by the teachings of the Quran and the Prophet and could not see how this could permit secularisation of national finances and education. Government taxes would cut into payment of religious taxes and secular education would undermine the teachings of Islam. The latter objection was met by the provision of article 19 of the constitution which banned any education that would prejudice Islamic teachings. Nuri's further objection that freedom of the press would be detrimental to the nation's moral and religious standing was also met by article 20 which restricted the press to the publication of material which was in the interest of Islam.[76]

Nuri secured the inclusion of his Islamic provisos by organising a series of agitations against the *Majlis*. Seminary students, *tolab*, demonstrated continuously outside *Majlis* parliament, and he formed a political society, *anjoman* to formulate their demands. Despite the compromises made by the parliamentarians, Nuri continued to agitate against what he saw as their attacks on 'the citadel of Islam'. Eventually he backed Mohamad Ali Shah's attack on the *Majlis* in 1906 and was hanged by the constitutionalists in July 1909.[77]

Although the constitution was revised to accomodate the objections of the conservatives, some of their opinions were countered by other leading religious figures such as Naini. On the critical question of equality, he pointed out that Islamic Law applied to all on equal basis and noted the necessity to distinguish between the human law and the laws of God. In the event the constitution was formulated largely along the lines of the Belgian model. But it retained a strong *Shia* texture. Not only was the official religion of the country recognised to be Shiism (article 2) but also a council of *ulema* was to vet all legislations to ensure that they remain consistent with Islamic dictum. Although the *Majlis* was to be representative, in accordance with the wishes of the *ulema*, the question of equality was abandoned. Religious minorities were given limited representation and women – who had participated in the revolution from its inception – were denied the right to vote. Thus the truce between the modernists and the *ulema* was finally achieved through the denial of equal rights to women and religious minorities and the establishment of a *Shia* constitution.

# 2 The Arms of the Bureaucracy and the Embrace of Theocracy

Constitutional government in Iran was to be short-lived in the first instance. The newly enthroned Qajar king, Mohamed Ali Shah, sent his Cossack regiment, headed by a Russian officer to attack the first *Majlis*, in 1908. He succeeded in closing the *Majlis*, and by doing so propelled the country into civil war. The constitutional revolution continued, with the clergy and the constitutionalists fighting side by side in pitched battles in most provincial centres. Finally in 1909 the constitutionalists led by Sattar Khan in Tabriz, in the north west, backed by the Bahktiari tribes from the south converged on Tehran. Mohamad Ali Shah took refuge with the Russians and his minor son Ahmad Shah was placed on the throne.

However, the success of the constitutionalists did not curtail the increasing foreign influence in Iran. In 1907 the British and Russians signed a secret treaty dividing Iran into three zones, the north for the Russian, the south for the British and a thin layer in between as neutral. They were most reluctant to relinquish their control. So, despite the success of the constitutionalists, the second *Majlis* was elected only to be dissolved in December 1911 under pressure from Russia. Russian and British troops marched into northern and southern regions. Despite demonstrations, attempts by Iranian women to set up their own bank and pay up the national debt, and calls for international help, parliamentary system was replaced by effective foreign control. The situation deteriorated severely during the first World War. In addition to the Russian and British troops, Turkish troops, supported by Germans, moved into the Western provinces of Iran. By 1917 the Russians controlled the north, the British the south. The Anglo-Persian Oil company, formed in 1909 after oil was discovered in the south-west of the country, ensured free flow of oil to the British – so much so that Churchill commanded the British navy to convert from coal to oil. The oil was secured by imported armed forces from India.

During the First World War, a third *Majlis* was elected and, under Russian pressure, dissolved. Iran erupted; there were riots and battles across the country, ranging from the tightly organised Jangali movement in the north to sporadic uprisings in most of the major cities.[1]

The Russian revolution of 1917 led to the decision of the Bolsheviks to pull out of Iran and renounce all Tsarist concessions. In 1918 a shortfall in the harvest was exacerbated by the decision of the occupying forces to channel all available surplus to their forces. A devastating famine followed which may have killed as much as one-quarter of the population in the north of the country. At the same time the British tried to step in and make Iran into a British protectorate. They began negotiating the unpopular Anglo-Persian treaty in 1919.

The clergy–modernist alliance held more or less firm throughout this period. Finally in 1919, in reaction to the attempt to make Iran a British protectorate, the nationalist movement in Azarbaijan and Guilan merged with the constitutionalists and guerrilla movements. The widespread discontent facilitated a coup engineered by the leader of the Iranian Cossack regiment, Reza Khan and the nationalist, Seyed Zia al Din, in 1921. Reza Khan was set to rise as the next leader of the country. In 1925 the *Majlis* deposed the Qajar dynasty in October, and in December Reza Shah became the founder of the Pahlavi dynasty.

Sheikh Mirza Mohamad Hosein Naini supporting Reza Shah and some of the clergy in Najaf suspecting his motives. Reza Shah himself abandoned his early republican stance in favour of a monarchist one. This shift was in part to placate the *ulema* who were wary of Ataturk's secular reforms in Turkey and were determined to prevent a similar process in Iran. Reza Khan conceded. Since, unlike the Qajars, he did not have a natural tribal support base, Reza Khan chose to placate the religious groups by posturing as the guardian of Islam and use this as a means of legitimising his claim to power:

> I and all the people in the army have, from the very beginning regarded the preservation and protection of the dignity of Islam to be one of the greatest duties and kept before us the idea that Islam always progresses and is exalted and that respect for the standing of the religious institution be fully observed and preserved...And we ultimately thought it necessary to advise the public to cease [using] the term republic.[2]

But once in power he began by curtailing both foreign and religious influences in the country's politics and economy. He reorganised the economy into a self-reliant and nationalist system, independent of foreign loans and foreign intervention. To do so, he curtailed the movement of capital, insisting that all investments should be made in the newly set-up nationalised industries and imposing realistic taxes which permitted a transfer of surplus from landed gentry to the modern capitalist sector.

At the same time Reza Shah embarked on building up a national administrative structure. The bureaucracy up to then had been rudimentary and intensely localised; in the rural areas it was organised along tribal and regional ties and fiefdoms with the tribal leaders paying some tax and undertaking to defend the borders.[3] In the urban areas a combination of religious laws *sharia*, proclaimed and enforced by the religious institution, and secular law, *urf*, enforced by government agents were accepted and more or less effective. Reza Shah, using the army as the buttress of his power, successfully attacked the various tribes. For centuries the tribes controlled the Iranian borders, guarded them against the enemy, and used this power as a political tool for influencing internal affairs. Defeated chieftains were brought back to Tehran and kept under the Shah's eyes. With the introduction of compulsory military service the army itself became one of the most extensive tentacles of the newly emerging bureaucracy. Youths from every village in Iran were conscripted into the forces. Drawn out of the villages, into urban areas; trained and often educated by the army, many chose to remain in cities working as drivers, mechanics or in other skilled or semi-skilled jobs. At the same time the forces themselves grew from five divisions totalling 40 000 men in 1926 to eighteen divisions with 127 000 men in 1941. As the armed forces grew, so did the Shah's power and confidence, to the detriment of the religious institution. By 1925 clergy lost the right to be automatically immune from conscription. By law the State was empowered to decide who did or did not qualify for military service. From then on the *ulema* were increasingly subjected to bureaucratic control.

Reza Shah used both the armed forces and the *Majlis* to set up a secular bureaucratic state and to undermine the pervasive power of the clergy. He organised a central, systematic, urban and rural taxation system and set about eroding the power and influence of the clergy. Religious schools were replaced by secular ones and religious courts by secular courts. The police, gendarmerie and armed forces replaced the clergy's *luti* (armed gangs) and *tolab*, (students) and gradually the *ulema* began returning to their mosques and withdrawing, willy-nilly from the political sphere.[4] Eventually in 1930 Reza Shah introduced a civil and a criminal code, both based on the *Code Napoléon*. The only area where Islamic laws prevailed remained in the matter of personal laws. Even there, the legal age of marriage for girls was raised from 9 to 15. The new laws were to be extended and interpreted by secularly trained lawyers and in 1936 when the Faculty of Law opened its door, it accepted both male and female students.

Secular education for all was the second extended arm of the new bureaucracy. Although the first secular schools in Iran had been set up in 1851, under Reza Shah the process gained momentum and Islamic teaching was significantly eroded and confined to seminaries. The clergy had, up to then, retained a firm foothold in secular schools. The education laws of 1911 had made instruction of Islamic sciences mandatory in all schools, and denied the right of religious instructions for minorities in schools (articles 7 and 17). Under Reza Shah new syllabi were developed for the newly organised primary and secondary tiers of education included Islamic teaching. But religion came second to the dominant ideology of nationalism and modernisation. Following a similar trend to Ataturk, Reza Shah was determined to modernise Iran; the new bureaucracy and the growing armed forces provided alternative sources of employment and political strength. Newly established industries were given much encouragement and gradually the power base of the *ulema* – the law, the educational system and eventually the *bazaar* – were eroded. Formal, secular qualifications became the required norms of education – so much so that by 1928 the law demanded the licensing of religious teachers and formal examination of religious students. This was followed by the 1931 law which established a core curriculum for seminaries. In 1935 a Faculty of Theology was set up in Tehran University.

This process was deeply contradictory to the prevalent methods of Islamic teachings in the seminaries, *maddares*, where teaching was on a dialectic principle of argument and counter-arguments.[5] Each leading Ayatollah held his own open courses and there were no examinations, no formal qualifications and no obligatory periods of training. Students continued until such time as the teacher felt that they had achieved all that they could. The gifted stayed on and the less able were sent off to various parts of the country to preach and represent the Ayatollah who had taught them. They collected religious taxes from his followers and selected bright prospective students to be sent to his seminary.[6] Part of the taxes was spent on paying stipends to the students in the seminaries and the rest was distributed as alms. Education facilitated an achievement-based entry into the ranks of the religious elite and many a humble student could find his way to the top of the hierarchy from the poorest and most distant of villages. Once there, a tendency to intermarry linked most of the highest-ranking religious leaders, *marja' taqlid*.[7] The formalisation of the curriculum and the introduction of a Faculty of Theology was seen as an intentional threat by the Shah to the fabric of religious education.

The central part played by the *ulema* in formulating and implementing the *sharia* (religious laws) was eroded by the secularisation of the legal codes in 1926. By 1936 judges were required to have a formal university degree in law. Thus seminaries were made even more marginal in the secularised state. Reza Shah firmly separated religion from politics. In this he found some support from Hassan Emami whom he appointed as the *Emam Jomeh* of Tehran. *Emam Jomeh*, which literally translated means 'the Friday imam', is the prestigious post of the city's public prayer leader, which had been in the gift of the monarch since the Safavid times. Hassan Emami, the son of the *Emam Jomeh* of Tehran, had a secular education, a Ph.D. in law. He shared the monarch's view that religion should be separate from politics. On his father's death, he accepted the post and sought to adjust religion to the contemporary circumstances.[8]

By mid-1937 the pervasive control of the religious establishment had been replaced by that of the bureaucracy. Law and education were secularised and the lucrative functions of notary public and registry had come under state super-vision, though the clergy continued to register marriages. Finally, in 1937 the secular Endowment Office was given full power of supervision over all public endowments, thereby extending State control over one of the last remaining important sources of income for the clergy. An equally important blow was the unveiling of women in 1936. Already the 1928 law on uniformity of dress had changed the male habit by demanding that men in general and civil servants in particular should wear Western clothes and hats. Strictly speaking such a require-ment was not un-Islamic. Women on the other hand have always been seen as the public face of national morality,[9] and many Muslims are of the view that Islam requires women to cover themselves under the Islamic *hejab*, veil. The banning of the veil and admittance of women to the newly opened Tehran University, at the same time as men, outraged the clergy who saw it as a final blow to the honour of the nation. Unveiling was a public statement of victory of secularisation. Ayatollah Hosein Qomi Tabatabai and Ayatollah Taqi Bafqi, a renowned teacher at Qom who included Khomeini among his disciples, began a campaign against the compulsory removal of veil. Reza Shah exiled the former to Iraq and the latter to Ray.

The formalisation of secularism was accompanied by marginalisation of religious ceremonies and their replacement with national ones. This marked a move from traditional mourning ceremonies to celebratory ones, military parades and public holidays to mark occasions such as the unveiling of women. In particular *dasteh*, public mourning demonstrations by flagellants and *taazieh*, passion plays, were first discouraged and then banned. But the recitations of the ills that befell the martyrs of Shiism during the battle of Karbala, *rozeh*, continued. These recitations by religious reciters, *rozeh khan*, were popular amongst the poor and were usually held in private houses during the month of mourning, *Moharam*. The rich gradually abandoned the practice, but amongst the poor it remained vibrant and a means of transmitting fundamentalist and radical messages at a time when most political parties were banned.

Reza Shah was deposed in the summer of 1941 by the Allied forces who once more marched into Iran and divided the country into spheres of influence. The British and Russian took their usual shares and the United States moved into the central parcel that had been neutral during the First World War. Reza Shah's 18-year-old son, Mohamad Reza, was placed on the throne to run a nominal government under the Allies' control.


## SHIISM AND SECULARISM, THE CONTROVERSY

The departure of Reza Shah was followed by a burgeoning of intellectual and political activities in Iran. The Communist party, whose founder-members had been imprisoned in 1937, came back to the fray as the Tudeh party, and a number of smaller and less-organised political groupings also emerged.

Once more the battle between modernist intellectuals and Muslim fundamentalists was joined on all sides. Ayatollah Hosein Qomi Tabatabai returned triumphantly to visit Iran and in 1944 the government removed the compulsory restriction on veiling. The *ulema* continued their attacks and in 1948, fifteen *mujtahed* issued a *fatwa*, forbidding unveiled women from shopping in the *bazaars*. The debate about Islam, the clergy and their rights to make political declarations and/or to govern was conducted through speeches and publications. Notable intellectuals such as the historian, Ahmad Kasravi, came to the defence of secularism by denouncing Shiism and clerical pretensions to authority. Religious leaders such as Khomeini countered with attacks on secularism. Kasravi published *Shiagari*,[10] (the Shia tendency) – a book which, according to the author, was written, using logic and common sense, to denounce the malpractices and foolish superstitions of the clergy:

We wish to praise the innocent name of the Creator and to erase idolatry...
Each statement in this book is supported by evidence and logic... Readers
should clearly understand what we have to say and think on it and allow
wisdom to be the judge and not turn away even where what we say goes
against their prejudices.[11]

Kasravi questions the very core of Shia belief. He argues against the misplaced
emphasis on the absolute wisdom and innocence of *imams* which entitled them
to rule, to judge and to interpret the laws of Islam – a right which was subsequently taken over and usurped by the *Usuli ulema* even though it had no
foundation in the *Quran*.

It is extraordinary that the Prophet of Islam openly states 'I have no knowledge of the unknown' but these clergy claim that their imams do have such
knowledge.[12] ...We should first ask: after the Prophet why do we need the
*imams*? Did the Prophet fail to accomplish his duties? Besides, which of the
activities of the *Imam* is worth bringing to the attention of the world? Which
failure have they ratified? How have they impressed the world? What
exceptional qualities have they shown to possess?
   It is true that Mohamad Ibn Ali and Jafar Ibn Mohamad [two of the *Shia
imams*], father and son, had a certain knowledge of *feqh*, Islamic law, but so
did Malek and Abu Hanifa and Shafei and Ahmad Ibn Hanbal [major theo-
logian and founders of different *Sunni* schools].[13]

The *imams* are the pure, the innocent and the undisputed leaders of *Shias*. Arguments which place the *Shias'* holy innocent and pure *imams* on a par with *Sunni*
theologians were, as far as the clergy were concerned, tantamount to heresy. As
to Kasravi, he argued that what the clergy were purveying was a form of idolatry:

If you discuss pilgrimage with these *mollayan* [a derogatory term meaning
clergymen], first they try to argue. When they get stuck they retreat to the next
trench and say 'we don't think of the imam and their descendants as God.
They are loved by God and we turn to them to act as intermediaries.' I reply
that this is nothing but idolatry. The idolaters of Qoreish gave this very same
excuse to the founders of Islam. They said 'We worship these to get closer to
God'. or 'They are our intermediaries.' We must say that idolaters are all the
same and they all come up with the same excuse.[14]...Now we must ask: those
who hold such beliefs, are they not misled? What can be more misleading
than to assume that unworthy corpses are God's assistants? We must ask:
what are the reasons for saying that *imams* are God's helpers? Who do you
think God is that he should need help?[15]

So Kasravi endorses the Sunni views and argues that *Shias* would do well to
abandon silly superstitions. He notes that God is not sitting in the heavens and
concentrating on Iranians to punish or reward them. He uses the same argument
when addressing the question of unveiling of women:

You say: because Iranian women have uncovered their faces God has punished us by sending a famine. I ask: How has God sent this famine?!... Has the rain not fallen from the sky?!... Have the plants not grown out of the earth?!... Has there been a plague of locusts or aphis to ruin the crops?!...In the absence of all these how can you say that God sent us hunger?...You can see with your own eyes that the foreigners [occupying allies] are taking the food...and yet you blame God... You unwise people! Would God take a grudge against the unveiling of Tehrani women, and take revenge on the women and children in Bushehre and Bandar Abas [cities in the south east]?!... This lot unveil and that lot have to bear the anger of God?! So why does the wrath of God not burn the women of Europe and America who are always unveiled? Why should God only get cross about the unveiling of Iranian women? How stupid can you get!

Kasravi systematically dismisses the very foundations of *Shia* beliefs as well as its practices and concepts of honour and innocence; he goes on to conclude that that *Shiagari*, the *Shia* tendency, is nothing but a shop-front to allow the clergy to get an undeserved income:

with all its turns and shades, *Shiagari* has concluded that authority and government of our time is in the hand of the absent *imam*. *Mollayan* follow this argument and say: we are the representatives of the *imam* and we should be the rulers today...but even though they think that they should govern, they don't and they cannot do so. They let someone else govern and undermine public confidence in the government.[16]...It is in their interest to have a government, as we have today, to run the country and at the same time to convince people that deep down it is the clergy who should be ruling and who should be paid to do so[17] ...But my... question is this: you the *mollayan*, you who will not govern and have sat doing nothing in a corner and are not taking any steps· forward, why do you still expect to be paid the *zakat*, religious taxes?... On what do you spend this *zakat* and wealth of the imam? Do you run the country? Do you fight a religious war, *jehad*?... Do you send lawyers and law-makers to the provinces?... These are what *zakat* and the share of the *imam* should be spent on. You don't do any of it, I can't think under what pretext you go on taking money from people?[18]

Kasravi had asked for reasoned debate, he invited the clergy to present their side of the argument, so that reason could be the judge. Rouhollah Khomeini was amongst those who sought to rebut Kasravi. He published *Kashf al Asrar* (Secrets Revealed)[19] and devoted large sections of it to defending every one of the beliefs and practices derided by Kasravi and attacking all secularisation measures. In particular, Khomeini warned his followers of the serious repercussions of unveiling women on their manhood:

the unveiling of women has been the ruin of female honour, the destruction of family and the cause of untold corruption and prostitution.[20]

Similarly mixed education:

> These schools, mixing young girls and young passion-ridden boys, kill female honour, destroy the very root of life and the power of manly valour [*javanmardi*], such schools are materially and spiritually damaging to the country and are forbidden by God's commandment.[21]

Dancing and music-making were also condemned:

> Music rouses the spirit of love-making of unlawful sexuality and giving free reign to passion, at the same time it removes audacity, courage and manly valour.[22]

Khomeini warned his readers of the dire consequences of secularism, which he described as submitting to foreign values and tearing down the moral barriers of the nation:

> They have put chamber-pot-shaped hats over your heads and gladden your hearts with naked women in the middle of the streets, and prostitution... This shameless unveiling...is materially and spiritually damaging to the country and forbidden by the laws of God and his Prophet.[23]

Countering Kasravi, Khomeini defended the clergy and their right to dictate political terms:

> No one but God has the right to rule or legislate. Reason dictates that God should form a government for the people and enact the laws. Such is the sacred Law of Islam.[24]

But although he demanded that all secularisation laws enacted by Reza Shah should be revoked, like many *Shias* before him, he fell short of denouncing the Shah and came to the curious conclusion that:

> Bad government is better than no government,... the *ulema* always cooperate with the government if that is needed.[25]

The political discourse, however, took a different shade on the streets. The cause of *Shias* was espoused by two Islamic-inspired groups, the *Mojahedin Islam* (Religious Warriors of Islam) led by Shams Qanatabadi, the son-in-law of Ayatollah Seyed Abol Qassem Kashani, and the secret underground movement, Fadayan Islam (The Martyrs of Islam) attached to Seyed Mojtaba Mirlahuti, known as Navab Safavi. Trained as a theological student in Najaf, Navab Safavi denounced all secularisation measures, advocated return to *sharia* and obedience to the teaching of the prophet and the return of women to domesticity. Like Khomeini, he feared the power of women in un-manning Muslims. He was of the view that:

> flames of passion rise from the naked bodies of immoral women and burn humanity into ashes.[26]

In addition to misogyny, Khomeini and Navab Safavi shared the demand of the prohibition of Western values and attitudes, which were said to include, prostitution, gambling, night-clubs, alcoholic drinks and modern music. Safavi considered modern music to be particularly dangerous:

> Immoral music weakens a person's strong nerves and undermines the intellect and the soul thereby threatening the nervous system of individuals and the mind and power of the society. Thus we must replace such exciting immoral music by calming gentle tunes which do not awaken sexual feelings, but rather calm the soul and make people aware of the greatness and values of truth and wisdom.[27]

Like Khomeini, the *Fadayan* regarded the West as a whole and the USA in particular as the cause of all evils. Navab Safavi argued that the import of American technologies had eroded Iranian know-how and undermined the development process of the country. In his book, *Hokumateh Eslami* (Islamic Government), he enjoined Iranians to avoid all Western products and become self-reliant. Furthermore, he demanded that those remnants of Westernisation that were not demolished, should be totally altered. Thus, for example, cinemas could be re-utilised:

> Should society find it necessary to use the film industry, then it could be employed to teach people about Islamic history and provide useful information and give lectures on medical care, agriculture and industrial training. The film industry should be cleansed and placed under the guidance of wise Islamic teachers who could ensure that what is shown accords with the best of Islamic teaching and provides morally acceptable material for public viewing.[28]

The *Fadayan* were to fight to the death for the total implementation of the *Sharia* laws, Islamification of the entire educational system and elimination of all foreign influences. To achieve this, they applauded the necessity of martyrdom and advocated the execution of anyone who showed any disrespect towards Islam.[29] But despite their accord on women's position, the Fadayan were on the whole antipathic to the *ulema* and attacked their monopoly of religious dictate and their stewardship over religious affairs. Unexpectedly echoing Kasravi, the *Fadayan* too suggested that *ulema* were redundant.[30]

The *Fadayan*'s methods were not one of public debate. Navab Safavi formed a tightly-knit small group of supporters who were trained as assassins. Their first target was Kasravi: what could not be resolved by reason was settled by blood and in the *Fadayan*'s second attempt, two founder-members Hosein and Ali Mohamad Emami, succeeded in killing Kasravi in 1946. After their arrest, their cause was espoused as a political ploy by some of the *ulema* who came to the rescue. Ayatollah Seyed Abol Qassem Kashani argued that they should be treated as national liberators since Kasravi was the known servant of the imperialists and Ayatollah Haj Aqa Hosein Qomi set about mobilising the Forces of the Godly and organising public demonstrations against their arrest.

The Emamis were acquitted and given *carte blanche* to continue, which they did. In pursuit of what they called a defensive *jehad*, holy war, the *Fadayan* was intent on rooting out all political leaders who were accused of acting as 'tools' or 'shields' for irreligious elements. The *Fadayan*'s manifesto declared:

We are able to send these traitors to hell, and to avenge Islam.[31]

It received support from the young illiterate, or semi-literate, poorer classes, particularly young disillusioned men who saw martyrdom and guerrilla activities as worthy causes to espouse with their lives. In this they were financially supported by a few wealthy merchants.[32] In February 1948 the *Fadayan* attempted to assassinate the Shah and failed; in September Hosein Emami assassinated Adbdol Hosein Hajir, a former Prime Minister and the Minister of court at the time. Emami was arrested and tried again. He admitted openly that he had assassinated Hajir and announced that he would welcome martyrdom with open arms. This time he was executed. The assassinations continued. In March 1951 Khalil Tahmassebi killed the Prime Minister, General Ali Razmara, who was negotiating an unpopular new oil agreement with the British.

Oil, always an important political factor, had once more come to the fore as the central question in Iran. The Allies had finally left Iran at the end of the war, though the Russians stayed on till 1946. But the bulk of the oil remained largely in the hands of the British, with the Russians negotiating to gain access to the northern oil-fields. After Razmara's death the *Majlis* passed the law for the nationalisation of oil. The bill was drawn up by Dr Mohamad Mossadeq, who came to power as Prime Minister in April 1951. During his tempestuous two years in power, Mossadeq sought to place the economy on a self-reliant basis and to curtail some of the extensive powers of the monarch.[33] In the ensuing confrontations, and street battles and demonstrations, Mossadeq formed a short-lived alliance with some of the *ulema*, like Kashani, while others like Ayatollah Mohamad Mousavi Behbahani were not prepared to back him

Kashani became the Speaker of the *Majlis* in the summer of 1952. He helped to release many of the *Fadayans* who had been rounded up and jailed in June 1951. In the autumn, Tahmassebi was released from jail through a bill passed by *Majlis*, which denounced Razmara as a traitor and servant of the imperialist powers,[34] and pardoned Tahmassebi. Tahmassebi publicly thanked Kashani for his release. By 1953 most of the top leaders of the *Fadayan* were released in 1953.

The final effort of the *Fadayan* was their attempted assassination of Prime Minister Hosein Ala in 1955, when he was about to sign the Baghdad pact agreement, a regional defence alliance with Turkey and Iraq. The *Fadayi*, Mozafar Zolfaqar, failed to assassinate the Prime Minister and there was a general round-up and execution of most of the *Fadayan*'s top leaders. Although the *Fadayan* had a small number of supporters, estimated at around 500,[35] they played an important part in delineating an Islamic line of action during a period when the majority of the clergy had chosen the quietist interpretation of Islam.

## ULEMA AND 'WESTOXIFICATION'

Mossadeq had been toppled by a CIA-backed coup in the summer of 1953. The arrest of Mossadeq and the return of the Shah to power marks the end of the era of independence, nationalism and self-sufficiency and the beginning of a blind pursuit of modernisation which came to be called *qarbzadegi* 'westoxification' or 'Euromania' by the author Jalal Al Ahmad.[36] The quest was made easier by the forcible elimination of all political opposition and by the establishment of the secret police, SAVAK, set up with a $4500 million aid package donated by the USA.

The new oil consortium, set up after the nationalisation, and revised by the Shah after his return, gave exploration and extraction control to a foreign consortium where the previously absolute control of the British was tempered by the participation of the French and US companies. In return for assisting the Shah to recapture his throne, the large US oil companies obtained 40 per cent of the new consortium. At the same time the USA saw this incursion as a means of securing a friendly base in the Gulf region and funding a friendly monarch:

> The security interests of the United States requires the United States petroleum companies to participate in an international consortium to contract with the Government of Iran, within the area of the former AIOC concessions, for the production and refining of petroleum and its purchase by them, in order to permit the reactivation of the said petroleum industry, and *to provide therefrom to the friendly government of Iran substantial revenues on terms which will protect the interests of the western world in the petroleum resources of the Middle East.*[37] [My italics].

The National Iranian Oil Company initially merely dealt with the distribution of oil in Iran and social and welfare organisation for its employees. It also ensured that there were sufficient funds to meet the Shah's ambitious modernisation plans for the the economy and the armed forces.

The armed forces were ruthlessly purged, the clergy were closely watched by the secret police and at the same time the country was placated by acceptance of generous foreign loan and a helter-skelter pursuit of growth and modernisation. The Shah ruled with the assistance of tame prime ministers and cabinets, that did not have to be constitutionally selected from parliamentary representatives. The parliament, manned by tame members, dutifully followed the royal command and the Shah began to move towards an absolutist form of government.

The decade of the 1950s was one where most of the *ulema*, with the notable exception of Kashani and Ayatollah Ali Akbar Borqeyi and Sheikh Hosein Lankarani, chose to keep their distance from most political issues, except that of opposition to women's liberation. All, except Borqeyi, remained united and effective in preventing the enfranchisement of women under a proposal by Mossadeq in 1952. Otherwise, under the leadership of the *marja' taqlid*, Ayatollah Mohamad Hosein Boroujerdi, a conference of leading clergy met in Qom in

1949 and adopted a firm non-interventionist political position.[38] Boroujerdi and his close ally, Ayatollah Mohamad Mussavi Behbahani, concentrated on developing Qom as a centre of religious learning and influence and establishing an amicable accord with the Shah and the state apparatus. In return the monarch and his government adopted a respectful attitude to the clergy and, as a seal of alliance, agreed to persecute the *Baha'i* minorities. In 1955 both Behbahani and Boroujerdi called for this 'heretical' religion to be made illegal in Iran. Baha'ism contradicts the *ulama*'s conviction that Islam is the last revealed religion and being perfect it can never be superseded. Therefore a religion that began with a break from Shiism in Iran in the first half of the nineteenth century could be nothing more than a heresy. Despite the opposition of the clergy, Baha'ism had gained ground and had been tolerated, but in 1955 it proved a useful scapegoat which gave the clergy the impression of having political influence and distracted public attention from the high returns that Iranian were going to give to the Western interests of the oil consortium.[39] The government acted decisively, sent in troops to occupy the *Baha'i* centres in Tehran and Shiraz and made Baha'ism illegal. In return the *ulema* endorsed the Baghdad pact agreement in 1955 and ignored the unfavourable terms offered by the oil consortium. Their quietism was less remarkable in the latter years of the decade which saw the country's first major economic boom. The period 1955–9 saw the resurgence of state power and the beginning of development strategies aimed at rapidly expanding the modern sector of the economy.

By 1961 the Shah, confident that the religious establishment would not oppose him and that the SAVAK would quash other political opponents, decided to force the pace of modernisation and rule unhampered by *Majlis* and politicians. He was feeling sufficiently confident to dissolve the *Majlis* and rule by edict. He initiated a number of major changes to the constitution, which reneged on his previous acquiescence to the clergy's demands. Political discrimination against minorities and women were to be waived. Restrictions against minorities whereby non-Muslim candidates were not entitled to Muslim votes were to be removed. Government officials were no longer required to swear an oath of allegiance on the Quran, but could do so on any divine book of an accepted faith. What was even worse in the eyes of the clergy, women were to be enfranchised.

But the Shah had miscalculated. There was an uproar, orchestrated by the *ulema* in general and Khomeini in particular. Initially the Shah retracted and his decision to abandon the enfranchisement of women was welcomed by the clergy. Khomeini applauded 'his Imperial Majesty's' decision to act according to 'the Quranic principles' and advised his followers to obey the Shah who was the 'guardian' of the constitution, independence and security of the country.[40] It appeared that Khomeini had not altered the views expressed in *Kashf al Asrar;* so long as women were kept out of the public arena, he was prepared to support the Shah.

But the truce between Shah and Khomeini was short-lived. Ayatollah Boroujerdi died in March 1961. With his death the damper placed on the *ulema* in general and Khomeini in particular was removed. Khomeini like all other leading *mujtahedin*, had married into the the the semi-closed élite that formed the pinnacle of authority. His daughter was married to Boroujerdi's son. Such familial link provided support and influence, but also demanded tacit cooperation and thus prevented Khomeini from stepping too far out of line, so long as Boroujerdi was alive. In November 1961 Shah gave the edict for implementation of the land reform policy, a policy that had been opposed by Boroujerdi and Behbahani in 1959. Its ratification by the cabinet of Dr Ali Amini in January 1962 met with ferocious opposition from the *ulema*. The land reforms threatened one of the last remaining major sources of income for the clergy. *Vaqf*, endowment, were still managed by them; besides many *ulema* were major landowners in their own rights.

The measures were countered by public demonstrations where the clergy and the intelligentsia once more linked forces. The Shah, determined to retain power, ordered the army to invade Tehran University, the site of one of the first uprisings. The brutality meted out by the army was such that the Chancellor, Dr Ahmad Farhad resigned in protest against the excessive 'cruelty, sadism and atrocity' of the forces.[41]

In July 1962 Amini resigned and was replaced by Assadulah Alam. In January 1963 the Shah decided to introduce his 'White Revolution'; a six-point programme which enfranchised women, continued the implementation of the land reforms, nationalised the forests and state industries and began a profit-sharing scheme for industrial workers and set up a rural literacy corps for the rural population. It was to be implemented peacefully and without bloodshed.

Predictably the religious institution mobilised once more, Khomeini in particular denounced the enfranchisement of women as 'a decadent trap' drawing women to the 'swamps of corruption, prostitution and destruction'.[42] Along with Jaafar Behbahani he also declared the land reforms to be un-Islamic. Other members of the religious establishment expressed a fear of return to tyranny. There were other factions amongst the *ulema* who held a more radical position and yet others who tacitly or openly supported the Shah. Besides the divisions were far from clear-cut and there were periodic readjustments as there had been with Khomeini and the Shah. Once more Iranians were to be divided into their traditional religious and modernist camps, but in this instance some of the intelligentsia sided with the Godly.

The emergence of the old alliance may be explained in part by the economic recession which began in 1960. Domestic trade, including most of the *bazaar*'s transactions, suffered most, whereas the newly developed modern sector was relatively unharmed.[43] With the death of Boroujerdi the apparent unity and quietism of the clergy had also come to an end. Jaafar Behbahani and Khomeini championed the conservative cause opposing land reforms and the liberation of women. Ayatollah Mohamad Kazem Shariatmadari and Ayatollah Mohamad Hadi Milani were primarily against rule by edict and feared a return to despotism; a third group including Ayatollah Abolfazl Zanjani and Mahmud Taleqani, had been active against the Shah since the 1953 coup and held what could be described as more radical views.[44] Others such as Ayatollah Khoeyi Najafi, Ahmad Khorassani and Marashi Najafi remained scrupulously apolitical until the mid-1970s.[45] The radical camps too were linked, some by Khomeini's pupils, Morteza Motahari and Mohamad Beheshti, who kept in touch with the social reformers and the *bazaar*. The court had its supporters, including the Friday prayer leader of Tehran, *Emam Jomeh*, and Ayatollah Mahdavi.

On the eve of the referendum for the White Revolution, there were demonstrations in many of the major cities. On 21 March 1963, the Iranian New Year day, Khomeini addressed a crowd in the Faizieh seminary in Qom, denouncing the White Revolution as un-Islamic. Once more it was the fear of women and their potentially dangerous role in unmanning the Iranian youths that was uppermost in his mind:

> The ruthless regime... is planning to endorse and implement a bill that calls for equal rights for men and women. This bill violates the fundamental principles of Islam and the *Quran*. This means that the regime wants to take 18-year-old girls for military conscription and force them into the barracks of soldiers... They want to degrade, imprison and destroy us... I warn this ruthless establishment, this despotic government, to step down because of its crime [in] violating Islamic principles and the constitution.[46]

The government responded by sending the army to attack Faizieh and many other seminaries. The White Revolution was soon going through a baptism of blood, the deaths were mourned by public ceremonies and mourning marches held at forty-day intervals and the unrest continued. In May Khomeini declared that the government should be impeached and asked his followers to use the mourning ceremonies as a political vehicle; students and devout Muslims joined forces in the mourning parades across the cities and once more Khomeini made a defiant call against the regime. In this he was ably assisted by the Islamic Coalition of Mourning Groups, *Hey'ateh Mootalefehyeh Eslami* organised by the Navab Safavi's followers, who had become Khomeini's followers.[47] This time he was arrested. His arrest coincided with the day after the major *Shia* mourning ceremony of Ashura, marking the death of the martyrs of Karbala. Protests and demonstrations broke out across the major cities in Iran and the army was sent in. In the ensuing brutal confrontation thousands lost their lives and many hundreds of opposition leaders were arrested. Khomeini was exiled first to Turkey and then he went on to Najaf in Iraq. The iron fist of the government suppressed most opposition, sending many underground. In retaliation, in 1965 in the classic *Fadayan Eslam*'s mode, one of the Mourning Groups' members, Mohamad Bokharayi, assassinated Prime Minister Hassan Ali Mansour. Bokharayi and four others were executed and over 100 members of the *Hey'ateh Mootalefeyeh Eslami* were imprisoned.

The decade that followed was one of prosperity, rapid modernisation and centralisation of the government power, expanding bureaucracy and underground political resistance by guerrilla movements such as the Marxist *Fadayan* and the

Muslim *Mojahedin*. The Shah used the hated secret police, SAVAK, *Sazemaneh etelaat va amniateh keshvar* (organisation for information and national security) who were given a free hand to throttle all political resistance. With the suppression of political opposition, the only possible form of resistance was through guerrilla activities or the religious establishment.

A group of *ulema* and Muslim intellectuals linked up to formulate the political and ideological grounds for an Islamic resurgence. The included Khomeini in Najaf, and Taleqani, Seyed Mohamad Beheshti, Morteza Mottahari and engineer Mehdi Bazargan in Tehran. They addressed both theological and political questions such as *imamat, marjayiat* (exemplariness of a religious leader to be followed by his disciples) and *ejtehad*, religious leadership. They also formed a number of religious societies, including *Anjomaneh Mahaneyeh Dini*, which held monthly meetings and *Nehzateh Azadi Iran*, Iran's Liberation movement, set up by Bazargan and Taleqani and associated with a revived opposition group – the Second National Front, a broad oppositional party that was reformed demanding democratic freedoms.

The Liberation movement recruited young professionals and members of the intelligentsia both at home and abroad and sought to synthesise Islam and political liberation. The monthly religious groups held regular meetings addressed by both clergy and non-clergy, including Bazargan and Ali Shariati who had joined the Liberation movement in Paris, and Mottahari, Seyed Mahmud Taleqani and Seyed Morteza Jazayeri. These discussions were collected and published in *Goftareh Mah* (Discourse of the Month) and widely distributed.

The ideas formulated by these leading theologians matched Islam and resistance and proposed a democratic Islamic alternative to the increasingly autocratic rule of the Shah. At the same time much of the discussion incorporated the distaste of the intelligentsia for the dependent forms of development, the devaluation of traditional culture and the loss of national identify, which could not be replaced by the denigrating views held by Westerners. Increasing Western influence, seen most clearly in the ever-increasing numbers of privileged foreign technocrats invited to run everything from the armed forces to the tourist industry, may have helped the rich, but was little help to the bulk of the impoverished population. The suppression of political forces, particularly the left, had created a vacuum which was readily filled by the religious institution. As government censors banned more and more publications deemed critical to the regime, so more religious publications arrived to replace secular ones. The anomie and loss of identity was channelled to wards a quest for Islamic Justice. Iranians were to set up a government that united God and his people in a specifically Iranian and equitable manner.

Resistance disguised as political discourse gained ground rapidly and reached a zenith with the establishment of *Hoseiniyeh Ershad*, a religious Forum, built by Mohamad Homayoun, a Liberation movement benefactor in Tehran. Preaching became the main vehicle of formulating public discontent and forgoing a new intellectual formation of Islamic ideology.

The most popular exponent of the new discourse was the French-educated Ali Shariati who took up the pulpit at Hoseiniyeh in 1967 and launched an Islamic version of Fanon's theories,[48] translating his views of colonialism and dependence in Algeria into an Iranian perspective.[49] Shariati called for a renewal of Islamic message, and a reconsideration of the *Quran* as a socio-political conception, rather than one dealing with worship and the metaphysics. The religious establishment initially supported Shariati and welcomed his rapidly rising popularity. But Shariati's insistence that Islam could be studied from differing methodological perspectives and did not demand a clerical training was a direct threat to the *Usuli* approach and was seen as such by the *ulema*, as was his radical reinterpretation of the religious texts.[50] In protest Mottahari resigned from the Hoseiniyeh, but Shariati continued to draw the crowds, which included large numbers of the middle class and professional men and women. In 1972 SAVAK closed down the *Hoseiniyeh*, arrested Shariati and banned his books. In 1975 he was released and placed under house arrest; in 1977 he was allowed to leave the country for London, where he died suddenly, either of a heart attack, or he was killed by SAVAK.

As religious discourse occupied the central ground in politics, so the decade of 1960 marked a rapid increase in mosques, seminaries and religious associations. By 1974 there were over 12 000 religious associations in the country, many funded by guilds or professions associated with the *bazaar*.[51] By the mid-1970s, perhaps for the first time in Iranian history, the religious establishment was large enough to be able to send preachers to the most distant of Iranian villages.[52]

What was emerging in the newly developing ideology was not a call for the establishment of a theocracy, but rather a collection of ideas that ranged from Shariati and Taleqani's views that Islam and socialism were compatible,[53] to Bazargan's carefully articulated notions of separation of political and religious powers in society,[54] to Khomeini's theocratic aspirations. Islam presided over the developing ideology both in a conservative and radical guise

## BUREAUCRACY AND CENTRALISATION

The Shah and his entourage seemed curiously oblivious to the politicisation of religion. Cocooned in the court and surrounded by flattering ministers, the Shah, like his father, concentrated on the expansion of the bureaucracy and the armed forces to buttress his regime.

Mohamad Reza Shah was brought up as an active officer in the forces and as early as the 1940s he took his constitutional title of Commander-in-Chief. He shared Reza Shah's faith in the forces, had a passion for armament,[55] and spent the next two decades in purchasing more or both. In 1962 the military ran to 200 000 men, by 1977 the total number in the armed forces had increased to 410 000. During the same period the annual military budget rose from $293m to $7.3 billion (at 1973 prices and exchange rates).[56] By 1977 Iran had the fifth largest military force in the world and the most up-to-date one in the Persian Gulf.[57]

Both industrialisation and urbanisation were growing at an ever-faster pace. The 1962 land reforms which entitled peasants to land-holdings, but dispossessed landless rural workers, *khoshneshinan*, increased the flow of rural urban migration. As a result, whereas in 1956 31 per cent of Iran's population lived in urban centres, by 1966 this figure rose to 38 per cent and it was 48 per cent by 1976. During the same period the cites themselves grew in size so that the percentage of towns with more than 100 000 inhabitants increased from 20 to 29 per cent in the period 1966–1977 and Tehran's population rose from 2.7 million to 4.5 million.[58]

As cites and their population grew, so did the educational system and levels of literacy. Whereas only 15 per cent of the population was literate in 1956, by 1966 the percentage had increased to 30, and to 47 in 1976.[59] The rate of literacy, was considerably higher in towns, so that for the same period the figures were 35 per cent, 50 per cent and 65 per cent respectively.[60] In the period 1963 to 1977 the education system grew more than threefold and by 1979 there were over 35 000 civil servants, working in schools, and universities and over 7.5 million students.[61] At the same time the decades of women's struggles began coming to fruition: the 1960s and 1970s marked the zenith of women's liberation in Iran. Female literacy increased from 22 per cent of all city-dwelling women in 1965 to 38 per cent in 1976 and 55 per cent in 1976.[62] What was more important, in 1962 women finally obtained the vote.

As modernisation gained momentum, so did the process of centralisation and extension of the state bureaucracy. By 1977 the State employed 50 per cent of the full-time employees in the country. The number of Ministries had increased from ten  civilian ministries in 1947, employing 90 000 full-time civil servants to twelve ministries with 150 000 in 1963 and in 1977, nineteen ministries with 304 000, of whom 28 per cent were women.[63]

The decade following the 1963 uprisings, was one of relative price stability, extensive growth of the economy, the wealth of the industrialist and the royal family, and widening social and economic inequalities.

The period marks an ever-increasing confidence of the Shah in his own power and authority and a belief in the economic miracle and its appeasing effects on the population. In 1971 the Shah threw the flamboyant 2500th birthday party celebrating the uninterrupted royal rule in Iran. Islam was to be relegated to the private and personal domain. Monarchy had been given the higher ground and to underline this in 1975 the Shah rejected the 1355-year-old Islamic calendar, marking the date that Mohamad migrated from Mecca to Medina in favour of a new 2535-year one; 2500 for the monarchy and 35 years for his own reign.

Khomeini denounced the birthday party, and the Shah as Ungodly and called on Iranians to rebel against such illegitimate use of power. He declared:

> The Tradition of King of Kings is the vilest of words. Sovereignty belongs to God alone. Resurgence against the Pahlavi dynasty is demanded of the people by the sacred laws.[64]

Undaunted, the Shah decided to expound his own version of Islam and set up a religious corps, *Sepaheh Din* to take the good news to the villages. Working under the auspices of the Endowment Organisation, *Sazemaneh Oqaf*, graduates from Faculties of Theology were sent to rural areas to serve their military service teaching about the official vision of religion and the State. They were supported and supervised by religious propagandists who were dispatched to advocate modernisation and denounce the old-style clergy.

In 1975 the Shah decided to mobilise political support for the regime by setting up the *Rastakhiz*, Resurgence, party. Iran was to have a one-party system and everyone was compelled to joint the party. The party apparatus was to penetrate in every sector, from the villages, to the *bazaar* to the intelligentsia. The party's ideology was to be the guiding line and the Shah the spiritual and political leader of the nation. Everyone had to join the party and pay membership dues. Those who could, including the *bazaar* merchants, had to make appropriate donations. The party was to set minimum wages for all workers and replace the merchants' High Council of Guilds with its own Chamber of Guilds which was tightly controlled and served as a means of transmitting the government's edicts to the *bazaar*. Khomeini sent a declaration denouncing the setting-up of the new party and the seminary students of Faizieh, in Qom, began a day of protest. Once more the armed forces were sent in and the demonstrators were dispersed. The demonstrations in Faizieh continued and finally the troops broke in, tore up the doors and the books, and closed the seminary.

On the same day Tehran University students also staged a demonstration to mark the anniversary of the 1963 army invasion of the university. Although Tehran university's demonstration passed relatively peacefully, the discontent was not to fade so easily. At the time the student population in Iran, numbered nearly 8 million in an economy that had few jobs to offer. The students at the seminaries had even less opportunity of linking into the prosperous parts of the economy. Their learning was viewed with scepticism by the modern sector, and many felt obligated to continue with their secular studies at the same time as attending religious seminaries. Nor were there long-term prospects for the flood of unskilled migrants. So long as the construction industry was booming, those made landless by the land reforms could be absorbed in the urban economy, but with the collapse of the construction boom in 1977 the numbers of unemployed quadrupled.[65] So long as the economy continued growing, with the vision of impending success and prosperity, it was possible to contain discontent. But in the wake of the vastly increased oil prices, the Iranian economy began to collapse under rapidly rising inflation.

THE REVOLUTION

The Shah's grandiose plans for joining the forefront of industrialisation fuelled a massive inflation. The oil boom encouraged the government to triple its investments and money supply increased by more than 60 per cent in the year 1974–5.[66] Goods and expertise bought at inflated prices created a class of largely foreign luxuriously paid experts,[67] helping the Iranian upper class with their conspicuous consumption, while the cost-of-living index jumped by 90 per cent in the period 1970–76.[68] The uneven development had disproportionately favoured the rich and the urban dwellers.[69] But the government's attempts at controlling inflation hit the rich and the cities and rapidly eroded the Shah's support base. Anti-profiteering measures threatened the commercial classes from the *bazaar* to the modern sector. Those who could began transferring their resources abroad and the *bazaar* intensified its support for the religious establishment's opposition.

The Shah, optimistic about his modernisation plans, and encouraged by the Carter administration in the USA, began relaxing the grip of the SAVAK and 1977 saw the renaissance of political groupings. Lawyers gathered together to form a secular pressure group advocating the abolition of the one-party system and press censorship, and demanded the release of political prisoners. Writers and intellectuals organised and sent open letters of protest to the Prime Minister, Amir Abas Hoveyda, demanding the revival of the Writers Association and freedom to publish. Judges sent open letters to protest against government intervention on the independence of the judiciary and demanded the disbanding of military courts for trial of political prisoners. A number of opposition leaders including Bazargan, Shahpour Bakhtiar and Ayatollah Haj Abolfazle Musavi Zanjani and Mahmud Taleqani linked the secular, modernist intelligentsia with the clergy and formed the Iran Committee for the Defence of Freedom and Human Rights. University Professors set up the national Organisation of University teachers to fight for academic freedom and *bazaar* merchants formed a society for merchants and craftsmen to curtail the Resurgence party's activities. The seminary students in Qom formed an Educational Society and demanded the reopening of the Faizieh and Tehran University, both closed because of student protest.

Various literary societies were formed, disseminating revolutionary materials. These were particularly influential among the university circles. The Iran–German cultural poetry reading was one; it held meetings attended by thousands of teachers and students. In these sessions the Shah and his government were openly criticised, the ruler was referred to as the Führer and his family named individually and their corrupt practices denounced. Although the armed forces were held ready and at hand, the State did not intervene until November 1977. A meeting of 10 000 students at Arya Mehre University was disrupted by the army. The students poured out into the streets, the army attacked, death, injuries and arrests ensued, followed by ten days of rioting. Tehran University students went on strike and demonstrators arrested by the police were acquitted by the civil courts. The student protests continued and gained momentum in January.

The Ministry of Information stepped in. In January, the daily newspaper *Etalat* was compelled to publish an anti-clergy article, naming Khomeini as a foreign spy. Qom seminaries and *bazaar* closed down in protest and thousands of students clashed with the police. Once more there were deaths and injuries.[70] Ayatollah Shariatmadari, along with other opposition leaders, called on the country to observe the mourning ceremonies on the fortieth day of the massacre of Qom, by staying away from work and staging peaceful demonstrations. Thus began the series of fortieth day strikes, protests, riots and demonstrations that continued until May.

The Shah and his government attempted to placate the clergy and reduce inflation. The Shah made a much-publicised pilgrimage to the shrine in Mashad and his Prime Minister, Jamshid Amouzegar, cut back government expenditure and succeeded in halting the astronomical rise in the cost of living and reducing it from 35 per cent in 1977 to 7 per cent in the first nine months of 1978.[71] Shariatmadari called for a return to constitutional government, without demanding the fall of the Shah and there was a short respite.

But the cutbacks resulted in severe unemployment for the poorest section of society, as well as restricting employment opportunities for the young and educated; thus both the professionals and the unskilled workers lost faith in the economy. The hope of ever achieving a prosperous future evaporated. The government, too, vacillated between a 'softly–softly' approach to the opposition and sudden brutal attacks. In July a mourning procession for a religious leader met with police intervention, broke out into riots and massacre and triggered off the fortieth-day cycle of demonstrations across the country. In August a cinema in a working-class quarter of Abadan was set on fire killing 400 people. The government blamed the fundamentalists, and the opposition blamed the government. There had been a pattern of attacks and arson on cinemas showing Western 'immoral' films, as well as banks and other 'agents of Western imperialism' by demonstrators throughout this period. But invariably people working or visiting these buildings had been invited to leave before the building were ransacked or burnt. Furthermore this particular cinema was showing a morally acceptable Iranian film. An estimated 10 000 people turned up the next day for a mass funeral.

The Shah reverted to the 'softly–softly' approach: all political parties, with the exception of the Communist *Tudeh* party, were unbanned, press censorship relaxed, political prisoners freed and Prime Minister Amuzegar replaced by Jaafar Sharif Emami. Sharif Emami, who came from a clerical family, began placating the clergy by closing down the Ministry for Women's Affairs as well as a number of gambling houses. He rescinded the Imperial calendar, sent some of the more notorious members of the royal family abroad, set up a new Ministry of Religious Affairs and turned once more to haunting the traditional scapegoats – women and the Baha'is. He also issued permission for public demonstrations on 4 September, *Eideh Fetre*, the feast day marking the end of a month of fasting, *Ramazan*. There were demonstrations and prayer-gatherings in almost every city in Iran. These were followed by ever-larger daily demonstrations with ever-angrier slogans. The Shah reacted by declaring martial law on 7 September, banning all demonstrations and issuing warrants for the arrests of all opposition leaders.

On Friday 8 September, Black Friday, the inevitable violent clash occurred. Over 5000 residents, students, and merchants staged a sit-in in the Jaleh Square, in one of the poorest quarters of Tehran. The army attacked with helicopter gunships and tanks, shooting to kill. The carnage ended all possibilities of peaceful negotiations between Shah and the people. Shariatmadari denounced the Shah and oil workers went on strike. They were followed by cement workers, and white-collar workers. All demanded higher wages, removal of martial law and the freeing of political prisoners. The employees of the central banks published a list of moneys transferred out of the country by leading industrialists and politicians, including, Sharif Emami. The rich were moving out and taking their money with them. By October Khomeini was forced out of Iraq and sent to Paris. Banks, industrial plants, mines and oil refineries were on strike. The fortieth day mourning ceremonies of Black Friday led to more carnage and the *bazaar*, schools, universities, banks, civil servants, the media as well as mills and oil installations went on strike. The poor and the middle classes, the illiterate and the professionals, the modern and traditional sectors had once more joined forces in strikes and daily demonstrations.

The Shah appointed General Qolam Reza Azhari as Prime Minister on 5 November and appointed six army officers to take over major ministerial posts. Shariatmadari refused to negotiate with the government as long as martial laws continued, and Khomeini held court in Paris where he met Engineer Bazargan and Karim Sanjabi, the secular leader of the National Front. They issued a joint declaration demanding the Shah's abdication and a national referendum. Strikes and violent demonstrations continued.

December coincided with the mourning month of *Moharam* and Azhari banned all demonstrations. Shariatmadari responded by declaring that Muslims did not need permits to mourn the death of *imam* Hosein, and Taleqani asked the faithful to go on rooftops and call *Allah Akbar*, God is Great. Moharam began on 2 December with violent demonstrations by day and the city calling to God by night. The ninth and tenth day of *Moharam* are the major mourning days of *Tasua* and *Ashura*, marking the martyrdom of *Shia imams* in Karbala. The government retreated into a softly–softly approach, released more political prisoners, kept the military out of sight and massive demonstrations took place.

By the end of December almost the entire civil service was on strike, though the government continued paying the salaries. Much of the industrial and service sectors were also on strike. Oil installations were placed under martial-law authorities, with little effect. Oil workers were only prepared to produce enough for home consumption. Almost all oil exports were halted.

The army was beginning to crack. The bulk of the 180 000-strong army were conscripts, with only 50 000 professional soldiers. The professionals had enjoyed many privileges, including good housing, medical insurance and privileged access to education. One of the first protests in Tehran University was against the privileged access which the army had to scarce places. Although with inflation and cutbacks, the privileges of the armed forces were eroded, the officers were still infinitely better off than the conscripts. Drawn from poor rural and urban backgrounds, they were paid little and required to do most of the menial jobs. They had little cause to have allegiance to the Shah and as the revolution progressed, more and more conscripts had to be kept confined to barracks, for fear of their joining the revolutionaries.

On 30 December the Shah appointed Shahpour Bakhtiar as Prime Minister. The National Front, who had refused to nominate a Prime Minister for the Shah expelled him. Bakhtiar, who feared the clergy and impending theocracy more than the Shah, tried to turn the tide. He released more political prisoners, and suggested that the Shah should go for a long holiday abroad. Although Shariatmadari was of the opinion that Bakhtiar should be given a chance to reinstate the constitution, Khomeini called for his removal and the Shah's abdication. The country responded with million-strong demonstrations demanding the removal of Bakhtiar. The Shah left for Cairo on 16 January, thousands took to the streets to celebrate and more than a million came out to ask Bakhtiar to leave. The Prime Minister tried to prevent Khomeini from returning, by closing the airport. Demonstrators took to the street and there was a final attack by the armed forces leading to more deaths.

On 1 February 1979 Khomeini made a triumphant return. On 9 February Air Force cadets and technicians mutinied and the imperial guards moved in to quash them. But, helped by the guerrilla organisations, the mutineers defeated the imperial guards. In the next two days revolutionaries attacked garrisons and police and army arsenals and firearms were distributed widely amongst the youths. On 11 February the Chief of Staff declared that the army would withdraw from the political arena and the revolutionaries declared the end of 2500 years of monarchy.[72]

Modernisation policies backed by foreign powers and interventions had clearly failed in Iran. The Shah had been identified as the lackey of the imperialist powers and the modernisation measures had created an ever-widening gap between the rich and poor. The oppressed, *mostaazefin*, had backed the clergy and were seeking justice. Khomeini had promised no wealth, but independence, self respect and an end to oppression. Once more Iranian politics were to be formulated by the clergy. Within 70 years once more a revolution had forged an uneasy alliance between the *ulema* and the intelligentsia against absolutism in Iran. For a second time in the century opposition to the West and its influence had been articulated through an Islamic political discourse. Yet again Iranians had initiated a revolution in pursuit of freedom and liberty and assumed that an Islamic allegiance would help them to secure these aims. Once more they were doomed to failure.

# 3 *Valayateh Faqih*: A Blueprint for Islamic Government?

The coalition of the clergy and the intelligentsia during the revolution was, as ever, an uneasy alliance, formed to oppose an enemy, shah and dictatorship, rather than to propose a path to follow. Although Khomeini had described it as a blueprint for an Islamic government, *Valayateh Faqih* (Rule by a Wise Religious Male Leader) in 1971, in fact it was little more than a criticism of the *status quo* and promises of a better form of government under the guidance of the clergy.

The religious establishment was of central importance in organising demonstrations, orchestrating grievances and publishing and distributing pamphlets and speeches. But the *ulema*, were themselves divided both in their criticism of the regime and in the kind of government that they wished to see as a replacement. As to the secular supporters of the revolution, their political allegiances stretched across the spectrum from the Communist *Tudeh* party and the Marxist *Fadayan*, to the secular National Front and the Islamic *Mojahedin*. All united to topple the shah, but each expected a different form of post-revolutionary State to follow. Thus, at the end of a year-long struggle, there were a number of competing models of government presented by the wide spectrum of pro-Islamic groups, many of whom were deeply wary of the clergy.

## THE 'WESTOXIFICATED' *ULEMA*

The intellectuals were particularly suspicious of the clergy whom they regarded as conservative, élitist and unsuited to sustaining a dynamic revolutionary process. Their entrenched traditionalism was thought to make them hidebound and reactionary. Some, like Ali Shariati and Jalal Al Ahmad, expressed their criticisms in terms that were supportive of Islam and critical of both hidebound traditionalism and unrestrained pursuit of modernisation; they were as critical of imperialist penetration and erosion of cultural identities and values, as they were of superstitious obedience to religious leaders. Thus, for example, the author, Jalal Al Ahmad, renowned for coining the term *qarbzadegi*, westoxification, argues that *rohaniat*, the clergy,[1] have always been the best-educated sector of society. But the nature of their learning and their views are such as to make them innately conservative and reactionary. So pervasive is their intolerance of any form of doubt, critical enquiry or revisionism that they would even drive their own children helter-skelter towards westoxification. Al Ahmad, himself born in a clerical family, seems to echo Kasravi's views:

> I was declared [by my family] to be *la mazhab*, irreligious, when I refused to put my head on a *mohre*, a prayer stone. I had thought to myself that to pray

40

on a stone is a form of idolatry, and Islam has banned all forms of idolatry. But in my father's eyes my comments marked the beginning of loss of faith. You must admit that when irreligiosity is so easy to achieve, one is tempted to go all the way, just as an experiment.[2]

But, unlike Kasravi, who derided the *ulema*, and whom he cites as a *qarbzadeh*, westoxificated, Al Ahmad notes the ability of the *ulema* to be politically active and to stand up against tyranny and defend the interests of Islam:

The *Shia* clergy do not see government and political activities as unsuited to their position. They openly contest and question all governments[3]...the *Shia* clergy have a concern for eternity and metaphysical values on the one hand and, on the other, Shiism sees the clergy as the vice-regents of the *imam* and as such entitled to claim the right to replace the rulers of their time. Thus by their very nature, and the nature of their faith, they represent an alternative to the government.[4]...The defence of tradition gives the Shia clergy the power to organise a resistance movement against the swarm of imperialism, which in the first instance robs each nation of its cultural heritage. The clergy form a barricade against westoxification of the intelligentsia and their unquestioning submission to the West and its rule. This helps and empowers those amongst the intellectuals who see the world, not through westoxificated eyes, but with anti-imperialist ones.[5]

But at the same time he deplores the clergy's inability to look towards dynamic change and progress:

The other side of this strength is a weakness – the weakness of unquestioning submission. This has burdened the clergy with a blinkered outlook which cannot deal with the complexities and extended interdependence of the present world...Thus we see that as contemporary scientific knowledge takes root in society, so religion and its values lose their foothold [6]

He argues that traditionalism has made the clergy too hidebound to be an effective force for change:

the clergy are the defendants of tradition. Therefore they oppose all change, progression and revision. This is why they are called the opiate of the masses. Since protection of tradition is a retrograde process, we observe that the clergy do not even protect the present situation. (For example the clergy have not yet come to terms with the unveiling of women or their enfranchisement and their right to participate fully in the public sphere.)[7]

In the final analysis, Al Ahmad is of the view that even though the clergy shun change, their activism may, willy-nilly, help society to move forward:

Thus we have occasionally seen them embark on violent protests and even uprisings against the temporal powers. But such a protest is not anchored in enlightened ideas, nor does it usually seek to alter the government or the society. Generally it is concerned with relatively minor issues. Nevertheless such repeated unrests and uprisings represent a form of progression towards enlightenment.[8]

Ali Shariati, a French-educated influential teacher and popular orator, who sought to synthesise Islam and socialism, is less charitable towards the religious establishment. He accused them of being the first examples of westoxification. Shariati argued that far from progressing, the Shia clergy have moved away from enlightenment. In his book *Tashiiyeh Alavi va Tashiiyeh Safavi* (*Alavi* and *Safavid* Shiism) he echoes Kasravi's scepticism and questions the very legitimacy of the *ulema*'s claim to represent the *imam* and act as the protectors of the oppressed and the needy. Shariati makes a distinction between the clergy before and after the *Safavid* period. The early *Shia* clergy, he says, were embattled and represented the people and the resistance movement. But in the sixteenth century, when the *Safavid* adopted Shiism as the official religion of the Iranian State the clergy became institutionalised. He notes that initially Shiism was a revolutionary force:

> Negation played a central role in shaping *Shia*'s embattled position in Islamic history...Shiism which began with this 'no' was an uprising against...the path of ignorance, *jaheliat*...*Shias* represented the oppressed and justice-seeking classes and the firm opponents of caliphate.[9]

But once Shiism became institutionalised, the religious establishment became part of the ruling élite. As such they undermined all revolutionary change:

> From the moment that Shiism succeeded in gaining formal recognition, from that moment it was vanquished...from the moment that the powers that had been ranged against it began to accommodate it, they absorbed it, it ceased to be a dynamic movement, it became a powerful ruling institution.[10]

Thus, instead of protecting the needy and forging a path against injustice, the clergy became the mouthpiece of the government:

> The *Safavid*-style clergy is a specialist in creating religious covers, *kola sharii*. He covers violence with a gown of piety [and justifies usury and similar practices].[11]

What is more, Shariati accuses the clergy of being the first to have been lured away by the culture of the West:

> The first westoxification was not in the nineteenth century, but in the sixteenth, when the *Safavid* created a formal ministerial post of '*rozeh khani*', reciting tales to mourn the martyrs of Karbala, and *taazieh*, passion play, and sent the Minister to Europe where he acquired the Western practices, hitherto unknown in Iranian culture, of passion plays and flagellants which were prevalent in Lourdes and elsewhere.[12]

They copied Western practices and lulled the people with the trappings and pomps and ceremonies of mourning and devotion, which completely undermined the revolutionary nature of Shiism. This westoxification turned red Shiism, a revolutionary colour bestowed by the martyrs to the movement, to that of black Shiism of tears and sorrows:

> The *Safavid* bewitched Shiism; they altered the nature of red Shiism – which is its eternal colour from Ali till eternity [having begun with his martyrdom] – to black Shiism which is the garment of death which in the name of mourning the *Safavid* have clothed it with...making *Ashura* a form of opium for the Iranians...[13]

Shariati is not the only one to deplore the public mourning marches of the flagellants and the passion plays. Even among the clergy there were some who viewed such practices with disfavour. As early as 1955 Ayatollah Heibat al Din al Shahrestani, the *marja' taqlid* of Najaf had issued a *fatwa*, decree, against the mortification of flesh during the observance of *Ashura*; he pointed out that there was no religious foundation for cutting one's head with a knife or for self-flagellation.[14] But with the suppression of all forms of opposition in the 1970s, religious processions became a major vehicle of social mobilisation and one that was condoned and even encouraged by the religious establishment. Shariati did not criticise the actual mourning for the martyrs of Karbala, but he objected to its transformation from a revolutionary process, as a symbol of resistance to the death, into a formal and organised procession which distracted people. It drained their emotions in tears, rather than inspiring fury, by emphasising sorrow and demanding pity rather than revolution. It made religion into an opiate of the masses rather than a quest for justice and fraternity.

Although it may have been too much to argue that the *ulema* were intentionally colluding with the government to lull the populace to sleep, it was nevertheless true to say that the religious institution had much to gain from the *status quo*. It was well-established and wealthy. By the mid-1970s the *ulema* were a more-or-less tightly knit élite who admitted newcomers to their ranks through their seminaries and tied them in by familial links. They offered extensive support for those whom they elevated to the ranks of *hojat el eslam* (proof of Islam), a title accorded to middle-ranking *ulema*, or *ayatollah* (sign of God) – a title accorded to leading clergy, or *ayatollah ozma* (greatest sign of God), title accorded to the highest ranking *ulema*.

By 1975 all seven first-ranking *marja' taqlid*[15] could be put on the same genealogy and linked to either wholesale merchants or landed classes, links which gave them access to formidable resources and influence across the country. The top ranks were on the whole quite well off. Abrahamian estimates that some 90 000 of the clergy could be classed as propertied middle class, linked by strong family and financial ties to the *bazaar*.[16] The clergy controlled a large and decentralised establishment, including 5600 mosques and six major seminaries in Qom, Mahshad, Tabriz, Isfahan, Shiraz and Yazd and considerable numbers of *vaqf*, private endowments. Shariati deplores this situation:

> The very same *ulema* and *rohaniat*, clergy, who always headed the battles against the governments and were always the shield-bearers against the raining arrows of the ruling institutions. The very same are now living the most luxurious of lives. They rule, shoulder to shoulder, with the government. Their opinions are sought by the political rulers. The ruler even justifies his own authority as one that has been bestowed upon him by the clergy who are the vice-regent, *nayeb*, of the Twelfth Imam.[17]

Furthermore, he argues that a combination of wealth, theatrical pretensions and westoxification has made the mosques into ostentatious works of art, rather than centres of revolutionary resistance:

> We see that the mosque which Islam, at the time of its foundation, disdained decorating, has become the house of golden and shimmering artistry and a museum devoted to ornate beauty. But the soul of Islam has long since abandoned these beautiful palaces with their moulded ceilings, glittering chandeliers and imposing chambers.[18]

Thus, although they were supposed to be the defenders of the oppressed, some of whom even paid them their *khoms*, religious tax, the *ulema* had gained a clear sense of their own superiority. Al Ahmad agrees with this view and illustrates it:

> A *rohani*, even though he may depend on the poorer classes, for him this dependence is in terms of leadership and management and not fellowship and equality…When my father was alive, it often happened that at sunrise, when he was going to pray in the mosque he would shout abuses or even hit the sleeping night-guard with his stick to wake him up. My father would tell him off for dozing off, instead of saying his prayers and guarding people's goods and chattels.[19]

But despite their self-importance, the *ulema* were dependent as a class on the contributions made by the devout as a whole and the merchants in particular. This dependence had two important effects, it obliged them to represent the interest of the merchants at all times. It also demanded that they addressed themselves to the masses and offer popular, rather than learned, discourses. This situation was not necessarily welcomed by the clergy. Sheikh Fazlollah Nuri, the well-known religious leader and opponent to the modernists in the first decades of the century, expressed the self-important view, shared by many of the *ulema*, that 'the masses are more benighted than cattle'.[20] Ayatollah Mottahari, the well-known *alem* and ideologue of the revolution, puts the same point in a less abusive way. He advocates abandoning *khoms*, since it enabled:

> The masses to control the clergy's income…[so that] reforming the structures of the religious institution would require their approval. Unfortunately for the

reformers, the masses have proved to be too conservative with regard to social change.[21]

Shariati makes a similar point when he argues that the clergy have abandoned learned discourse for populist sloganisms to pacify the more wealthy and influential among their supporters:

Just as the clergy moved from the very heart of the people into the centres of government, so the Shia scholar, *alem*, became a *rohani*, clergyman...a Christian term. A clergyman is pious, devout and virtuous. He is a Godly person who prays and has a clear conscience and a serene nature; the people kiss his hand and admire the clarity of his gaze. He does not have to be learned, the spirit shines through him...but spiritualism has nothing to do with scholarship.[22]

The *Shia* scholars throughout the history of Islam were renowned for their accessibility and willingness to argue and debate and engage in scholarly disputes and discussions.

At a time when all the educational and propagandists resources were controlled by their opponents, they embarked on developing the strong logic that they offered in support of Shiism – it was this very openness of discourse and debate that enabled them to argue their points convincingly and present their views logically and clearly. By contrast the clergy of *Safavid* Shiism is scared of probing questions...The *Safavid* clergy – though seemingly learned and wearing the garb of the *Shia* scholar – is always addressing the bulk of the ignorant people even in his supposedly scholarly discourses. He is wary of the true scholar. He has usurped the position of the Shia scholar and claims to be the source of emulation for people in all matters. But his only source of reference is the ignorant people. He is the official mouthpiece who pronounces the commands that have been gathered by his followers. He commands that we should not read a certain scientific book because it is against the principles of Islam.

We ask: 'where does it contravene our beliefs?'

He says: 'I don't have the time or the patience to read it, but a number of respectable and reliable people from the *bazaar* have repeatedly told me that this book is harmful and corrupting. They wanted to know why I had remained silent? Why I do not denounce it? Why I do not tell you all not to read it?'[23]

It is worth noting that this criticism applies to Khomeini's *fatwa* against the book, *Satanic Verses*. Khomeini could not read English, and had never read the book. Nevertheless he ordered the death sentence for Salman Rushdi because others told him that a chapter in the book was heretical.

If the clergy have become the mouthpiece of the ignorant, then their commentary and interpretations of Islamic laws, *ejtehad*, can no longer be universally accepted. Shariati deplores the demise of real scholarship and the failure of *ejtehad*. Initially used by the true *Alavid* ulema to deduce appropriate solution for new situations by studying the principles of Islam, *ejtehad* had helped to maintain the dynamic nature of Shiism and prevent it from stagnating into a backward-looking faith. But, Shariati argues, the clergy have turned this practice on its head and use it to maintain old traditions or apply it to peripheral and irrelevant questions:

> So that at a time when the question of women is paramount and the debate is about human rights and their socio-political role and the part that women should play in society and the problems of sexual freedom and marriage and family and their relationship with men. When there are grave questions as to whether women would embark on a revolutionary or a seditious path. At such a time, the best and most learned of our clergy are concentrating their attention on distinguishing the differences between the blood after childbirth and the blood of menstruation.[24]

A clear example of such preoccupation is Khomeini's teaching. In his *Toziholmassael* (Explanation of Problems) Khomeini warns his followers about women. They should not be believed when they make statements concerning their own menstruation. The faithful can recognised menstrual blood as it 'pours out with pressure causing a slight burning sensation'. They can distinguish it from the blood of an abscess by inserting cotton wool in the vagina: 'if tainted in the left-hand side it is menstrual blood, on the right hand it is an abscess'.[25]

Having denounced the clergy for being ignorant, superficial and in collusion with the government of the time, Shariati dismisses both their right to interpret the holy texts and set an example, *ejtehad*, and the requirement that their example should be followed, *taqlid*. Shariati argued that before the institutionalisation of Shiism *taqlid* enabled the masses to find a leader and enabled the learned to discuss differing approaches to deal with each problem. At the time, Shariati argues, learning was valued for learning's sake and all could participate in the search for the correct path. There were diverging views and out of the discussions certain ways for dealing with new conditions emerged. In any case, Shariati is adamant that *taqlid* is only about emulating the leading clergy on matters of secondary importance and that the principles of Islam have never been blindly followed. Matters of principle and faith were to be understood by each person individually and Shariati reiterated the belief that Islam did not place intermediaries between people and their faith:[26]

> It is a sin to copy, *taqlid*, in matters concerning the principles of faith ...individuals must, according to their personal ability, knowledge and learning and their own personal logic and reason, decide for themselves. It is only in secondary and tertiary matters of jurisprudence that one should follow the example set by the clergy. Even then such *taqlid* should not detract from independent reasoning and free-thinking and logic and open-mindedness....What is dangerous is blind imitation, intellectual imitation...Humanity has been given the characteristic ability to think independently and to choose freely, imitation kills both these gifts [of a free mind and a free will] in human beings and turns them into nauseating monkey-like creatures.[27]

Although both Shariati and Al Ahmad have been rehabilitated by the post-revolutionary state in Iran, they distrusted the clergy and presented some of the most trenchant criticism of the clergy. Both denounced them for losing sight of the plight of the very people they should be representing and of being lured by the trappings of wealth. Shariati's criticism caused a great deal of anger amongst the clergy and he was the butt of much abuse by the religious institution during his lifetime. Not only did Mottahari resign from the *Hoseinieh*, because he objected to Shariati's teachings, but also the clergy published many abusive pamphlets questioning Shariati's right to interpret Islamic dictum and to teach about religion. Shariati was unrepentant:

> They say: 'dear man, are you a *moqaled*, imitator or a *mujtahed*, religious leader? If you are a *mujtahed*, where is your *ejazeh* [formal signed permission granted by an Ayatollah] to indicate that a pupil is fully trained and permitted to embark on *ejtehad*? Having a Ph.D. and specialising in history, sociology, economy and philosophy and the like indicate that you are a *jahel*, ignorant ...*jahel* is in no position to enter into debate with the clergy'.[28]

So Shariati concludes that the intelligentsia should beware of the clergy who are divisive and self-interested and who are setting 'traps' and 'snares' for the Muslim people: [29]

> Our intellectuals should not take the words, the rationalisations and the example set by these [*Safavid* clergy]...as representing religion, Islam and specially Shiism. They must be warned. These are the institutionalised clergy of the *Safavid* ilk...who give Shiism a bad name.[30]

Not surprisingly Shariati viewed a potential new theocracy, which he called the despotism of the clergy, *estebdadeh rohani*, as 'the worst and the most oppressive form of despotism possible in human society'.[31]

## THE *MUJAHEDIN*

The teachings of Shariati, and his brand of revolutionary Islam, was one that formed the ideological foundation of the *Sazemaneh Mujahedin Khalq*, the people's holy war warriors' organisation. The movement began with the 1963 carnage. Its chief ideologue, Mohamad Hanifnejad, had gained a state scholarship to study engineering at Tehran University. He joined the Islamic Students Movement and Bazargan's Liberation movement and was imprisoned for his political activities in 1963. In prison he met Ayatollah Mahmud Taleqani and embarked on studying the *Quran* under his guidance. Although they held different political views, the association was of lasting influence for both of them.

The ideology that was developed through this prison association, was one that did not define religion as the opiate of the masses. On the contrary it saw it as a socialist, democratic and egalitarian ideology.[32] Hanifnejad and Said Mohsen gradually developed an ideological framework for the *Mujahedin* that was disseminated through pamphlets and study groups amongst the members of the party.

The *Mujahedin* combined Marxism and materialism to develop a new anti-thesis. They posited a historically deterministic law of evolution, whereby the contradictions between the means and relations of production propelled society into constant motion. This in turn produced qualitative changes which destroyed old social systems. At the same time they maintained that the concept of class struggle was an integral part of Islam.

It was God who set in motion the law of historical determinism. It was God also who periodically sent Prophets to enable humanity to move towards better social systems. Mohamad was the ultimate Prophet who sought to move the world towards a free and egalitarian world.

Shiism in particular spearheaded the battle against oppression and martyrs of Shiism had died for the cause of justice and equity, as devout Muslim–Marxists, the *Mujahedin* should do no less. Thus combining Islam and Marxism, the *Mujahedin* endorsed the guerrilla tactics advocated by Che Guavara and reinterpreted them into their call for liberation through Islam. The ideology that evolved was also much influenced by Frantz Fanon's ideas that the poor had, under the influence of imperialism, become the 'wretched of the earth' damned to subordination.[33] The term 'wretched of the earth', *mostaazefin*, adopted by the *Mujahedin*, was to become a major political concept in the revolution and a cause for all to defend.

Hanifnejad shared Shariati's view that the clergy had lost the way and the Islam that they preached was radically different from the Islam of the Prophet; that what was needed was a revolutionary organisation which would once more ignite the flame of 'negation' and say 'no' to despotism, capitalism, colonialism and conservative clericalism.[34] Like Shariati, the *Mujahedin* made a distinction between the preachers and the religion and argued that it was not Islam, but the clergy who were the opiate of the masses. One of the young *Mujahedin*, Mehdi Rezayi, in his defence speech, before he was sentenced to death, explained the synthesis that they had drawn from Marxism and Islam:

> Marx knew nothing of Islam and made no reference to it...He criticised Christianity and we share his views. He talks about a false Christianity which advised people to submit to oppression on this earth and to be patient in the knowledge that would be rewarded in the next world. But this view is not shared by Muslims. Islam is the religion of action. Islam teaches us that those who are shamed in this world will be shamed in the next. Islam teaches us that peace and calm for the believers can only be gained at the cost of bloodshed and battles against the enemies of God and his people.[35]

In the *Mujahedin*'s view it was precisely this dynamic and vigilant nature of Islam that had been covered by the traditional clergy with a veil of sorrow and static conservatism:

Unfortunately the traditionalist have treated these texts (the Quran and the Teachings of the first Imam Ali) as dry dogma and public tranquillisers.[36]

The clergy had forgotten the vibrant messages of the seventy-three martyrs of Karbala, who fought to the death for justice. Echoing the views of Shariati on red Shiism, the *Mujahedin* state that martyrdom is an act of religious devotion, conducted bravely in pursuit of a just cause. Self-sacrifice and battle to the death were required if people were to be freed of the yolks of injustice. Such martyrdom ensured eternal life for the heroes who gave their all for a just cause. *Mujahedin* were returning to the central concern of Islam with the class struggle and with the injustice meted out to the oppressed:

> God warns us to beware of sedition and requital will not be only for those who were the oppressors, but also for those who allowed injustice and exploitation to occur and continue without breathing a word of protest. They too will be punished...As Ali (may he rest in peace) has said...God depends on those who see these inhumane social problems not to remain silent, not to tolerate the unheeding gratification of the unjust and the hunger and misery of the oppressed...We have responded to the call of the Almighty and the injured and the oppressed people.[37]

In this they required no clerical intermediaries between themselves and the holy texts:

> For us the texts [of the *Quran* and Ali's teachings] are not static and dogmatic commandments, to be obeyed to the letter. They provide guidance and inspiration for dynamic and revolutionary action.[38]

Their revolutionary action, the Mujahedin claimed, was in direct response to the teachings of the Quranic verse which stated:

> Why do you not engage in battle to serve God and those who are oppressed – men, women and children – those who call to God to send them friends and helpers to deliver them from sorrow in a land where they are being oppressed.[39]

In his defence speech, Rezayi, who was to be one of an entire family of martyrs of *Mujahedin*, explained that it was in response to this very verse that the movement had launched its attacks on the State. Like Shariati, the *Mujahedin* saw themselves as the successors of the pre-*Safavid* clergy, crusaders for the defence of the people who loved and supported them:

> We are funded by the people. Many of our friends have to go short themselves, to scrimp and save to help us. Our supporters offer us their hard-earned honest incomes because they believe in our Islamic and Quranic ideology.[40]

The *Quran* had promised that the *mostaazafin*, would inherit the earth. To achieve this end God sent the Prophet Mohamad to establish a new society of Muslim people, *umma*. Stretching over all national boundaries and encompassing all Muslims, this dynamic society was in constant motion towards social justice and the achievement of both united monotheistic religion, *mazhabeh tohidi*, and a classless society *nezameh tohidi*. In this the martyrs of Karbala, as well as Fatima and Zainab, respectively daughters of the Prophet and the first Imam Ali, represented crusading examples of selfless devotion to the cause.

So the revolutionary Muslims, as represented by the *Mujahedin*, like the Muslim intellectuals, as represented by Shariati, distrusted the *ulema* and offered an alternative, direct and fundamentalist route to faith and revolution.

## ISLAMIC POLITICIANS

Much of the political discourse of the revolutionary era took Islam for granted. The questions posed by the *Mujahedin* and many of the libertarians was not whether a future government should be secular – that is, without a declared national religion. On the contrary the argument was that the failure of the State under the Pahlavis to recognise and value its Islamic adherence had resulted in the emergence of dictatorial rule. Thus Islam was equated with liberalism and with the exception of Khomeini's entourage no one advocated a theocratic rule as a viable alternative to dictatorship.

The age-old divergence between the modernists and the traditionalist and the clergy and the intellectuals was not even addressed by those avowed Muslim intellectuals who had, for decades, sought to resolve the differences between secular forms of politics and the implementation of Islamic laws. Disagreement about a post-revolutionary government divided the *ulema* and extended to an intellectual divide between politicians such as Mehdi Bazargan and Abol Hassan Bani Sadre and the orthodox clergy, headed by Khomeini. Bazargan, who played an important part in the revivalism of Islamic thinking in the 1970s, was a devout Muslim and an active participant of the monthly-gathering groups of theologians. He was wary of the deep penetration of secular bureaucracy into every aspect of daily life and the loss of faith that followed the marginalisation of religion and its rituals and representatives in everyday life. Bazargan was determined to reconcile the intelligentsia with Islam and the people with their faith. He argued that:

> The state's total control to regulate life from birth to death...[means that] unless there is a change of pattern, politics will annihilate religion.[41]

To secure such change, he and the radical religious leader Ayatollah Taleqani organised the Liberation movement of Iran, *Nehzateh Azadiyeh Iran*, in the early 1960s and linked it with the National Front. The Liberation movement aimed at meeting people's 'religious, social and national needs'.[42] Amongst its early members were some of the future leaders of the Mujahedin and their newspaper, *Mojahed*, published the aims of the liberation movements:

> We are Muslims, Iranians, constitutionalist and Mossadeqists: Muslims because we refuse to divorce our principles from our politics; Iranians because we

respect our national heritage; constitutionalists because we demand freedom of thought, expression and association; Mossadeqists because we want national independence.[43]

But in terms of practical politics, the Liberation movement and Bazargan envisaged a clear separation between faith and its rituals and government and the state. Far from seeing the clergy as the obvious potential candidate for government Bazargan viewed the secularist National Front as a suitable vehicle for establishing a new political rule. The main aim of Bazargan and his movement was religious enlightenment, not religious government. He noted that although there were 'linkages and contradictions between religion and politics', care was needed in:

treading the fine line between religion and politics and creatively interweaving them together without fully integrating them into a monolithic whole.[44]

In fact Bazargan was extremely wary of an enforced imposition of religiosity on people:

Islam ran society through its members' deep and sincere commitment to its implementation. Therefore it has never been imposed [on people] against their will and their nature...It has often been said of Islam that it conquered by the sword. But it cannot be said that it ruled and governed by the sword...The Prophet of Islam ruled...and according to his rule...there has never been any compulsion in accepting religion, there were no...religious inquisitions ...Islamic governments did not rule in the shadow of fearsome organisations such as the Gestapo to secure their survival...the government of the just is protected by God and the people themselves.[45]

What Bazargan denounced was all forms of autocracy. His movement intended to return the country to its constitutional base and secure the implementation of a constitution which guaranteed the freedom of all individuals and the welfare of all nationals, even the non-Muslims:

Ali (the only rightful caliph) not only permitted his opponents to express their views, but also allowed them to have a share of the public wealth, *beytolmal*.[46]

For Bazargan opposition and discord was of the essence and nowhere in his writing is there room for envisaging an absolute rule by the *faqih*, learned religious leader. Bazargan denounces all submission:

When people in a country think themselves powerless and ineffectual, they feel that they are led by, and according to, the wishes of others. Even if it were a good leadership, they would still lose hope and self-respect. They lose confidence in themselves and their own action.[47]

This democratic view is deeply contradictory to the fundamentalists' position on Islam. If God has made all laws already, then there is no room for legislation, what is required of the Muslims is submission to the will of God,[48] and what is

required of the clergy is appropriate interpretation of such laws.[49] There is no
room for democratic control and diffusion of power. But both Bazargan who led
the very first post-revolutionary government, and Abol Hassan Bani Sadre, the
first President of the Islamic Republic, had been raised on a different political
ideology. Both sought to integrate Islamic faith and Islamic justice with
democratic government and politics. Both denied that an Islamic government
could ever be envisaged as the autocratic rule of one person, albeit a *faqih*. Bani
Sadre in his *Eqtesadeh Tohidi* clearly explains this position:

> The society has never been given the right of owning individuals, and it is not
> allowed to deprive any one of the right to live, work, think etc. That is, Islam
> has not elevated the public, *jam'*, to the position of the Deity, *nor does it
> recognise such a right for any imam*. If a freehold over the life and death of
> the individual falls into the hands of the *imam* (the party or whatever), then he
> is no longer the *imam*, he is a *taqut*, an absolute and arbitrary holder of the
> reins of power.[50] [my italics]

Thus for Bani Sadre *imam* is a symbol of consensus, but does not have the right
to impose himself and create a coercive state – very much the same kind of
political analysis as Bazargan. Similarly, Bani Sadre, in his manifesto of the
Islamic republic, advocates a diffusion of power amongst the people who are to
supervise the government at all times.[51]


## THE ANTI-THEOCRATIC *ULEMA*

In the tumult of the pre-revolutionary period, the clergy presented a united face,
but in practice they remained as divided as ever. In particular, they differed over
the future model of government. There was a wide division between those who
expected a secular democratic government to follow and those who perceived a
theocratic future. Amongst the democrats, there was also a division between the
more left-wing group, including Ayatollahs Abolfazl Zanjani and Taleqani, and
the more conservative group, including Ayatollahs Mohamad Hadi Milani and
Shariatmadari.

Ayatollah Mahmud Taleqani was at the extreme left of the clerical group.
Unlike most other clergy, Taleqani was neither totally dismissive of Marxism,
nor of the view that it was essentially incompatible with Islamic belief and
practices. In 1935, when Taleqani was imprisoned for the first time, he shared
his prison cell with the future leaders of the *Tudeh* party. Ever after he saw 'true'
communism as consistent with the revolutionary dynamic and anti-exploitative
nature of Islam:

> In terms of its true and authentic linguistic meaning, communism, that is, com-
> munal family life, is rooted in Islam...The issue of communism is different
> from that of materialism and whether or not it is scientific. If we consider
> Islam as being so weak that it cannot even confront materialism...then

clearly we have not understood Islam, or we are failing Islam by thinking it inadequate.[52]

This empathy with Marxism, made Ayatollah Taleqani an important spiritual source of inspiration for the *Mujahedin*. Like Shariati, the other source of socialist Islamic ideological inspiration for the movement, Taleqani had been holding open discussion series. From 1960 onward Taleqani taught at the Hedayat mosque. The mosque was built by a number of *bazaar* merchants including Haj Sadeq, who was a friend of Taleqani and the father of Nasser Sadeq, one of the Mujahedin's leadership cadre. These classes were attended by many future members of the *Mujahedin* including Mohamad Hanifnejad and Ahmad Rezayi, intellectual leaders of the movement. Their scholarly dialogue continued after the imprisonment of Taleqani in 1975. There he met and worked closely with Hanifnejad – collaboration that continued after Taleqani's release in 1978.[53] Taleqani, whose son, Mojtaba, joined the *Mujahedin*, worked actively to collect funds to help the relatives of those who were in prison. He had much admiration for these young guerrillas:

I respect such selfless and strong people who make so many sacrifices and lay down their lives for the cause and are prepared to endure imprisonment for a quarter of a century. I respect them from the human point of view and not because they've espoused a particular ideology. We do not, ever, reject anybody.[54]

Very much in the same mould as Bazargan and Bani Sadre, Ayatollah Taleqani and his brand of Islamic revivalism, advocated democracy and freedom and argued that every group, including the Communists who 'without a doubt had a share in this struggle' would have the right to be represented:

Islam, the Islam that we know, the Islam that emanates from the *Quran* and *sunna*, customs and practices of the Prophet, does not restrict freedom. Any group which does not want that despotism, imperialism and exploitation to be uprooted, has not understood Islam.[55]

For Taleqani there was no conflict between a representative secular government and the demands of Islam; the very worst scenario would have been an autocratic theocracy:

The most dangerous of all forms of oppression are laws and restrictions forcibly imposed on people in the name of religion. This is what the monks, in collaboration with the ruling classes, did to people in the name of religion. This is the most dangerous of all impositions, because that which is not from God is thrust upon the people to enslave and suppress them and prevent them from evolving, depriving them of the right to protest, criticise and be free.
Islam is the religion of freedom. Its goal is peoples' liberation. If a religion aims at liberating people from all forms of bondage, it cannot itself be made a chain for keeping people in bondage.[56]

The Islamic society that he had envisaged there was room for a spiritual religious leader, but not for a theocratic one:

> No single division or party has the right to impose its self-righteous control over others...In the Islamic system of government it is possible for a person to be in a position of leadership, but he has no right to control and dominate people.[57]

He was emphatically against the formation of a theocracy and felt that the clergy ought to concentrate on religious teachings and, once the revolution had been successful, return to their mosques:

> It is not advisable for the *rohaniat* to take up governmental posts and respons-ibilities. The mosque is the best fortification and the strongest base for the clergy. We hope that once the situation is under control and a government has been formed, the clergy will shun governmental duties and will return to its main responsibilities and will be entrenched in their mosques.[58]

During the revolution Taleqani remained very active. After his release from prison in 1978, his house was one of the revolutionary headquarters, organising the demonstrations and communicating with Khomeini. In December 1979 Taleqani told mourners that they should defy the martial laws and make it a day of political protest. But he did not endorse the concept of *Valayateh faqih*, gov-ernment by religious leader. In this he was supported by others amongst the clergy, who did not share his left-wing tendencies, but had a high regard for a constitutional democratic form of government. The best-known among this group is Ayatollah Kazem Shariatmadari.

Shariatmadari headed the group of liberal clergy. He had close ties with the well-to-do merchants and was the *marja' taqlid* of the Azarbaijanis, the power-ful minority group of the north-western provinces. Based in Qom, Shariatmadari was first and foremost a scholar; politically he demanded a return to the 1906–9 constitution. He did not think it necessary for the clergy to govern the country at any time, and thought it sufficient for them to supervise the temporal powers. For him, politically, the clergy were the providers of protection for people against injustices by the government; their role was an oppositional one. During the revolution, Shariatmadari began by demanding reforms and return to parlia-mentary democracy. Like Khomeini in the 1950s, Shariatmadari in the 1960s sought a just government, but did not wish to topple the shah. He was, however, sympathetic to and supportive of the revolutionaries and gave shelter to Bazargan and secularist political activists.

Once the government began targeting the clergy in its attack, Shariatmadari rose to their defence. In January 1978 he condemned the government for slandering the clergy and the police for behaving in an un-Islamic manner:

> if wanting a return to constitutional government is a sign of black reaction then I must confess to being a staunch black reactionary.[59]

The excesses of the government so angered Shariatmadari that he threatened that he would personally deliver the dead bodies of the revolutionaries to the royal palace unless the government ceased attacking the clergy and their supporters. The response was not particularly favourable. In May 1978 troops pursuing demonstrators in Qom, invaded his house, violated the rights of sanctuary and killed two students. Shariatmadari protested vehemently and the government offered a public apology. In June 1978 he was sufficiently mollified to repeat that he did not care whether or not the Shah went, what he wanted was a return to constitutional government.[60]

But the truce was short-lived. As the troops continued murdering the revolutionaries, so Shariatmadari's opposition became more vocal. In November 1978 he refused to negotiate with the shah and called upon the country to observe the fortieth-day mourning ceremonies.

After the revolution, Shariatmadari called for a pluralist political system where all groups could participate and elected officials, and not the clergy, wielded power. He conceived of the *faqih* being consulted in cases of major crisis and the clergy intervening only if the government contravened religious laws:

> *Valayateh Faqih* must not be so interpreted as to deny the firmly established rights invested in people to govern themselves. Nor should *Valayateh Faqih* be devoid of legal source and lawful logic. Since every principle that concerns Islam must derive clearly from the canonical sources, the *Quran* or the *sunna* of the Prophet. At the very least such laws must rely on well-known *fatwas*, religious decrees, issued by leading Muslim jurisconsuls.[61]

Both Taleqani and Shariatmadari and their supporters had assumed that the collegiate accord of the clergy would continue after the revolution and would check any excesses that any one leader may indulge in. In this they appeared to have been supported by Khomeini himself who in *Valayateh Faqih* argues that since no *faqih* can dismiss the opinions of another *faqih*, then the 'guidance of the just government would be collegial'.[62]

## KHOMEINI'S DISCIPLES

Khomeini's vision of an Islamic government was advocated by a group of his disciples, who had been taught by him and successfully disseminated his teachings. These included Ayatollah Mohamad Hosein Beheshti, and Ayatollah Morteza Mottahari who had been trained in Qom and Tehran University, Ayatollah Hosein Ali Montazeri, Mohamad Reza Mahdavi Kani, both of whom had been imprisoned both in the aftermath of the 1963 rebellion and in the 1970s and Hojatoleslams Ali Khameneyi, imprisoned in the 1970s, and Ali Akbar Rafsanjani, imprisoned in the 1960s. All came to play central roles in Iranian politics after the revolution and all supported Khomeini's vision of a theocratic state.

The most prolific propagandist and popular speaker of all in this group was Mottahari. Reputed to have been Khomeini's favourite pupil, he was involved in setting up the monthly religious discussion meetings at the Faculty of Theology in Tehran and in formulating and advocating a specifically Khomeini-style

Islamic ideology. In this perspective there is no room for Marxism and the left, and Mottahari devoted a series of pamphlets to denouncing Marxism.[63] Mottahari viewed the dialectic analysis as fundamentally contradictory to Islam and could see no way of resolving what he chose to call the relativist position of the Marxist, with the absolutist one of the Muslims. For Muslims the laws of God had been given once and for all and were not subject to any form of alteration. Human beings were created by God as a masterpiece. They were given a soul and a conscience which raised them above squalid economic classifications and subjected them to God's eternal commandments. There was no room for evolution and development and improvement on the laws of God:

> The Marxist argument of dialectic evolution of society suggest that as society changes so should its laws...when society reaches a new stage then its laws should be altered accordingly to meet the needs of the time since the laws of the previous mode no longer apply. Such views categorically contradict what we say about the eternality and universality of Islam...dialectical analysis negate the very foundation of Islamic teaching. Therefore those who pretend that Islam and Marxism are compatible cannot be right.[64]

Nor were people necessarily the best judges of what laws should govern them. Echoing the classical fundamentalist views, as expressed by Madudi and others, Mottahari argues that the laws of Islam are not 'conditioned by the socio-economic context of the Prophet's life'. They were absolute and irrefutable commandments to be obeyed for ever by all Muslims: [65]

> What do you mean by saying that the laws should be subject to the needs of the times? If the laws obey the times, then who should the times obey?...That would imply that the laws should follow the wishes of the people. But one of the functions of law is to control and conduct society...humanity is capable of moving forward, or veering to the right or the left or stopping and regressing...This free will means that humanity is capable of making many mistakes...This is precisely why we must not be submitted to the will of the times. We must rely on absolute values...We have faith in and rely absolutely on the knowledge that our series of laws and practices are eternal...We regard religion as an absolute and as independent of the economics and political circumstances of the time.[66]

Nor could Mottahari endorse the Marxist idyll of a classless society. In the first instance, he considered class to be relevant, but not central to the discourse on an Islamic political system:

> No doubt humanity is subject to change and alteration, but this change does not occur without the intervention of human will. We argue that humanity will have an essence of self which is higher than power, money or material wealth. Marxists fail to see this and insist on anchoring people in their class.[67]

The path that Mottahari delineated was to be distinctly separate from that of the Marxists. Unlike Taleqani, Shariati and the *Mujahedin*, Mottahari does not think that it is possible to form a religious–political synthesis between Islam and Marxism and warns his followers of falling into such a trap:

> We already have a movement, each movement must have its own intellectual and cultural foundation, otherwise it will fall prey and be trapped by movements that already have a cultural heritage and will be annihilated by them. We have seen how those who lacked an Islamic cultural foundation fell, like flies, in the web of others. Besides, the Islamic culture that is needed must be anchored and developed in our own ancient Islamic culture and not in alien traditions. It won't do for us to take a bit from Marxism and a bit from existentialism and a bit here and a bit there and then put an Islamic cover on it all ...Beware of those who have not been taught by us and are not sufficiently learned about our school, *maktab*, and who are deluded by a series of foreign views and ideas. Knowingly or unknowingly they hide these ideas under the cover of *maktab*, and offer them to us...They write in the name of Islam, but they advocate a foreign morality...and a foreign philosophy and politics.[68]

Mottahari, and Khomeini, like Nuri, the fundamentalist *alem* of the 1906–9 constitutional revolution, do not have an egalitarian view of humanity. Mottahari refers to the verse in the *Quran* which, according to his interpretation, shows that from the beginning of time God wished human beings to have different talents and differing status:

> Do they divide the wealth and kindness of the Creator (is it theirs to give the honour of Prophecy to whom they chose?) We have given them material and moral means, so that some have supremacy over others in aptitude, so that some conquer others. The benevolence of the Almighty is greater than all that they gather.[69]

Mottahari argues that the idea here is that different human beings would join forces and conquer each others' shortcomings and form a united society which is rooted in complementarity of talents and attributes, and not in equality. This inegalitarian perspective he calls 'positive equality' and describes as:

> the kind experienced by disciples of a just teacher who is equally kind to all. Should they provide equally good answers, they would be equally well-rewarded, but should the answers be of differing quality then each is rewarded according to his ability.[70]

This notion of a benevolent ruler is central to the political analysis of *Valayateh Faqih*. Mottahari, like his teacher Khomeini, was of the view that only the clergy had the cultural background and the fundamental fairness to become the natural leaders of any future Islamic government:

> It is the rich and magnificent Islamic culture that can and must be the foundation of our movement. It is the Islamic clergy who know this magnificent culture and have been educated by it and who are able to understand our contemporary society who could and should be its leaders...the leadership must be cognisant with true Islamic vision, only those who have been raised

in the heart of the Islamic culture...only the clergy have the necessary quality and ability to lead the Islamic movement.[71]

In this analysis the intellectuals can only participate as followers and not as leaders:

> Some argue that the leadership of the Islamic movement should be transferred from the clergy to the intellectuals. But our society in Iran today is an Islamic one. Iran today is like Europe in the fifteenth and sixteenth century, in that it is rooted in religion and its culture; it can only respond to religious calls. The religion of this people is Shiism which is a revolutionary faith...Our intellectuals think of Iran as a counterpart to contemporary Europe. It would be quite irrelevant to offer solutions suggested by intellectuals such as Sartre or Russell that are appropriate to the West. Iran today is much more like the Europe of the fifteenth and sixteenth century...it can only respond to religion which echoes through the minds and lives of people. Besides we have our own Shia religion which demands dynamic revolution, and calls for the blood of martyrs in its holy war for freedom...But beware, Islam is not a means to an end...it is the correct path that must be followed by all.[72]

But, like Khomeini, in his earlier writings, Mottahari still envisaged a form of collegiate rule by a group of religious leaders (of whom he would have been one) and in his writings and sermons always presented a united clerical front to the faithful:

> The Islamic movement is proud of its current leadership who are *marajeyi* [plural of *marja*, leading clergy who should be emulated] who are learned, who are embattled and recognise the needs of our people and understand their sorrow, who are impassioned by Islamic exaltation. They bar the way to fear, discouragement and loss of faith which are the battalions of Satan.[73]

The list of 'embattled' clergy drawn up by Mottahari includes the entire spectrum among the *marajeh taqlid*, indicating the will on the part of the theocratic group to enlist the names, if not the wholehearted support, of all their colleagues. Thus Mottahari includes the most eminent religious leaders, Ayatollah Mohamad Kazem Shariatmadari, Ayatollah Shahabedin Marashi-Najafi, who were linked to wealthy *bazaaris* and Ayatollah Mohamad Reza Golpayegani who was related to small landlords and married into a family of shopkeepers. Even though they were not all at the forefront of the revolutionary struggles, enlisting their support provided legitimacy for the claims of the theocratic group.

Khomeini's faction were particularly aware of the fragility of the clerics' control over the administration and were determined to overcome that. They were all too aware of the secularisation that followed the previous linking of the modernists and the religious establishment, and were determined that history should not repeat itself:

> Sadly the clergy failed in one respect in the past. They championed the Islamic movement to victory and then ceased to lead it and returned to their own cus-

toms and practices and allowed others, even those who were the enemies of Islam, to benefit from the fruit of the clergy's toil...The Iranian constitution was the fruit of the labour of the Iranian clergy, but they did not stay on to tend it and soon a savage dictatorship came to ravage their crop and there was nothing left of their constitution but a name...Now the intelligent people are worried. They fear that once more the clergy will leave the task unaccomplished.[74]

Thus, unlike the other leading clergy, the theocratic group were determined never to return to their mosques. For them the time to take political power in their own hands had come and there was to be no turning back.

## THE BLUEPRINT FOR ISLAMIC GOVERNMENT?

Despite a great deal of talk about a post-revolutionary theocratic state, Khomeini and his group did not offer a coherent political alternative. Mottahari,like the rest of the group, talked of a united monotheistic, *tohidi*, future:

*Tohidi*, united, both in terms of individual practice and in terms of social practice. It will secure unity for individuals in the worship of one God and denial of all other forms of submission, be it for faith in money, power, pomp and ceremony or the heedless pursuit of carnal desires. The society will unite in its opposition to devilish wealth and inequalities and injustices. Individuals and society will not rest or reach contentment until they reach such unity.[75]

But it was not clear how this united government would emerge, operate and be funded. Khomeini's lectures and the book, *Valayeteh Faqih*, government by the religious jurisconsul, was not particularly helpful. He dismisses monarchy and hereditary forms of government as being un-Islamic. This view may be open to question for Shias who began with the argument that the imamate ought to be hereditary and Muslims should be led by the descendants of the Prophet.[76] It is as stewards to the knowledge transmitted from the Prophet, through the hereditary *imams*, that the clergy claim the right to become the legitimate rulers of the country; a view held firmly by Khomeini himself:

God has entrusted to [the Prophet] the task of government and command, and accordingly, in conformity with the interests of the Muslims, he arranges for the equipping and mobilisation of the army, and appoints and dismisses governors and judges.
This being the case, the principle: 'the *foqaha*, religious leaders, are the trustees of the Prophet', means that all tasks entrusted to the Prophet must also be fulfilled by the *foqaha*, religious leaders, as a matter of duty...Just as the Most Noble Messenger (peace and blessing be upon him) was entrusted with the implementation of divine ordinances...and just as God Almighty set him up over the Muslims as their leader and ruler, making obedience to him obligatory,

so too the just *foqaha*, religious leaders and jurisconsuls, must be leaders and rulers...No one can doubt that the *imam* (peace be upon him) designated the *foqaha*, religious leaders, to exercise the functions of both government and judgeship.[77]

It is noticeable, that Khomeini appears to endorse a notion of collegiate government by a united group of clergy. Repeatedly he refers to the *foqaha*, religious jurisconsults, 'who are just and ascetic and who fight in God's way to implement the laws of Islam and its social system', as the natural leaders of the Islamic government:

So long as they do not concern themselves with illicit desires, pleasures and wealth of this world... it is only the just *foqaha* who may correctly implement the ordinances of Islam and firmly establish its institutions, executing the penal provisions of Islamic law.[78]

Furthermore Khomeini states that no religious leader has:

absolute authority over all other *foqaha*, religious leaders, of their own time, being able to appoint or dismiss them. There is no hierarchy ranking one *faqih*, religious leader, higher than another or endowing one with more authority than another.[79]

It is not easy to foresee the rise of a single theocratic leader to be the natural outcome of the model of government that Khomeini sets out. Much of his arguments about *Valayateh Faqih* refer to *foqaha* rather than *faqih*. He only mentions the singular, male, *faqih* as a possibility, but a remote one. He notes in passing:

When a *mujtahed*, religious leader, who is just and learned struggles for and succeed in establishing an Islamic government, he will have the same rights and authority in the affairs of society, that were enjoyed by the Prophet. It will be the duty of the people to listen and obey this *faqih*. He will hold the supreme power in the government and management and control of social and political lives of the people in the same way as the Prophet and Ali.[80]

But Khomeini is adamant that such a government will be no more than a burden for the *faqih*, one that would not bestow high status and would merely demand responsibility and time. Like Mottahari, Khomeini has a notion of guardianship of minors, a paternalistic rule by a kind theocrat. 'There is indeed no difference between the guardianship of a minor and that of a nation'.[81] This simplistic approach to government is indeed the hallmark of the Islamic government as outlined by Khomeini. There are no elections and no legislation: it is the *faqih* who rules and everyone obeys willingly:

Islamic government is the rule of divine law over people...Herein lies the difference between the Islamic government and constitutional monarchy or republican government. In these regimes people's representative or the king take charge of legislation, whereas in Islam this power is the prerogative of

God...Since all Muslims wish to follow God's law, Islamic government does not depend on force but merely serves to map out the programmes.[82]

What Khomeini and his followers are quite clear about is that just as no woman is entitled to become the guardian of her children, a right that is the preserve of men, so at no time could a ruling *faqih* be a woman. One of Khomeini's disciples, Ayatollah Javadi Amoli, insists that the burden of government is one that would be too heavy for any woman to carry:

There are many kinds of administrative work that are suited to women, but *valayat* [to rule] and *valy boudan* [to be a ruler], and governing are a different category of activities. There is no impediment to women taking charge of the administration of women's affairs, in fact they enjoy the right of priority there Similarly should a woman ever achieve the high rank of learning that would entitle her to be called a *faqih* then she may be allowed to go to consultative arena such as the *Shorayeh Negahban*, The Council of Guardians, or the *Majlis*. But it is indicated that the six leading *faqih* are amongst the leading men and that is because they are capable of tolerating hardships and it is not necessary for men and women to keep mixed company. It may be, however, that the views of leading religious women are, on occasion, sought. It is possible for a woman to reach the very pinnacle of wisdom and learning without becoming a *marja' taqlid*, source of emulation, but her pupils can become *marja' taqlid* and that is how it is...It is obvious that the leader of Muslims must be a man. He has to have the power to order men to go to war. He has to be able to mix freely with people and it is of the essence that a man takes charge.[83]

Of course the implicit idea is that the devout would not follow a woman to the grave. Nor would they be so willing to pay their taxes. Financial matters too are assumed by Khomeini to have been simply regulated by God and obediently implemented by the devout as a matter of devotion. Shias are supposed willingly to offer one-fifth of their surplus wealth in religious taxes, *khoms*:

*khoms* is a huge source of income that accrues to the treasury and represents one item in the budget...It applies equally to the greengrocer with his stall outside the mosque and to the shipping or mining magnate. They must all pay one-fifth of their surplus income, after customary expenses are deducted, to the Islamic ruler so that it enters the treasury. It is obvious that such a huge income serves the purposes of administering the Islamic state and meeting all its financial needs.[84]

A state with people who willingly pay their taxes and willingly obey the rule of God clearly does not require an extensive bureaucracy or judiciary. So the blueprint for Islamic government envisages the dismantling of both institutions, as well as the armed forces:

Superfluous administrative organisations and the administrative method accompanied by fabrication of files and bureaucracy which are alien to Islam, have imposed expenses on the state budget, which are...inadmissible...this administration system is remote from Islam.[85]

The judiciary too becomes unnecessary:

The procedure prescribed by Islam for adjudication, settlement of disputes, imposition of punishment and penal code are simple, practical and fast. When the Islamic legal procedure was practised, a religious judge in a city with two or three officials, a pen and an ink-pot, would settle the disputes and send the people away to conduct their daily lives. But God knows how vast the administrative apparatus of justice and its formalities are, yet without achieving any results.[86]

Thus, in *Valayateh Faqih* Khomeini postulates a future government by a group of like-minded, and high-minded, clergy, who submit themselves to the will of God and merely prescribe the Islamic dictum for the population to follow. People, assumed by Khomeini to be deeply devout, simple-minded and intellectually docile, accept the rule of the clergy and follow their instruction to the letter. Religious taxes meet all the state's expenditure and religious courts dish out justice on an immediate and satisfactory basis. There is no need for elections and representative government, because the laws are prescribed by Islam and the clergy have emerged as the best guides and have reluctantly accepted the burden of government. People willingly abandon malpractices and, if necessary, occasionally accept exemplary death sentences being meted out to the few who step out of line 'in order to make men submit to laws that are beneficial for human beings'.[87] Women are confined to 'women's affairs' and the sphere of domesticity and charged with protecting the public face of Islam, and everyone is happy.

Clearly such a simplistic Utopian view of a future Islamic society could not provide a blueprint for a post-revolutionary state in Iran. Once more the historic divide between the intelligentsia and the clergy had temporarily closed to oppose injustice, and oppression. But, once more, the vision of the future remained very different for the different participants in the revolution. Even the clergy were divided in the expectations for the future and, with the exception of Khomeini and his group, few had envisaged a theocratic future for the country.

# 4 Theocracy Defeats its Opponents

Khomeini's Utopian rule of a just *Faqih* was to remain between the covers of his book. In reality after the revolution there was no evidence of any form of submission to the rule of the *Faqih* by the Iranians. The assumption that the society of Muslims would be a homogeneous, quasi-tribal, hierarchical, respectful and obedient to the laws of God, as interpreted by the *Faqih*, proved fallacious. Secular people and the intelligentsia were regrouping and were even securing support among some of the religious classes. The *Mujahedineh Khalq, Fadayaneh Khalq* and the *Tudeh* party were finding footholds among the armed forces and jockeying for political influence. The *ulema* remained divided and regional minorities began agitating for autonomy. Everyone expected the revolution to deliver their particular version of the future and there was no visible administrative or political machinery for attaining any of these aims.

*Valayateh Faqih* has assumed a division between a submissive, puritanical people and its superior, united religious leaders. Now the Islamic state had to synthesise the simplistic views of the leader with the complex and far from submissive reality of the revolutionary nation. A central dilemma was to reconcile Populist demands with the need to create an ordered government.[1] Khomeini did not have a disciplined organisation at his disposal nor a detailed programme to implement. His supporters on the ground were divided. His successful propaganda campaign and his stay in Paris had been engineered by liberal-minded individuals such as Abol Hassan Bani Sadre and Sadeq Qotbzadeh. The revolution in Iran had been orchestrated by radicals and fundamentalists, in a temporary coalition that fell apart almost as soon as Khomeini returned.

While in Paris Khomeini had relied on a few of his disciples to act as his representatives in Iran. They included *Hojatoleslam* Mohamad Javad Bahonar, Ayatollah Mohamad Hosein Beheshti, Ayatollah Mohamad Reza Mahdavi-Kani, Ayatollah Abdol-Karim Musavi-Ardabili and *Hojatoleslam* Ali Akbar Hashemi Rafsanjani. On his return on 31 January 1979 he appointed them to form a Revolutionary Council to govern the country. Khomeini himself stated that he would withdraw from political life, and withdrew to the holy city of Qom.

Initially the Council included a number of secular politicians, such as Mehdi Bazargan and six opposition leaders associated with him as well as generals Valiolah Qaranai and Ali Asghar Masud. But soon Khomeini realised that the secular group could hamper the Council's more conservative approach. He separated the secular group from the religious-minded members, by asking Bazargan and his colleagues to form a provisional government in February 1979. They were replaced at the Council by Mir Hosein Mussavi, Habibolah Payman, Abol Hassan Bani Sadre, and Sadeq Qotbzadeh, all avowed followers of Khomeini. Qotbzadeh was in fact the man who accorded the title, *Imam*, to Khomeini. Though normally used by the *Sunnis* to denote religious leadership, '*Imam*' for *Shias* represents notions of purity and infallibility. These character-istics had enabled the twelve Shia Imams to delineate the correct path for their followers and to provide eternal political and spiritual leadership. Since the occultation of the twelfth *Imam* no other religious leader had used this title. But Khomeini, who saw himself as the Shadow of God on earth, was all too happy to adopt the title as his own.

In marked contrast to the Council, Bazargan's cabinet members were either secular, or liberal Muslim professional men from the Liberation Movement and the National Front. It was essentially a cabinet of bureaucrats and professionals. There was no representative from the left and only one member was proposed by the clergy; he was the Minister of Education, Qolamhosein Shokuhi. They set out to repair the damages incurred by the state and administration during the previous year of dissent, strikes and revolution. The cabinet sought a gradual orderly change. A number of religious leaders, including Ayatollah Mahmud Taleqani (who died suddenly in September 1979) and Kazem Shariatmadari supported Bazargan's views that even in the context of an Islamic revolution, the state and the religious classes should be clearly separated and the integrity of the boundaries between religion and government should be maintained,[2] a view not shared by Khomeini's disciples in the Revolutionary Council.

The majority of the clergy resented their exclusion from government by Bazargan and relied on the Council to represent their interests. The initial worries about the political inexperience of the *ulema* and their traditional anti-political stance were short-lived. Ayatollah Mohamad Hosein Beheshti, a leading advocate of theocracy, argued convincingly that the existing bureaucracy could provide the expertise, while the religious establishment delineated the political aims. Soon it was the Council who was making all the legislative and executive decisions.

The provisional government's search for an orderly and regulated move towards state formation was countered by the *ulema*.[3] A diffusion of political control, similar to that which had always existed amongst the religious classes, was reflected in the rapid increase in the authority of local revolutionary *komitehs*. The *komitehs*, who called themselves the Operational Headquarters of the Temporary Revolutionary Government, had become, from the inception of the post-revolutionary era 'one of the powers in the land'.[4] They had begun as revolutionary cells set up in all neighbourhoods to help to organise the street battles in 1978. Each developed its own regulation and local means for its enforcement and employed its own guardsmen.

Bazargan was made the target of a barrage of criticism emanating from the *komitehs*. He noted that they eroded his influence and 'made our days into night'.[5] By the summer Bazargan had to admit that he could not control the *komitehs* and could not establish a new order. His failure marked a major defeat in the post-revolutionary struggle against totalitarian theocratic rule in Iran. In August

Khomeini denounced all those who criticised the rule of God and threatened them with the Wrath of Allah. He closed down all independent newspapers and banned the publications of material that contravened 'the will of the people' – a term that in Khomeini's language was understood to mean 'the dictate of the Imam'.

Finally Bazargan, the long-term supporter of Islam and the revolution, was deemed not sufficiently theocratic by the *Imam*, who withdrew his support. The final *coup de grâce* was to brand him 'pro-American'. Bazargan had sought to maintain some diplomatic contact with the USA who had been the main trade-partners of the country. But Khomeini was adamant about cutting all ties. He insisted on the removal of all diplomatic protection for US citizens. Bazargan protested, to no avail.

Much of Iranian economy had been interlinked with US resources and international markets: the armed forces were almost entirely equipped by the USA. The links of the armed forces with the USA were never truly cut. Soon after the revolution American military experts and technicians began trickling back into Iran to help to run the country's advanced weaponry and there was even an agreement reached to secure supplies of spare parts.[6] With the downturn in the economy, Bazargan had sought a political accommodation with the USA. He had arranged to meet the American National Security Advisor, Zbigniew Brzezinski, in Algeria in November.

But all efforts at *rapprochement* were abruptly halted. Washington allowed the ailing Shah to go to the USA for medical treatment. Bazargan's opponents and particularly the youths who had spearheaded the street fighting during the revolution, took matters in their own hands. On 4 November 1979 the 'students following the line of the Imam' occupied the US embassy in Tehran. Overnight Iran became an international pariah. Two days later Bazargan resigned to become – and remain – one of the few public personages who have continuously criticised the regime's failings.

## THE CONSTITUTION

With the demise of the monarchy in February 1979, the revolution needed to establish some form of legitimacy and build up its own institutions of government. Khomeini was of the view that the revolution had sought to establish an Islamic government and that there was no need for further consultation. The rule of God did not require legitimisation by the people. Islamic government had never been considered a democracy. The most for which one could hope was a consultative process whereby the institutions for planning and delineating the path of Islamic development would be ratified.[7]

Faced with demands for democracy by the technocrats and democrats in the cabinet, Khomeini agreed to a national referendum provided it was staged to endorse the Islamic Republic. Accordingly in the referendum of 30 and 31 March, the people were not offered a choice between democracy and Islamic government. What they had was the option of endorsing the replacement of the monarchy by an Islamic Republic. They were asked 'Do you approve of an Islamic republic?' In strict Islamic terms this could be interpreted as demanding a consensus, *ijma*. According to the strict interpretation of the creed, Muslims cannot legislate, since all the necessary legislation has been done by God, and conveyed to the Prophet Mohamed at the inception of the faith. But by convention they may endorse certain measures and practices through consensus, *ijma*. The wider the support, the more likely it is for such measures to be practised.[8] Khomeini claimed a 98 per cent majority in favour of his government and instructed the provisional government to draw up an Islamic constitution.

The first draft of the constitution was prepared largely by the Minister of State for Revolutionary Affairs, Yadollah Sahebi. Based on the 1906 Iranian constitution and that of France's Fifth Republic, it made no mention of *Valayateh Faqih* and reserved no special privileges for the ulema. The draft, which was completed in June, was seen by Khomeini who initially appeared to acquiesce. He did, however, insist that the draft be altered to ensure that women were barred from becoming judges and from the Presidency.

A Constitutional Assembly was to discuss and ratify the constitution. Khomeini wanted the Assembly to be a small group of some forty of his selected *foqaha*, religious jurisconsults, appointed to revise the text according to his teachings. But Shariatmadari and other liberal-minded members of the *ulema* were of the view that the text should be scrutinised by an elected representative Assembly of about 500 members before final ratification. In addition to the division amongst the *ulema*, other secular and revolutionary parties were also concerned about securing an institution which would allow a truly democratic, rather than a theocratic, constitution to emerge. After much bitter wrangling Khomeini agreed to the election of a 73-strong Assembly to amend the constitution.

In the discussions that ensued, at the Assembly and in the media, lawyers and human-rights activists argued for a symbolic Presidential post and a powerful Parliament as well as an independent judiciary and local autonomy for tribal people and minorities. Most expected a degree of political and cultural freedom. The Kurds in particular argued vociferously for autonomy. The resistance groups, *Sazemaneh Cherikhayeh Fadayiey Khalqeh Iran* and *Sazemaneh Mojahedineh Khalqeh Iran* offered more radical versions of the constitution and declared their intention of mobilising people against the more conservative provisions of the draft constitution.

Khomeini realised that his assumptions about a passive, willing, body of followers poised to obey his every command had been false; *Valayeteh Faqih* was not going to emerge as a matter of course and there was a real possibility of the revolution moving towards a democratic system, with little room for the religious institution to dictate policies. He reacted quickly by publicly criticising the draft constitution for being insufficiently Islamic. He called on the religious classes to redress the balance in favour of God. His supporters responded by stressing the requirement of adhering to the rule by *Faqih*, as the *sine qua non*.

The conservative clergy-dominated Assembly then embarked on a revision of the constitution which emerged in November and was a blueprint for a theocratic state. Twelver Shiism was declared to be the religion of the State – not a controversial point since well over 90 per cent of the population are Shias and this provision had been included in the previous Iranian constitution of 1906. But the new constitution firmly rejected the principle of equality of sexes. Women were barred from becoming judges, governors or President. The *Faqih*, Khomeini, was given undisputed political and spiritual supremacy. Islamic law was to form the foundation of all legislation (article 4) and a twelve-man Council of Guardians, *Shorayeh Negahban*, was to ensure that no legislations contravened Islamic law and practices.[9] The Council was to consist of six clergymen appointed by the *Faqih* and six experts in Islamic law, appointed by the *Majlis*, to work for an initial period of six years. The Constitutional Assembly was subsequently replaced by another Assembly, *Majleseh Khebregan*, the Assembly of Experts. An elected body, it was to be responsible for the appointment of a future *Faqih*.

The constitution gave competing powers and responsibilities to the President and the Prime Minister. Both were subject to the control of the *Faqih*. The President was to be elected directly to the office and was empowered to appoint a Prime Minister who could nominate his own cabinet. However, the appointments of both the Prime Minister and the cabinet were subject to the ratification of the *Majlis*, whose elected members were entitled to act as the nation's legislature, but remained subject to the final verdict of the Council of Guardians.

In effect, the constitution failed to solve the basic contradiction that is inherent in the concept of an Islamic government. If God is the sole source of all laws; and if the law of God must be unquestioningly obeyed, then how can an Islamic government accommodate any notion of democracy, least of all that of a representative elected legislature? All that a Parliament can do is to plan institutions and delineate administrative paths.[10] To accommodate this problem, the constitution designated the *Majlis* to be an elected representative body who would delineate the path for the implementation of Islamic laws. To ensure that this single constituent assembly does not deviate from the straight path, its decisions were subject to ratification by the Council of Guardians and the *Faqih*.

In essence the constitution was rewritten in the constitutional Assembly by Ayatollah Beheshti as a vote of confidence in Khomeini. The *Faqih* was given a central place in the political order and was given vice-regency (regency belonging to God alone) and the leadership of the nation (article 5). He was the designated leader and supreme guardian with power to vet all presidential candidates, to endorse the winner and to dismiss him if he judged it to be in the nation's interest. The *Faqih* was also appointed to be the Commander-in-Chief of the armed forces with the right to declare war (article 87). Even Khomeini, when writing *Valayateh Faqih* had assumed that the Islamic ruler would be elected and would be de-selected if he failed to be just. But the Constitution made no provision for dismissing Khomeini who was deemed to have been selected by the revolution. A future *Faqih* was expected to emerge naturally. Failing that, however, the Assembly of Experts was to select three to five suitable jurisconsults to take over the reign. The religious classes were given a firm hold over the political destiny of Iran. They were empowered to dismantle all that they perceived as un-Islamic. Thus, along with alcoholic drinks, they banned playing cards, Western music and unveiled women. Soon the fundamentalists set about dismantling the country's educational system and cultural heritage and liquidating its Western-educated intelligentsia.

There were a number of people like Bani Sadre in the Constitutional Assembly who argued against the fusion of religion with politics. Shiism would only permit political leadership to the *ma'soum*, those descendants of the prophet who are protected from sin.[11] Even Khomeini could not claim *ma'soumiat*, freedom from sin.

But on this issue, as on that of popular sovereignty, the revised constitution remained in contradiction with the *Shia* dictum. Even though Bani Sadre's views were supported by Khomeini's own son, Ahmad, who publicly challenged the extensive temporal powers invested in his father. Ahmad Khomeini pointed out that it was perfectly possible for the leading religious figure of *Shia* not to be an Iranian; his father's predecessor, Ayatollah Sheikh Mohsen Hakim, had been an Iraqi citizen living in Najaf. Thus the new constitution enabled an Iraqi, Pakistani or Kuwaiti *alem* to nominate the President of Iran and exert absolute power over the government. Khomeini had a vision of a united Middle East, where such an eventuality would not have mattered: since the community of Muslims, *umma*, is unified by faith, national boundaries are irrelevant. But Ahmad did not share his father's optimism and expectation that the Iranian revolution would spearhead a series of revolutions and forge a unified empire of Islam in the region. Ahmad Khomeini's comment on this scenario was:

If you tell me that Islam knows no boundaries, then it is a joke.[12]

The religious establishment remained divided on this issue. A number of grand ayatollahs, including Ayatollahs Mohamad Reza Musavi Golpayegani, Shah al-Din Hosein Marashi-Najafi, Baha al-Din Mahalati, Abolqassem Musavi Khoi and Abdollah Shirazi had maintained their distance and a degree of silence. They had neither condoned nor condemned *Valayateh Faqih*. With the exception of the Ayatollah Kazem Shariatmadari, the venerable religious leader of the Azarbaijan region, and the most eminent Ayatollah, and Ayatollah Abdollah Shirazi, most of the *ulema* did not openly criticise the constitution.

But minorities such as the Kurds, the Turkomans and the Baluchis, who had not been given recognition or any degree of autonomy fiercely denounced the constitution. Although religious minorities, such as Jews and Armenians were allowed to elect their own representative to *Majlis*, as they had done before the revolution, tribal peoples, such as the Baluchis and the Kurds were not even permitted to do this. Nor were the latter allowed to publish newspaper and books or teach their own languages. The Kurds responded by boycotting the subsequent referendum and preparing for armed conflict.

## POLITICAL OPPOSITIONAL GROUPS

In the early days there was little certainty as to who would be the final winner. Bazargan and his cabinet had the advantage of experience and familiarity with the existing bureaucracy. Khomeini and his disciples ruled over the hearts and minds of the masses, but did not appear to have the necessary organisations to take over the reins. Nor were the religious classes entirely united. Both Ayatollah Taleqani and Shariatmadari were of the view that the religious establishment should only have a consultative part in the running of the country. Furthermore they considered it necessary to have a collegial group of jurisconsults to act as a collective advising the *Faqih*, rather than any single individual becoming an absolutist ruler.

The anti-theocratic Muslims formed a political party, the Islamic People's Republican Party, IRIP, to try to secure a pluralist political system. Symbolically it was based in the holy city of Qom.[13] The party sought to entrust political power to elected representative officials, rather than the *ulema*. The Islamic Jurisconsults were only to intervene in the country's affairs in times of crisis or when officials failed to implement the laws of Islam. At such times, the party argued that the *ulema* should act along the lines suggested by Shariatmadari. He emphasised the collegial nature of the religious classes' scholarship and enlightenment and the collective nature of their political activism.

Shariatmadari was the only outspoken critic of the new constitution and the rule of the *Faqih* amongst the *ulema*. He stood firm in denouncing the public executions of pregnant women and the young and the very old as well as the practices of public whipping, press censorship and purges of academics and civil servants.

Eventually in December 1979 Shariatmadari's supporters in Tabriz resorted to open rebellion. The Ayatollah, who was a firm supporter of non-violence, wavered. The revolutionary guards attacked Tabriz, took over the broadcasting station, shot and killed the demonstrators and put down the uprising. At first Khomeini announced that there was a distinction between Shariatmadari, who was to be respected, and his supporters, who were denounced as 'imperialists and counter-revolutionaries' and were attacked mercilessly. Shariatmadari was urged by Khomeini and many influential members o the religious establishment to disband the Muslim People's Republican Party (MPRP).[14] Finally, in January 1980, Khomeini banned MPRP, and like the Shah before him, confined Shariatmadari to house arrest. Subsequently Khomeini went considerably further than anyone had thought possible. For the first time ever a ruler divested a leading religious figure of his clerical rank. Khomeini himself in his treaties had always maintained that no one, not even the most high-ranking of religious leaders, could ever dismiss an Ayatollah, let alone an *Ayatollah ozma*. Yet he did so and this unprecedented act was not condemned by any of the leading religious figures. Although without precedence or legal or religious justification, such excesses were consistent with Khomeini's new perception of his own *nolo porq* ´

unlimited powers and *imamiat.* The historian, Homa Nateq, has underlined Khomeini's statement in *Valayateh Faqih*:

> If a just ruler orders the arrest of any person or burning down of the house of another, or the extermination of a community which is detrimental to Islam and Muslims, his order is just and must be obeyed.[15]

But, in the early vision of Islamic rule, such orders were never to apply to an eminent religious leader. However, despite a reputation for steadfastness that Khomeini had carefully cultivated, he was willing to make any move that was necessary, however contradictory, if it helped to tighten his grip over the national politics. With the death of Talequani and the removal of Shariatmadari, Khomeini's most eminent opponents left the political stage and the firm grip of autocracy tightened in Iran.

The *Mujahedin* and the Marxist guerrilla organisation, the *Fadayan Khalq*, and the *Tudeh* party, though excluded from it, initially supported the provisional government. At the time they tried to reach for power by attempting to consolidate their support amongst workers and in the case of the *Fadayan*, among feminist groups. Both guerrilla organisations also sought to infiltrate the armed forces and some of the neighbourhood *komitehs* that had been set up during the revolution. The *Fadayan* were demanding that a new people's army should replace the old armed forces.

Different groups reacted to different edicts and attempted to secure various strongholds. By March the *Fadayan* seemed to have secured a niche for themselves. The mass rally organised to mark the anniversary of Dr Mossadeq, attended by the entire cabinet, was marshalled jointly by the guerrilla organisations.[16] The *Fadayan* were instrumental in storming the US embassy on 4 November 1979 and starting the process of examining its secret documents. The raid was organised by the *Fadayan* and the *Mujahedin*. It followed the gutting of the Israeli mission earlier in the same week. But they were soon supplanted by the revolutionary guards who emerged as the undisputed guardians of the new theocracy.

*Mujahedin*, who had began by giving their conditional support to the government, were attracting the young intelligentsia. Their leader, Massoud Rajavi, who had been a student of Ayatollah Taleqani, gave a series of lectures in Tehran University which proved enormously popular. Rajavi reiterated the earlier teachings of the *Mujahedin* about historical materialism, class struggle and their hopes for achieving a classless *tohidi* society, a society that believes in one God and is united in its faith. The *Mujahedin* were moving into the socialist religious forum. Rajavi was demanding political freedom, he was championing the cause of democracy and supporting the women and demanding the elimination of all forms of discrimination. Like the *Fadayan* and the *Tudeh* party, the *Mujahedin* had organised cells amongst the industrial workers, amongst the bazaar guilds and their own women's organisation and were preparing for both overt and covert political resistance.[17]

The National Front and the Iranian Freedom Movement both sought to secure parliamentary representation and form loyal oppositional parties. A more radical party, the National Democratic Front, was set up after the revolution by Dr Mossadeq's grandson, Hedayatollah Matin Daftari. This party was advocating freedoms for individuals, the press and political parties as well as demanding the curbing of powers of the revolutionary guards and *komitehs*, a decentralised government and economic programmes to benefit the poor.

## THE ISLAMIC REPUBLICAN PARTY

On his return, Khomeini did not have a disciplined cadre, nor a clear political agenda. He had been the champion of the cause which for many was more about rejecting a regime, than adopting an Islamic alternative. The multiplicity of aims and purpose was clearly seen in the deep divisions between Khomeini's views of Islamic Iran and those of his Prime Minister, Mehdi Bazargan. The dual sovereignty exercised by Bazargan and Khomeini through the cabinet and the revolutionary council was doomed to disintegration. But it provided Khomeini and his disciples with a little time to clarify their own position and organise their support-base.

Within a week of his return, Beheshti set up the Islamic Republican Party (IRP) as a first move towards establishing a theocracy. Thus began the split between the government and its theocratic masters – a division that was to undermine the provisional government and all subsequent attempts at setting up any form of liberal government.

The Party provided a point of contact for the dispersed supporters of Khomeini in workplaces, cities and regional centres, within the bureaucracy and amongst the newly emerging militiamen. Rooted in the traditional support base of the *ulema*, the party was financed by the bazaar and the *petit bourgeoisie*.

Beheshti formulated IRP's Populist Islamic, *Maktabi*, ideology. This denotes a devotion to the totality of Islamic principles, rules and values. *Maktab* literally translated means the religious primary schools run by the clergy, which preceded the secularisation of the educational system. IRP used the term *Maktabi* as self-designation to denote the need for asserting the supremacy and the prevalence of the traditional Islamic doctrine as a primary goal. This was expressed by the term *tohidi* which means united by faith in a single God and could only be secured through the rule of the *Faqih* over a united country.

To gain momentum and mass support, IRP declared itself to be firmly opposed to capitalism, imperialism and economic oppression. It projected a return to an Islamic idyll envisaged in terms of the Mohamadan rule in Medina. Like all revivalist Islamists, it adopted an idealised image of a past, that could never have been as golden as it depicted, and promised a future, which could never be as bright as it claimed.

In the meantime IRP advocated the nationalisation of all forms of 'dependent capitalism'; the eradication of 'westoxification' through a cultural revolution and the return to pure Islamic values. All efforts were to be directed toward helping the deserving poor and the *moztaazefin*, the oppressed; this term was borrowed from Ali Shariati, who in turn had coined it as a translation of Frantz Fanon's 'wretched of the earth'.[18]

In practice, the IRP was a highly centralised and authoritarian organisation which could not accommodate any of the other oppositional forces. Its enforcement agency was the *Hezbollah* (The Party of God). In many ways the *Hezbollahis* were like the *lutis* of the bygone days.[19] Recruited amongst the poorest residents of the slums in south Tehran, they professed a fanatical devotion to Khomeini and the cause of Islam. One of their leaflets describes the typical *Hezbollahi* as an omnipresent angry man:

> a wild torrent surpassing the imagination. He [the *Hezbollahi*] is a *Maktabi* disgusted with any leaning to East or West. He has a pocketful of documentation exposing the treason of those who pose as intellectuals. He is simple, sincere and angry. Stay away from his anger which destroys all in its path. Khomeini is his heart and soul, not an idol, but an older brother and above all the *Imam*.
>
> The *Hezbollahi* does not use eau de cologne,[20] wear a tie or smoke American cigarettes. The proletariat and the bourgeoisie mean nothing to him. He knows our painted women. You might wonder where he gets his information. He is everywhere, serving you food, selling you ice cream.[21]

They were exalted by the IRP as the embodiment of militant Muslim virtues. They formed armed bands which the *Guardian* reporter, David Hirst, describes graphically:

> The *Hezbollahis* are at their most striking in cavalry formation, riding in great armadas through the streets on their motor bikes, traditional shi'ite black flags and banners held aloft, and sometimes preceded by a *mullah* in a bullet-proof Mercedes[22]

They were organised by the IRP to interrupt meetings and demonstrations held by secular political organisations. In the early years they were sent to ransack the opposition's bookshops and head offices and undermine their political activities. Even the Islamic *Mujahedin* were viewed as too left-wing to be accommodated within the new party.

In April 1980 the *Hezbollahis* attacked student offices at Shiraz University. They accused the students of being too left-wing and were so brutal that 300 students had to have hospital treatment afterwards. In July the *Hezbollah* occupied the National Front's Headquarters. They arrested the party's leader Abolfazle Qassemi, and closed down the party and its newspaper.

The *Tudeh* party's offices were also ransacked, but it was allowed to resume operations for a short period before being outlawed. In February 1980, the *Mujahedin* were singled out: the *Hezbollah* attacked their offices, burned their newspaper, *Mujahed*, and killed and maimed those who were selling or distributing its publications. In June Khomeini denounced the *Mujahedin* as polytheists and hypocrites. The attacks on the *Mujahedin* intensified and they went underground.

The brutal and unwieldy suppression of all oppositional parties intensified the use of terrorism as a means of asserting control. In June 1981 Beheshti was killed. But by then the IRP had been firmly established as a directive force in Iranian politics. It dominated the institutions of the State, media, *komitehs* and revolutionary guards.

## LAW AND LEGAL STRUCTURES

The revolution was more effective in dismantling legal structures than in replacing them with an effective alternative. In the first instance the 'ayatocracy'[23] was determined to introduce Islamic laws. But besides barring women from the judiciary, it enacted little positive legislation and allowed revolutionary *komitehs* and the hanging judge, *Hojatoleslam* Sadeq Khalkhali, to create a blood-bath into which anyone accused of un-Islamic behaviour was to drown. A firm supporter of Navab Safavi,[24] and of the *Fadayan* Islam's uncompromising views on the implementation of *Sharia* laws, Khalkhali was a founder-member of the Militant Clergy of Tehran who were committed to total Islamification at all costs.

[Trials by secret tribunal resulted in instant execution of many of the shah's supporters and leading army generals. The killings began five days after Khomeini's return on 16 February; by 14 March, seventy people had been executed; by November the death toll had risen to 550.[25] The judgements handed down by self-appointed revolutionary tribunals were meted out indiscriminately in Tehran and the provinces by the burgeoning revolutionary *komitehs* and their guardsmen.]

The *komitehs* had been the local nucleus of activities during the revolution and they remained the most effective revolutionary units. [They policed the cities, looted the houses, arrested people at will and killed without compunction.] The *komiteh* guards themselves were purged in the summer of 1979. To eradicate the influence of the guerrilla movements who had infiltrated the *komitehs*, Khomeini ordered a massive purge which led to the dismissal of some 40 000 *komiteh* members. But thousands of fanatical devotees of Khomeini remained to continue the reign of terror. In the words of Bazargan:

[The *komitehs* are everywhere and no one knows how many exist, [they create an atmosphere of] instability, terror, uneasiness and fear...turn our days into night. They upset our apple-cart.[26]]

Ayatollahs Shariatmadari and Hassan Qomi Tabatabayi joined a number of eminent lawyers to protest against the unruly tribunals and their deadly decisions. But the tribunal continued their midnight meetings, immediate executions and perpetuated the atmosphere of terror in the country. Although the government had appointed official courts and prosecutors, they had no control over these tribunals. The Revolutionary Prosecutor-General, Ayatollah Ali Qodussi, and the Head of Tehran's Revolutionary Courts, Ayatollah Mohamed Mohamadi Guilani, tried to control the tribunals without any visible degree of success. Even Ayatollahs Mohamad Beheshti, the Chief Justice of the supreme Court and Mussavi Ardabili, the Minister of Interior, despite their considerable power and influence, could not being the tribunal to order. The divergent centres of power and control, which was to become the hallmark of the post-revolutionary state in Iran, were exemplified by the judicial system.

In the words of the well-known scholar, Shaoul Bakhash, the judiciary 'was in a shambles', revolutionary courts dished out judgements at will, no two regions had similar sentences for similar crimes, prisons were full to overflowing,[27] and the courts seemed more like bandits than law-enforcement agencies.

Liz Thurgood reporting for the *Guardian* from Tehran on 4 November 1979 described the situation:

> Iranians are now witnessing a gradual breakdown of the fragile power structure that emerged in the wake of the February revolution. Orders issued by Ayatollah Khomeini frequently do not get beyond the holy city of Qum, and thieves, bandits and Muslim extremists feel increasingly at liberty to rob, kill and terrorise in the name of the mosque...The iron fist in the velvet glove has not worked and neither has the Islamic sledgehammer.

## WOMEN

The first to lose by the new constitution were the women. As had been the case in the revolution of 1906–9, so once more, despite their massive presence in the anti-shah demonstrations and their support for the revolution, women were to be legally marginalised. Although they were permitted to retain their hard-won right to vote, they lost all the other legal and social ground that they had wrested from unwilling governments in the past century.

Khomeini's misogyny was already clear from his writings.[28] He was personally responsible for the alteration to the constitution that excluded women from becoming judges and governors. His position, however, is one that has a long and highly respected antecedence in Islam. The opinion that women are evil and inferior to men, though not substantiated by the *Quran*, is one that dates back to the early days of Islam. It is a view firmly voiced by the Prophet's son-in-law and the *Shia*'s first *Imam*, Ali ibn Abu Taleb. He has been quoted as saying that women:

> are deficient in faith, deficient in shares and deficient in intelligence. As regards the deficiency in their faith, it is their abstention from prayer and fasting during their menstrual period. As regards deficiency in their intelligence

it is because the evidence of two women is equal to that of one man. As for the deficiency of their shares, that is because their share in inheritance is half of men's. So beware of the evils of women. Be on your guard even from those who are reportedly good. Do not obey them even in good things so that they may not attract you to evils.[29]

Ironically Ali himself was the husband of Mohamad's daughter, Fatima, and all subsequent *Shia imams* claimed that *ma'soumiat*, innocence, and legitimacy is through descent from Fatima, since Mohamad did not leave a surviving son behind. At the time of the sermon Ali was denouncing women because Ayesha, the Prophet Mohamad's favourite wife, was contesting Ali's right to the caliphate. She had raised an army and taken to the battlefield against Ali. But although Khomeini had not been initially faced by a female-led army, he remained rooted in the misogynic tradition. He opposed the enfranchisement of women and led a procession in 1963 to denounce the bill for granting of vote to women. He had declared at the time that:

Women's emancipation and women's right to vote is against the laws of Islam and the laws of the country.[30]

and

This bill violates the fundamental principles of Islam and the *Quran*.[31]

But above all Khomeini was an astute politician; so as gradually more and more women came to support his cause, he realised the potential benefit of their political support and in December 1978 he announced that in an Islamic society women could be permitted to vote. However, this concession was the only one that he was willing to make.

Within days of his return, on 26 February, Khomeini issued a decree to suspend the Family Protection laws of 1967 and 1975 which referred all matters related to marriage and divorce to family courts and removed the husband's automatic and unilateral right of divorce and custody over children – a point that he reiterated in a speech in Qom in March 1979. A few days later, on 7 March, the *Faqih* announced that Islam demanded that its women should be veiled in public. At the same time Khomeini also issued a decree barring women from becoming judges, and the Minister of Defence, General Ahmad Madani dismissed all women conscripts and released them from military service.

On 8 March, to celebrate International Women's Day and to protest against Khomeini's declaration about the veil, some 15 000 women took to the streets in Tehran. They were met by the new forces of law and order, the revolutionary guards, who attacked them physically and fired in the air to disperse them. The demonstrations continued on the following days. On 10 March Bazargan issued a statement indicating that the Khomeini had been misunderstood and the wearing of the veil was not compulsory. On 11 March, 20 000 women turned up on another protest rally at Tehran University. This time it was the fanatical

Muslim men, *Hezbollahis*, who attacked the women and eventually dispersed them.

The *Fadayan* and other secular Marxist-wing groups also supported the women's campaign. But the *Mujahedin*, the liberal members of the religious institution, including Ayatollah Mahmud Taleqani and even Abol Hassan Bani Sadre, all supported Khomeini and declared the imposition of the veil to be an appropriate symbol for demonstrating the nation's rejection of imperialism. Women and their garments were chosen as the public face of the Islamic revolution.

In the meantime the process of segregation continued. All games and physical activities were segregated. This resulted in barring women from all sport since they could not travel on the same coaches or use the same facilities as men, and there were no alternatives available for women. In May the Ministry of Education outlawed all co-education. This led to many technical colleges expelling their female students. Since their numbers did not justify setting up separate classes, these women had to abandon the hope of completing their studies. In June, married women were barred from attending high schools. This was accompanied by a lowering of the age of marriage to 13. The combination could conveniently reduce female participation in secondary schooling.

In June, women nominees for judicial posts, who were no longer eligible and were therefore not appointed, staged a sit-in protest which continued for five days with no results.

At the same time more and more organisations closed down their nursery and crèche facilities. Because these facilities were deemed by Khomeini to have been dens of corruption,[32] organisations were released from the pre-revolutionary legal compulsion of providing child-care for their employees. Women who protested were threatened with mass lay-off.

In the summer of 1979 seaside resorts began to segregate the beaches. Women who transgressed and swam in the men's section were publicly flogged. At the same time the State began to execute women accused of prostitution or corruption.

In October 1979 the Revolutionary Council ratified the new family laws. These gave men the exclusive right of divorce, unless women demanded and obtained the right on marriage and stipulated it in their marriage contract.[33] The official age of marriage for women was lowered from 18 to 13. Polygamy was once more made legal; men could marry four permanent and any number of temporary wives. Men regained the automatic right of custody over their children after divorce, for daughters after the age of 7 and for sons after the age of 2. Husbands were empowered to bar their spouses from taking employment.

Women reacted by organising more demonstrations and sit-ins. Once again the demonstrations were attacked by the *Hezbollahis*. There were women's sit-ins at the Ministry of Justice and a Women's Solidarity Coalition was set up to fight the new retrograde measures. The authorities cut off the electricity at the Tehran Polytechnic where the Women's Solidarity Coalition was holding its meeting. Despite extensive protests, demonstrations and sit-ins, the Islamic government was determined to use women as the public face of the faith and the firm process of legal and social subordination of women continued apace.[34]


## INDUSTRIAL ACTION

In the early wave of resistance to theocracy groups of factory workers, some assisted by Marxist groups such as the *Fadayan Khalq*, *Tudeh* and *Peykar*, also joined the agitations for greater democracy on the shop floors. The modern industrial sector had grown rapidly during the Pahlavi era and already by the 1960s there were over 70 000 manufacturing enterprises,[35] 20 per cent of which employed more than ten workers.[36] During the course of the revolution, workers in the larger industrial units had formed strike committees, *shora*, and staged many strikes. After the revolution a number of these committees organised the take-over of factories. Between December 1978 and February 1979 workers' committees took charge of industrial units in Azarbaijan, Guilan and Tehran. In Amol and Sari these committees forged a wider political base and allied themselves with other groups such as teachers, traders and civil servants.[37] But these *shoras*, committees, did not link up with the neighbourhood *komitehs* which had also sprung up during the revolution.

Within the first week of its inception, the provisional government was faced with 50 000 workers on strike. So, as a matter of urgency, it set about curbing the power of workers by preventing strikes. In the first instance it requested a return to work; on 8 January, the railway workers refused to do so. It was obvious that the working class were not the docile believers that Khomeini had assumed they would be. So on 20 January 1979 the Provisional government established the Committee for Coordination and Investigation of Strikes to negotiate with the strikers. The committee included many of the old liberal members of the National Front, including Bazargan, Karim Sanjabi and Ali Akbar Moinfar as well as some influential members of the religious classes including Ali Akbar Rafsanjani and Mohamad Javad Bahonar. It recommended the resumption of work to the oil and transport workers. The CCIS urged the strikers to continue 'the production of people's urgent needs', and ensure the survival of the nation.[38] Transport workers accepted and went back to work, agreeing to carry only essential goods. By the end of the month CCIS had persuaded 118 production units and a few public services to resume work.[39] In return the minimum wage was doubled and average wages rose by 53 per cent.[40]

The struggle between the government and the workers' organisation continued. On 1 March 1979 the Founding Council of All Iran Workers was formed with a twenty-four point programme. The Council demanded government recognition of the *shoras*, the right to strike and shorter working weeks, 40 hours, longer holidays, sick pay, tax-free housing, and free canteen. In Guilan and Tehran the workplace committees linked up through the council of workers' committees to provide some basic coordination. The council held its meetings at the pre-revolutionary government-controlled Trade Unions Office. The building was soon occupied by unemployed workers and called the employment house, *khaneyeh kar*. The revolution was asked to meet some of the aspirations of its supporters.

Initially, the Islamic government appeared to have conceded to some of the demands and accepted working-class participation. The Revolutionary Council ratified a 44-hour week and initially accepted the *shoras'* proposal for profit-sharing schemes and a major year-end bonus. Constitutionally, article 104 recognised the *shoras* 'composed of representatives of workers, peasants and other employees as well as the managers' and ratified their formation in industrial and agricultural units. The only qualification was that 'decisions taken by the *shoras* must not be against Islamic principles and the law of the land' (article 105).

The workers used their legitimised prerogatives and there were more than 350 industrial disputes in the course of the first year of the post-revolutionary government. But faced with a rapid flight of capital and with a working class that was far from the submissive image that Khomeini had, the government responded with an all-out attack on the *shoras*. Despite some support from religious leaders such as Taleqani, Khomeini encouraged the government to introduce the law of Special Force, in May 1979. The law barred the *shoras* from intervening in 'the affairs of management'. In July, Khomeini banned unauthorised demonstrations and in August strikes were made illegal.

With the collapse of the economy and industrial production and rising unemployment, the *shoras* lost much ground. Although there were mass demonstrations by the unemployed, these were denounced by religious leaders as being anti-revolutionary. The *shoras* were also attacked during the conservative backlash against left-wing organisation in the course of the summer of 1979.

At the same time, the religious classes began setting up their own alternative workers' organisations in all factories and workplaces. These Islamic association, *Anjomaneh Eslami* sought to secure the new *Maktabi* (clerical) line of Islamic management, which was nothing more than an affirmation of the government's support for the bourgeoisie. From September 1979, there was a gradual return to management from above, and a gradual demise of the *shoras*. The Provisional Government set up a special force, *nirouyeh vigeh*, to dismantle the *shoras* and replace them with the Islamic associations which facilitated a form of Islamic corporatism. In August 1980 the Minister of labour, Ahmad Tavakoli, announced the priorities of the Islamic Associations, which included cooperation with the management and strictly limited the association's activities to cultural events. This measure was accompanied by the announcement that workers could be dismissed for objecting to or staging protests against 'any of the country's political or social systems'.[41] The Islamic government was tightening its grip in a determined move to control the working classes and curb militant organisations. Since the working classes had not willingly submitted to the will of *Valayateh Faqih*, the religious-minded workers, and through them all production units, were to be pulled into line. Khomeini had denounced the wealthy for being corrupt, but he wished the maintain economic activities and was not about to tolerate a working-class take-over of assets. It was of the essence that workers did not create trouble and strife for the Islamic state. The *shora* leaders were very clear about their role. Assef Bayat quotes two different leaders making very similar points; the one at Amazon factory declared:

> should the aim and intentions of a *shora* member be contrary to the interests of the Islamic Republic or violate laws, and disrupt the order of the company, it will be the Islamic and canonical duty of the other members to report him to the employer through the mass meetings.[42]

The *shora* leader of the ITN company explained the same point:

> The revolution we made was an Islamic Revolution. We didn't make a Communist revolution. Therefore [the *shora* members] must act within the Islamic framework and ideology. The objective must be to implement an Islamic economy, which is neither a capitalist economy nor a socialist.[43]

But the quietism advocated meant that a capitalist strategy draped in an Islamic garb was being imposed. It proposed to transcend class conflict by integrating the economic motive as a unifying force accommodating the interests of the state, capital and labour. The arguments were couched in the language of Islamic *tohid*, unity. This approach is similar to fascist corporatism. They both encompass non-plural, hierarchical relations between state and capital.[44] It advocates an anti-antagonistic approach well-suited to Khomeini's vision of a docile, obedient, Islamic workforce

The Islamic associations announced their opposition to capitalist management, and declared their alliance with the state on the basis of the *Maktabi*, clerical, approach. They adopted a Khomeini-style notion of idealised Islamic equity which became popularly known as the *Imam*'s line. It was strongly anti-democratic, anti-Communist and committed to the teaching of the *Imam*. The approach, which is in the mainstream of what is commonly called fundamentalist Islam, claims that all Muslims are equal, undivided by class, caste or nationality. All are united to serve in God of Islam. If such service requires the industrialists to make a little more profit and the workers to work a little harder, then that is how it should be. In this framework exploitation as a concept has been replaced by cooperation. The enemy is not the enemy within – a Muslim, exploiting another Muslim – but rather it is the enemy without – the imperialists aligned to exploit all Muslims. Any deviation from opposition to foreign interests, any undermining of the united front of Muslims, is seen as an unacceptable threat to the whole community.

The *Maktabi* approach delineated the framework of the new Islamic corporatism. It postulated that managers were people of high moral standing who had obtained their position not because of skill or experience, but because of their ideological purity. This in turn prevented them from exercising any form of exploitation and enabled them to act as the political, social and spiritual guides and leaders in the workplace. Such pious managers would not merely seek to maximise profits, their main aim would be to direct the workers towards the correct Islamic path.[45]

In practice the *Maktabi* school failed to find managers of such high moral probity. Yet the approach remained *dirigiste* and demanded the total submission of the workers. It could not accommodate the *shoras* and other democratic institutions. So the Islamic associations, rapidly, and often forcibly, displaced the *shoras*. At the same time the earlier benefits accorded to the workers were discarded by the government. The first to go was the year-end bonus which was abolished in February 1981 to be replaced by an incentive pay based on the length of service and current wages; this worked out to be a lower payment than the bonus. According to one estimate, whereas wages rose by 12 per cent in real terms, for the year ending March 1980, the cost of living for the working classes rose considerably faster, at 42 per cent for food and over 100 per cent for some goods. In reality the buying-power of the workers decreased by over 30 per cent.[46]

The workers responded by staging wild-cat strikes, walk-outs and protests in the months that followed. In October and November they organised massive demonstrations outside the office of the Prime Minister and the Minister of Labour. These were countered by revolutionary guards who fired into the air, and by stern warnings from the government.

By the end of the year unemployment had soared to 3 million and there was a mood of disillusion and despair amongst the workers. As one factory worker told the Sunday Times reporter:

> As for us workers things are not much different from what they were before the revolution…What we are offered is a bourgeois constitution. What we need is a socialist constitution.[47]

Nevertheless the workers continued to resist. In the period 1979–1980 there were 366 industrial incidents.[48] The Islamic Associations helped to block many more, though they were not always successful. The case of the Car and Tractor Factory in Tabriz, was typical of events at the time.

On 29 April 1980 a group of factory workers organised a demonstration calling for the workers to follow the line of the *Imam* and join the Islamic associations. The next day this 'spontaneous' move was backed by a cleric – IRP *Majlis* representative, Abolfazl Mussavi – who arrived at the factory to announce a 'cleaning up' *paksazi*, programme. A committee was set up and a Mr Mirzayi announced that he was the regional head of the *paksazi*. On 31 March at closing-time loudspeakers of the factory announced the names of those who had been sacked. They included those who had already been thrown out by the workers on suspicion of collaboration with the SAVAK as well as the members of the workers' council.[49]

There were, however, some successful strikes, such as that of the Tehran Regional Water Authority Workers in July. In response to the cuts in their allowance and bonus payments, the 7000 workers went on strike and held their head-office director-general hostage in his office. The government conceded to their demands and their wages and conditions were restored.[50]

But gradually the numbers of strikes diminished. The Islamic associations embarked on a programme of indoctrination and elimination of the politically active, non-Islamist, labour force. They were instrumental in 'ejecting' the 'deviant elements' opposed to the revolution and identifying the 'reliable individuals'. In the following five years they executed some 300 workers.[51] They mobilised the Islamic workers to break strikes, to enforce Islamic corporatism and to undermine unions and the *shoras*. Their success can be seen in terms of the dramatic fall in numbers of strikes; these were nearly halved in a matter of a year and were down to 180 for the year 1980–81, and more than halved again to 82 in the years 1981–82.[52] By spring 1981 the Islamification process was reinforced by making participation in public prayers compulsory in all factories and offices.

At the same time the hard-line Islamic Minister of labour launched an Islamic programme of work, pay and entitlement. According to Tavakoli, Muslim labourers were duty-bound to view their labour as a commodity that is hired out for a rent, *ojrat* rather than one that is sold for a wage, *dastmozd*. The Muslim labourer had to embark on work as an Islamic and spiritual duty, one that would make the labourer an active part of the great Islamic nation, *umma*. Khomeini endorsed these views and went so far as to describe the performance of work as a form of devotion, *ebadat*, a means of repaying the individual's debt to the martyrs of the revolution.[53] What these eulogies indicated was that work carried its own spiritual reward and did not entitle the worker to demand high wages. Ahmad Tavakoli even tried to change the word worker, *kargar*, bearer of labour, with its socialist connotation to, *karpazir*, capable of accepting work. The latter denoted a passive recipient who accepted employment as a religious and a national obligation and would find the work itself to be sufficient reward. Therefore such a worker would have no wish to engage in collective bargaining, which was denounced by Tavakoli as un-Islamic. In the unlikely event of needing slightly more money, the Islamic worker would prefer to explain his predicament in individual negotiation with the *Maktabi* manager.

To facilitate the move away from unions and national bargaining, Tavakoli announced in May 1981 that trades and crafts were no longer subject to the labour-law restrictions. Eventually the Islamic labour Laws that were introduced in December 1982 even permitted child labour. Article 53 allowed managers to negotiate employment contracts with the parents or guardians of under-age workers. Tavakoli also cut wages and bonus payments of the better-paid workers, offering them instead an incentive rate of pay based on productivity. At the same time the job-classification scheme which benefited skilled workers, was dismantled.

Although, when faced with massive opposition by the workers, Tavakoli repudiated his plan for individual wage negotiation, Islamic corporatism had come to stay. In May 1981 the *shoras* were barred from intervening in the affairs of management; in August strikes were made illegal and in February 1981 Tavakoli suspended the formation of all *shoras*. This despite the provisions of article 104 of the constitution which endorsed the formation of *shoras*, provided their activities did not contravene Islamic laws.

By June 1981 Bani Sadre had been dismissed, the mass execution of all opposition had gained momentum and many *shora* representatives had been killed by members of the Islamic committees or the Revolutionary guards and the path cleared for the restrictive Islamic Labour Laws that were to be introduced in the subsequent year.


## THE ECONOMY

Despite the year-long strife and strikes in many industries including oil, rising oil prices helped to minimise the fall in revenues. Income form oil and gas fell from $21 billion in 1977–8 to $19 billion in 1978–9 and 1979–80. But the buoyant prices meant that it was only after the war in 1980–81 that income from oil and gas plummeted to $12 billion.[54] nevertheless the 1979–80 budget predicted a $15 billion shortfall. This was partly caused by the strikes and largely by the flight of capital. In the year leading to Khomeini's return, there was an estimated $4 billion outflow from banks in Iran.[55] By the time the new government was formed, the situation had become quite critical. As Bazargan noted:

> The owners and shareholders have gone; they've taken their money and run and have left us with a heritage of debts and deficits.[56]

The problem was made all the more difficult by the government's total confusion over its economic policies. Though all too eager to repudiate the modernisation policies of the Shah, initially Khomeini offered no practical new solutions to replace them.

In the years leading to the revolution ideologues such as Bani Sadre and Ayatollah Taleqani had formulated certain economic perspectives. But in practice these proved both contradictory and unrealistic. In theory, Islamic economics was to be based on the *Quran*, committed to social justice, result in an equitable distribution of wealth and defend the interests of the poor. Ayatollah Taleqani and Bani Sadre both saw Islamic economy as being anti-capitalist, and redistributive.[57] Neither had predicted the emergence of a *dirigiste* and corporatist economic model after the revolution. Nor had they proposed a clear alternative programme. In practice all the revolutionary government did was to respond to the exigencies of the time and make its economic policies on the hoof, a practice that has continued throughout.[58]

The 1979 budget was drawn up on a monthly basis and the government dealt with short-term goals as they came up. In June 1979 Bani Sadre and the Revolutionary Council decided to establish an Islamic form of banking. They nationalised all banks. The twenty-seven privately owned banks, thirteen of which were jointly owned with foreign interests, were merged with government banks to form central bank and nine other banks, all committed to charging 'service charges' or 'sharing profit' instead of paying or charging interest.

In industry as in banking, as the State moved in so foreign interests and much Iranian expertise moved out. Some industrialists simply left the country. Others were ousted by the militant workforce. *Ajr* consumer durables, *Minou* biscuits, and the textile firm, *Jahan Chit*, were amongst those that were taken over by the workers and handed over to the government.[59]

In June 1979 the Revolutionary Council authorised the government to appoint managers to all enterprises that had been closed, or could no longer operate or whose owners had gone abroad. In July the Council passed a law for the protection and Expansion of Iranian Industry. The law permitted the nationalisation of heavy industries, including metallurgics, cars, chemicals, shipbuilding, aircraft and mining as well as industries that were in economic difficulties and unable to meet their liabilities. In addition over fifty industries belonging to 'corrupt' individuals and families were also taken over. As a result the Republic became the owner of the largest part of the country's private industries.

The nationalisation process gained momentum in August, when *Majlis* authorised the government to take control of secondary shares in national industries. The law enabled the government more-or-less to write off these shares as worthless. Subsequently pharmaceuticals, cold-storage warehousing and trucking were also nationalised.

Once more there was a diffusion of controls. *Bongaheh Mostaazafin*, the Foundation of the Dispossessed, was established in March 1979 to administer the expropriated properties of the members of the royal family and their associates. Soon it became actively involved in physically ousting factory-owners and taking over the control of many large industrial concerns. But, though very effective in expropriating industrialists, the Foundation was lamentably ineffectual when it came to running these concerns. Despite its vast assets, in the early years of the Revolution the Foundation consistently made enormous losses. Although cases of embezzlement by the Foundation were discovered and widely discussed, it continued unhindered.

By the end of 1982 the government sought to rectify matters and set up the National Industrial Organisations to administer the nationalised industries. By this stage only the smaller firms had stayed in private hands. Most large industrial concerns that had been joint Iranian and foreign productions, like the copper complex in Kerman which was only half-built, were making an estimated loss of about $10 billion.[60]

Thus in the early years of its inception the Iranian theocracy seemed to be facing a number of severe crises. Industrial growth had disappeared and been replaced by negative economic growth. Those industries that were still operating were mostly producing at 50 per cent capacity. Lay-offs and close-downs had resulted in some 2.5 million men and women losing their jobs. With no welfare and social provisions to fall back on the unemployed began protesting and staging marches.

Women were already protesting about the severe curbs that were placed, in the name of religion, on their civil rights. The opposition parties were attempting to gain support amongst students, armed forces and factory workers. The first Prime Minister had resigned and become one of the most influential critics of the government. The peace and serenity predicted by *Valayateh Faqih* showed no sign of appearing and Khomeini did not seem to have practical solutions to the complex political and economic problems that had emerged.

# 5 The Revolution Betrayed

Far from creating a coherent Islamic society, obedient to the teachings of its leader and satisfied in the achievements of the Islamic republic, by the end of its first year, the government was faced with seething discontent. Dissatisfaction amongst women, workers and minorities was reflected in division amongst the governing institutions. The provisional government was at loggerheads with the Assembly of Experts. Neither was able to control the spontaneous Islamic courts, *komitehs* and the students who ruled in the name of the followers of the line of *imam*.

There was an unbridgeable divide between the aspirations of the different groups who had launched the revolution. Khomeini had not promised a democracy, or a socialist government. His revolution was for the establishment of a theocracy and he was satisfied with nothing less. Many of his allies within the religious and secular spheres had different expectations. The constitutional battle and the removal of the technocrats from office were but two of the many hurdles that had to be cleared before the theocracy could take firm roots. Khomeini had a clear understanding that the country, like the faithful, would have to follow the teachings of the *Faqih*. In the style of the dominant *Shia* school, citizens had the right to chose the *alem* whose teachings they were willing to follow. But they were not entitled to make their own political decisions. That much had already been established by the *Shia ulema* in the nineteenth century,[1] and they were not about to retreat once they had obtained political power.

The problem was that those who had followed Khomeini's call had done so for different reasons. Even his own entourage had not expected the leader to succeed in imposing his will. He devoted the early years of the post-revolutionary rule to removing the obstacles. This meant that soon the revolution had to devour its own children. It did so by undermining the first political structures it had set up and denouncing the technocrats, the liberals and all oppositional organisations, and at the same time creating a profusion of commands to serve differing warlords, all of whom claimed allegiance to 'the line of the *Imam*'. Khomeini proved to be a pastmaster at divide-and-rule strategy, which in any case was the traditional form of control exercised by the *ulema*.

The killings began early in the revolution, gained momentum and in a year became torrential. Revolutionary tribunals sprung up across the country, there was no right of representation for the defence, no clearly defined regulations about the process and no judiciary in evidence. Army officers, political leaders, including ex-Prime Minister Amir Abas Hoveyda who had presided over the modernisation policies of the 1970s, and individuals accused of 'moral turpitude' were unceremoniously executed. There were protests by Ayatollah Shariatmadari and Ayatollah Hassan Qomi Tabatabayi, as well as lawyers and opposition groups. Even the Revolutionary Prosecutor-General, Ayatollah Ali Qoddusi accused these tribunals of 'looting in the name of confiscation.[2] But these pleas fell on deaf ears. Khomeini did little to curb the rising tide of blood. He denounced the demands for open trials as anti-revolutionary and allowed the courts to take their deadly toll. The new Constitution had given citizens unconditional freedom of thought and expression, the right to form political parties and to oppose the government (articles 21 to 27), almost as soon as they were ratified, these rights were disregarded. The citizen's protection against arbitrary arrests (article 23) though enshrined in the constitution, was similarly forgotten.

## THE REVOLUTIONARY STATE AND PROFUSION OF COMMANDS

The revolutionary courts system was one amongst a multiplicity of command centres that sprang up after the revolution. The *ulema* had for centuries had a tradition of accommodating discord by allowing difference; competing centres of authority had emerged and for years conducted the faithful concurrently. Despite Khomeini's insistence on the supremacy of the *Faqih*, the post-revolutionary state in Iran adopted the more traditional pattern of the religious establishment. Khomeini's own deep distrust of the existing bureaucracy and awareness of the inexperience of the *ulema* in conducting affairs of State, led to his endorsement of the burgeoning revolutionary organisations, *Nahadhayeh Eqelabi*, which became popularly known as self-propelling organisations, *Sazemanhayeh Khodkhoroushideh*. These units began operating as an alternative to the bureaucracy. They developed parallel powers and organisations, but unlike the civil service, they were generally not controlled by the government. They created a new administrative élite who owned their allegiance to the revolution and competed with the old bureaucracy for jobs. Some like the Ideological Centres, *Dayereyh amre beh marouf va nahi as monker*,[3] functioned as a morality squad within all government organisations.

Others, like the revolutionary courts, replaced the Western-style professional judiciary. Within months of his return Khomeini sacked all women judges. Just as women were deemed not be suited to governing, so they were seen as unable to judge rationally. Though men and women were both subject to the laws, women were not entitled to act as lawyers. As one of Khomeini's disciples, Ayatollah Javadi Amoli, has explained:

> Women may reach the heights of learning, they may even be allowed to train judges. but since being a judge is an active judicial role, women are not to become judges. It is like saying that when it comes to cutting a thief's hand, it is appropriate that women should not draw the dagger.[4]

In the early post-revolutionary flux, Khomeini closed down all the legal institutions including the Lawyers' Association, *Kanuneh Vokala*, and eventually the Faculty of Law. The laws of Islam were to prevail. They were applied, even before they had been codified and legislated. In the absence of trained

Muslim lawyers, seminary students were to take over the courts. Their decisions were enforced by the *komitehs* and their guards. Soon the country had three different kinds of revolutionary laws; one administered by the revolutionary Prosecutor-General. Assisted by a team of armed guards, he served warrants, made arrests and guarded prisoners. At the same time spontaneous local revolutionary courts ran their own armed guards and executions. A number of powerful clergy also had their own armed forces, reminiscent of the *lutis* and administered their own laws.

Friday prayer leaders used their platform to issue decrees and spread political doctrine. They issued ration cards, mobilised recruits for the army and often headed the local IRP branches. Their power overshadowed the authority of the government and all Bani Sadre could do was complain:

> Where in the world, in which religion, where in Islam and in which Islamic country are there six types of imprisonment?... Why has a delegation not yet been formed to study these prisons and see if there is any torture? As soon as we ask these questions a number of ignorant people step forward to call us 'liberals'. But the liberals are those who do not abuse their power when they are powerful and do not submit to the powerful when they are weak.[5]

The liberals had lost much ground to the *komitehs* which frequently shared the same offices as the IRP, and operated as a form of spontaneous local government. Their more lucrative activities, those of taking over the properties of the rich, were soon hived off by another revolutionary organisation, *Bongaheh Mostaazefin*, the organisation for the protection of the dispossessed. The organisation's largest holdings were the properties of the Pahlavi Foundation, *Bongaheh Pahlavi*. Almost the entire personnel of the organisation was replaced by revolutionary experts. But these newcomers, though zealous enough, lacked management expertise. Not surprisingly, though the organisation controlled 140 industrial units and 11 mines with a labour force of 34 000, *Bongaheh Mostaazefin* could only register losses.[6] The also took over factories and industrial units. This activity was duplicated by another revolutionary organ, *Sazemaneh Sanayeh Meli*, the nationalised industry organisation, which did no better. By the end of 1981, they registered a loss of 76 billion rials (£380 millions).[7]

In fact as industrialists left, so various agencies took over their concerns; some 500 production units, banks and insurance companies and numerous large-scale industries amounting to some 70 per cent of the value of the total output were supervised chaotically by fifteen revolutionary organisations. In some cases the management of a single factory was shared by five or six organisations. Not surprisingly in the period 1981–2 the state industries lost a further 60 billion rials.[8]

In May 1980 the Revolutionary Council empowered the government to control certain categories of goods such as essential food and textiles. The Ministry of Commerce established twelve procurement and distribution centres which controlled 40 per cent of the imports. The Centres were licensed to deliver 30 per cent of their consignment to the government and sell the rest directly to the public at specific profit margins. In May 1981 the government set up the Foundation for Economic Mobilisation, *Bonyedeh Bassijeh Eqtessadi*, to take over domestic distribution of all consumer goods. This organisation duplicated the centre's work and was in competition with the mosques which were also engaged in distribution of consumer goods.

Another self-propelling organisation, *Jahadeh Sazandegi*, the reconstruction crusade, had taken it upon itself to develop the rural areas. To counter the ever-rising pressure of population in towns in general and Tehran in particular, Khomeini called for a return to the villages and instructed a group of devout students to rebuild the necessary infrastructure to attract the villagers back home. Duplicating the responsibilities of the Ministries of Agriculture and the Ministry of Cooperatives and Rural Development, they were to link the villages to the national electricity grids, get clean water, good irrigation, satisfactory housing and generally raise the rural standard of living. There was some financial backing for the new venture, they facilitated housing loans and declared a minimum wage. They took over the lands of absentee landlords, who had left the country, hounded out 'anti-revolutionary' elements, who were usually the landlord' representative in the village, and set up rural *komitehs*. Their methods were similar to their urban counterparts and their zealous endeavours led Ayatollah Qomi Tabatabayi of Mashahd to denounce publicly the 'cruelty and oppression' perpetuated by the crusaders.[9] But despite much publicity and effort, the organisation managed to provide some jobs for the urban revolutionary youths, but it failed to turn the rural–urban migration tide, or meet the needs of the peasantry.

A more successful rural programme was launched by the *Fadayan* who organised the peasants in the Northern Iranian Province of Turkomanestan to take over the lands of the absentee landlords and farm them cooperatively. They formed over 300 Guerrila Councils, *Shorayeh Chariki*, where with the peasants' collaboration they produced the crops and administered the holdings. They provided loans, seeds, fertilisers, and supervised the production of crops, appointed local youths to guard the harvest and marketed the produce.[10] Using the slogan, 'peace, land and freedom', they encouraged different minorities in the region to work together. They included Persians, Turks, Baluchis, Zabolis and Turkomans in their projects. Turkomanestan was the only region in Iran where production of crops increased after the revolution. But with the persecution of the *Fadayan*, this sole example of success of revolutionary organisation was subsequently smashed up.[11]

The Turkomansahra experience clearly demonstrated that the revolutionary organisations were not necessarily encouraged to serve the people or even the post-revolutionary government. Their main role was to provide an alternative executive, and to undermine the existing administrative organs. But, with the flight of much of the intelligentsia, the persecution of many more, there was a critical shortage of know-how and expertise. These organisation were run by devout young people who had much zeal and little else to offer. The revolution had thrown up a challenge to the youths who had fought on the streets for the cause, but were unable to deliver its promises.

## BANI SADRE: THE HOSTAGE CRISIS

The rise and fall of Bani Sadre presents a clear example of the importance of diffusion of power and authority in enhancing the political control of the theocracy in Iran.

Bani Sadre had been instrumental in the success of Khomeini in the pre-revolutionary days. Khomeini's journey to Paris, from whence he orchestrated the revolution, had been organised by a number of Muslim intellectuals who, though not clerics, were devout followers of his teaching. These included Abol Hassan Bani Sadre, Sadeq Qotbzadeh and Ebrahim Yazdi. They formed part of a small Western-educated clique who helped the Ayatollah during his stay; they ran the press conferences, translated his views into acceptable statements and generally secured a favourable and well-publicised projection for him and his policies. They were particularly adept at translating the Ayatollah's autocratic views into revolutionary concepts. This entourage was convinced that given care and good management Khomeini would remain a spiritual leader and that on their return, they, the intelligentsia would take over the government.

Unlike Khomeini, this group expected to set up a form of democratic socialism in Iran. Bani Sadre, like Ali Shariati, combined a firm belief in Islam with a conviction that Islamic rule would be representative, democratic, and welfare-orientated – views that he had already expressed widely in his writings on Islamic politics and economics.[12]

In the first six months of the revolution the optimism of this group appeared to have been well-founded. While theocrats were attempting to form different centres of control, the provisional government of Bazargan had managed to push through a number of radical measures. Bani Sadre who had control over the eight Ministries involved with finance and economic planning, was attempting to implement his vision of an Islamic economic order. He was a young man in a hurry, as he told the French reporter, Eric Rouleau:

> Following *Imam* Khomeini's instructions, the Revolutionary Council has decided to continue working as if its mandate were eternal and spread good as if it might disappear the next day.[13]

He announced the nationalisation of banks and insurance companies and placed the nationalisation of foreign trade on the political agenda. To free Iran of 'imperialist' control and in the name of Islam, Bani Sadre was determined to curtail the control of merchant and finance capital in the country. He proudly declared that the profit motive was to be removed from the face of Iranian economics:

> The underlying principle in Islamic economics is to satisfy the needs of all human beings, unlike other economic systems where the objective is the concentration of wealth and profit-seeking. In Islam economic is a tool which must be used to attain the objective of bringing man closer to God.[14]

Interest rates were abolished and replaced with a standard 4 per cent commission and 7–8 per cent profits. Any profit over and above that was to be shared with the banks, workers and customers. The banks were to be reorganised into five groups, the two large national banks and three other groups dealing with industry and mining, housing and agriculture respectively.

Bani Sadre's economic vision included efficiency and productivity. He was going to clean up the bureaucracy and turn the one-million-strong civil service into 'productive' and useful members of society.[15] Yet he himself acted without ever consulting his own senior colleagues. The nationalisation of trade and banking had not been discussed with the civil servants at the Ministry of Finance; they knew nothing about it until they heard the policy announcement on the radio. Deputy Minister Cyrus Ebrahimzadeh, who had been all too aware of the need to set up the necessary framework first, before 'very cautiously' nationalising trade,[16] had to admit that he knew nothing about these measures.

Nor had Bazargan's cabinet been consulted. Even at this very early stage the cabinet did not speak with one voice. The diffusion of power, which was to characterise the decade, had begun. The nationalisation of the banks and insurance companies and intention to nationalise foreign trade was announced by Bani Sadre on the same day that the Minister of Commerce, Reza Sadre, was introducing measures to encourage investment in trade and industry by the private sector.

When questioned on these contradictory government policies, Bani Sadre argued that the nationalisation of trade was a constitutional measure. He was merely implementing Article 44 which placed foreign trade in the domain of the public sector. The only person informed about these radical changes was the head of the central Bank, Ali Reza Nobari, who had been appointed to the post by Bani Sadre.

At the same time the guerrilla movements, *Mujahedin* and *Fadayan* were advocating far more radical moves and the Communist *Tudeh* party, while supporting the government, was standing ready to take over. As the power struggles continued, so did the rising tide of discontent and public protests. As early as February 1979 thousands of military personnel, backed by the *Fadayan* and *Mujahedin*, were taking to the streets demanding the democratisation of the army. The 'line of *Imam*' dictated brutal reaction and suppression of all opposition. Demonstrations by women, workers, the minorities, and the unemployed were met with uncontrolled attacks by the *Hezbollah* and summary executions by kangaroo courts set up spontaneously by the *ulema* and the revolutionary guards in every city in Iran.

Khomeini countered the unrest by evoking the cry of 'the enemy at the door' and calling directly on the people to defend the national interest; a ploy that remained central to his rule throughout the decade that followed. At such times, all opposition to the theocracy was projected as a threat to the stability of the country itself and every devout man, woman and child was called upon to take to the streets.

There was a century-long tradition of negotiating Iranian politics at the street level,[17] and the *ulema* were adept at manipulating the crowd. Thus when the unrest began spilling into the streets, and women and the unemployed staged public protests, Khomeini diverted the attention away from them by focusing on the imperialist enemies in general and the USA in particular. By May 1979, organised marches were heading to the US embassy in Tehran on a regular basis. Anti-Americanism was to become 'the cement for the Iranian regime'.[18] Khomeini called for the demonstrations, the IRP organised and orchestrated them and the *hezbollah* stamped out all counter-demonstrations. To silence criticism, in August 1979, forty opposition newspapers and publications were closed down.

By November the anti-imperialist rhetorics had been whipped up to a crescendo. Matters were not helped by the US decision to allow the Shah in for medical treatment. Khomeini called on the youth and the students to 'force America to extradite the criminal shah' and on 4 November, they responded by attacking and taking over the US Embassy compound in Tehran.

Those staff who were in the compound were taken hostage, others took refuge in the Foreign Ministry where their diplomatic immunity was still recognised. The students announced that they accepted no law other than the will of the *Imam* and were and responsible to none other. Yet another centre of political command was set up and foreign policy was to be made on the hoof by the students for the next year.

Bazargan's position became untenable. His Foreign Minister, Ebrahim Yazdi, had began a cautious programme of *rapprochement* with the USA and had met the American national Security Advisor, Zbigniew Brezezinski, in Algiers. There was even talk of resumption of arms deals. But within days of the hostage crisis, on 11 November, Bazargan felt compelled to resign. He announced that he had been 'pushed over the edge'. Khomeini immediately appointed the Revolutionary Council as a caretaker government and instructed them to forge ahead with plans for 'fundamental social and economic changes' as well as the purge of all 'corrupt elements of the former regime'.[19]

The process of making policy on the run was briefly halted by the December referendum on the Constitution. Already much of the opposition had been muzzled. Even Ayatollah Shariatmadari's announcement that he would vote against the Constitution was countered by Tehran radio's declaration that the venerable religious leader had changed his mind. In the event, the constitution was ratified by a massive 2 million vote, though the turn-out fell short of the 98 per cent 'yes' vote cast in support of the revolution in March 1979. The Kurds who had already taken up arms against the government in November 1979, and the *Mujahedin* boycotted the referendum. The tribes were all dissatisfied with the Constitution, which not only did not allow them any autonomy, but went even further than the pre-revolutionary constitution in depriving them of the right to teach their own languages or maintain their own cultural integrity. Despite the confusions in the nature and character of political power, the constitution indicated the determination of any future government to enforce the supremacy of the Persian-speaking majority and the control of the centre over all minorities. In February the Kurds began their armed insurrection and launched massive attacks against the government forces in Pishavar, Bijar and Sanandaj.

Still the profusion of commands continued. Constitutionally the *ulema* were ensconced, in both the Assembly of Experts and the Council of Guardians and thus controlled all policies. But Khomeini was unwilling to allow clerical competition when it came to ruling the land. As the *Faqih*, he remained at the apex. To maintain his own political and spiritual supremacy he decreed that members of the religious establishment could not stand for the post of President.

This unexpected decision, made almost on the eve of the Presidential election, blocked IRP's obvious candidate, Ayatollah Beheshti and threw the party into disarray. The IRP then nominated Jalaledin Farsi as its candidate, only to find him disqualified because his father had been from Afghanistan and he was deemed not to be 'a true Iranian'. They hastily found a replacement, Hassan Habibi, an unknown figure who in the event failed to get many votes.

Khomeini's decision paved the way for an entirely secular field. But he banned the *Mujahedin*'s leader, Massoud Rajavi, from standing, on the grounds that the group had refused to endorse the constitution and could therefore not run a Presidential candidate. Bani Sadre's candidature was opposed by Admiral Ahmad Madani, the Governor-General of Khuzestan, and Foreign Minister, Sadeq Qotbzadeh.

In the event Bani Sadre gained 75 per cent of the votes cast and began the struggle to curtail the power of the 'multifarious' centres of political control. Supported by Bazargan, the intelligentsia and much of the middle classes, he sought to limit the controls of the religious classes and dislodge the students from the US embassy. He began by denouncing the students as irresponsible schoolchildren who should return to their schoolrooms. He was vociferously supported by Bazargan who, in speeches on the television and at *Hoseiniyeh Ershad*, expressed his fervent wish:

> May God save our country, our revolution and our President from these brats.[20]

The students in turn began denouncing the technocrats that Bani Sadre and his cabinet had appointed. The battle for the minds of people launched by Khomeini was spearheaded by the students. The political format for the coming decade was taking shape; spontaneous, self-propelling revolutionary institutions were to pop up at all levels to contest the authority and legitimacy of both the legislature and the bureaucracy.

There was a degree of direction provided by the religious establishment. But given the divided nature of the establishment itself, the slogan of anti-imperialism was used as a convenient cover for a power struggle both amongst the ulema and between them and the technocrats. In the meantime the students and the revolutionary guards, who were interchangeable, had taken it upon themselves to 'clean up' the anti-revolutionary elements and did so by attacking and arresting all those whom they had denounced as traitor. A disproportionately large number amongst these were Bani Sadre's allies. They included the Minister of Information, Nasser Minachi, arrested in February and extracted from prison after much argument by the President who complained:

If the students want to cleanse Iranian politics, if they intend to continue making revelations concerning certain prominent personalities, then they should use the normal judicial channels. The Constitution that the students are trampling on guarantees citizens the right to their lives, their property and their dignity.[21]

The students responded by parading their revolutionary credentials:

The people will continue to support the students by demanding that they keep unmasking the lackeys of imperialism.[22]

Bani Sadre had hoped to form a democratic government based on relatively independent administrative and executive arms. But the revolutionary organs spinning uncontrollably across the political and administrative arenas left little room for manoeuvre for the President. Like the students, he had to resort to the revolution and the will of the people. He told reporters that:

If, with the support of the Iranian people, he was eventually to order the hostages' release, he was confident that the militants in the US embassy would obey.[23]

The students countered that the President:

has no competence on this question. Only the people can decide what will happen to the hostages, their will being expressed nobly through the *Imam*.[24]

Within days of the Presidential election, the students were showing their determination to run 'a state within a state'. Throughout the hostage crisis, they remained independent of the President, but often acted in collusion with the IRP.

Bani Sadre had also to contend with the Revolutionary Council who showed no sign of withering away after the election of the President. A stronghold of the IRP, the Council backed the students and generally curtailed Bani Sadre's power. It argued that the President could not take his oath of allegiance until he received a vote of confidence from the forthcoming General Assembly, where the IRP expected to gain the majority of seats. Bani Sadre insisted on the confirmation of his post and eventually he took the oath before Khomeini, at his hospital bedside. But the Revolutionary Council remained determined to hold on to power which they were only willing to relinquish to the future *Majlis*.

Bani Sadre was faced with a collection of redoubtable rivals at the Council. Members of the religious establishment who had been checked by Khomeini's ban from gaining access to the Presidency or challenging the *Faqih* himself were lining up against Bani Sadre. They included Beheshti, who represented the IRP's interests, Rafsanjani, who ran the Ministry of Interior and Ali Khameneyi who was in charge of the Ministry of Defence. None were willing to hand over their posts to Presidential nominees. Beheshti explained the situation by telling a *Le Monde* reporter that:

according to our constitution, the President counts for nothing.[25]

The fourteen man Revolutionary Council looked likely to prolong its life indefinitely. The President had to admit that his 'hands were tied' and that 'the multiplicity of decision-making centres and the discussions within the Revolutionary Council' hindered his every move.[26]

Khomeini remained firmly on the fence. He was wary of the *ulema* and suspicious of the liberals. So he played one against the other and prevented either side from gaining the upper hand. He appeared to come to the rescue by appointing Bani Sadre to chair the Revolutionary Council. But within days of doing so, Khomeini blocked Bani Sadre's attempts to negotiate a deal for the hostages with the UN Secretary-General, Kurt Waldheim. On 23 February 1980 Khomeini decided to side with the theocrats; he announced that only the as yet un-elected *Majlis* had the authority to decide the fate of the hostages.

The Parliamentary elections were to decide the balance of power. Assured by his own massive majority, Bani Sadre expected to see the democrats well-represented in the *Majlis* and hoped that the election would spell the death sentence of the IRP and the Revolutionary Council. He called on the eighteen organisations and fronts that had supported his candidacy to form a front and field candidates for the *Majlis* elections.

The IRP was determined to recapture the ground lost over the Presidential elections and to ensure that the President had no more power than the 'king of England'. It used both the media, which it largely controlled as most oppositional newspapers had been closed down, and its own extensive organisation through the mosques to the grass root, to mobilise votes. Muzzled by censorship and lacking an effective party machinery, all Bani Sadre could do was to denounce the 'scandalous censorship' of the radio and television and lament his own lack of authority to 'restore freedom inside this body'.[27] He used his own daily paper, *Enqelabeh Eslami* (Islamic revolution) which for a while escaped the censors, to warn the voters eloquently of the dangers of theocracy. Using a discourse reminiscent of Ali Shariati he signalled the threat posed by 'religious fascism':

> seeking to re-establish political despotism under the guise of religion.[28]

The elections were conducted in two rounds in March and May. Those candidates who gained less than 50 per cent of the votes had to go to a second round. The rounds were interrupted by the bungled American attempt to free its hostages in April – a débâcle that enabled the IRP to renovate its cry of 'the enemy at the door' and denounce all democrats as potential lackeys of the satanic USA.

The final round of the elections secured a resounding success for the IRP. Bani Sadre supporters got 74 of the 270 seats and Rafsanjani was elected as Speaker of the *Majlis*. Bani Sadre's meagre support was further cut by the *Majlis*' rejection of the credentials of several candidates, including the previous Presidential candidate, Admiral Ahmad Madani.

The tussle for power between the President and the IRP-dominated *Majlis* was exacerbated. Constitutionally the Prime Minister and his cabinet had to be approved by the *Majlis*, but they could be selected by the President or the *Majlis*. In a last-ditch attempt at consolidation of control, Bani Sadre obtained Khomeini's approval to select a Prime Minister and a cabinet 'designed to stabilise the country's disjointed power structure and consolidate the government's position'.[29] Bani Sadre suggested that Khomeini's son, Ahmad, should accept the Premiership, but the *Faqih* refused. Eventually in July 1980, when the Shah was being buried with pomp and ceremony in Cairo, the IRP moved to impose its own choice of Prime Minister on the President. He was one of their *Majlis* representative, Mohamad Ali Rajai, IRP representative for Tehran. Rajai was a maths teacher with no previous administrative experience. He was a devout Muslim and had attended Ayatollah Taleqani's classes and had been imprisoned in 1963. In prison he had met Ayatollah Mohamad Javad Bahonar and had become one of his firm followers.

There was little common ground between the Premier and the President and for the next months they tussled over the selection of a cabinet. Initially, of the twenty men proposed by Rajai, Bani Sadre was willing to approve only six, who were already serving as ministers in his own cabinet. Rajai suggested that both the Foreign Minister, Qotbzadeh, and the Oil Minister, Ali Akbar Moinfar, should be replaced, the former by Mir Hosein Mussavi, editor of the IRP newspaper *Jomhouri Eslami*, and the latter by 27-year-old Asghar Ebrahimi. Even those appointees who were approved by them both needed to secure the support of both the students and IRP. Those suspected of pro-Bani-Sadre tendencies were likely to meet with a barrage of criticism. To secure its own base within the administrative branch, IRP had set up Islamic Societies in every Ministry. When the Minister of National Enlightenment, *Ershadeh Meli*, questioned this practice, he was pilloried by the students. The Minister asked:

> In a Muslim country, where everyone claims to be a Muslim, what is the point of having an Islamic society in every institution? It is the minority non-Muslims who should form such organisations... It is quite pointless to set up such a society in a government office. What are they suggesting? Are they claiming that they alone are Muslims? Are they questioning the piety of other Muslims?[30]

The students responded by accusing him of imperialism and arguing that any questioning of their views merely highlighted the Minister's anti-revolutionary attitude:

> Such questions merely show that the Minister, like his Ministry, has not changed his attitude – like the Ministry of Tourism and Information becoming Ministry of National Guidance. It is all a pretence, merely a change in name and not a change in its nature.[31]

They were supported by Khomeini who complained that:

> Nothing has changed... the same bureaucrats who had misruled Iran for the Shah are still at their desks writing their endless memos on paper with the imperial crest.[32]

The leaders' plaintiff words dislodged an avalanche of retributions. The IRP redoubled its efforts to control all Ministries; 150 purge committees were set up and over 1400 officials were sacked. The Foreign Ministry, which was still harbouring some of the US Embassy members, lost 800 of its total of 2000 civil servants. By September 4000 civil servants had been purged.[33]

Bani Sadre sought to counter these purges. Eventually, in December 1980, he pushed through a bill which limited the grounds for dismissals of civil servants. Earlier, he also tried to form a broad oppositional coalition by a *rapprochement* with the *Mujahedin*. The IRP retaliated by condemning all oppositional parties – a move supported by Khomeini who dubbed the *Mujahedin* 'pseudo-Muslims' and denounced the rest as imperialists. These criticisms were backed by attacks by the revolutionary guards and *hezbolahis* who beat up demonstrators who took to the streets in support of the *Mujahedin* in June 1980 and subsequently stormed the offices of opposition organisations. They killed the officers and looted the files. Eventually they forced the Communists, the *Mujahedin* and the nationalists to close down their offices and go underground. The fascism of religious control had raised its ugly head.

By mid-September, Bani Sadre had approved fourteen members of Rajai's cabinet. But he refused to endorse one-third of the nominees on the grounds of youth and inexperience. The Ministries of Economics, Finance, Commerce, Labour, Oil and the Plan and Budget Organisations remained without the cabinet seats. But already power and authority had shifted away from the Constitutional organs.

The closing-down of oppositional parties went directly against the constitution. The *Mujahedin*'s newspaper, printed underground and distributed surreptitiously, was publishing such subversive material as the text of the constitution; article 9 prohibited all officials from abrogating civil liberties and article 26 enshrined the right of oppositional groups to associate and operate freely.[34]

But with the government in disarray, the judiciary in revolutionary hands and the administration under attack, there were no laws and no law-enforcement agencies to come to the rescue of the constitution. On the contrary the arbitrary death sentences, which had temporarily subsided, began gaining momentum. Bani Sadre appointed Sadeq Khalkhali to head the anti-narcotic campaign on the 20 May. Within weeks there were 127 executions.[35] By the end of August the total reached more the 200. They included members of Marxist organisations such as *Forghan*, who were captured after open warfare on the streets. Other prisoners were sent to their death for 'crimes' such as 'indiscipline' or even for staging hunger strikes. Eventually Khalkhali, who is known as the 'hanging judge', was forced to resign in December 1980. He was unable to account for over $14 million that he had seized through drug raids, confiscations and fines.

Ayatollah Ali Qodoussi, the Revolutionary Prosecutor, made some attempts at curbing the torrent of executions. The IRP responded by sending in their strong men to rifle through his office and to organise a strike by Evin prison guards. Qodoussi was in a quandary:

> Should we dance to the tune of Amnesty International who ask why we kill and not grant amnesty, or to the tune of these gentlemen who ask why we grant amnesty?[36]

He decided to allow the revolution to take its course.

By September, Khomeini had removed the hostage negotiations from Presidential control and appointed his own aide, Sadeq Tabatabayi, to deal directly with the hostage release, which was finally completed on 20 January 1981, the day of President Ronald Reagan's inauguration.

In November the erstwhile Foreign Minister, Sadeq Qotbzadeh, gave an interview denouncing Islamic fundamentalists and their censorship of the State-run media. The revolutionary guards promptly arrested him and forcibly removed Bani Sadre's appointees from the television and news programmes. The Prosecutor-General, Mussavi Ardabili, then took it upon himself to appoint a new director and complete the IRP take-over of the media.

These excesses were countered by protests from the anti-clerical groups. These included close relatives of the *Faqih*, leading secularists and even members of the religious establishment who were against the excesses of the IRP. Bani Sadre could count on the support of Khomeini's immediate family including his son, Ahmad, his brother, Morteza Pasandideh, and his son-in-law, Shahab al Din Eshraqi. In the *Majlis* he was backed by a handful of representatives including Bazargan, Ebrahim Yazdi, Yadollah Shahabi, Ahmad Sadre, and Ali Akbar Moinfar. They protested against Qotbzadeh's arrest and organised a petition with 3000 signatures, including those of many influential merchants, demanding his release. The President, assisted by Khomeini's son, Ahmad, intervened and pleaded with the *Faqih*, and secured the Minister's release.

There were also a few *alem* who still questioned the legitimacy of arbitrary arrests and executions. In addition to Ayatollah Shariatmadari, they included Ayatollahs Abolfazl Zanjani, Hassan Qomi Tabatabyi, Abdollah Shirazi, and Hassan Lahuti. They questioned both the legitimacy of the State as an instrument of oppression and Khomeini's supreme position. They emphasised that *Shias* had always pursued justice, and countered *zolm*; no *Shia* State could legitimately pursue the methods and policies of IRP and the revolutionary courts and remain true to its doctrine.

Bani Sadre tried to pull together these different oppositional strands. He set up a network of Offices for Coordination of People's Cooperation with the President in Tehran and the provinces. He also began addressing the public directly both through his newspaper, *Enqelabeh Eslami*, and by calling up large rallies to denounce the rising tide of execution and the drift towards dictatorship. By November 1980 the dual government of Iran was in open warfare internally and externally, while its borders were attacked by Iraq.

## THE WAR AND THE DEMISE OF DEMOCRACY

The Iraqi attacks began in April and gained momentum in September. Relations had been strained for some time: the Iraqi government feared interference by Iran, which was publicly encouraging all *Shias* to follow the revolutionary path. Iraq, 50 per cent of whose population were *Shias*, saw itself as the natural target of the revolutionary propaganda. In fact, though Khomeini sent several resounding messages to call the believers to rise and demand their rights, these were not backed by any material help.[37] Iraq itself was keen to take over the oil-rich southern provinces which had traditionally been occupied by people by Arab descent and, since they bordered on Iraq, seemed a relatively easy target. So the Iraqi government sent armed Arab dissidents to Khuzestan to stir up rebellion.[38] In April the Iraqi government deported 1300 Iranians and Iran withdrew its diplomats from Baghdad.[39] This was followed by skirmishes into Iran and finally on 10 September 1980 the Iraqi forces crossed the border into Iran.

Saddam Hosein, who had been President for about a year, expected his highly disciplined and well-equipped forces to rout the dispirited and much-purged Iranians and score a rapid and decisive victory, annexing the oil-fields in a matter of weeks.

In the event these calculations proved wrong. The war provided a last ray of hope for the President to resist the tightening grip of theocracy. He had already gained much support amongst the regular armed forces for his moves to shield them from the excesses of the successive purges. The army had traditionally been the bastion of support for the Pahlavi regime,[40] and on coming to power Khomeini remained extremely wary of the forces and their potential for staging a military coup. The penetration of the *Fadayan* and the *Mujahedin* into different sectors of the armed forces and their success in organising revolutionary cells both in the air and land forces did nothing to allay Khomeini's fears.

The Revolutionary Council singled out the army for savage purges in the early days of the revolution. By September 1979 government figures showed that 248 military persons had been executed and 302 officers ordered to retire.[41] These purges resulted in the removal of 80 per cent of the officers.[42]

The purges, justified on the grounds of ideological purification, were pursued vigorously by the Provisional government's Minister of Defence, Mustafa Charman, who came to power in September 1979. Assisted by his deputy Minister, *Hojatoleslam* Ali Khameneyi, by February 1980 they purged some 6000 military personnel.

At the same time the revolutionary government decided to create new allegiances by setting up ideological purification units run by members of the religious establishment to direct and police the army ideologically. The move was opposed by the forces who demanded the right to elect their own councils, along similar lines to the workers' councils, and to direct their own affairs and conduct their own investigations. To obtain this right some 2000 army and air force NCOs occupied Tehran University mosque for a week in early February. Bani Sadre attempted to step in the breach and act as mediator between the government and the army. Khomeini appeared to condone the move, and on 19 February, appointed him as the Commander-in-Chief of the armed forces. In return, Bani Sadre addressed the demonstrators, insisted that the army must maintain order and discipline,[43] and agreed to support their demands for the reorganisation of the armed forces.

But here as in other spheres of the government, he was unable to halt the surge of Islamification, despite the continuing battles with the Kurds and the Iraqis. His position was made more difficult by an attempted army coup in June, by an organisation called *barandazi*, overthrow, at the Pishavar garrison in Kurdistan. The discovery led to a new surge of blood-letting and over 127 executions within weeks.[44] Bani Sadre intervened and obtained an order for a general amnesty for the forces from Khomeini. But in July another attempted coup, planned by the air force at Shahrokhi and Mehreabad air bases, was foiled. The revolutionary courts responded by an accelerated purge at the rate of some 100 soldiers per day.[45] By September 1980 over 12 000 army personnel had been purged.

Nevertheless Bani Sadre continued to support the forces. The revolutionary guards, zealous, devout and willing to die for the cause were singled out as exemplary soldiers by the IRP and its organs who continuously denigrated the army. Khomeini seemed uncertain; his son-in-law, Eshaqi, declared publicly in favour of the President, announcing that he was of the opinion that a war could not be fought 'with sandals and prayer beads',[46] while Prime Minister Rajai defended Islamification, declaring it preferable even to victory.

Bani Sadre attempted to side-step the IRP propaganda and party machinery and appeal directly to the people. From September onward, he divided his time between visits to the armed forces at the fronts, and organisation of public meetings in the capital and the provinces. He too was seeking to negotiate the terms of the nation's political discourse at street-level. He began by criticising the IRP for its stranglehold on the press and media; he argued that the revolution had sought to deliver 'structures that allowed people to take part directly in the decision-making process.[47] The IRP responded by sending in the *hezbollah* to attack the meetings addressed by the President and other liberals. In December a number of academics, members of the National Front and bazaar merchants called for the resignation of Rajai and forty members of the *Majlis* signed a petition asking the government to prevent violent disruptions of public meetings. But their protests were of no avail. Even religious leaders such as Ayatollah Hassan Lahuti were not immune. Hezbollahis disrupted his sermon the northern city of Gorgan, in February 1981, and held him hostage for two hours. The surge of fanaticism had gained such a momentum that even calls by Ahmad Khomeini to curb 'these club-wielding extremists' failed to have any effect.

Newspaper editors, authors, members of the intelligentsia muzzled by censorship, resorted to distributing hand-written letters of protest to the representatives of foreign press. One such letter signed by eminent writers like Ahmad Shamlou, a renowned left-wing author, and former newspaper editors, Massoud Mohajer and Firouz Gouran, denounced the Revolutionary Council for:

> major acts of tyranny, monopolisation of power, rigged elections, suppression of freedom of expression, assembly and of the press... as well as widespread purges, barbaric suppression of minorities, closure of universities and imprisonment and torture of militants.[48]

The guerrilla movements resorted to violence. The winter of 1981 was marked by pitched battles between the *Fadayan* and the Marxist guerrilla group, *Peykar*, and the revolutionary guards in the streets of Tehran. But already the Revolutionary council had reinstated the shah's secret police SAVAK, now renamed SAVAM,[49] which purported to defend the national interest. It was hard at work spying and pinpointing the hide-out and activities of all opponents of the regime. With its help, and that of the local *komitehs* who policed every street in every city, the guards began finding the guerrillas' safe houses and moving in armed with the best that the country could afford to destroy them. Painfully and after much carnage the guards began gaining ground.

Their success strengthened the hands of the IRP who continued to undermine the President. By February, Bani Sadre was ruefully telling the *Sunday Times* reporter:

My hands are tied in most respects. These days you see that if anyone hails the President, he'll be immediately arrested and imprisoned.[50]

Khomeini tried to reconcile the government's feuding parties by asking them to come together and join forces to defend the country. But he remained more wary of Bani Sadre and the intellectuals who supported him than the club-wielding *hezbollahis*:

the club of the pen and the club of the tongue are the worst of clubs.[51]

IRP was determined to remove Bani Sadre. The débâcle was staged at a Friday prayer addressed by the President on 5 March 1981, on the occasion of the birthday of Mohamad Mossadeq. Some IRP hecklers who were trying to disrupt the meeting, were arrested and thrown out of the meeting. The hecklers decided to press charges of intimidation and illegal activities against the President. In a country where intimidation and illegal activities were the norm and the legal machinery had seemed powerless, there was a sudden surge of legality. Khalkhali and Beheshti secured the agreement of the Prosecutor-General, Musavi Ardabili, to investigate.

Khomeini sided with his henchmen and warned everyone, including the clergy against supporting Bani Sadre and ordered him to 'desist' from 'plotting'[52]. The noose was tightened by the closure of Bazargan's newspaper, *Mizan*, in April. Beheshti accused the President of self-aggrandizement and of projecting himself as the sole intellectual power in the land – a view echoed by Khomeini on 27 May when he publicly rebuked Bani Sadre for indulging in a personality cult. Immediately a number of Presidential aides were arrested, including one who was compiling a dossier listing the cases of torture and illegal executions. In June, the Minister of Interior closed the offices of the cooperation of People and the President. At the same time the few remaining newspapers likely to support Bani Sadre, including the *Enqelabeh Eslami*, were closed down and all publications 'inciting public disorder' were banned.

Already by November 1980, Bani Sadre had been well aware of the problems; in a prophetic speech he asked a mass rally:

> Who would think that insulting the President would be rewarded, but protesting would lead to imprisonment? Who could believe that a television interview would result in arrest and imprisonment afterwards, but if masked, clubwielding people attack the *Mizan* newspaper they would be rewarded? ... Where else in the world could officials order the censorship of the President's message and use weapons to ensure that it is done? What is strange is that it is these very same people who get all the promotion.[53]

The National Front tried to mobilise popular support for Bani Sadre by organising a public demonstration on 15 June. Khomeini denounced the move as 'an invitation to insurrection', [54] and the *hezbollah* moved in and violently attacked the demonstrations and routed the rally.

On 20 June the *Majlis* moved to impeach the President. *Guardian* reporter, David Hirst, described the scene:

> When Parliament, ostensibly scrupulous in observation of conventional forms, was debating Bani Sadre's impeachment, *Hezbollahis* formed part of intimidating throng outside, or having deposited knives and knuckledusters at the entrance, filled the galleries. When one deputy, Ali Moinfar, had the courage to defend Bani Sadre, the crowd began to shout 'death to Moinfar, death to the liberals' while a beaming Ayatollah Khalkhali, the Hanging Judge, appeared at the balcony and symbolically grasped his throat.[55]

In the event only one deputy, Salahedin Bayani, voted for the President, 13 abstained, 25 absented themselves, and 177 representatives voted against. Rafsanjani, Khalkhali and Hadi Qafari came to the *Majlis* balcony to announce the decision to a cheering crowd who took up the Ayatollah's call and chanted 'death to Bani Sadre'.

Within a month Bani Sadre and Massoud Rajavi, the leader of the *Mujahedin* fled the country to form the National Council of Resistance in France to fight against the Islamic government.

THE REIGN OF TERROR

With the impeachment of Bani Sadre the last obstacle to theocratic fascism was removed and the revolution plunged into its bloodiest phase. The fundamentalists decided to use every possible means to eliminate all opposition.

The *Majlis* Speaker Rafsanjani declared that:

> The ex-President was not gifted for politics and together with his liberal allies did much damage to the country. Now we can show the world what Islam can do in government.[56]

The 'normalisation' process included a massive purge of the administration. Over 200 journalists were dismissed from the State-run radio and television and newspapers. Score of managers were sacked and hundreds of trusted men were appointed to run national industries.

The guerrila organisations launched an all-out counter-attack with a spectacular hit on 28 June.[57] A bomb destroyed the central headquarters of the IRP while a meeting was in full swing. In one blow Ayatollah Beheshti and a whole throng of his supporters were killed. This attack was followed by another on the Prime Minister's Offices whilst a meeting was in progress. Mohamad Ali Rajai, and the new IRP chief, Mohamad Javad Bahonar, and Hushang Dastgerdi, the Chief of Police, were killed. A week later the revolutionary Prosecutor, Ali Qodussi, was assassinated.

The regime retaliated by open attacks, warfare and mass execution. The Islamic Prosecutor, Assadolah Lajevardi, spelled out the terms:

> The Islamic revolution had not been aimed at creating democracy, liberalism and other Western diseases desired by that ridiculous Bani Sadre and his pathetic hangers on... Don't count on us to show any mercy, Islam has no mercy for wrongdoers. We shall not spare even 9 year-old girls... The authorities will not hesitate to shoot hundred of people each day until the word of Allah is fully obeyed in this land.[58]

Ayatollah Sadeq Khalkhali, the Hanging Judge, reinforced these views by giving every citizen the right to become an executioner:

> executions should be left to the faithful themselves, who should dispense with troublesome formalities.[59]

The executions gained momentum and the legal age for executions reduced. In June a 9-year-old girl, Zahra Mossayeli, was executed for attacking a revolutionary guard. Within a month 540 people had been killed[60], and 6000 people jailed.

There was some opposition to this carnage from the *ulema*. In July, Sheikh Ali Tehrani published an open letter to Khomeini warning him about his irreligiosity:

> It appears as if, in order to retain power, you have chosen to act contrary to your own religious decrees and Islamic principles.[61]

At the same time several other leading figures, including Ayatollahs Abolfazl Zanjani, Hassan Qomi Tabatabayi and Abdollah Shirazi denounced the tribunals, questioned the doctrinal grounds for the legitimacy of the state and Khomeini's supremacy in the constitutional order and his infallibility in interpretation of laws. Ayatollah Qomi reiterated the long-standing *Shia* tradition wherein:

> The real clergy do not seek power... real clergy do not support those amongst the religious leaders who rule over us. The real task of the *ulema* is to enjoin people to do good and enlighten the people and prevent them from doing evil.[62]

But their pleas and views fell on deaf ears.

The *Mujahedin* suffered a major blow in mid-August when following a three-day siege in West Tehran over 100 of their members were killed and many of their leaders were captured.[63]

By late August over 8000 people had been executed, the majority were in the 18 to 35 age group.[64] Members of resistance groups were shot for such charges as 'possession of burned papers'; not stopping when told to do so;[65] 'speaking to foreign media'; 'using a car as an ambulance during demonstrations' or even 'causing disturbances in prison'.[66] The *Mujahedin* denounced the massacres and 'the dictatorship imposed on the people in the name of religion'. They argued that the regime was drowning in the blood of the innocent and was both corrupt and Fascistic. It had already 'swallowed' more than $15 billion[67] and was conducting the worst forms of spying by asking school-children to report on their own families.

The Chief Prosecutor responded by issuing a general death warrant for all members of the guerrilla organisations whom he called the 'corrupt of the earth' and 'at war with God'. He decreed that they should be executed without trial,[68] a view echoed by Ayatollah Mohamadi Guilani, a Tehran revolutionary Court Judge who recommended that:

> rebels wounded in the streets should be 'finished off' and those who take part in demonstrations should be 'put against the wall and executed on the spot'.[69]

He reiterated the same view in a television interview in November announcing that:

> All of the *Mujahedin* must be executed, even if they are unarmed, because of their opposition to the Islamic government. They should not be taken prisoner, but should be killed off.[70]

Yet this Ayatollah's sons, Mohamad and Kazem, were active members of the *Mujahedin*. They promptly denounced their father who had tried to bribe them away by offering them huge sums of money, cars and houses. Their refusal had led to the Ayatollah's venomous order for the round-up and indiscriminate execution of all the *Mujahedin*.

The *Fadayan* launched a major attack on many fronts in September 1981; they attacked revolutionary guards and even took over Amol in the north of Iran. The government redoubled its attacks on safe houses and demonstrators and accelerated its mass arrests and executions. The numbers executed reached about 50 a day and on 19 to 20 September 182 people were killed.[71]

The list of those who were executed, arrested or in hiding, read like the Who's Who of the original revolutionary coalition that opposed the Shah. The dissidents published an open letter in London, addressed to Khomeini, it read like an appropriate epitaph to the revolution:

> Our revolution was against the police State and aimed to create a united and safe land for all. We feel nothing but shame and guilt when we see the foreign media interview the mothers of the young idealists who are being executed.

Such murders do no more than highlight the terrors of this reign of fascism where all spirituality and higher values have been undermined. Why do you permit that unique flight of spiritually and idealism which sparked off the revolution, to be turned into such relentless, fierce and degrading oppression and materialist rule? Executions ...executions every day... explosions and executions and more executions... Is Islam not the religion of justice and love? With so many bloodthirsty murders how could anyone conceivably believe that you who allow such iniquitous killings to continue, have any respect for Islam?[72]

After Rajai's death, Khomeini appointed Mohamad Reza Mahdavi Kani, the Minister of Interior, chief of Tehran's *komitehs* and head of the Association of Militant Clergy, *Rohanianeh Mobarez*, to act as interim Prime Minister. He was replaced after the October elections. The IRP's candidate, Hajatoleslam Ali Khameneyi, became President and he appointed Mir Hosein Mussavi as Prime Minister. Clearly, the IRP had gathered all the reins of government to form a single party state. It was already closely associated with the *komitehs* and with the self-propelling organisations. It had a near-monopoly control over the instruments of coercion and was backed by the tribunals and could use the revolutionary guards and the *hezbollah* to assert control. It ran the ideological purification bureaux of the civil service and the armed forces. It used the mosques through which it contributed rations to create a network of support amongst the poorer sections of the society.

The rule of terror continued for some 18 months. In April 1982. Qotbzadeh was executed for plotting with army officers to bomb Khomeini's home. Ayatollah Shariatmadari was accused of condoning the plot. His Centre for Islamic Study and Publication in Qom was closed and he was placed under house arrest. In an unprecedented move, Khomeini took it upon himself to strip Shariatmadari of his right to act as *marja'*, leader of *Shias*. There are no religious grounds for any religious leader to deprive a colleague from the right to lead his community. *Shias* do not have hierarchy of interpretation, even the highest Ayatollahs, *Ayatollah ozma*, achieve this rank as a result of public recognition and clerical endorsement. Once selected as a *marja'*, there are no legal ways of removing one – a view that Khomeini himself had repeatedly endorsed.[73] Yet, in another of his many *volte-faces* the *Faqih* who prided himself on his steadfastness, did that which he had declared unacceptable, when he would have been the likely victim. In the climate of terror at the time, no one moved to defend Shariatmadari.

The climate of fear and merciless killings created a general revulsion inside and outside the country. There was open disillusionment with the revolution and the combination of fear and poverty made most people apathetic and ineffective. Participation in the elections fell dramatically, despite Khomeini's decree that voting was a religious duty, the reduction of the voting age to 15, and the presence of revolutionary guards who supervised the elections, and stamped the ration cards of the voters. The economy was slowly grinding down and the brain-drain accelerating. Eventually in December 1982 Khomeini issued an eight-point decree aimed at curbing the excesses of the revolution. He set up a committee chaired by the Prime Minister to ensure that the commandments were implemented and gradually the wave of executions subsided.[74]

# 6 The Armed Forces: Divided We Rule

The reign of terror and the invasion of Iran by Iraq effectively secured Khomeini's rule in the decade that followed. Wary of the army and its potential for staging coups, Khomeini chose the *komiteh* guards to secure his hold on the country. Khomeini's initial idea, that his revolutionary message was sufficiently powerful to arouse all Muslims and create a united Islamic revolution across the Middle East, proved hollow, as did his initial declaration that a revolution rooted in the people would need no army for internal security. He soon changed his mind on this, as on most political issues, but he was wary of what he regarded as the Shah's army and secret police. So, in a move not unlike that of the formation of Hitler's SS, Khomeini organised his own personal alternative armed forces. He gathered the youths who had already armed themselves by ransacking the Shah's arsenals and had spearheaded of the US Embassy occupation to form the Guards Corps of the Islamic Revolution, the revolutionary guards, *sepah*. They were declared to be:

> the popular organ which has emerged from the core of the revolution, to protect it and its ideological purity and to act as the powerful arm of the Islamic revolution and the protector of the oppressed the world over.[1]

Devout, fanatical and wedded to the cause, the guards were given extensive powers and privileges. They were empowered to administer spontaneous justice, act as the strong arm of the revolutionary *komitehs* and combine the functions of police, secret police and firing squads. They replaced the army as a ready ladder of upward social mobility. For those who had no qualification other than a fanatical faith in the person of Khomeini and for the deprived illiterate slum-dwelling youths, service in the guards provided not only a regular salary, but also cheap housing, free medical care and extensive powers and authority. 'Spiritual discipline' replaced 'the superfluous discipline in the form that was seen under the shah'[2] and death for the cause – martyrdom – provided an additional bonus by allowing direct entry to heaven.

But strong-arm tactics caused havoc in the early years of the revolution and during the reign of terror that followed the departure of Bani Sadre. Their arbitrary searches and arrests, on the spot executions and excesses made them amongst the most-hated groups in society. The liberal interpretation of the extent of their powers enabled the *komiteh* guards to burst into people's homes, ransack houses in search of alcoholic beverages, playing cards and Western tapes or records, or even photographs of female members of the household in less than Islamic garb, stashed away in albums. They carried out similar raids on work-places, rounding-up large numbers of 'suspects' and condemning them to death or imprisonment.

Their excesses were such that even their commander, Morteza Rezayi, was obliged to admit that they tended 'to interfere in some affairs that they should not'.[3]

But the ubiquitous presence of the *komiteh* guards was extremely useful in securing the survival of Khomeini. They effectively undermined the *Fadayan* and *Mujahedin* resistance groups' activities in Iran and remained a high-profiled, well-armed agent of government control. Though aware of the need to improve their public image, Khomeini – unlike the Shah – was not deceived by his own rhetoric. He occasionally tried to restrain the guards and advised them:

> as a father, and a brother to tread the path of righteousness... to treat people with good manners, kind deeds and open countenance and courtesy.[4]

But whereas the Shah, in the firm belief that the prosperity created by oil money had secured his future, dismissed the anti-riot unit of the army, Khomeini remained all too aware of the need for an effective anti-resistance force and insisted that they should have the necessary powers:

> to enable them them to fulfil their constitutional duties of fighting against internal and external enemies.[5]

In 1982 the *komiteh* guards were officially placed in charge of all police precincts. At the same time they were also placed under the supervision of the

> *ulema*, to safeguard them, and prevent them from straying from the path of virtue.[6]

However, the *ulema* did not check the excesses of the guards. Even Khomeini's eight-point decree in December 1982 did not curb their power. Though intended to ensure the safety of the citizens, the decree was more effective in reinstating some sacked civil servants than in controlling the guards.

The eight-point decree had made it illegal to tap telephones, prosecute people without a valid warrant and trespass into homes or places of work. In the decree, Khomeini had announced the end of the reign of terror and declared that all private properties were safe and protected by the Islamic government. The decree demanded the immediate legislation of an Islamic criminal code and a general check on the qualification of the many revolutionary judges who had sprung up over the country. It banned arbitrary arrests, denouncing them as 'sinful'; prohibited 'the treatment of people in an "un-Islamic manner"', and insisted that the Committees to Redress Grievances pursued his commandment diligently and to the letter.[7]

The Central Committee for Redressing Grievances, *Setadeh Markaziyeh Peygirieh Farmaneh Imam*, chaired by the Prime Minister, Mir Hosein Mussavi, included the Prosecutor-General, Mussavi Ardabili, and Khomeini's son, Ahmad. It was empowered to sack anyone who failed to implement its decisions. Within days of its inception, twenty committees, each consisting of three men, including a representative from the militant clergy, the judiciary and the executive branches of the government, were dispatched to different parts of the country,[8] and a civil service Justice Tribunal, *divaneh edalateh edari*, was set up in every Ministry. *Hojatoleslam* Emami Kashani was appointed to head the tribunals and promptly declared that all the appointments and dismissals organised by the *Heyateh Gozinesh*, the appointment committees who had purged the civil service, were illegal and subject to review by the tribunals.[9] The central follow-up committee called to task the Tehran, Qom and Ilam Prosecutors as well as the under-secretary of the Ministry of Labour.[10] But, even in its heady days, few revolutionary guards were asked to account for their actions. An exception was the head of the Revolutionary guards of Bukan who was accused of interfering with the election process.[11]

The *komiteh* guards remained unrestrained, even their staunch supporter, Ayatollah Montazeri, was obliged to warn them that:

> any wrongdoing by the guards is seen as a fault in our revolution…the guards must treat everyone, even the counter-revolutionaries, according to the clearly defined Islamic code of conduct.[12]

This view was echoed by Hojatoleslam Ali Khameneyi:

> the guards should behave in such a way that would endear them to the people, since the guards can only survive and be effective if they are loved and respected.[13]

Love and respect, however, have not been the lot of the *komiteh* guards. The general discontent with the guards led to what was termed a 'radical review' in 1984. All 'unsuitable people who did not have the necessary revolutionary principles' were purged to create 'a new revived and committed force',[14] and in 1985 the functions of the *komiteh* guards were formally ratified. They were required to fight all corruption and corrupt ideologies, deal with all crimes and misdeeds, fight narcotics, protect key installations, control riots, strikes and all undiscipline, eradicate all opposition groups and take charge of policing. These powers were so wide-ranging that, not surprisingly, they continued to claim that they did not have a 'clear idea about the extent of [their] duties'.[15]

> There are no clear limits imposed on the *komiteh* guards in dealing with corruption and Godlessness… Some people continue to accuse us of bad faith… But the forces of law and order are never loved by the populace… The *komiteh* guards are obliged to deal with the law-breakers in our society and it may happen that, God forbid, they may behave in an undesirable way in their encounter with a guilty brother or even one that is innocent… But people can always complain to us and we'll review the matter.[16]

Some of the *ulema* tried to add the *komiteh* guards to their own group of supporters and *lutis*. The hanging judge, Sadeq Khalkhali, was the first to try to use them in an unsuccessful political assassination plot. Others made less-publicised attempts to gain the guard's support. Eventually, to cut the links between political leaders and the guards, the *Majlis* decided in December 1984 that *komiteh* guards could not be used as personal bodyguards by anyone.

There were considerable similarities between the *komiteh* guards and Hilter's SS soldiers, as were the many methods used by the regime to secure what Khomeini called 'a 36 million-strong police force'. Children were required to report on their parents, neighbours to spy on neighbours and the guards were allowed to keep an eye on everything. Not surprisingly the *komiteh* guards have been the focus of general hatred in spite of the 1984 clean-ups and the decision in the same year to send some of the guards to serve at the fronts. This move was useful; selected guards were sent out of the cities in the hope that some of the popular sympathy for war heroes would be channelled towards them. But the strategy was not successful, despite the 'martyrdom' of thousands of *komiteh* guards at the fronts.[17]

There were sporadic attempts by the resistance groups to kill and undermine the *komiteh* guards. But, after the early years, these attacks were met by the guards redoubling their brutality – a tactic that ensured their continuous unpopularity; so much so that they began having severe difficulty with recruitment. By 1987, despite the high general levels of unemployment, they could only fill 2 per cent of their vacancies.[18] The *komiteh* guards' deputy-commander-in-chief, Mokhtar Kalantari, attributed the problems to the bad press that they were getting:

> We wish to fight against wrongdoers but all the propaganda machines are in the hands of our enemies.[19]

But all evidence suggests that they were too zealous in their pursuit of wrong-doers. By 1987 Rafsanjani was still trying to control the guards by telling them that he 'expected' the 'law-enforcement agencies' to:

> behave in a way as not to go against the people-based principles of our revo-lution. They must love and respect people... People judge the government by the way its law-enforcement agencies deal with them and we hope that in the future we may improve the standards of these agents in our society.[20]

Once more his expectation was in vain. By 1988 the guards were accused, by *Majlis* deputies, of arresting 'fathers of martyrs', and of brutally mistreating 'honest traders and citizens'.[21]

To improve matters the guards had decided to raise the standard of education within their ranks and in 1984 they had launched a nationwide recruitment drive for university-educated personnel. They decided to set up their own university and teach psychology, sociology, psychoanalysis, and courses on law and the judiciary, and history.[22] In doing so they extended the existing multiplicities of educational sources.[23] But their campaign enjoyed only a limited success. By 1987 when the *komiteh* guards became formal civil servants, the best they could do was to recruit middle-school graduates. All they had managed thus far was a total of 3000 men with more than primary-school levels of education, to add to their 20 000 who had less.[24]

Despite their lack of education and expertise and their all-too-evident unpopularity, the *komiteh* guards have remained an essential agent of government in Iran. Khomeini was all too aware of the potential threat of a counter-revolution. Like many Populist governments, the regime sought for nearly a decade to resolve all political disputes at the level of the street and by mobilising the crowds.[25] Khomeini called repeatedly on his people to participate in street marches and public demonstrations to exhibit their support and the success of his regime. But his popular base was an uncertain cross-class and ideological combination which could prove volatile and unreliable. So the marchers were often renumerated by mosques and *mullas* and closely supervised by the guards who marshalled supporters and disrupted demonstrations by opposition groups – a task in which they were greatly helped by the *hezbollah*, God's party. Occasionally, however, the guards were used to check the excessive righteousness of the fundamentalist groups. The *hezbollah* tended to organise 'spontaneous' attacks on 'undesirable elements' such as poorly veiled women.[26] Sometimes these attacks contravened the official mood of moral relaxation, which was sporadically adopted to encourage the middle classes to return from exile and run the economy. Then, although many of the guards themselves shared the *hezbollahis* views, they were obliged to step in and impose the line of the *imam*, which varied according to the moods of the *Faqih*.

## THE GUARD CORPS

Although *komiteh* guards viewed service at the front as a severe punishment, the guard's battalions, known as the Guard Corps, were considered to be the emergent heroes of the revolution. Created at the same time as the *komiteh* guards, they, rather than the army which Khomeini considered less than reliable, were initially directed to fight the tribal uprisings in Kurdistan and Turkomanistan. But it was in the first year of the Iran–Iraq war that they succeeded in covering themselves in glory. As Bani Sadre sided with the regular forces, so Khomeini encouraged the guards and relied on them. They were instrumental in recapturing the oil town of Abadan by December 1981 and Khoramshahre three months later. They played a central role in pushing in the Iraqis out of much of southern Iran and staging a 'human offensive' in an attempt to overwhelm the Iraqis by force of numbers.

They gained Speaker Rafsanjani's whole-hearted support and even when the war was not going well for the Iranians they retained Khomeini's help; he declared:

> I can assure you that if this revolution is to stay then the guards must stay. The guards are part and parcel of this revolution, they are embodied in it and are not an external organ... The guards were born of the revolution they grew with the revolution and will stay with it.[27]

Increasingly the guards acquired the characteristics of the armed forces under the Pahlavis, and obtained similar privileges.[28] After the general call-up in 1982, they began extending their activities and preparing the grounds for forming an alternative force to the army. Unlike the Shah, who mistrusted and feared his armed forces, the clergy competed with each other in praising the guards. Rafsanjani announced that:

> The government is and remains indebted to the guards for the role they have played in buttressing the revolution from its inception till today. If our Islamic revolution is to remain true to its principles then it must ensure the survival of its most important backer and agents of security, namely the Guardian Corps of the Islamic Republic... The guards are and always have been in the active arm of the Imam. These large numbers of devout and devoted men have offered their lives and have been active in the battlefields. They are the firm basis and the insurer of the survival of the revolutionary rule.[29]

Even Ali Khameneyi declared:

> The guards brought rays of hope into the most desperate moments of the war, whenever the battle conditions caused doubts or weakened expectations. The Guards Corps have secured the success of all the leaders of this country and are respected by our venerable and illustrious leader.[30]

In this war, which did not recognise its heroes until late in the decade, it was the Guards Corps that spearheaded the heroics. While the army used military strategies, with greater and lesser degrees of success, it was the guards who furnished the 'wave of human force' which swept across the minefields to invade Iraq. By 1981, of an estimated 150 000 guards, 11 000 had 'achieved' martyr dom,[31] However, in subsequent years, the honour of such wholesale 'martyrdom' was reserved for the younger or inexperienced militiamen. The Guards Corps used their glory to help them expand and by 1986 form their own alternative air, sea and land force.

Although theoretically egalitarian, and informal, in practice the Guards Corps became a professional, well-funded and well-equipped force. But through most of the war they retained equal ranks, with no formal stratification and with the commanders remaining, at least in name, 'brothers'. As early as 1982 they began planning to set up their own naval units and by 1985 Khomeini allowed them to start their own air force and take charge of the war industries. They remained the privileged bastion of Khomeini's power. Their road to grandeur was paved by the establishment of the Ministry of Guards in 1982. Typically, Khomeini did not appoint the Guard Corps' leader, Mohsen Rezayi, to the ministerial post, choosing instead to give the job to Mohsen Rafiqdust, thus creating tension at the top of the hierarchy. To mediate between the two, Khomeini appointed a third man, Qassem Ali Zahirnejad as the *Imam's* representative on the Supreme Defence Council, which was set up to oversee the war and which controlled the top echelons of the guards. The rift between Rezayi and Rafiqdust was both public and ever-widening. Finally, the Minister was made responsible for foreign affairs and the commander for internal and operational matters. Both remained subject to the control of the *Imam's* representative who, though theoretically in charge only of ideological matters, in practice exercised great authority.

The foreign-relations dimension was translated into the provision of military training for the guards in Syria and Libya, while access to formal budgetary allocation and cabinet level enabled the guards to obtain equipment for their anti-aircraft, telecommunication, artillery and air force and naval units. The guards replaced the military in terms of access to resources. Khomeini relied on them to win the war and offered them the best that the revolution could afford. They had their own hospitals, including the latest and very best-equipped one in Tehran; access to subsidised housing and preferential treatment by government agencies, and their own university and training courses.

In fact, Khomeini went much further than the Pahlavis in creating a firm military basis of personal support. Like that of the Pahlavis, Khomeini's regime offered an entire gamut of schooling to potential guards. Not only have young boys been able to join as 'honorary' guards from primary school onwards, but also, in an unprecedented move, the guards set up their own boarding schools in a country with no tradition of sending its children away for education. The boarding schools, with places only at the secondary levels, are open to boys who have had high average passes in their school grades, pass the guard school entrance exams and prove their worthiness during a short camping expedition. The successful pupils then board at schools in Tehran, Sanandaj, Tabriz and Zahedan. The students have free board and lodging and health care as well as a basic grant. They can specialise in Islamic knowledge, or mathematics, physics, or experimental sciences. The young men are expected to stay for four years at these schools, to undergo compulsory ideological and military training and, if successful, to apply for tertiary education at the Guard's university. All applicants must be male, Muslim and in good health.[32] High-school students who wish to join the guards without going to boarding school may also apply for grants. Once more, access is through competitive entrance exams.

Symbolically, as an assertion of supremacy over the USA, the boarding school in Tehran is located at the former American Embassy, now called 'the den of spies' and denounced as 'a centre of treason against the people of Iran' – a curious aberration since it was from this very place that the resistance of the high-ranking generals of the Shah was organised by a representative of USA; one of the many reasons why Khomeini chose to call the USA the Great Satan.

The guards played a dominant part in the war, and repeatedly attempted to defeat Iraq by sheer force of numbers. They staged a major attack in 1984 to try to cut off Basra from Baghdad; this was countered by chemical attacks from Iraq and failed. In March 1985 the Guards' leader, Rezayi, with Rafsanjani's support, masterminded the Karbala attacks – a series of forays the earliest of which ended disastrously for the Iranians who, according to the Iraqis, suffered

90 000 casualties.[33] The next move was the war of the cities. Iraq began launching missiles at several major cities in Iran.

By June the Iranians were beginning to show signs of war fatigue. The Iranian anti-aircraft weapons proved quite ineffectual against the Iraqi missiles. Mehdi Bazargan protested about the unnecessary carnage and prolonging the war. He made speeches in the *Majlis* and sent open letters that were only reported by the foreign press. But his criticisms were stifled by *hezbollahis* who attacked and ransacked his offices and banned him from making any public communications. Nevertheless, the sporadic protests against the war continued and in May 1985, in response to a call by the exiled Prime Minister, Shahpour Bakhtiar, the middle classes in Tehran staged an anti-war demonstration by car and jammed all the streets in the wealthier quarters of the city. Within weeks the slum-dwellers in the southern parts of the city, who had suffered the brunt of the Iraqi air raids, were also staging spontaneous street demonstrations.

It was evident that unless Iran regained access to better military equipment, it was bound to lose the war. The initial expectations that the war would be won by sheer force of numbers began to wane. The political divisions within the country made it all the more difficult to form a firm war policy. In particular there was a new power struggle developing between Ayatollah Montazeri and *Hojatoleslams* Rafsanjani and Khameneyi about who would succeed Khomeini. Khameneyi remained close to the armed forces, who continued to be underfunded. Montazeri formed an alliance with the students following the line of the *Imam* and the more fundamentalist groups, including the *komiteh* guards, and Rafsanjani continued to back the Guards Corps – a liaison that proved particularly successful when in February 1986 the guards captured the island of Fao in Iraq and marked a notable success for the Iranians.

But, given the official US ban on arms trade with Iran, and the heavy dependence of the forces on American products, there were severe shortages of sophisticated military equipment. Finally in May 1986, Rafsanjani began secret negotiations with President Reagan's former National Security Advisor, Robert C. McFarlane, and White House aide, Lieutenant-Colonel Oliver North, to get some US military equipment. In July McFarlane made an abortive visit to Tehran where 'the students following the line of the *Imam*' and supporters of Montazeri hounded him out. Nevertheless there was a second clandestine visit in September.

Rafsanjani was taking a calculated risk in dealing with the Americans. Already, the first post-revolutionary Prime Minister, Mehdi Bazargan, had been forced to resign for doing the very same thing. The 'followers of the *Imam*' were unlikely to remain silent, even though quite possibly in this, as in most other matters, Khomeini may well have changed his mind. The secret rapport between the Speaker of the *Majlis* and the representatives of the Great Satan were denounced by the Islamist groups headed by Ayatollah Montazeri. Mehdi Hashemi, an aide to Montazeri and his brother, Hadi Hashemi, who was Montazeri's son-in-law, leaked information about these meetings to the media and started the Irangate scandal. Undaunted, Rafsanjani ordered the arrest of the

Hashemis. Montazeri, working behind the scenes, mobilised the students follow-ing the line of the *Imam* and they held a congress in Tehran accusing Cabinet Ministers Ehtashemi, *Hojatoleslam* Rayshahri and the Commander of the Guards Corps' land forces, Colonel Ali Shamkhani, of plotting against the interest of Islam and arresting the Hashemis. The students also called on Rafsanjani to explain his actions and forced the Speaker to make an official statement in *Majlis* about the visits. Brazenly, he announced that the US representatives 'were thrown out of Iran before meeting any of the nations' leaders',[34] a position that Rafsanjani could not maintain when questioned by the Western press. He admitted: 'They met with our arms-dealing representatives' but insisted: 'I did not negotiate and was not their counterpart'.[35]

Khomeini must have known about these meetings, since he appeared unper-turbed by the *rapprochement* with the Great Satan. He counselled care and called on the two sides to unite:

> the enemy has failed at the fronts. But they have not lost hope and are seeking your destruction by spreading divisive rumours amongst you. Beware of divisiveness from whomever it may be. Be it a holy man, be it a sacred mouth, be it the words of a prayer leader... these are the words of the devil... the Defence of the Islamic Republic depends entirely on your unity... unity between you and all social classes of this country...[36]

However, in the context of the post-revolutionary state in Iran, unity was not a matter of consensus or negotiation; one side had to win and the other had to acquiesce. Eventually Rafsanjani won the day. Whereas in the USA, North and others were hauled up before the House of Representatives to account for their deeds, in Iran Rafsanjani got away. Like the bad old days, using typical secret police and SAVAK tactics, it was Mehdi Hashemi who was made into the culprit. Like the resistance fighters in the days of the Pahlavis, Hashemi was made to appear on television to confess to a series of grave misdeeds which secured him the death sentence. Furthermore, in December 1986, Khomeini publicly announced that he had decided that Montazeri was not the appropriate person to follow him as the *Faqih*.

Much of the American arms were used in the Karbala-5 offensive in January 1987. This battle resulted in the gain of 40 square miles and its success enabled Rafsanjani to discard the blame for dealing with the Great Satan.

At the time, the guards had already embarked on an extensive drive for self-sufficiency which included taking over the management of industrial complexes and organisation of the production and equipment and ammunition. In 1986 the first consignment of Iranian heavy, semi-heavy and light armaments were dispatched to the fronts and the guards claimed that they were producing 80 per cent of the weapons and ammunition that they required.[37] A year later they were firing home-produced land, sea and anti-tank missiles.[38] By 1988 they claimed that they were meeting 90 per cent of the light armaments required by all the fighting forces and were making hunter fighter aeroplanes, bombers, helicopters and land-to-land missiles with 140-kilometres range. Finally in September the Minister, Mohsen Rafiqdust, announced the end of arms imports.[39]

By 1988, the guards had the first graduates of their own helicopter-piloting training course, as well as others who had completed the Corps' air force training courses. The guards had put the days of fanaticism and blind allegiance behind them and embarked on the road to professionalism. They were trying to become an élite force and were doing their best to recruit better-educated and more highly qualified personnel. Applicants for trainee places in the Guards Corps had to have above-average high-school grades, a good school record with no failures at any level and had to pass the competitive entrance exams. Nor were they now even required to be Muslims; they merely needed to reiterate their absolute faith in Khomeini and the Islamic government. Those who failed the exams could join the Guards' infantry.

## BASIJ

As the guards became more professionalised and their numbers of 'martyrs' were reduced, so the *basij*, volunteer mass-mobilisation militia, were called on to furnish fanatical devotion to the cause and the rush to eternity. Thus whereas by 1988 the guards' losses at the fronts were down by 10 per cent over the previous year and considerably more over the early years,[40] the *basij* provided the bulk of the 79 644 non-army men 'martyred' in the war.[41]

*Basij* was formed in November 1979. It was envisaged as small-scale neighbourhood defence units of about 20 men each, working in four or five household cells. They were to operate under the guidance of the local mosques who were to organise rudimentary training courses and enlist the help of off-duty soldiers in teaching them hand-to hand combat methods. Some of these units were taken over by resistance organisations. In June 1980 the guards were put in charge of the *basij* cells and they began by a thorough purge which cut down the cells considerably and what was left became an integral part of the guards forces.

After the outbreak of war the Ministry of Guards, decided to use the *basij* organisation to get the much-hailed and never-seen 20 million-strong popular militia. Article 151 of the Iranian constitution already required that all citizens should receive a thorough grounding in military techniques. Accordingly Khomeini ordered the general mobilisation in 1982 and in the first year of the call-up some 800 000 were reported to have been trained and 300 000 of these organised in specialised battalions.[42] Most were not sent to the front. Those too young to join the army or too illiterate to become professional soldiers offered their services to the *basij* and they were unlikely to make good soldiers.

Of necessity the training was minimal; it consisted of courses on ideology, and theory of warfare provided after hours at schools, offices and factories, followed by a three-day practical course at local army camps, at the end of which participants received a certificate which registered them as members of the *basij* and subject to call-up. Before going to the fronts, volunteers obtained further 'high level training'. In the early days the training consisted of two days at the camps. In 1985, the period was extended to four weeks.[43]

Primary-school children and teenagers too young for conscriptions formed a major intake of the militia. By 1987, the head of the *basij*, Ayatollah Mohamad Ali Rahmani was claiming to have 3 million youngsters on his register and boasted that 9000 of these were already selected to act as battalion leaders.[44]

Amateurism was the hallmark of the *basij* and a matter of pride. The men referred to themselves as the 'shunners of qualification' and claimed to glory in the avoidance of 'classical warfare methods'.[45] As a *basij* leader explained:

> As *basij* forces we are led by a twelve-year-old boy whose small heart is more eloquent and more powerful than a thousand words. Unhampered by classical specialisation, with a bomb tied to his belt he braves the enemy, runs under the tanks killing the foe and draining the cup of martyrdom himself.[46]

Unpaid volunteers, untrained, barely armed and without uniforms, followed the drum, initially in their hundreds and subsequently in dozens. By 1984 *basij* leaders boasted of 2 25 000 men with general training. Of these only 420 861 had obtained even the rudimentary battle training that was on offer. Although there was virtually no age barrier and no male was considered too young or too old to join the *basij*, the total of volunteers did not increase according to plans. The Minister of Guards had expected:

> to accommodate the deluge of volunteers and rapidly send forth a thousand fresh battalions to *basij* warriors to bring victory to this war.[47]

In the first years tens of thousands of *basij* men went to the fronts, with 60 000 in 1984 and 1986, and even an estimated 100 000 in 1987, but despite the obligation for all employed men to volunteer for the *basij*, the numbers never even remotely approached the hoped-for millions of warriors each year. Schools and the education sector consistently provided 60 to 70 per cent of the *basij* forces,[48] 20 per cent were from factories and offices but there were hardly any clergy, intellectuals or traders.[49] By 1988, of the expected 20 million, only 4 million had shown up for the initial training and most of these did not go to the fronts.[50]

Since the faithful were not forthcoming, it was no longer possible to hope for success by deluging the Iraqis with a 'human wave'. As early as June 1986 the period of service at the fronts for *basij* men was extended from three to four months. As Rafsanjani pointed out:

> Of course since the *basij* men are volunteers we cannot compel them to serve longer at the fronts... But all government offices must take note of the requirement to participate in the war effort, even if this results in temporary closures.[51]

But the numbers of volunteers continued to fall. Even the arrival of the US navy in the Gulf in 1987 failed to re-ignite the lost enthusiasm for martyrdom. Rafiqdust resorted to praising the heroism of the *basij*, boasting that their bravery compensated for the paucity of numbers:

> Each of our *basij* men has the ability to take on the largest US ship single-handed. Our people have no fear, the only notion of fear for us is fear of God and none other... Each of our *basij* men is a missile in himself and we have the means to sink the entire US naval forces.[52]

A remarkable expectation when of every 3000 *basij* trainees only 100 gained any seafaring skills.[53]

In September 1987, Mohsen Rafiqdust announced the imminent addition of 2 million of these redoubtable *basij* forces to 'deprive the enemy of peace of mind',[54] a view echoed by President Khameneyi:

> The Western media call us the 'demented soldiers', that is, soldiers who are crazed by this complete and unrecognisable passion, the selfless love of God and devotion to the path laid by the line of the *Imam*.[55]

There was not much substance to be seen. Fewer, than 2000 men joined and the number of volunteers plummeted to one-seventh of the previous year.[56] In November Prime Minister Mussavi declared a week of preparation to defeat the USA and counter the attack of 'the Great Satan at our gates':

> Of course the Americans are in a very weak position in the region and the murder of the captain of the Sharje fishing-boat indicates that in the Gulf the Americans fear their own shadows and are scared stiff even by a mere fishing-boat which they classify as an aggressor.[57]

The Guards' propaganda machine warned:

> People should note that we have the USA at the gate and Saddam, heartened by the enemy of Islam, has extended his attacks on civilian targets. It is our duty to rise against these usurpers and their chemical warfare and defeat the enemy.[58]

But still no sign of the 20-million-strong army. Khomeini had expected all the male population to join the war. But most did not. By mid-November, Rafsanjani was forced to provide some excuses for the failures:

> We do not call this a general mobilisation. That is the next stage. This is merely a change in the war.[59]

However, the war was devouring the forces and more men were needed at the front. So in January 1988 government offices were instructed to increase the 10 per cent of their workforce required to serve at the fronts at all times to 20 per cent. The *ulema*, university students and professionals were asked to remember their duty to serve the revolution. But, despite repeated efforts, the *basij* failed to recruit the middle classes. In November 1982, in response to a call from

Ayatollah Montazeri, the *ulema* had sent 350 of their junior members from Qom to the fronts. But since then avoidance of military service had gained an epidemic momentum amongst the clergy. As the head of the Political Ideology section of the guards commented in November 1988:

> Those who call themselves the guardians of Islam must necessarily have an Islamic approach... There are reports of critical cultural weakness amongst the forces currently at the fronts. We invite the political ideological cadre of the guards to embark on a cultural mobilisation and serve in two- to three-monthly turns at the fronts.[60]

As the numbers of volunteers decreased a substantial element of rounding-up of volunteers increased. Tribal people were put under considerable pressure to join up and undergo what the government called 'training suitable to their temperament'.[61]

Since the proliferation of the forces and the attempt to create *two* land, air and sea forces was already placing a heavy drain on the military budget, the *basij* was not only to be manned by volunteers, but was also to be funded by popular donations. Khomeini and other leading *ulema* launched various appeals for collecting money which they described as the 'vital life-line of the war'. Different groups were targeted at different times. Khomeini personally headed the project, *tarheh labik*, unity project, which encouraged men of all ages to express their unity with the *Imam* by paying for and joining the *basij* forces.

The most successful programme was that of the school-children. In 1987, militia training was made part of the core curriculum of all boys' schools and pupils were encouraged to join the *tarheh qolak*, money-box project, and save their pocket-money to buy military equipment. Backed with extensive propaganda the project was reported to have been very successful. Some 200 boys from the provincial town of Shahinshare were photographed with their cheque for 60 000 rials for the project, a sum which was equivalent to two months' salary for the average civil servant.

But such small donations fell far short of the growing needs of the *basij*. Eventually the guards announced that people who were physically able but unwilling to go forth as volunteers were to pay money instead and offer what they could towards the war effort. Those who could afford to do so, were entreated to shoulder the responsibility of paying the expenses of a warrior. This was included in the ten-point programme for funding the war which was launched in November 1987. It announced:

> We expect all those who for valid reasons such as illness, physical disability or people such as housewives and those who cannot be at the fronts to help the war effort financially... Each financial unit is a warrior who, when we consider arms, ammunition and infrastructural facilities, costs of digging trenches and building living quarters would cost us more than 100 000 tumans every three months. But we only ask for the paltry sum they receive as salary

and the cost of individual equipment for each warrior such as boots and flask and torches etc. which only amounts to 20 000 tumans for three months. Those who can afford it should pay for at least one warrior for three months, some may take on 10 or 100 or even a battalion of 1000.[62]

Khomeini's son, Ahmad, was amongst the numerous *ulema* who had avoided war duties. He promptly announced that since he did not have 'the physical strength to serve in the ranks of the warriors of Islam', he would fund fifty men for 3 months – a considerable sum for the honest son of an Ayatollah who demanded austerity of his followers and had his eyes firmly on the next world, to muster at such short notice.

All government establishments were instructed to report the concrete measures that they were taking in support of the war effort. There ensued a flurry of advertisements with each and every office announcing its commitment to the war. It was interesting to note that announcements by private institutions were few and far between. By far the largest donation came from the Industry and Mines section of the *mostaazefin*, the organisation of the deserving poor, which funded 1300 warriors;[63] the Martyr Organisation, *Bonydaeh Shahid*, took on 500, but the martyrs' families, who no doubt were no longer receiving their dues from their organisation, could only pay for 14. The Ministry of Foreign Affairs took on 700 and the Reconstruction Revolutionary Unit, *Jahadeh Sazandegi*, 500.[64] A cynic could argue that more than anything else the announcements indicated the areas where there was money to be made within the bureaucracy. Khomeini however declared his satisfaction with the results by announcing the imminent demise of Saddam and the Americans:

Saddam is going and neither the Americans nor the others can keep him in place.[65]

## THE ARMY

As the guards climbed up the ladder of social privilege and prestige, so the armed forces moved down. Whereas only high flyers, who had passed competitive entrance exams were eligible for joining the guards' training courses, the armed forces could recruit amongst those who had failed their high-school certificates.[66] As the guards became more professionalised and better-equipped, the army became more 'Islamified'. Ideological purification sections were set up at every level, run by the *ulema* who both supervised and controlled much of the activities of the troops and regulated them according to Islamic dictum. According to the head of the Political Ideology Section of the navy, Mussavi Kashani, the forces:

welcomed these units with open arms, because these enabled them to fulfil their social and political obligations as well as their military duties.[67]

As the guards rose in status, so they discarded the requirements of Islamification. In an attempt to recruit the best for the guards' newly formed air and sea forces, they dropped the requirement that all applicants should be Muslims. What was required was to believe in the Islamic Republic and pass examinations in mathematics, sciences, languages, etc. By contrast the armed forces were 'placed on the path of the Islamic mainstream'[68] and were made to 'gain spiritual depth'.[69] Not only did their recruits have to be Muslims,[70] but they had to be devout. New recruits only needed to pass an IQ test, but they had to sit a written and an oral examination in 'Islamic perspectives'.

Eventually the Armed Forces Law of 1987 tightened the grip of the *ulema* making the ideological sections responsible for 'evaluation and selection' of personnel and for appointments, promotions and foreign posting.[71] In addition, in a move that mirrored the Shah's secret police in the army,[72] an information unit was set up to:

> Make security checks on military personnel; discover and recognise all political activities of members of the armed forces and assess the impacts of political events on the forces and their organisations.[73]

Like SAVAK under the Shah, so the information organisation under Khomeini was:

> to serve directly under the national leader who would select the person who should head the unit and will have the sole authority for ordering the Head of the Armed forces to sack him.[74]

For much of the war the army remained the butt of clerical suspicion. For years it fought, lost men and equipment and braved the enemy without any rewards or promotions. Until 1987 its forces were headed by mere colonels: Hassan Shorabi, who served as the head of *gendarmerie* till 1985 and then became the Commander-in-Chief of the forces; Ali Sayad Shirazi, head of the land forces; Mansur Satari, head of the air force, and Mohamad Hosein Malekzadegan, the head of the navy. Eventually in May 1987, at the insistence of Khameneyi, the army received its first promotions and ten of its officers were elevated to the rank of Brigadier-General. The only one to become Major-General was Qassem Ali Zahirnejad who had been Army Chief of Staff in 1984 and the representative to the *Imam* in the High Council of Defence for a period. Malekzadegan, the head of the navy, which had been singled out for praise for its heroic defence of the Persian Gulf, was also promoted to the rank of Rear-Admiral.

## CONSCRIPTION

The bulk of the armed forces was provided by conscripts. Iran had had compulsory military service since the 1920s and this was not abandoned despite Khomeini's mistrust of the armed forces. Since the general call-up in 1982 all young men over the age of 18 were required to serve at least two years with one of the forces. As the war continued the length of service was extended as was the age-range of potential soldiers. Initially those up to the age of 36, then 46, and finally 50, had to show up, serve their two years – subsequently extended to two and a half – and remain available as reservists.

The *komiteh* guards and the *gendarmerie* zealously pursued draft-dodgers in towns and villages. Failure to report for military service was classified as desertion and those who were caught were treated harshly. A certificate of completion of service, or exemption, which applied to very exceptional cases, was required at every turn. It was necessary to obtain health care, educational certificates, employment, piped water, telephone, electricity, gas, insurance, driving licence or any form of official registration of birth, death or marriage. The employers of deserters were subject to punishment as accomplices to treason.

Yet, as the war went on, more and more men avoided the fronts. In 1985, all deserters were given a general amnesty and invited to come forward, serve their terms and become reservists for an additional two years as a penalty,[75] with no result. So in January 1987 the *Majlis* amended the Public Conscription Act increasing the punishment for draft-dodgers and all those who help them in any way and instructing the *komiteh* guards to intensify their search for these 'war criminals'.[76] In July, there was a further call-up, which appealed to reservists as well as potential conscripts to come forward for the extra six months of compulsory service. The only exemptions were for only sons with dependent elderly parents, married persons with two young children to support, or married men who had a brother or father in active service, or freed prisoners of war.[77] But the take-up remained low and most of the better-off youth managed to contract some form of severe disability, pay the appropriate bribe and obtain the certificate without ever seeing the fronts.

## MARTYRDOM

It was hardly surprising that most of the youth did their best to avoid the fronts. For the entire period of the war the government and its myriads of ideology sections did their best to develop the theme of martyrdom and make death appear desirable. But since, at the same time, the great venerable leaders cultivated the art of front-avoidance, it became harder and harder to sell the idea to the youths.

The government took to referring to the country as 'the land of the sufferers', 'the land of tears and mourning', 'the birthplace of martyrs' and 'the embattled land of the oppressed'. Admittedly the traditional *Shia* discourse lends itself splendidly to these notions of death and sorrow that Ali Shariati has called 'black Shiism'.[78] But the *ulema* went further than ever before in developing the custom of celebrating death. The discourse is centred on death and destruction, on suffering and the willingness to espouse death, to drink the sherbet of martyrdom, to join the forces of heaven, etc.

The more bloodthirsty aspects of Shiism were brought to the fore and stage-managed hysteria was integrated into the very culture of the nation. Islam is historically a religion of wars. Mohamad conquered his followers as much by the sword as by the word and gave himself the right to declare a holy war against the unbelievers whenever necessary. *Shias* themselves were born of war and martyrdom. Mohamad's cousin and son-in-law, Ali, had sought to follow in his footsteps and become the Caliph of Muslims. But on the way he had to go to war with Mohamad's wife, Ayesha, a battle that he won, and then against his own followers, the *khavarej*, who deserted him because he went to arbitration about the caliphate. In this war, Ali showed no compunction about killing God-fearing Muslims, who had deserted him. Qolam Hosein Naderi, the *Majlis* representative from Najaf was only too glad to offer a detailed description:

> The day Ali *alyhasalam*, may peace be upon him, realised the danger posed by them (the *khavarej*), he announced in a fierce and deadly voice 'only I have the strength to cut through the protection of faith, enhanced by daily prayers; only I can cut open their heads with my sword and shatter their frail bodies which are protected by years of fasting and devotion'; and he proceeded to do so.[79]

Thus, fighting other Muslims has a perfectly respectable precedence, as has martyrdom.

After all, Hosein, the revered third *Imam* of the *Shias*, and the son of Ali and grandson of the Prophet, rose against the unjust usurper of power, the Sunni Ummayad Caliph, Yazid. On 10 October 680 the Caliph's 4000-strong army was opposed by Hosein and seventy-two armed men, women and children of his family. Almost every one of them lost their lives in this heroic battle in the desert of Karbala and since the Safavid era the Iranians have held annual pageants and plays mourning the martyrdom of their favourite *Imam*. So it was an easy matter to appeal to this tradition of tears and sorrow and celebrate martyrdom and the war.

The newspaper, *Kayhan*, carried a daily feature, complete with photographs, purporting to be the last will and testament of a martyr. Yet another young man each day wrote of his longing 'to embrace and angel of death', 'to serve his country by offering his worthless life for the cause' and of 'winning the battle against the infidels by interposing his body between them and his people'. Parents of martyrs took to advertising their deaths, using a similar language, as that used for wedding and birth announcement: the 'pride of giving their sons to the country', 'the honour of offering a mere life in the service of the *Imam*', etc. Those who had lost a third or fourth son made the front pages and 'invited' their compatriots to share 'their joy and sorrow'. The mourners were 'congratulated' and condolences were offered for 'the sweet experience of death and the bitter one of living'.

In this war without heroes, all the unsung heroes were publicly and spectacularly mourned. Every town and every village had public mourning ceremonies. Every Thursday there was a procession of martyrs' coffins wending its way through the main thoroughfares. Where the parents of the martyr did not have a whole body to bury, they paraded the parts they had. An arm or a leg would be placed on the coffin and mourning and the burial completed. Wealthier families organised grander mourning processions, providing transport for the mourners from different parts of town and following the cortège in cars rather than on foot. The poor simply walked the miles to the burial grounds, flaunting their sorrow and the glory of death. It was a weekly demonstration of devotion, of willingness to suffer, of showing solidarity with the government. The larger urban areas had to have two mourning days each week.

Black-clad women hurled the traditional moans, *shivan*, at the crowd, tore their hair out and offered their younger sons. Young boys aged 4 or 5 walked besides them wearing the red armband which indicated that they were preparing for the fronts. Women had become the guardians of the coffins and the cradles, the symbols of suffering and endurance.[80] Widows gave long interviews about the wondrous state of martyrdom and the heavenly experience of bereavement for Islam. Many declared their absolute faith in the paradise that is specially made for direct entry by Iranian martyrs to which all should aspire to go.

In the meantime the burial-ground of Tehran was given a red fountain, symbolically pouring out the blood of the martyrs to show that Iran was willing to go on offering its dead to the war.


THE DENOUEMENT

Despite enthusiastic reports about public donations and attempts to highlight the imminent dangers faced by Iran, and the never-ending death ceremonies, public support waned and gradually disappeared. The government had to consider alternative solutions, but to the last the rhetoric remained voluble. Defeat made it impossible to portray Khomeini as the conqueror of the Islamic world, so now he postured as the valiant defender of the faith, the country had to back him and its people had to put their lives on the line to defend the cause:

> The line of defence is the main battle line against the enemy who is threatening the very existence of the Islamic Republic of Iran...Defence is no less important than our next step which is the planning of a major offensive against the enemy...Despite the very base pyschological battle that international aggressors and enemies of the revolution are conducting against the Islamic Republic of Iran, a solution which carries even the slightest shade of degradation or contempt for Islam would be unacceptable, and would totally negate the Islamic revolution and the Islamic Republic and all the values and principles that we hold dear...We are defending the honour of this land. The defensive move of our Islamic Republic will continue and the final outcome of the war will be determined by the will of the people and their faith and sincere belief in their righteousness; a faith which is lacking in the Iraqi forces who are faced with impending doom.[81]

So long as the war continued as an unending struggle between two Middle-Eastern countries, the guards continued to shine. For almost seven years Iranians and Iraqis fought each other, lost vast numbers of people and achieved nothing. The Iranians managed to recapture the oil city of Khoramshahre in April 1982 and the Iraqi retreated. The UN Security Council called for a cease-fire in July, but the Iranian government rejected the resolution and went on the offensive in 1983 and 1984, with little or no success. Iraq retaliated by bombing the oil-tankers in the Persian Gulf, to cut Iran's financial life-line. The following year Iraq began bombarding Iranian cities, including Tehran and Isfahan and many Iranians began questioning the need to continue the war. Mehdi Bazargan protested in the *Majlis* and Ayatollahs Hosein Qomi, Golpayegani and Morteza Haeri cast doubt on its legitimacy in Islamic terms.

But the government remained committed and in February 1986 the guards attacked the Iraqi oil port of Fao and captured it. The Iraqi countered by major attacks on Iranian oil installations. The result was severe shortages of power and fuel and petrol-rationing in Iran. In January 1987 the Iraqi began once more to bombard Iranian cities. In July the UN approved resolution 598 calling for withdrawal of the forces. This time Iraq refused to comply. At the same time the US navy, ostensibly in response to the Kuwaiti request for protection for its oil-tankers, allowed them to use the American flag and moved into the Persian Gulf to convoy tankers using its flag. Though nominally impartial, in the months that followed they only ever attacked the Iranian forces. An anguished editorial in the newspaper, *Kayhan*, asked the question:

> When, even according to the Western media's reports, it is largely the Iraqi forces who attack the tankers, and it is the Iraqis who break the international laws, why is it Iran that is the butt of the US attacks? Why are the Americans blaming the Iranians?[82]

The American forces continued to attack the Iranians. Yet they made no response when in May 1987 Iraqi missiles hit their ship and killed thirty-seven US marines. In October they engaged the Iranian guard's naval forces. The disarmed and arrested the guards, and then proceeded to destroy two Iranian oilplatforms in the Gulf.

The guards were no match for the American forces. Their first encounter was a disaster. The Iranian Commander of the guards' navy, Alayi, had the unenviable task of explaining why the valiant, martyrdom-seeking soldiers of Islam were so badly routed by the enemy:

> A number of the guards' patrol boats were conducting their normal duties on the west of Farsi island when they were attacked by dozens of US helicopters. The Americans fired rockets and machine-guns at our petrol boats. The attack lasted over 20 minutes and resulted in a number of injuries and martyrdoms... Dozens of petrol boats sunk as a result of this unwarranted attack. But the barbaric Americans continued firing on our warriors who were struggling in

the waters and all were hit by the enemy fire. Some managed to swim ashore and the Americans captured and imprisoned them. The guards defended themselves by firing stinger missiles which brought down US helicopters and a number of Americans were killed... The prisoners have been extensively and barbarically tortured by the Americans. Those returned to us report that the Americans were so scared of our men that they had tied them down hand and foot to prevent them from attacking the American forces. Although they were all injured and in great physical pain, our guards were subjected to severe physical and mental torture... the Americans fired guns at them, knifed them and dug 10-centimetre nails into their bodies.[83]

Once defeat began looming on the horizon, the Guard Corps lost its heroic aura. Though there was still lavish praise for them as the 'guardians of the revolution', their expenses began coming under scrutiny. Suddenly the *Majlis* realised the considerable cost of arming two separate and competing fighting forces. The Guards Minister's credentials were questioned when the 1988 cabinet came to the *Majlis* for ratification. In the disillusionment that had followed the defeat of the guards, Rafiqdust was accused of condoning corruption within the ranks. He was held responsible for low-calibre personnel in the guards, for their poor managerial skills, their ineptitude in dealings with foreign arms-dealers and their inability to provide satisfactory accounts and their complete ignorance of the strategic needs of the forces and failure to provide logistical back-up.

Rafiqdust was put in the unenviable position of defending what had not been of his doing. Suddenly revolutionary zeal and willingness to give their lives to the cause no longer justified the existence of the revolutionary guards. Their lack of education, inefficiency and gullibility in their dealings with foreign arms-dealers were considered unforgivable. Rafiqdust boasted that there were 3000 graduates in the guards' 25 000-strong Corps. He pointed out the long and honourable services of the non-graduates who had spent years at the front before being promoted to take charge of arms deals and noted their devotion to the cause:

> We do not pay high salaries, all those who come to us do so for the love of God and offer their services to Him. They come to serve the revolution and the *Imam*.[84]

But despite his protestations, Rafiqdust was replaced by the Head of the guards' land forces, Ali Shamkhani, no doubt as a reward for Shamkhani's solidarity with Rafsanjani. Otherwise this choice would have been a surprising one since the land forces had been the poorer relation in the Guards Corps' hierarchy. It was where those who failed their exams were sent to serve.

In fact, the land forces had planned to train 1500 battalions; in July 1987 they began recruiting conscripts and in December they open a national 'Eternity Saving Account', to fund their recruitment and other activities. Devout believers were asked to contribute to the account to secure a place in heaven for themselves and to qualify for the lottery draws which offered prizes such as journeys to Mecca, Syria or Mashed. At the same time, to deal with the expected rush of volunteers who could join as conscripts, honorary guards or regular guardsman, the infantry opened a round-the-clock answering machine to facilitate recruitment.[85] But by then the country was tired of heroics and neither the expected tens of thousands, nor for the matter the fund, ever materialised.

By June 1987 Iraq had recaptured all the areas that the Iranians forces had gained, including Fao. After the loss of Fao, Khomeini dismissed the Head of the Iranian military staff, Brigadier-General Esmail Sohrabi and appointed Rafsanjani as Commander-in-Chief of the forces and empowered him to integrate the various guards and armed forces.

Eventually Rafsanjani had to admit that the war could not be won. In a major admission of failure, which he described as being 'like drinking poison', Khomeini accepted Rafsanjani's advice and on 18 July 1988 Iran agreed to a ceasefire and invited the UN observers to come to Iran.

But even in August 1988, when the UN ceasefire observers arrived at the borders, President Khamenyi remained adamant. Iran had not been defeated, the aggressor had not been conquered (yet) and all *basij* 'defence' forces were required to stay at the fronts.[86] Daily reports of large donations to the war effort, and men being sent to the fronts continued. But by September 1988 instead of the millions, or even thousands, that used to be the unit of fighting manpower in Iran the new recruits were being counted in 'tens of units of fresh *basij* men'.[87] The love of martyrdom that fired the imagination of the young and the devout and took the lives of thousands and thousands of believers had gradually died the death of failure and monotony. Thousands of mutilated war heroes returned to a life of nameless drudgery. Several factors combined to make the war less than glorious: the total absence of recognition of any heroism other than death; no rewards other than eternal peace in paradise; minute pensions to only some of the parents of martyrs; and the careless discarding of returnees to the haphazard mercy of charity. For the returnees, the widows of martyrs and the mutilated there was no pension, no welfare, no social security and no jobs.

Typically the only response was to set up yet another revolutionary organ, an ex-servicemen's charity organisation called *Gordaneh Ansarel Mojahedin*, the defence of warriors battalion. Muslim brethren and even sisters were called upon to form assistance battalions to help the families of the warriors of Islam:

> You could play an essential part by helping the dependents of our warriors and lightening their heavy burden of responsibility and care for those they love and leave behind. Such selfless support on your part would please the sacred heart of the Messenger of God and show our unity with our Leader.[88]

Although there were those who were moved to action, many were too involved in their own daily battles for survival to seek to please God or his Messenger. Women in particular, deprived of the opportunity to be recognised as a suitable workforce, had for the past decade been more and more marginalised and had been forcibly reduced to the worthy but unpaid roles of mothering heroes and burying martyrs.[89] Some had served as cooks, cleaners and nurses behind the lines, but although there were stirring photographs of many more marching with guns over their veils, in practice this had been a war which, unlike the ones in the West, had not brought economic opportunities for women. Unlike their Iraqi counterparts,[90] Iranian women did not find empty places on the job market. The war in Iran had been accompanied by a slow and continuous process of under-development and women had been specifically excluded from the only growing sector, the war industry. Of course, not having work did not mean that the women did not have to eat or in many cases support the families they headed. It simply meant that they had to work longer and harder in the badly paid informal sector. So, not surprisingly, most did not have the time nor the means to respond to the call of duty and help their brethren.

## THE RETURNING EX-SERVICEMEN

Matters got worse as slowly and continuously more and more ex-servicemen trickled home. The great warriors came back to no work and faint praise. Many were illiterate and unskilled, but all had expected some recognition. Rafsanjani did pay them lip-service and told the *basij* men:

> You self-sacrificing men are the symbols of a long period of resistance and martyrdom... your resistance has been invaluable to our society and has changed the course of our history.[91]

But respect for the men was soon replaced by disillusionment and blame. The days when bravery and zeal were the hallmark of success had long since gone. Whereas once lack of discipline had been hailed as the crowning glory of the *basij*, suddenly it was held up as a major contributory cause of defeat. Rafsanjani announced the new policy in December 1988.

> Lack of discipline in military units undermines their strength in the battle-fields. *Basij* commanders have noted the need for firm and hardened, steel-like, discipline and coherent action in the battlefields and I must warn you about the central importance of discipline.[92]

Nor were the returning men respected for their bravery and zealousness. Ellias Hazrati, *Majlis* representative for Rasht, complained in Parliament:

> The *basij* returnees are under heavy attack from counter-revolutionary forces and there is no one in this land to protect them. You should see how many of these youngsters who have spent eight years at the battle-fronts are now spend-ing their days in prison. The charge is usually that they have warned some sinful infidel about corrupt practices and have sought to lead sinful people to the path of righteousness. All they get for this is to be locked up in prison. It seems that law officers and court officials see it as their duty to arrest and imprison any *basij* man who has been attacked by a sinner.[93]

Eight years of war had drained Iran of much of its economic resources; unemployment was high and rising and, with the exception of the war industries, all other sectors of the economy were in decline. To deal with some of the problems of the *basij* returnees, the government acted as it had always done, by setting up yet another revolutionary organ. At the request of the organisation of Martyrs of the Islamic Revolution, *Bonyadeh Shahid Enqelabeh Eslami*, in November 1988 the government formed yet another self-propelling unit, *nahadhayeeh khod khoroushideh*, the Personnel and Administration Organisation. The organisation was to act as an employment agency; it was to remind every employer of their duty to meet the needs of 'our self-sacrificing beloveds' and provide education, training and employment for them.[94] Rafsanjani endorsed its role by calling on employers to:

> consider it their revolutionary duty before God to provide the maximum facilities for comfort, education and employment of our self-sacrificing people.[95]

The believers were to inform the organisation who was to match vacancies with available heroes. In a country where nepotism was about all that was left for many, the organisation's roles proved pretty difficult. The private sector employed its own friends and relations and the government had been cutting back on the civil service for almost a decade;[96] it was impossible to provide instant employment in the public sector.

As a result, the *Majlis* was asked to ratify a bill enabling the Civil Service to open some of the posts that had been frozen over the past years. Of the new jobs 50 per cent were earmarked for the relatives of martyrs, or prisoners of war or missing personnel and self-sacrificing combatants who were unable to work themselves. Also included were warriors with nine consecutive or twelve interrupted months of service at the fronts – a stipulation that effectively excluded all the *basij* men who had done their regular four-months stint and no more. Furthermore the Civil service was required to take on only the suitably qualified men. Only the health and education sectors were permitted to employ the wives or sisters of martyrs.

The only advantage that the warriors gained was that the organisation for the Oppressed, *Mostaazefin*, provided a special row of seats in the cinemas it controlled for 'those self-sacrificing warriors who have put their lives on the line and the disabled returnees'.[97] As for the public sector, the Ministry of Education decided that war experience should count as an extra academic qualification. Thus, a primary-school graduate would be equivalent to a civilian with some secondary schooling and a secondary-school graduate equivalent to a non-warrior with first-year university training. The returnees who lacked all qualification could count each year of school attendance as one-year service with the civil service. In addition those who amongst them who wished to study were to be entitled to enter the university without sitting any entrance examinations. If they lacked the necessary qualification for entrance, they were entitled to a year's intensive tuition to prepare them for university.[98] But none of these promises were ever realised.[99]

As to the Revolutionary Guards, in many respect history has come full circle. Gone are their days of prosperity and grandeur, gone too their days of success. They managed to take over some of the war industries producing small arms and ammunition. But the problems of running two separate forces proved insurmountable.

The huge costs of running two parallel forces put severe strains on the national budget. A new language of efficiency began seeping in as did a new respect for training and professionalism; all by-words of the Shah's army. Eventually moves began to merge the forces. But the factionalism in Iranian politics is such that despite the obvious necessity to cut back on the costs of maintaining and operating two alternative armed forces, the merger is yet to come. For the army, as for the rest of the state bureaucracy, the revolution has brought a multiplicity of commands and directions obtained at high costs and for little benefit to the country as a whole.

As the war receded, so did the importance of the armed forces. By 1993 although the government still paid lip-service to the forces, the military budget was cut back to 10 per cent of the total planned national expenditure; with $850 million earmarked for arms deals.[100] At the same time the forces were encouraged to present a more peaceful profile and engage in the 'reconstruction' process and the head of the armed forces, Major-General Ali Shahbazi, announced that the experiences gained during the war, both in terms of scientific and practical know-how would be put to civilian use to rebuild the nation.[101]

# 7 *Valayateh Faqih* in Disarray

Khomeini's theories about a future polity, as described in *Valayateh Faqih*, proved untenable in practice. But his political ingenuity, flexible loyalty and ability to play various supporters against one another, helped to sustain him in power. Khomeini was well-versed in the skills of political manipulation, which had traditionally facilitated the accommodation of differing shades of opinions, under the guise of collegiality, within the religious institution. He maintained uneasy alliances by ruthless purges of the army, the removal of all the top echelons of the civil service and a relentless killing of all dissidents.[1] From the very first years, all opposition groups were driven underground. By August 1979, Khomeini had decided that the wrath of Allah should fall on all conspirators, and immediately closed down all independent publications for 'contravening the people's will'.[2] Within a year of his return, the regime issued a press code which made it a crime to criticise Khomeini. At the same time the Ministry of Information was renamed as Ministry of National Guidance. Its remit was to ensure that the media supported the Islamic Republic, acted as an efficient propaganda tool and did not report the rapidly growing factionalism within the government.[3] Though not often reported, the differences remained unresolved.

The Islamic government, having arrived precipitously, found itself embroiled in a prolonged war on its borders, and a continuous struggle for direction within the state. Khomeini saw the Islamic state as an undisputed theocracy where he, as the representative of God on earth, would direct the people without necessarily dictating the day-to-day policies. Such details were left to a number of theocratic councils, consisting exclusively of religious leaders, placed at the apex of the judiciary, legislative and executive branches, with the duty of ensuring that Islamic rule was observed at every level. The high profile adopted by him, as the *Faqih*, the undisputed religious leader and source of inspiration, meant that from the beginning the only clear guidance concerned itself with the necessity of total submission of the Muslims to Khomeini's decrees.

One of the first targets for subjugation was women. Within days of his return, Khomeini issued a decree annulling women's right to demand custody of their children after divorce. Strictly speaking, Islamic dictum accords fathers and paternal forefathers the undisputed right of custody of their descendants. The next move was to impose the veil on women. As the public face of the Islamic Republic, women were burdened with the duty of demonstrating its modesty and righteousness to the world, by covering themselves from head to foot.[4] Furthermore the preamble to the constitution clearly noted that men and women were not equal. Women were 'freed' of the objectification imposed on them by the West; identified as the targets of Islamification; given the 'critical duty' of motherhood; and placed firmly in the home. They were to guard the family, which was declared to be the fundamental basis of the Islamic Republic.[5]

As for the State, through its early years it lurched from goal to goal and programme to programme without any clear idea as to whether the revolution was to serve the *ulema*, the *bazaar* or the people. 'The masses', said the rhetoric; 'no', said the Council of Guardians, who had been appointed to ensure that all legislation was strictly Islamic and to defend private property rights as sacrosanct. They regarded the *bazaar* and private enterprises as the natural beneficiaries of the revolution.

## THE COUNCIL OF GUARDIANS

When the constitution was formulated,[6] the tensions between the theocrats and the bureaucrats had been resolved in favour of the former and the Council of Guardians was appointed to 'guard Islamic laws';[7] without its ratification the *Majlis* could not legislate.[8] The Council of Guardians, *Shorayeh Negahban*, consisted of six *alem* appointed by Khomeini and six Muslim jurisconsults chosen by the Supreme Judicial Council and the *Majlis* to serve for six year.[9] But the laws of Islam, for all the claims that they made to eternality,[10] were not necessarily suited to the needs of the twentieth century. Nor was their strict defence of private property consistent with the aims of the revolution to empower and protect the dispossessed. The *Majlis*, with its 270 representatives, serving for four years, sought to fulfil its duty to the electorate, while the Council of the Guardians defended the eternal rights of the Almighty.

The battle between the conservative Council of Guardians and the more radical *Majlis* began at the inception of the Islamic Republic and has raged unabated ever since. The *Majlis* had the duty of defining the extent of the duties of the Judiciary, the Executive and the Council. Once it had done so, it had to obey its dictate. Khomeini was categorical on this point. He told the *Majlis* deputies in 1981.

> Do not any of you dare to transgress. Beware! No one has the right to say that they do not accept the Council of Guardian's decisions. No one has the right to defy the Council of Guardians. Over sixteen million of our people voted for the constitution that installed the Council and the Council is here to stay ...Anyone who opposes the Council is opposing the constitution and betraying our people.[11]

The *Majlis*, however, did not always find it easy to toe the line. In the ensuing rows, Khomeini generally intervened in support of the Council, but always invoked the name of the masses. After all, in the context of an Islamic government, the *Majlis* would be merely charting the rule of Islam and the Council would ensure that the process has been done correctly. The law-maker would be the God of Islam whose divine rule was established for ever and required no revisions:

This *Majlis*, which was nourished by the blood of our Muslim people and has been hailed by the sound of *Allah akbar* (God is great) has no right to diverge from the path of Islam and the Muslims...We must submit to the will of the *Majlis* and that would be submitting to the will of Islam and the Muslims... Obeying the *Majlis* and its laws is part and parcel of our religious rituals and duties and is like paying homage to God.[12]

But Khomeini was not convinced that the *Majlis* would fulfil its divine duty unaided. He expressed the hope that:

the *Majlis* would be one where religious rites, rather than devilish might, would prevail.

Speaking to the deputies, he warned them that the *ulema* would be vigilant; the *Majlis* was sovereign only as long as it followed the Islamic doctrine. The country would remain a theocracy. Dismissing the decade of political struggles by a whole gamut of political forces, Khomeini told the *Majlis*:

Never forget that the militant clergy operate throughout this country. The moment that a devout respected religious leader calls the people of this land, every last one would follow him. Do not dare ever to attempt to by-pass the *ulema*. What have you achieved in this country in the past year (with your secular President and government) to show that you know better than the religious leaders?... You've done nothing but talk and bicker... Its been the religious leaders who've continued the struggle against injustice; they did it under the Pahlavis and they've done it since ... It was the religious leaders that pulled the people on the streets; it was for the sake of Islam that people gave their lives and shed their blood... no political group or party could have called on so many people, no other cause would have been worth the blood of our martyrs... No politician could have brought out so many willing martyrs.[13]

In May 1981, just before the final débâcle of the Bani Sadre Presidency, Khomeini delivered a firm homily to the recalcitrant *Majlis*:

Our people died for Islam, they volunteered to embrace martyrdom for the cause of Islam and to establish the rule of Islam. Should you fail to follow the Islamic path paved with the blood of our martyrs this follower of Islam for One [i.e. Khomeini] would oppose you with all his might. I asked you gentlemen [*sic*] at the beginning of the year to ensure that the constitution is implemented to the letter. It is our duty to delineate the legal constraints that it poses on the President... Then should he step beyond those limits, I'd personally oppose him. Even if the whole of the population rise up in his support, I'd still oppose him. Similarly the Prime Minister must know his limits, should he transgress I'd oppose him too.[14]

Within a month Khomeini had sided with the Prime Minister against President Bani Sadre who had to flee the country.[15] Then Khomeini reinforced the hold of the *ulema* over the state by removing his earlier ban on the members of the religious institutions standing for the Presidency. From then on the Iranian Presidency was held by members of the religious institution; the longest-lasting one was to be one of Khomeini's disciples, *Hojatoleslam* Ali Khameneyi.

But the uneven division of power between the Prime Minister and the President made cabinet government a virtual impossibility. They were both responsible for the Executive and for presenting programmes to the legislative, but neither could overrule the other. Regularly the country turned to the *Faqih* to sort out this tangled political web.

The *Shia* problem at the core of *Valayateh Faqih* was not resolved. Khomeini was yet to convince many of the leading ulema about the validity of his form of theocracy.


## THE ISLAMIC REPUBLIC PARTY

The *Shia* doctrine had developed over the centuries as a revolutionary antithesis to government and temporal authorities,[16] it was not easy to complete this ideological *volte face* while maintaining the *tohid*, unity, that Khomeini demanded. Nor was the clergy helped by the constitution which had retained declarations about freedom of the press, except where the interests of Islam were at stake;[17] and freedom of association and party political activities, again except where such activities were deemed to counter the interest of Islam.[18] This proviso had helped the government to close down the free press, control the radio and television and drive underground or ban most parties. After Bani Sadre's departure the Islamic Republic Party seemed poised to take over the apparatus of powers. But in June 1981 its headquarters were blown up.[19] The attack killed the flamboyant Ayatollah Beheshti and with him the obvious theocratic successor to the President. With the demise of most of its top echelons, the uneasy alliance of the *ulema* in the IRP began to crack. At the same time as the state itself was seeking to define the limits of authority of different political organisations, a struggle for power began within the IRP.

The party split between the *maktabi*, and the *hojatieh*.[20] The former, using the term, *maktab* (the old-style Islamic school) to mark its traditional and orthodox character, advocated absolute obedience to the person of the *Faqih*. The term, *maktabi*, was adopted by the IRP as a self-description in 1979. After the fall of Bani Sadre, the *maktabi* style was associated with the more populist and revolutionary elements in the IRP.

The *hojatieh* had its antecedence in the 1950 anti-Baha'i activities. In the post-revolutionary era it was not a recognised group. It was the sectarian designation applied by the *maktabi* faction of the IRP to those whom they accused of secrecy and of adherence to a restrictive *Shia* interpretation. Vali and Zubaida in their detailed study of this group conclude that the *hojatieh* had much in common with the traditional *ulema*. The common ground included their theological reservations about the *Valayateh Faqih* and its endorsement of the right of any religious leader to claim political leadership. They held more orthodox views of the imamate and the state;[21] adhered firmly to the sanctity of ownership and were therefore against all forms of nationalisation, redistribution of wealth or land reforms which they criticised for being socialist measures. They were accused of having quietist tendencies and favouring a separation of state and religion and of seeking a wider support-base amongst the conservative *ulema*, the *bazaar* and land-owners. The *maktabi* argued that the *hojatieh* faction was attempting to use this base to wrench power away from the *ulema* and thus deny the revolution any real success.

The *hojatieh* group made few public statements. The *maktabi* section was convinced that the *hojatieh* was infiltrating the civil service and government agencies, with a view to disempowering the *maktabi* elements. The accusations continued and finally, in July 1983, Khomeini, whose determination to Islamify the land had never wavered, intervened. He warned the *hojatieh* by announcing that those who believed that *Shia* Muslims ought not interfere in politics during the period of occultation of the Twelfth *Imam* did so at their peril, since quietism merely prolonged the rule of injustice and the period of occultation.[22] The *hojatieh* responded by a public statement in the Tehran Press announcing an end to its activities.

Nevertheless, although open factionalism in the IRP was laid to rest, the divisions continued, not only within the party but also amongst the *ulema*. There were no easy ways for resolving the central contradiction between the tenets of Shiism and *Valayateh Faqih*, or between it and the ideals of democratic politics and elections of party-based political representatives to run the legislature and the government.

Khomeini had based his blueprint for government on a short-lived period of rule by the Prophet Mohamad and his son-in-law, Ali, in Medina, some fourteen centuries earlier, which lasted only 15 years.[23] His ideas sat uncomfortably in the post-revolutionary, twentieth century Iran, with its eighty years of struggles against despotism and for parliamentary representation. He was wary of giving any organisation too much power and the IRP was beginning to act as the national power-broker. So the *Faqih* opted for a policy of *tohid* (national unity) and announced that party political activities in the elections would contravene this 'paramount' political aim. The *tohid* that Khomeini demanded was not forthcoming. Nor could Khomeini dispense with elections altogether. So he tried enforcing unity by eliminating all parties:

Parties are irrelevant to our politics. Parties can neither secure absolute probity, nor would their absence be indicative of political failure. Elections must be conducted in the interest of the Muslims, and not that of any party. Elections are about the selection of individuals who are of good character and whose faith in Islam is absolute and who have a clear understanding of Islam and its needs and its interests in this country…that is all that matters.[24]

Since elections were merely a confirmation of the trust of the nation in its leader, they had to be conducted in an atmosphere of accord and unity. Ayatollah Montazeri confirmed this view:

> The important question in the election has nothing whatever to do with party affiliations of any candidate, but much to do with each individual's capabilities and their personal commitment to Islam and the revolution.[25]

He began campaigning for a more lenient approach to politics and for allowing non-party-members access to power:

> We need parties and organisations, but electioneering candidates must work towards unity. We should allow all candidates, including the independents, to have a platform and have their say.[26]

But the IRP had its defendants, not least the Islamic republic's President *Hojatoleslam* Ali Khameneyi, who was also the General Secretary of the IRP. Khameneyi argued that a single centralised party would act as a cohesive element rather than a useful ladder of upward mobility for ambitious religious leaders. Khameneyi pronounced that the IRP was the best means of securing a united Islamic rule:

> The party is a neccessary base for the Islamic Republic and those who attack IPR have failed to understand the country's urgent needs.[27]...

> The party belongs to the revolution. It participates in the elections as the flagship of unity ... We are not here to seek power, but only to serve our country.[28]

> The party is a necessary base for the Islamic Republic...All those who attack the party have failed to understand the most important political needs of this country.[29]

The elections delivered a majority of IRP representatives. Musouvi was re-elected as Prime Minister and Rafsanjani remained the Speaker of the *Majlis*.


THE SUCCESSION

With so much authority vested in Khomeini, the question of succession became of central importance to the politicians. The constitution required the Council of Guardians to set up an Assembly of Experts, *Majlesseh Khebregan*, with eighty-three members[30] elected to choose a successor for Khomeini.[31] Should a natural leader emerge, and be accepted and endorsed by the Council of Guardian and the people, then he could take on the mantle of the Prophet. Failing that, the constitution returned to the traditional solution usually adopted by the religious institution, namely that of having a collegial leadership.[32]

The Assembly of Experts was chaired by the Friday prayer leader of Qom, Ayatollah Ali Meshkini, and included the Speaker of the *Majlis*, Hashemi

Rafsanjani. It took some time for a future leader to emerge; the most eminent religious leaders, Ayatollahs Abolqassem Mussavi Khoyii, Mohamad Reza Mussavi Golpayagani and Shaheldin Hosein Mar'ashi Najafi, were not deemed sufficiently 'radical' and were in any case all in their eighties. Eventually, in November 1985, the Assembly selected Ayatollah Hosein Ali Montazeri, as the heir-apparent. One of the youngest of the leading Ayatollahs, Montazeri had an impeccable revolutionary background. He had been imprisoned by the Shah in 1964 and again in 1972 and had stayed in prison till 1978. But, though politically correct, wily, and learned, Montazeri did not have the charisma that would have made him an obvious choice. Nevertheless he had been trying conscientiously to counter the worse of the excesses of the regime and to woo the middle classes. He had emerged as a champion of the educated, the intelligentsia and the 'liberals'. By 1983, in the wake of Khomeini's eight-point decree,[33] and the demise of the *hojatieh*, he began building bridges between the traditionalists and the 'radicals' and set about counselling the more extreme elements to become less zealous:

> I have said repeatedly that we must try to attract capable people and not reject them.[34]

> I am all too aware that the activities of some secret societies have proved most detrimental to us. It has led to the dismissal of some of the very best amongst the educated people. If this process continues the revolution will suffer an irrevocable blow. We hear again and again about people in schools, universities or the armed forces being interrogated and purged. This means that we are actively preventing the best from serving this country while we suffer critical shortages of skilled, educated and trained personnel...We must stop this folly once and for all...Of course we have a duty to support the government and the President and the Prime Minister. This is a national duty. But we must not assume that this entails gagging everyone and not coping with constructive criticism. No one should be prevented from pointing out the difficulties and offering solutions...If we don't deal with the problems, as and when they arise, then this revolution will be doomed to failure.[35]

This was a view that was going further than the earlier relaxation of the reign of terror announced by Khomeini and Rafsanjani, both keen to regain the confidence of the Iranians and even inviting the exiles to return. In the wake of his eight-point decree, in December 1982, Khomeini had already stated:

> Nobody should be afraid to come back and engage in business...Islam does not allow private property to be seized.[36]

Rafsanjani had echoed the *Faqih*:

> Now we have paved the way for all the people in our country to live in peace, to know that their homes will not be invaded, their children will not be thrown out of school, and workers will rest assured that they will not be thrown out of

factories. Now that the country has calmed down, people must know that they are safe in their homes and in their jobs and that so long as they obey the laws, no one will harass them... Now we must make sure that people's privacy is not invaded... We must forget about past mistakes. We must forget and forgive... We must not break into people's home in search of the odd illegal musical instrument or the photographs of naked women on the beach lurking in albums here and there. We must not denounce people for immodesty and shame them in public. We can do without this kind of public humiliation. The time has come for law-abiding citizen to feel safe in their homes.[37]

But neither wished to relax the grip of censorship or allow critical debates to enter the political arena. The only permitted criticism was vented against minor officials. The daily paper, *Kayhan*, published a weekly complaints page in which readers could take various Ministries to task for failure to provide hospital beds, clear water or properly paved and lit streets. But no one was allowed to criticise the Islamic government and its 'morality'. Rafsanjani was categorical on this point:

People are in full support of the Islamic dictum against the liberals... they abhor the liberals' low standards of morality; their lax attitude to such matters as veiling our women goes directly against the core of the honour of our nation. Their immorality is reminiscent of Western culture and its paucity of values and arouses the suspicion and abhorrence of our devout Muslim people.[38]

In the context of Iranian politics, Montazeri's 'liberalism' and Rafsanjani's 'fundamentalism' were not directly translated into their strategies on foreign policy. There, it was Montazeri who was for a world-wide Islamic revolution and a strictly anti-American position, and Rafsanjani who was not. Finally, in October 1986, these opposing stances brought Montazeri into collision with Rafsanjani over the Irangate debacle when Mehdi Hasheini, a relative and close aide of the heir-apparent leaked Rafsanjani's *rapprochement* with the USA to the world press.[39]

Although the scandal was hushed up in Iran, Rafsanjani had an uncomfortable year ahead of him. Even the pro-Islamic magazine, *Pasdar* (the Revolutionary Guard) confronted the Speaker of *Majlis* with some probing questions; the answer was far from enlightening:

Q. Some people think that you have taken a very gentle tone in one of your interviews with the Western press. This seems to contradict your earlier unequivocal opposition to the West.

A. What I try to do in my interview with Western journalists is two things; one to address the Westerners, the US citizens; I have no wish to make them fear us, I do not want the people of America to think that we are on an eternal war-path against them... We must make it clear that it is their government and not their people that we opposed. The second point, the one on which we stand firm, it is not against them, it is addressed to their government. Where the US government and its supporters are concerned, then there is no malleability. So we have two different ways of saying the same thing to two different audiences.[40]

But despite their political differences, the alliance between Rafsanjani and Montazeri seemed to be holding up. On 29 July 1987, the Assembly of Experts held its fifth annual meeting, with Meshkini in the chair and Rafsanjani as his deputy, and once more it opted for Montazeri. Rafsanjani went on record declaring his support for Montazeri and disclaiming any pretension to the throne of the *Faqih*:

> I have none of the high qualifications that Ayatollah Montazeri enjoys. But even amongst the highest ranking *ulema* there is none that can be compared to him. The Assembly of Experts...has confirmed Ayatollah Montazeri as our future leader...No one is standing against Mr Montazeri, no one opposes him. He is the undisputed future leader of our revolution.[41]

In *ulema* parlance denial of animosity is merely a delaying tactic, Rafsanjani was not yet ready to wrest power away from Montazeri.

## *VALAYATEH FAQIH* IN DISARRAY

The election of a successor to Khomeini did little to alleviate the chronic constitutional quandaries. The struggle for power between the *Majlis* and the Council of Guardians continued; as did the remnants of the arguments for and against party-based elections, as well as a less-orchestrated, but equally insoluble, struggle for power between the Prime Minister and the President.

The departure of Bani Sadre had not solved the permanent dispute between the two over the selection of the cabinet. Article 87 of the constitution stated that it was the duty of the President to ask the *Majlis'* approval for the cabinet, but there was no clearly stated method for selecting Ministers. The assumption had been that, as in the pre-revolutionary period, the Prime Minister would select his cabinet, which would not necessarily have to be from Members of Parliament. But the battle for selection of Cabinet Ministers, which had raged throughout Bani Sadre's era, continued unabated. By the end of the decade, in 1989, Prime Minister Mussavi and President Khameneyi spent a year arguing over the selection of a Minister of Trade, without coming to any conclusion. There was no constitutional solution to their problem. *Majlis* deputy, *Hojatoleslam* Ali Movahedi Savoji explained the predicament:

> The executive has had great difficulties... in clarifying the limits of Presidential and Prime Ministerial authority and their relation with particular Ministries.[After the Leader, the President is the highest political office. He is the head of the executive and responsible for the implementation of the laws

and for liaising between different branches of the government. But he lacks authority. His limited powers make him seem more like a ceremonial than an active head. The position of the Prime Minister too is far from clear. As the head of the cabinet he must supervise and coordinate the work of ministers; but he does not have the executive powers to intervene in the running of ministries. Yet he is held responsible by the *Majlis* for Cabinet decisions. It is far from clear what his powers are where the Cabinet is concerned. The Prime Minister can nominate a Minister, but he needs the President's ratification; should the two disagree there is a deadlock which cannot be resolved.[42]

A similar discord had raged between the Council of Guardians and the *Majlis*. The Council of Guardian behaved very much along the *hojatieh* lines, and its continuous struggles against the *Majlis* reflected the divide that remained between the traditionalists, who feared 'socialism' in any guise, even an Islamic one, and the elected representatives who had to deliver some redistributive measures to keep the ideals of the revolution alive. As *Majlis* deputy, *Hojatoleslam* Mussavi Khoyiniha complained to the press:

The orchestration of an unnecessary fear of Marxism has created a pernicious atmosphere... where all the ideas that would benefit the poor and the dispossessed are dismissed as Marxism. Even when, in this time of war and shortages, *Majlis* attempted to control trade and help distribution of goods, as we have been bound to do by our constitution,[43] we are accused of moving the country towards socialism.[44]

The result was inaction and unjustifiable caution on the part of the Council. After all, as Seyed Hosein Ghazizadeh Hashemi, himself a non-clerical *Majlis* representative, pointed out:

Article 96 of the constitution appointed the Council of Guardians 'to ensure that no parliamentary law contradicts Islamic laws'. But the Council has interpreted this to mean that all laws must accord absolutely with Islamic dictum. The problem is that many laws, which do not contradict the laws of God, would at the same time not necessarily strictly accord with them.[45]

The embattled Prime Minister, Mussavi, complained that all attempts to combat commercial hoarding and inflationary practices had been blocked by the Council of Guardians and there was no constitutional way of overcoming their opposition:

*Majlis* has been constantly seeking to create social order and establish the rule of law. After the revolution, our revolutionary needs allowed various organisations to interact and intervene in one another's affairs. But from its inception the *Majlis* has been trying to regulate these organisations and place them on some sort of legal footing...But *Majlis* does not have the authority to intervene in the details of the executive branch. So we have ended up in a quandary. We cannot even move one administrative unit from one Ministry to another without producing a Parliamentary bill and going to the Council of Guardians for ratification. This slows down the whole process and ties our hands... With the multitude of problems that we face we should have the power to act quickly and decisively.[46]

*Majlis* was not even permitted to have supervisory authority over the executive. Seyed Hassan Ghazizadeh gave an example:

> The way things are turning out every institution passes the buck. They all claim that someone else is responsible for law enforcement...Here we are in urgent need of controlling inflation and spiralling prices and who should make sure that people do so? The government point the finger at the judiciary, the judiciary blames the legislature, and the *Majlis* complains that the Council of Guardians have declared it un-Islamic to control prices... meanwhile the people go on suffering[47]

> *Majlis* passed a law whereby representatives of each province were given the responsibility to keep an eye on the way the administration executed the laws in the region. The Council of Guardians objected saying that *Majlis* did not have the right to appoint its members to act as inspectors with extensive powers to ensure that laws are implemented. So the *Majlis* failed to secure any means of ensuring the effective implementations of the laws of the land... Yet *Majlis* must ensure that the laws of the land are properly implemented and has the right to obtain the relevant information about implementation of its laws.[48]

A measure that repeatedly failed to get ratification was land reform. The sanctity of property rights in Islam was used by the Council to curb any distribution of holdings, or even control of land prices, or expansion and regulation of rural cooperatives.[49] After repeated attempts, *Majlis* and Council came to an uneasy compromise which minimised the amount of land that could be distributed; put no limits on the size of ownership by landlords; and only earmarked the lands of 'collaborators', in exile for distribution.[50]

As the guardian of Islam, the Council usually insisted on the eternal validity of the laws of God and rejected every bill that attempted to give some rights to the oppressed against the landlords, factory owners and employers. The revolution was delivering its promise of Islamisation, but many of the *Majlis* deputies were distraught. One of them, Haj Yahya Sultani, told the press:

> We submitted our labour laws to the Council of Guardians. These laws sought to offer some protection to our deserving workers and to make the employers responsible for the provision of some welfare for their employees. Why does the Council of Guardian argue that this law must not apply to existing contracts and worker?[51]

Moving beyond the rhetorics and establishing an Islamic government in terms of practical day-to-day politics posed a problem that had no obvious solution. As Seyed Hosein Ghazizadeh Hashemi, a disgruntled *Majlis* representative, told the daily paper, *Kayhan*:

It is not possible to run a political system according to two kinds of laws, the laws of God and the laws of our time.[52]

The central dilemma was that if the laws of Islam were eternal, as the orthodoxy believed and Mottahari had argued vehemently in the pre-revolutionary era,[53] then there should have been no question of changing them according to the needs of the time. But the rule of what *Shias* accept as the true Islam had been short-lived, and was clouded in the glory of the distant past. Although the very glorification of this golden past had been the cornerstone of fundamentalism, and is the core of revivalist Islam, it is more useful in creating illusions of grandeur than in forming a practical bureaucratic machine. As to Khomeini's own thesis on Islamic government, it was proving inoperable at every turn. Yet the Iranians were told repeatedly that it was 'a sin' to transgress from its dictates, because of their duty to 'submit' to the laws of God.

A classic example was the ever-present problem of taxation. Khomeini in his thesis on Islamic government had assumed that payment of religious taxes, *khoms* and *zakat* would be ample enough to meet all the needs of a much-trimmed-down bureaucracy.[54] But, far from cutting back the bureaucracy, the profusion of command and proliferation of self-sustaining revolutionary organisations had expanded the state apparatus by about 300 per cent in less than a decade.[55] The Islamic government's policies, though formulated along monetarist lines and seeking to cut down public expenditure, had reduced welfare and social services, but could not cut taxation.[56] The government needed an ever-larger income to fund the war and the state, but it could not legitimise its demands in Islamic terms.

The *Shias* are expected to part willingly with one-fourth of their surplus worldly goods, *zakat*, and one-fifth of their surplus liquid cash, *khoms*, each year, to meet the needs of the poor and the needy; not those of the state and government. So the religious dues are paid to a religious leader of one's choice and never find their way to the coffers of the state.[57] Twentieth-century Iranians were not quite as forthcoming as they should have been, and the *ulema* saw no reason to pass what they obtained to the government. At the same time declining oil revenues, which had halved between 1984 and 1988, necessitated an increase in taxation. Eventually Khomeini was obliged to use *ejtehad*, interpretation by a religious leader, to extend the religious duties of believers to the domain of payment of secular taxes; he announced:

> Payment of state taxation is a religious duty. Just as the Muslims have an obligation to pay their religious dues, so they must also pay their national taxes to the Islamic government.[58]

This wholesale addition of secular duties to religious ones, and the admission of the relevance of the nation-state to the Islamic discourse, created a new problem for Khomeini's supranational vision of Islam and its government. Did his support for the secular state apparatus amount to a denial of his earlier teachings? The religious institution closed ranks and Friday prayer leaders began constructing a rationale around the question. The Yazd preacher, Ayatollah Khatami, reiterated the duty of obedience that *Shias* owed to their religious leaders and their God:

Islamic government is about the implementation of the divine commandments and it would be a cardinal sin to oppose such a government; it is the Islamic duty of all believers to obey this rule.[59]

The Shiraz Friday prayer leader, *Hojatoleslam* Mohin al Din Haeri Shirazi, provided further guidance:

When the question of taxation was discussed the *imam* of the *umma* (people of Islam) declared that the government must do more than merely implementing the basic rules of Islam; taxation is a matter for government to take on board... Once the *imam* has spoken, and so long as the twelfth *imam* is in occultation, it is our duty to obey the *Valayateh Faqih*.[60]

Khatami concurred, distinguishing between the 'basic' rules and temporal laws:

There are some absolute immovable laws of God that are eternal and never-changing; but the laws which govern the day-to-day administration of the land may well change over time... different historical periods demand different regulations.[61]

No doubt this view would make Ayatollah Mottahari turn in his grave. After all, the pre-revolutionary arguments had all been about the fallibility of people and their perceptions of the needs of the time, and the absolute necessity to have faith in the eternal truth and rulings of Islam,[62] a view that includes the grave doubts that traditionalists have always had about innovation, *ibd'a*,[63] be it political or otherwise. Yet in less than a decade, the Islamic government had to come to uneasy terms with the changing needs of time. In this it was much assisted by the concept of *ejtehad*.[64] As *Hojatoleslam* Hassan Marashi, member of the High Council of Judiciary explained:

Where there are legal shortfalls, our constitution permits the jurisconsults to pass a judgement based on religious texts and principles. This ruling is then a binding law... In Shiism *ejtehad* is a basic and invaluable principle which enables the jurisconsults to remedy all legal shortfalls and fill up all the legislative gaps.[65]

In terms of *Shia* politics the *ulema* provide the only means of adjusting the laws of God to the needs of people. It is the religious institution that guards the interests of God on earth, and by doing so no doubt benefits itself. Ayatollah Montazeri chooses to see this process as a coincidence of Godly and clerical interests:

It is the duty of the religious institution and the *ulema* to the politically aware and active and to shoulder their share of responsibility for the Islamic government. They must ensure that their decisions benefit society and do incur irrevocable damage to the Muslim countries. It is the duty of the believers to support the *ulema*, to elect them and to demand that they fulfil their political duty [66]

This emphasis on *ejtehad* linked with *ulema* as legitimate elected representatives seeks to remove the contradictions between theocracy and democracy.

But the *Majlis* had numerous non-clerical representatives and the Prime Minister himself was not a member of the religious institution. In practice, it was not possible to bypass the electorate and the Council of Guardian's continuous blockings of *Majlis* legislations were not accepted mutely. But whenever the matters got too difficult, Khomeini issued a new *fatwa*, providing the directive for the next move. Occasionally he would order the Guardians to reconsider. He did so in January 1988.

After a long and acrimonious bout Khomeini declared that *maslehat* (national interest), demanded that the Guardians be more circumspect. He instructed them to reconsider a series of bills that they had rejected outright. There followed frenzied meetings and public statements. Initially the Council seemed to have forgotten its duty of absolute obedience to Khomeini and his commandments and he found it necessary to remind them:

*Valayateh Faqih* and its legitimate right to rule is a primary article of faith in Islam.[67]

Given the difficulties of substantiating this claim in terms of religious doctrine, the Council and its spokesman retained a dignified silence. For this they were fiercely criticised by Khomeini's supporters. The temporary Friday prayer leader of Mashad declared:

Islamic commandments are sometimes asserted regardless of the needs of our nation and government. Up to now the Council of Guardians has based its rulings on Islamic laws of government. But now that the *Imam* has ordered the government to take into account the needs of the poor and the dis-possessed, the Council must adjust its decisions accordingly...It is essential that this nation follows the wishes of the *Imam*.[68]

Shiraz's temporary Friday prayer leader reiterated the duty of Muslims to obey:

The *Valiyeh Faqih* has the authority to decide every detail of the govern-ment...and in the absence of the twelfth Imam all believers have the duty of obeying him...The cabinet must delineate the path for government and the Parliament must pass laws and the Council of Guardians must ensure that the laws accord with Islam. But ultimately it is the *Imam* who decides the limits of the duties of the Council and dictates the terms of government in this country.[69]

When it came to practicalities, the rule of Islam had to be discarded in favour of the rule of Khomeini.

Islamic government is legitimised by the *Valiyeh Faqih* who leads it. It is the *Valiyeh Faqih* who is responsible for everything and rules over everyone and is in charge of our nation... Islamic society is ruled according to the views of the *Valiyeh Faqih*. He is not required to consider anyone else's views and opinions.[70]

The Islamic student's associations denounced the Council's spokesman, and Temporary Friday prayer leader of Tehran, *Hojatoleslam* Emami Kashani, for not responding to Khomeini's *fatwa* and not endorsing the role of *Valayateh Faqih* during the Friday prayer.[71]

The Council had taken its religious duties too seriously and forgotten that it was Khomeini and not Islam that ruled the land. With the majority of the *ulema* gagged, the press controlled by the *Faqih* and his henchmen and the organs of government competing powerlessly against one another, the Council had no hope of holding firm. Eventually it admitted defeat. Emami Kashani announced the Council's absolute submission:

The Council had always been a follower of the line of *Imam* and has obeyed his dictate to the letter, and would never intentionally transgress. Accordingly the Council is prepared to review every bill that has been previously rejected. We are all too aware that the saintly *Imam* is *Valiyeh Amre*, our ruler, and the main source of emulation, *Marja'eh taqlid*,[72] and his decisions are final and absolute and no member of this Council has the right to go against them.[73]

This view was reiterated by the Council's Secretary-General, Ayatollah Safi. He went to Khomeini, vowed their obedience and extracted a conciliatory comment from the *Faqih*. Matters returned to normal. Khomeini declared:

The Council of Guardians has always had my support which is in no way diminished. They have a duty of remaining constantly vigilant in the service of Islam and the Muslim nation.[74]

Although the dispute between the Council and Parliament was momentarily silenced, the problems of power, authority and conflicting responsibilities remained unresolved. The recurring problems were: first, whether the *Majlis* was any more than a charade: and, second, whether the religious institution could both govern and claim to guard the dispossessed, as the *ulema* had traditionally claimed to do? Furthermore it was not clear whether Khomeini's absolute rule left any room for delegation of powers and responsibilities, even to the *ulema*. Khomeini's insistence on the overriding importance of the *Valiyeh Faqih*, the sole true representative of God on earth, left little room for anyone else. Even the pro-government, conservative daily newspaper, *Kayhan*, began to ponder about the logic of the political situation. An editorial comment said:

The question arises as to whether the honourable representatives of the *Valiyeh Faqih* have any right to make independent decisions or must they always turn to the *Faqih*? Is the Minister of labour not allowed to deal with the problems of employment and can he not institute any measures without consulting the *Faqih* at every turn?

What about the Councils of Guardian and Judiciary? Can they solve the daily problems that come before them on their own, or must they also turn to the *Faqih*? If they cannot act independently then can we govern without ever delegating any responsibility? Would such a conclusion not make a nonsense of the *Valayateh Faqih*?[75]

This question was perennial. It was raised first by Rafsanjani in a series of open letters to Khomeini in October 1981. The response had not been enlightening. Khomeini had not planned to set up a democracy and the tangled web of the Islamic constitution allocated responsibility to all without giving anyone other than the *Faqih* any powers.

President Khameneyi sparked off another national debate by requesting that the *Faqih* 'clarifies' the respective responsibilities of the government and *Valayateh Faqih*. Khomeini responded by affirming his own supremacy and demanding that his position as *Valayateh Faqih* should be discussed by the nation as a whole. Everyone was to endorse his absolute right to exercise an undisputed command over all Muslims. The *ulema* responded with rounds of applause and attempts on all fronts to establish obedience to *Valayateh Faqih* as a matter of religious doctrine and duty.

But amidst the cacophony of support there were a few dissenters. Some, like *Hojatoleslam* Seyed Ali Mohamad Dastqeibi, the Fars representative on the Council of Guardians, quoted the Holy *Quran*:

No believer has the right to exercise personal judgement on matters where there has been a commandment delivered by God and his Envoy.[76]

Others tried to distinguish between Khomeini, the *Imam*, and Islamic government.The Friday prayer leader of Semnan, *Hojatoleslam* Abas Ali Akhtari explained:

The government is the government of *Feqh*, Islamic law, and not the government of *Faqih*. The *Faqih* rules because he has knowledge, Islamic knowledge. It is this knowledge and not the individual as such who is ruling over us. Islam gives the *Faqih* the right to issue *fatwas*, Islamic decrees, and to legislate and to determine policies. These are rights granted to him by the virtue of his extensive knowledge of Islam. It is his superior learning and knowledge which legitimises his rule. That is why if the *Valayateh Faqih*, the pinnacle of Islamic wisdom, disagrees, then the *Majlis* and the Council of Guardians lose their legitimacy. By virtue of his knowledge and wisdom, God has entitled the *Faqih* alone to rule over the Muslims.[77]

Ayatollah Montazeri allowed his students to publish extracts from his lectures which also seemed to question the unilateral right of the *Faqih*, as a person, to hold undisputed reign. Montazeri reverted to the only *Shia* solution that had existed, that of collegiality:

*Valayateh Faqih* does not mean that the *Faqih* alone and single-handed would do everything, rather it means that the *Faqih* is the core and anchor who delegates responsibility to the legislative and administrative organisations, but keeps a keen supervisory eye to prevent carelessness, shortcomings and failures. But in making important decisions the *Faqih* consults with experts and the learned to ensure that his decisions are beneficial to society as a whole and do not incur irreparable damage to the social fabric of Muslim nations.[78]

In the event Montazeri's views, reminiscent as they were of Shariatmadari's insistence on the collegial nature of Islamic rule, was to precipitate his downfall, as they had in the case of Shariatmadari before him.[79]


## THE REVISED CONSTITUTION

Although the Council of Guardians toed the line and reviewed some of its decisions, it was obvious that the division between two interpretations of what the revolution had been for was unlikely to disappear. Khomeini's interventions, always conducted in the name of Islam, did little to shed light on the matter: it was more in the nature of a cover-up than an enlightening judgement: the important points, beside the assertion of Khomeini's right to absolute rule, had been the question of delegation of power and authority and the delineation of the national interest, *maslehat*. The disagreements looked set to go on and national interest appeared to be less than clear. Eventually, in February 1988, Khomeini set up yet another Council, *Shorayeh Tashkhisseh Maslehat*, Council of Arbitration (literally translated: the council for identification of national interest) to resolve the problems. The twelve-member Council included President Khameneyi; the Speaker of *Majlis*, Hashemi Rafsanjani; the President of the Supreme Court, Mussavi Ardabili, as well as the outspoken *Hojatoleslam* Mussavi Khoyiniha, who was at the time the General Prosecutor, and *Hojatoleslam* Tavakoli. Decisions were to be taken by majority vote. Khomeini's son, Ahmad, was to sit in at the meetings and report the proceedings to his father.

But despite the proliferation of councils, there was no solution to be found. The debates on *Valayateh Faqih* had merely highlighted the centrality of Khomeini to the survival of the system and had made Montazeri seem less than absolutely obedient. Khomeini was getting ill and frail and Khameneyi and Rafsanjani, both favourite disciples of the *Faqih*, felt themselves to be vulnerable should Montazeri come to power. Montazeri was clearly the most scholarly of the three and if it was *Feqh*, knowledge of Islamic law, that was to determine who should rule over the country, then the President and Speaker of the House, both *Hojatoleslams* – that is, in the lower echelons of Islamic learning[80] – had much to lose. Besides Rafsanjani could not expect Montazeri to forgive him for the execution of his colleague, Mehdi Hashemi, over the Irangate affair.[81]

At the same time Montazeri's 'students' were serialising his lectures in the daily paper, *Kayhan*. They used the series to voice dissenting views about

Islamic government, the role of the ruler and the limits to his power. Rafsanjani used these and the Irangate episode to convince Khomeini that the chosen heir, whose name ironically means 'the expectant', should never become the nation's leader. The *coup de grâce* was precipitous; on the night of 26 March 1989, during the Iranian New Year holiday period, the leaders of the Assembly of Experts were summoned to Khomeini's bedside to discuss the future of the leadership. The meeting lasted an hour.

Khomeini conveyed his decision by an open letter to Montazeri: in the name of Islam and because of his 'unsuitable entourage' and, of course, the 'national interest', Khomeini felt compelled to dismiss his successor. But, as an act of kindness, the benevolent theocrat was willing to allow Montazeri to continue functioning as a religious leader. Unlike Shariatmadari he was not to be illegitimately stripped of his theological rank. The letter stated:

In Islam the interest of state takes precedence over all other questions...I consider it to be in the best interest of the state and the revolution that you should remain a religious leader from whose opinions the people of this revolution would benefit...In order not to repeat past mistakes, I advise you to bar the way to unsuitable people who have been encircling you and cleanse your domain from people who frequent you and, in the name of their love of Islam and respect for the revolution, sow the seeds of discontent and oppose the interests of the state. You must take much greater care in choosing those whom you befriend.[82]

Montazeri immediately offered his resignation. Reporting the matter to *Majlis* on 9 April, Rafsanjani said that Montazeri had given *maslehat*, national interest, as the reason.

Montazeri's departure precipitated a constitutional crisis; there was no other suitable candidate to fulfil the functions of the *Faqih*. According to Khomeini's thesis he – and it could only be a male theocrat – had to be 'the most learned' and 'the most disinterested', religious leader who would not only have to shoulder, albeit unwillingly, the responsibility of office; but also to lead the nation both by his own exemplary virtue and by his extensive and superior learning and knowledge.[83] The much-publicised debates in January and February 1988 had underlined the extensive power and authority of the *Faqih*, thereby making it even more difficult to find a suitable successor. The constitutional solution had been collegial;[84] if a single *Faqih* 'who is so recognised by the majority of people' had failed to emerge, a council of three or five religious leaders would take charge of the leadership. In 1988, however, such a council consisting of the leading *ulema* selected on the basis of knowledge and learning, would not have included either Khameneyi or Rafsanjani. Neither individual was likely to command public, let alone religious, backing.

It was imperative, in their interest if not in the national interest, to change the constitution. Khomeini, who did not expect to live much longer, agreed to the expediency and on 25 April 1989, he appointed a new Council, this time to revise the constitution, *Shorayeh Baznegary*. The council brought together old companions of the leader and devout followers of his views. This time there was going to be no secular/religious divide about the constitution. All but two of Khomeini's nominees were reliable members of the religious institution. The non-clerics were Prime Minister Mussavi and Hassan Habib, the rest were ardent Khomeini supporters and included well-known personages such as Rafsanjani, Khameneyi, Mussavi Ardabili, Ali Meshkini, head of the Assembly of Experts (all fellow-prisoners in the last years of the Shah), Mussavi Khoyiniha, Taheri Khoramabadi, Mohamadi Guilani (one of Khomeini's notorious hanging judges),[85] Khazeli Yazdi, Emami Kashani (spokesman of the Council of Guardians) Amini, Jonati, Mohamad Reza Mahdavi Kani (member of Khomeini's first secret revolutionary council),[86] Ahmad Azari Qomi (Tehran's revolutionary prosecutor) Mohamad Tavassoli, Mehdi Koroubi,[87] and Khomeini's grandson, Ayatollah Yahya Nuri. The *Majlis* was permitted to nominate an additional five members to the council.

The council was to disentangle the proliferation of command, delineate the limits of power and responsibilities of the President, the Prime Minister and the leader and sort out the problem of the succession. To clarify the situation, it was instructed by Khomeini to change the name of the House of Representatives from *Majlis Shorayeh Melli* (The National Consultative Assembly) to *Majlis Shorayeh Eslami*, (the Islamic Consultative Assembly). This change was to emphasise that Iran was a country ruled by God whose legitimacy is accepted by people, rather than one that required popular legitimisation.[88]

The revisions were completed by July 1989. The new constitution dispensed with prime Ministerial responsibilities by handing them over to the President. After the leader, the President holds the highest post in the land,[89] and is in charge of both the Cabinet and all branches of the government.[90] Ministers are hired and fired by the President, subject to *Majlis*'s ratification.[91] But the President cannot take over any Ministerial portfolio,[92] thus avoiding a concentration of powers in one hand.

As to the leader, the collegial option was removed,[93] and the idea of *Valiyeh Faqih* was radically revised. Khomeini's insistence that the leader would have to have immense religious learning and vision and be a 'reluctant' politician was replaced by the need to select a person who had 'the correct political vision'. The new leader no longer had to be a fearless source of enlightenment, *marja*, or exemplary in terms of justice and probity; instead he had to be 'prudent' and have good political judgement and 'sufficient' religious knowledge.[94] Once the leader becomes a mere human being, a fallible political appointee, then he no longer holds power forever and can be dismissed if necessary. Should this occur, a council consisting of the President, the head of the Judiciary and a religious leader from the Council of Guardians, can take over temporarily; with the proviso that council members of the religious institution had to be in the majority.[95]

The demotion of the leader to the ranks of mere mortals posed a serious problem of legitimacy for a state which is run on the basis of absolute obedience to the laws of God and to the decrees of his shadow on earth, the *Valayateh Faqih*. If the *Faqih*, the highest source of emulation, is not one and the same as the *Vali*, the ruler, then who has absolute authority and the right to rule in the name of God? There was a public debate conducted in the press about the legitimacy of a mere ruler to govern the Islamic Republic. An outspoken opponent, Dr Sholeh Saadi, the *Majlis* representative for Shiraz made the obvious point that according to Khomeini's own thesis, it was inconceivable that the country could be ruled by a mere fallible, and removable religious leader:

As the *Imam* has stated in his book on *Valayateh Faqih* the powers of *Valayateh Faqih* are in no way inferior to those exercised by the Messenger of God and his son-in-law, Ali; his power and authority to govern is exactly the same as theirs, neither more nor less.

Just as it is imponderable for the Islamic constitution to place limits on the rule of the Prophet, so it is unacceptable to place limitations on the rule of the *Faqih*...The Islamic government has no legislative authority. No one has the right to legislate...the most we can hope to achieve is to propose plans and programmes and provide some kind of expertise. But power and authority is entirely in the hands of the leader and there is little else beyond that...It is pointless to talk about separation of powers since it is the leader who is the executive and the judiciary...as to the legislature, our laws are the laws of God and religion and decisions are made by the religious leader's decrees, *fatwas*. These *fatwas* are absolute and binding from the moment they are pronounced; they are not subject to anyone else's opinions; neither [those of] the Council of Guardians nor the *Majlis*.[96]

It was the assumption of infallibility of the leader that had made obedience to his ruling a religious duty; without it how could people be expected to be obedient? Seyed Hosein Hoseini, the Majlis representative for Shahroud raised this point:

Our leader has repeatedly saved this country from terrible dangers. He has been able to do so because of the absolute obedience of [the] people to his ruling. His commandments have been above and beyond the law and the constitution. No council or government could lay claim to such sanctity and infallibility...We cannot separate the leadership from *marja'yiat*, being the source of Islamic knowledge and emulation. It is because of his wisdom and religious learning that our leader has our unquestioning obedience. I have no right whatsoever to legislate. Legislation in the first place is the prerogative of God and it is only the Messenger of God, the *imams* and the *Valiyeh Faqih* who can initiate legislations on his behalf...Furthermore it is only the *marja'* (source of emulation) who has the right to ratify legislations. It is his sanctity which legitimises the legislature in the eyes of God and secures the absolute and unquestioning obedience of the people.[97]

The revised constitution was going to appoint a mere human being, without sanctity, without superior religious learning and without absolute probity, *ma'soumiat*, to rule over the country. Yet the people were still expected to obey this ruler as if he were a *Valiyeh Faqih*. *Hojatoleslam* Mussavi Khoyiniha tried to shed light on the problem:

> Whether or not the leader is a *marja'eh taqlid*, we must be all be ruled by him. Provided he is a religious leader, *mujtahed*, and he is just, then we must obey his decrees...On matters of politics and the state it is the leader who rules absolute. We must all obey him as a matter of duty and we have no right to question his judgement, even if we are better scholars of Islam and higher ranking *ulema*. Just as now the *imam*'s decrees are binding, so in the future it is absolutely essential that we obey the decisions of our future leaders...In terms of Islamic laws it is the *Valiyeh Amre*, the person in charge of government, who rules. The *Valiyeh Amre*, who must be a suitably qualified religious leader, like our *Imam*, has, according to our faith, a canonical right to determine the best interest of the nation and rule accordingly...In addition to this God-given right, the ruler enjoys the support of our people. So the suitable leader has not only the God-given prerogative to govern, but also has this right endorsed by the faithful.[98]

The only protection offered to the people by the General Prosecutor was the vigilance of the ulema:

> So long as the Islamic State ... relies entirely on the laws of Islam ... it will have the full support of the Muslims and the religious leaders... Should it ever, God forbid, fail to do so, then the religious leaders and the people of Islam will rise as one and defeat it.[99]

But the revised constitution, having removed the theocratic councils heading each sector of the state, had undermined the bureaucratic means of securing such vigilance. Just as the collegial leadership was removed, so the constitutional overhaul removed most of the other collegial provisions which had permeated the original constitution. The different branches of the government were to be headed by a single Minister, rather than a supervisory council, and the President was to be in charge and to liaise between departments.[100] Even the High Council of Defence was disbanded.

The nation's leading religious figures rushed to the media to denounce collegial government. The Judicial High Council came in for much vilification. The Public Prosecutor, *Hojatoleslam* Mussavi Khoyiniha, asserted that where God was the source of all laws, consultation was unnecessary and collegiality merely an obstacle to efficiency:

> Collective leadership simply cannot work. It may have a place in the context of the *Majlis* where decisions are made by majority voting; but it certainly has no place in the judiciary. Our decision-making is not a consultative process, it

is a matter of personal interpretation of the laws of God. We might seek advise, but the decision is taken by one person and independently.[101]

Strictly speaking this is the case: *Shias*, unlike the majority of *Sunni* Muslims, do give the jurisconsults the right to use *aqle*, reason, and his personal discretion in interpreting the laws of God.[102] But the Islamic government's first constitution had failed to note this basic article of faith and had thereby caused delays and deficiencies. Seyed Hosein Hoseini, the *Majlis* representative for Shahroud, blamed the backlog of unresolved cases on the collegial nature of the judiciary:

> If one person on the high council of the judiciary disagrees with his colleagues then we have an impasse. Major decisions need the unanimous endorsement of the council; where this is not forthcoming crucial decisions are simply shelved. One obdurate member can prevent the other four from handing down a sensible judgement and everything is left in limbo.[103]

The insistence on unanimity accords with the Islamic reliance on consensus, *ijma*, as a means of coming to a correct legal solution. But once more the laws of God and faith fell short of the needs of the country. The head of the government inspectorate, *Hojatoleslam* Mohaqeq Damad joined the fray:

> The collective nature of responsibility in the judiciary has prevented the government inspectorate from getting to the root of the problems and operating effectively.[104]

But the revised constitution was not going to abandon its Islamic posture. So the judiciary ended up with two heads. The high judicial council was replaced by a religious leader who was appointed for five-yearly periods to supervise the courts and the Minister.[105] It was the religious leader, and not the Minister, who was empowered to appoint judges,[106] including the Head of the Supreme Court, and the National Public Prosecutor, both of whom had to be religious leaders.[107]

Thus the revised constitution removed much of the Islamic practices, if not its polemics, from the government. The day-to-day business of the republic was to be conducted by bureaucrats and elected representatives and only the judiciary was under the direct control of a theocrat for all time.

But the Council of Guardians retained its hold. The presence of many of its members on the revision council ensured that it extended its role by taking charge of elections both to the *Majlis* and to the Assembly of Experts.[108] To deal with the unavoidable clashes that were to arise between the Guardians and *Majlis* the new Council, the *Majmaeh Tashkhiseh Masslehateh Nezam*, the Council for identifying the national interests of the government, was to continue. The Council's membership was to be determined by the leader who could appoint its members on a permanent or temporary basis and who could also go to it for advice. The Council's role was to arbitrate between the laws of Islam, as expressed by the Guardians, and the political expediency, as expressed by the *Majlis*.[109] Thus, in the final analysis, despite all the efforts to concentrate power and responsibility, the *ulema* returned to the traditional collegial solution to deal with the unavoidable problems that the theocracy was going to face in its attempt to adopt a democratic guise.

The revisions were completed just in time; the final version was presented in July 1989, a month later Khomeini was dead. Rafsanjani took over the Presidency and Khameneyi, who, without ever presenting the necessary Islamic thesis, elevated himself overnight to the rank of Ayatollah, became the national leader; one that was neither a *Faqih* nor an acceptable *Valiyeh Amre*, in Islamic terms. Within a year the cabinet had lost most of its Islamist members; Prime Minister Mir Hosein Mussavi's post was abolished; Minister of Interior Ali Akbar Mohtashemi, and Behzad Nabavi, Minister of Heavy Industries, had been replaced as had Abdol Karim Mussavi Ardabili, the former Prosecutor-General. As to the *Majlis*, in the 1992 elections for the fourth session most, if not all, of the old guard were either disqualified by the Council of Guardians, or were not elected. Influential representatives such as Mehdi Karubi and Ali Akbar Mohtashami lost their seats. Khomeini's son, Ahmad, lost much of his political predominance and Khomeini's blueprint for government proved worthless. Within a decade the Iranian government had had to abandon all but the pretence of being Islamic.

# 8 Freedom, Culture and Education in Khomeini's State: What Price Islam?

Khomeini intended to build a thoroughly Islamic state, yet – despite the rhetoric – by the time he died, in terms of real politics Islam had become more of a posture than a reality. When it came to debts, matters of welfare, health, housing, economic planning then it was not Islam but the economist and IMF's monetarist policies that dictated the terms.[1]

There were two major spheres, however, in which the process of Islamification made a more lasting impact; these were education and the media. In these cases the post-revolutionary state, guided firmly by Khomeini, set about changing the parameters and the contents and concepts; all challenging views and ideas were to be eradicated for being 'pro-Western' and 'imperialist' and, in the name of Islam and unity, a bland conformity was to be forcibly imposed on intellectuals, authors, film-makers and educationalists.

As early as 1980 the theocracy had closed down all opposition newspapers,[2] and had established ideological units and Islamic societies,[3] acting as a kind of 'thought police' in work places and throughout government agencies; these units were set up to maintain the Islamic line and report on dissidents. All educational material was revised to eliminate traces of un-Islamic attitudes. The Islamic State had launched its programme for the 'purification' of the minds of its people. That these measures contravened the essence of freedom, liberty and democracy did not concern the nation's leader. In his political thesis *Valayateh Faqih* Khomeini had already dismissed democracy as a Western ploy for undermining the politics of Islam and defended his right as *Faqih* to dictate the political agenda. In a series of public speeches after the revolution, he set about contesting the public's right to freedom; to justify this Khomeini chose to equate freedom with immorality and present it as the poisoned chalice of the West and the source of all evil. Thus liberty was equated with imperialism and retrospectively rejected as being counter-revolutionary.

It is worth noting that Khomeini's attempts to define liberty in terms of restrictive practices is very much part of the mainstream revivalist thinking. Ali Shariati too was concerned about the confusion between *azadi*, freedom and *rahayi*, liberty:

> We must not confuse freedom with liberty. Liberty denotes the absence of constrains, it has a negative sense, it indicates the existence of a situation. By contrast *azadi*, freedom, is an essential quality, a characteristic of human

153

progress which can only be achieved through struggles and hardship and wisdom and growth.

The difference is like that of a person who escapes from prison. That is liberty regardless of the kind of person that the prisoner is. It can be a thief who is at liberty or a slave or even an enemy of freedom. Similarly a progressive, noble and conscientious person, a free-thinker, may be caught, imprisoned and deprived of his liberty. Yet one remains a libertine, in prison or otherwise and the other a freedom fighter. They cannot be equated as one and the same.[4]

The Islamic intelligentsia had to forge its own version of moralistic, constrained, yet acceptable vision of freedom. In this Khomeini went considerably further away from Western views than Shariati had done.

## FREEDOM ACCORDING TO KHOMEINI

Khomeini was of the view that the revolution had not been about freedom from oppression, so much as about leading the misguided people of Iran back to the correct Islamic path. Therefore, he was not going to stand by and allow woolly-minded intellectuals to bar the way to Islam and its rule.

Khomeini singled out the secularised education system which he accused of producing an 'anti-Islamic' intelligentsia for over fifty years. All intellectuals, authors and educated people were suspect because they had been nurtured by this pro-Western educational system which lulled them into an alcoholic and narcotic Western-style torpor. Khomeini was adamant that they should not be allowed to continue in that vein:

> They should arise from their slumber, our youths, our thinkers, our authors, our intellectuals. They must change themselves completely and line up to serve this country.[5]

Khomeini's claim that the revolution had been for Islam and not for liberty or independence is a simplistic rewriting of the revolution's history. It disregards all the Marxist, radical and nationalist groups who came together during the revolution and attempted to negotiate and form a different political system afterwards.[6] What is more, the Islam he espoused and advocated was not of the enlightened and libertarian variety adopted by many of the revolutionaries.[7] Khomeini's revolution demanded absolute devotion and the very life of its adherents; it dealt out death and destruction to its supporters who gave their all to achieve success, and to the opponents who barred the way.[8] Blood and violence were its hallmarks and there was little room for liberty:

> Our aim was not mere freedom. Our aim was not mere independence... We did not want to be free like Sweden; they may be free, they may be independent, but they have no Quranic awareness... What do you suppose the Iranians wanted? Did they want Islam?... Did they die for the *Quran*?... We did not shed the blood of our youths for mere material gains... Our martyrs

gave up their lives, they willingly espoused death, to make this the land of Islam. They did not die for freedom or liberty, they died to make this an Islamic State and we will make sure that their death is not in vain, that it is not made pointless by the libertines who survived.[9]

The survivors are condemned by Khomeini for having a false idea of freedom and for espousing immorality in the name of liberty. Khomeini can see no difference between freedom and immorality. In his eyes the young were divided between those who died or put their lives on the line for the cause and the others, the 'westoxificated' ones:

The kind of youths who spends their time in the movie houses making day into nights... the kind of youths who find their dreams and their goals in the Western cinemas and have no idea about our own culture and its wealth of resources. The kind of youth that is willingly exchanging our oil, our very economic blood, for Western weavers of fantasies and immoralities, for material goods that are squandered on these dream machines ... The kind of youth that remains supine while our best resources are sucked away by the imperialists.[10]

Polluted by Western materialism, he argued, these youths are praying to false Gods in the name of freedom; they are asking for the kind of freedom that must be denied:

These advocates of freedom who wear out their pens in praise of liberty. What is it that they are really asking for? They want free access to gambling halls; they want our youths to spend its time in drinking houses. They are out to corrupt our youths in every possible way. They want free access to prostitution... This kind of freedom would devour our youths, would destroy our national identity... If we give them a free hand they would corrupt our youths to their very core. They would lead them to the opium dens and an alcoholic mess.[11]

Such uncontrolled pursuit of pleasures had to be stopped and the Islamic Republic was to do so as a matter of national and devotional duty. Khomeini was unequivocally opposed to their kind of freedom:

The freedom that they are asking for is nothing but the road to corruption. It is the path to ruin for this land and for this people. We will deny you this freedom. The freedom that you want... the freedom to undermine our revolution, to raise an indifferent uncommitted youth who is willing to try and do anything at any time for any reason... A youth that would drown in worldly pleasures while squandering the wealth of this nation on corrupting pastimes... that is the freedom that we will deny you with all the might of the Islamic State and its revolutionary forces[12]

He argued forcefully that the freedom-seekers were merely enslaved by their obsession with the pleasures of the flesh; an obsession that 'unmanned' the young men of the revolution and opened the gates to the enemies poised to undermine the revolution and its prospects:

> The kind of freedom that they advocate is the freedom to annihilate our workforce... while our youth are indulging in the pleasures of the flesh and indulging in carnal exploits they'll take away everything we've ever had and there would be no one to stop them. While the youth dance their lives away, they scoop our wealth away.[13]

By equating freedom with immorality and apathy, Khomeini justifies his determination to restrict intellectual activities and to forbid much of what would normally be seen as individual liberty. In the name of Islam the arts, literature and poetry were to be curtailed and initially music was banned. Along with ideas, women, whose freedom was seen as a most corrupting element,[14] were to be restricted and confined to the home. In his last will and testament, Khomeini firmly condemned any move away from his Islamification programme:

> We must be wary of Western-style freedom; it will ruin our young men and lead our women astray. Leading the youth astray is against the principle and the spirit of Islam; it is condemned by our faith and condemned by our reason. It is not permissible to undermine our national honour and modesty by books, speeches or pictures and magazines that would pollute our honour. It is the duty of the Islamic government to be vigilant against corruption and freedom. The kind of freedom that threatens our revolution and is contrary to our beliefs and our religion.[15]

Thus Khomeini justified his insistence on the imposition of severe restrictions on clothing, which had to be universally 'modest', and all-covering for women; outings, which had to be the exclusive prerogative of males, or females accompanied by their spouses or male parents; and on cultural activities, which were defined strictly in terms of religious feasts, mourning or passion plays. All this was done in the name of the alternative sort of freedom that Khomeini had in mind. He took on the adversaries:

> So what is it that they are denouncing as restrictions? Merely our devout wish to save our youth, to save our future from these dens of corruption. We are going to take our youths away from the corrupting pleasures of the flesh. We take them from the bars and send them to the war fronts... We drive them out of the cinemas and away from the dream machine and take them to the battlefields where they can make real contributions, where they can place their lives on the line to defeat the enemy and defend our nation... We will take them and arm them and send them to the battlefields. That is the kind of freedom that we need in this country.[16]

But if the new morality was to be imposed effectively, then the Islamic Republic had to instill these values in its youth and educate them to equate restrictive practices with freedom. It was not going to be easy to impose puritanism on the Iranians, a people renowned for its sense of humour and fun.

No sooner had the revolution taken hold than the country began reverberating with anti-clerical jokes that were passed on through the grapevine and, defying the censors and morality laws, repeated on all occasions. Khomeini blamed the intellectuals, the Western-style media and most of all the educational system. He launched a cultural revolution which began by reforming educational materials and went on to the closure of all universities.

## THE CULTURAL REVOLUTION

Within a year of the establishment of the Islamic Republic, Khomeini set up the High Council of the Cultural Revolution; its first duty was to revise the entire educational system. It began by closing down all schools and universities. Then it attempted to check all text-books and remove any trace of un-Islamic opinion and illustration. This in the first instance meant covering up all the photographs of women, and rewriting Iranian history to glorify the Muslims rather than the Persians. Until then the Arabs had always been depicted as uncivilised invaders who conquered Iran and were educated and trained by the Iranians, who soon returned to their tradition of royal rule and dynastic imperialism. The new version hailed Islam as the liberator of the people and denounced monarchs as oppressors. But the re-writing did not extend to biology text-books; they did not introduce an anti-Darwinian and pro-Islamic interpretation of evolution. There was however an attempt to simplify the curriculum and make it more *maktabi*, in the old style of clergy-run schools where learning had been by rote and dutiful acceptance of the teacher's views.

## SCHOOLS

The education system, like the pre-revolutionary bureaucracy, was initially purged to the core; all foreign-run schools were closed down and anyone suspected of un-Islamic tendencies was sacked. But, along with the re-establishment of other civil servants, some of the teachers were gradually allowed to return to their desks.[17] Initially an estimated 40 000 teachers were expelled or compulsorily retired. But acute shortages led to many of them being reinstated, some after attending courses on Islamic education.[18] The schools were segregated and the curriculum was intended to have more of a home-economics orientation for girls. Although the constitution undertook to make schooling available to all school-age children free of charge, these high ideals were not realised. Private schools re-emerged almost as soon as the schools were allowed to re-open and many of these bypassed the second-rate provisions stipulated for girls.[19]

To ensure continuing ideological purity, every school, like every factory and other work-places, was obliged to establish an Islamic society which policed its members. But their powers were to some extent curtailed by the reality of the crisis in education; lack of funds and a rapidly growing population placed an ever-heavier burden on the system. There simply were not enough teachers. Even the Islamification process itself had to come to a halt. A decade after the launch of the cultural revolution, Minister of Education Mohamad Ali Najafi had to admit that he was still looking for another 4000 qualified teachers of *Quran* and religious ideology capable of teaching the subject in any depth.[20]

The demand for ideological purification and integral Islamic education, which was central to the cultural revolution, had to be accommodated in the context of increasing numbers of students, and deteriorating conditions in the schools. The birth rate was rising by an average of 3.2 per cent a year and the numbers of pupils spiralled from 5 million boys and 3 million girls in 1979 to 7 million and 5 million respectively in 1989 and a total intake of 17 million in 1992.[21] Yet the numbers of schools remained almost static. This was initially because of the ideological closures; but, from the mid-1980s onward, many schools were repossessed by landlords for failure to pay the rent. The courts had to recognise the Islamic rights of ownership and grant eviction orders. Each time some 600 to 1000 pupils were thrown on the streets.[22] Not surprisingly, by the end of the decade there were over 1.5 million children who could not go to schools at all.[23] By 1986 38 per cent of the population was illiterate.

For those who did go to government schools, which offered the most strictly Islamified teaching, the situation was particularly abysmal. Classes had grown in numbers to seventy or ninety pupils, while the classrooms, built to accommodate twenty to thirty, stayed the same size. In Tehran, which had the fastest-growing population of all, only 350 new schools had been built since the revolution; while many had been turned out of their rented accommodation by the landlords. The remaining ones were engaged in an unequal battle teaching in two, three, four or even five shifts each day; which meant that some pupils had 3 hours education or less a day.[24] Even then the classes were packed beyond their capacity. As a primary-school teacher, Manijeh Amini, explained in 1991:

> In the classroom the teacher has nowhere to sit; the pupils are packed in four to five at a desk to within 30 centimetres of the black board. To give you a clear picture all I need to say is that in a room 12 metres square we pack in forty pupils.[25]

Qolamreza Soleimani, a secondary-school teacher described a similar situation:

> We have to pack sixty pupils in the class. There is no room for anyone to move; I can't call them up to the blackboard and I can't get to the back of the classroom to see what they are up to. I have them piled up one against the other with hardly any room to breathe.[26]

As for recreational facilities, there were none to be had. A physical-education teacher told *Kayhan*'s reporter:

Not only do we not have the grounds and the sport facilities, but in over 20 000 schools you wouldn't even find a football to kick around. Not when the average physical education budget per pupil is 10 tumans a year and a football costs over 200 tumans.[27]

Those teachers who obtained jobs after the cultural revolution stayed, even though frequently they were better Muslims than educationalists. Whereas before the revolution 69 per cent of secondary-school teachers had graduate degrees, by 1990 only 17 per cent were graduates. Critical shortage of qualified and experienced teachers meant that those with equivalents of 'O' or 'A' levels could still apply for headships provided they had 5 to 7 years experience. In fact many head-teachers were secondary-school graduands.[28] It was not easy to become an experienced teacher. With large classes, poor facilities, little encouragement, and budgetary restrictions imposed by the government, the teaching profession was not attracting many new recruits. Existing teachers were highly disillusioned. The head of Payameh Shahid, Mohamad Mokhtari, told a journalist:

My teachers are going hungry; those on short-term contracts had to start teaching in October, but they were not paid till the following March... And what do you suppose they get? They are contracted to teach twelve hours a week at 40 tumans per hour. Now they are doing us a favour and raising the rates to 70 tumans per hour and they've raised our taxes from 10 to 15 per cent. This in a country where a kilo of potatoes costs 50 tumans.[29]

There were some 15 000 low-paid teachers on short-term contracts in Tehran alone; it is hardly surprising that university graduates did not seek a career in teaching.

The problem was that although the politicians paid lip-service to the need to educate and train the population, the economists regarded the education sector as mere 'consumers' and in the monetarist atmosphere that prevailed consumerism was not to be rewarded. The Under-Secretary for Education, Mr Ebadi, put the blame squarely on the monetarist planners:

The reason for the delay in the pay of the short-term contract teachers is that the Plan and Budget Organisation is of the view that the whole education system should be reorganised. They refuse to see education as a productive sector; they define it as a consumption sector and therefore do not see any need for further investment there. In fact they are of the view that any increase in teachers' salary would be inflationary. When I tell the Plan and Budget Organisation that our teachers have not been paid, they ask me 'well what did the ones who did get paid produce?' Over the past year they have in fact cut 1 per cent off our budget because they think that we are overstaffed and should administer some cuts.[30]

After the war, the need to absorb the returnees and help the unemployment statistics meant that, despite the Plan Organisation's structuralist views, education gained more resources and was given a higher priority by the government. Even teachers' salaries were increased. In 1989, 18 per cent of the national budget was allocated to the Ministry of Education; in 1990 this was increased to 24 per cent. Of this amount, 88 per cent had to go towards teachers' salaries; leaving relatively little for books and educational materials or for construction of schools.[31] But the Minister, Dr Najafi, announced that the bulk of the increased was to go towards improving the staff/student ratios, giving better terms to part-time teachers and contracting 300 000 new personnel over the next five years.[32] By 1992 President Khamneyi was claiming that there was 850 000 teachers and head teachers providing education for the country's 17 million pupils.[33] The following year the education sector's construction budget was doubled.[34] Nevertheless the Ministry's school-construction sector had to admit that the funds were unable to meet the shortage of 20 000 classrooms that impeded education in Tehran alone.[35] As to the rural areas, the Ministry of Education had to admit that absence of schools meant that only 10 per cent of young girls in these areas obtained any schooling at all.[36]

The Islamic Republic was unable to deliver on its commitment to free Islamified education for all, even though article 3 of the constitution guaranteed the rights of all citizen to 'education and physical training, free of charge for all at all levels'. Lack of public resources has meant that the government had to condone private schools charging fees. The regime could not even deliver cheap textbooks, pads and pencils, or inexpensive uniforms. A 100-page exercise book cost 100 tumans – that is, more than the average hourly pay of many teachers. So September was always a difficult month for parents. As the parent of two school-children told a reporter:

> I have been saving a month's wages to pay for the children's school-bag and uniform. But I have been going through all the shops and no way can I afford to pay. Even the poorest quality school-bag costs 300 tumans, and I know it won't last the month. As for the material for school uniform, at 400 tumans a metre... Never mind the clothes, I can hardly afford the school exercise books which cost anything between 15 tumans for a 40-page book and 100 for a larger one... I just don't know which way to turn.[37]

The government could do little about the costs. There were attempts at providing cheaper exercise books through cooperatives, but these had little impact. By August 1991 even school text-books could not be obtained. The Minister of Education, Dr Mohamad Ali Najafi, was obliged to order the first 32 pages of secondary-school texts to be printed and distributed, while he tried to sort out the rest.[38]

The Speaker of *Majlis, Hojatoleslam* Korubi, deplored the imposition of fees and declared them to be 'detrimental' to the interests of the vulnerable groups in society. He demanded that the *Majlis* and the Ministry of Education did its best to remove this heavy burden from the shoulders of the needy.[39] But although the education budget was increased much of the rise was absorbed by galloping inflation. There were simply not enough resources to pay for building new schools. So the government resorted to asking the private sector to build 'non-profit-making' schools. The Deputy Minister of Education in charge of Finances, Mohamad Taqi Movayed, announced that the government had to renege on its duty to provide free education for all:

> The government budget cannot meet the cost of education. Without help from parents and charitable organisations we simply cannot offer free education and will be forced to charge fees.[40]

This point was emphasised by Hashem Razfar, the Director of the Ministry's school construction programme. He declared that without private assistance, no new schools would be built:

> Without help from charitable people and organisations the shortages will get continuously worse. As it is we need 20 000 new classrooms.[41]

The government offered people the option of allocating up to 30 per cent of their taxes to pay for construction of new schools; the religious institution declared that about 33 per cent of religious taxes could also go towards building schools. Some 100 sites were made available in Tehran for private charitable schools. People willing to set up non-profit-making schools were allowed to borrow up to 10 million tumans for building each school and 750 000 tumans for equipping it. They could then charge fees of 12 000 to 25 000 tumans per term. By September 1990 the government and the private sector together had completed plans to build 155 new schools and there were another 500 in the pipelines.[42] By 1994 the government expected some 614 000 pupils to be attending the independent schools.[43] But the crisis did not abate. In 1993 a Ministry of Education official was complaining that people had not been willing to pay the back taxes they owed by building schools; nor had the government organisations contributed 2 per cent of their annual profits to help the construction of educational sites.[44] There simply was not enough space to accommodate the ever growing numbers of potential school-children.

## TERTIARY EDUCATION

The universities were also put through the cultural revolution. But whereas schools reopened within a couple of years, the Universities remained closed for over four years and then began reopening quite slowly. Though presented as a process of Islamification, the closure of the universities was in fact a political ploy to scatter the militant youths who had begun to express their dissatisfaction with the system within a year of Khomeini's return. They were proving most resistant and unwilling to accept the rule of the theocracy and internalise the new definitions of freedom, and control. By June 1980 the High Council retaliated and set up a *Jahadeh Daneshgahi*, (Universities' holy war) to purify the system. Its stated aims were to 'link the universities to the mass of the people and ensure the prevalence of Islamic faith in every aspect of university life'.[45]

But the real purpose of the move was to eliminate the strong core of young Marxist opponents who were vehemently criticising the regime.

Khomeini set the stage by denouncing the universities as hotbeds of left-wing, Western-orientated and corruptive influences. On 18 April 1980 he made a public speech demanding the purification of universities. The next day the ever-ready *hezbollahis* (members of God's party) attacked Tehran's Teachers Training College and Universities in Shiraz, Mashad and Isfahan.[46] On 21 April there were pitched battles in Rasht, Ahvaz and Tehran Universities; over 100 students were injured and many were killed.[47] But the Islamic government succeeded in quashing the rebellion and with President Bani Sadre's blessing, the *Jahad* went into action. All universities were closed and the staff had to retrain. By 1983 *Jahad* had devised a suitable one-year course – only those who gained high grades in the qualifying examination were permitted to return to their posts.

Most of the Western-style technocratic faculties, such as medicine and engineering, were reopened within three years. But humanities and social sciences were identified as the 'corrupt' areas which took considerably longer to be purified. It was no coincidence that the humanity and social science students had been at the core of the dissidents who were demonstrating against the regime and working with the *Fadayan* and *Mujahedin* guerrilla groups underground.

A couple of years later, Rafsanjani admitted that Islamification was not about curricular revision so much as about the elimination of oppositional forces:

> We have been criticised for closing down universities... but these were the very centres of corruption and Western-style pollution of ideas. It was the people who demanded the purification of our intellectuals... But when we reopen the universities you'll see that we were right to close them down. We have been clearing out all the corrupt elements, but have kept the good ones and even those who were half-way decent, since we know that the righteous will lead them to the correct path. We are even willing to allow people who have gone abroad to come back. Should they wish to return, we'd welcome them in the name of God and forgive them their past... Once we start again the world and everyone will realise that we are not against science and technology and real learning; nor are we against university education. What we eradicate is corruption, instability and terrorism which used to flourish in the universities.[48]

The result was rather spectacular. In 1978, just before the revolution, there were 17 000 university students, of whom 40 per cent were women. By 1983, as the universities were slowly allowed to reopen, the numbers of students had plummeted to 4500 only 10 per cent of whom were women. During the same period the numbers of university staff had been reduced from 8000 to 6000.[49] Gradually the numbers of public-sector university teachers increased to 14 454 full-timers, 9474 part-timers and 4980 hourly-paid tutors.[50] Amongst the beneficiaries of the Islamification and expansion of education, there were also some women. For example the requirement for Islamic teaching enabled

Maryam Behrouzi and Mrs Dabbagh to occupy chairs of 'Islamic Studies' at the Universities of Shaheed Beheshti and of Science and Industry respectively.

But the government planned a rapid increase in its educational sector and aimed to put 270 000 students through the tertiary system within five years. They did so by opening new universities, and by redefining tertiary education to include every college and institution that offered post-high-school courses. Over the five-year period the tertiary level's intake rose to 44 000 in 1986, and to 60 000 in 1988.[51] To accelerate the process in the period 1985–9, eight new universities were opened with eighty-five faculties and room for an additional 15 000 students. But the real increase was to be absorbed by the private sector. Two fee-paying universities were opened, the Free Islamic University, *Daneshkadeh Azadeh Eslami*, and the Open University, *Payameh Nour*. By 1988 90 000 students, 30 per cent of the total tertiary students, were enrolled at private universities; of these 4700 were enrolled at *Payameh Nour*.[52] By 1992 the Free University alone had 700 000 applicants, of whom 125 000 were offered actual and conditional places.[53] By 1993 the Plan Organisation was proposing the privatisation of all universities and the 'running of universities along management lines suggested by the investors'.[54]

Despite the increased places, there was stiff competition and applicants had to take a series of demanding entrance examinations. Even the fee-paying Free Islamic University, *Daneshgaheh Azadeh Eslami*, had 380 000 applicants for its 57 000 places,[55] and the *Payameh Nour* (the Radio University) had 35 000 applicants for 10 400 places.[56] There was also a marked increase in the numbers of *jahad Daneshgahi*'s personnel. By the time the war ended it had recruited a staff of 2000 of whom 25 per cent had been serving at the war-fronts controlling the *ad hoc* classes set up for the soldiers.[57]

The government had set up fifty-seven war-front classes and by 1987 it claimed to have sent some 120 000 students and 4000 teachers to provide education at all levels; from basic literacy to advanced classes.[58] Soldiers with at least three months active service were allowed to attend 20 day-long residential courses at some of the universities near the front. As to the teachers, participation in the programme entitled them to a special priority quota scheme for university entrance examinations.

The *Jahad* was influential in helping teachers and returnees to obtain the much-coveted entrance examination places. In 1989 over 620 000 people applied to take part in the universities' entrance examinations. They included war returnees and children and relatives of martyrs who had a 60 per cent priority quota as well as people from deprived regions of the country who had their own special quota. But the quotas and the definitions of entitlement changed so often as to make the system extremely difficult to understand. In addition to *Jahad*, there were specialist consultants, who set themselves up, charging fees ranging from 600 to 5000 tumans, and tried to advise applicants which quota would give them the best chance of getting a place.[59] It is interesting to note that women, who were entitled to few places, still topped the marks in the entrance examinations. In 1989 women came first in physics and mathematics and second in humanities and arts.

Some effort was made to provide segregated tertiary education for women. In March 1991 the Fatemieh Faculty of Medicine was opened in Qom with an initial intake of 110 students. This women-only faculty was to work with an 800-bed hospital which was to be built in the city to serve the faculty and a new women-only college of nursing. But this was an exception: on the whole women were severely discriminated against. In a letter to the women's weekly, *Zaneh Rouz*, in 1990 two university students claimed that women were barred from ninety-seven academic areas, including agriculture, banking, accountancy, archaeology, veterinary sciences and 66 per cent of the engineering courses. In twenty-two other areas they are allowed a very restricted quota and overall they suffered from unfair discrimination in 119 subjects.[60]

The pressure of demand for university places and the conviction that it was possible to provide cheap simple *maktabi* teaching had contributed to the government's decision to back the alternative private Islamic university. Funded by fee-paying students, the Islamic university was committed to the *maktabi* approach and initially declared that it would admit students, aged from 12 years upwards, to do any course they chose. They planned to use any cheap location that they could find, including religious halls, *takiyeh*, generally used for sermons and performance of the traditional passion plays. It was to be totally self-funding and Rafsanjani proudly announced in 1989:

> This university has had a spectacular success without imposing the slightest financial burden on the government. It has filled a wide gap in the tertiary education system and has achieved high standards.[61]

The Islamic University estimated that it courses would cost about 33 per cent or even 16 per cent of other educational institutions, though it admitted that its student staff ratio was three to five times higher than the average of 32 student per staff at other places, with the exception of the Open University which had the highest ratio of all.[62] The *maktabi* nature of the university meant that its staff were almost all male; the only areas where it allowed women as well as men to apply for jobs were secretarial posts and those of librarian and laboratory assistants.

The problem for the religious institution was that the *ulema* were still debating whether or not, strictly speaking, women's voices should also be (metaphorically) covered by a veil? One of the leading theologians, Ayatollah Javadi Amoli, writing in the magazine, *Zaneh Rouz*, argued that an old woman, provided her hair was covered and she avoided eye contact with men, could perhaps be allowed to speak to a mixed group of students. But younger women, whose voices could sexually excite men, should avoid doing so.[63] So although silent, invisible, young women were permitted to attend courses, they were not to assume that they could also teach them!

In the event of the Islamic University had to revise its entrance requirement; it raised the age of entrance to 18 and set entrance examinations. But although there were many who wished to register, those who got in were dissatisfied. The newspapers were flooded with letters from students about the appalling student/ staff ratios and the high costs. Fees had been rising steadily over time, from 2500 tumans to 3000 tumans per term in 1989 and from 300 tumans per unit taught to 800 tumans in 1992.[64] A typical letter said:

> My husband ...managed to get a place at the Free University, but he did not know what he was letting himself in for. Studying at the Free University needs money at every turn... He is a school-teacher, but he has to pay all his salary to pay for three days' University fees... To pay for our livelihood, he has had to take on extra work and work to 2 o'clock most mornings. I cannot tell you the hardships that we have had to go through to get him this far.[65]

*Payameh Nour*, the Open University, was cheaper to register for, charging 2000 *tumans* fee per term, but it charged an additional 200 tumans per course and 350 *tumans* for each examination. The students could take five to ten courses each term, and could expect to complete their undergraduate degree in six to ten years. The national television refused to cooperate with the Open University, making it totally dependent on the radio and a very small skeleton core of 400 full-time staff who were supposed to teach some 60 000 students. The ratio was to worsen considerably with a planned recruitment of a further 200 staff to teach a projected 500 000 students.

The proliferation of courses and universities did little to improve the quality of tertiary education. By 1989 the Ministry of Education had come to the conclusion that the intended and unfunded increase in the numbers of students had 'not been thought through carefully'[66] and that the rate of increase in student intake had to be lowered from 15 per cent per year to 6 per cent. The old-established Universities continued querying the validity of degrees issued by the newcomers and insisted on emphasising the demarcations between universities and tertiary colleges. They insisted that even teachers' training colleges could no longer be called universities. They also questioned the ability of the Islamic University to teach the many subjects it claimed to teach. In particular the Faculties of Medicine refused to allow Islamic University's students access to their teaching hospitals – a measure endorsed by the Minister of Health and Medical Education, Dr Iraj Fazel, who announced that the government would no longer issue permits for setting up Medical Schools and demanded that the Islamic University build its own teaching hospitals. He also insisted that before graduation, the Islamic University's medical students had to sit qualifying examinations similar to those at the Faculties of Medicine elsewhere in the country.[67]

The imposition of high standards was confirmed in 1989 by the Minister of Education, Dr Mustafa Moin, who declared:

> We will deal firmly with the Islamic University to ensure that it maintains high standards of education. Only if and when the Islamic University achieves standards similar to that of the University system across the board, will this Ministry be willing to ratify their degrees. It is not that we wish to refuse

people access to a universal education, but it is our duty to ensure that University degrees are not devalued in the process.[68]

Nevertheless for the academic year 1992–3 the intake of medical schools rose to 15 000, of which 12 000 were admitted to the Free University,[69] and only 3000 to formal academic institutions. An estimated 100 000 students were by then studying medicine in the variety of faculties;[70] though inevitably most of them were destined not to pass Tehran University's standards or even gain access to practical training.

What the Islamic University lacked in terms of intellectual rigour, was to be compensated by excess of Islamic zeal. But shortages of trained personnel and waning of revolutionary fervour across the board made this difficult to achieve. The University staff were (and are) closely monitored by the students to prevent 'affront' to Islam. In October 1992 the Professor of Islamic History at Tabriz's Islamic University got the sack for joking about heaven and hell. Reporting the event, the daily paper, *Kayhan*, wrote:

> Dr Jaafar Pour... while discussing the Islamic wars stated that nowadays the infidels have invented such new technologies that they could cool the terrible heat of hell and transfer it to heaven and *vice versa* so that it would be those who'd gone to heaven who'd burn till eternity while the hell-dwellers enjoy the soft breeze of heaven... Following the disrespectful talks of the said professor some of the misguided students began to laugh, while the fervent Muslims felt slighted and very angry and protested... The Islamic Cultural Society and the disciplinary committee of the Free University reported the matter to Tehran and in a commendable move the central organisation sacked Dr Jaafar Pour for showing disrespect and affronting the Muslim community.[71]

A few months later *Kayhan* allowed this lecturer to exercise his legal right of response and on 2 February 1993 published his letter. He denied the accusation and pointed out that the only evidence provided to justify his dismissal was the *Kayhan* report. In the meantime graduates from the Free Islamic University were finding themselves heavily indebted and unable to find jobs. As one of them told *Zaneh Rouz*:

> The Islamic University's chiefs tell me that all government departments accept their degrees. But I have presented my BA from their university to several government organisations none of which are willing to accept the document as a valid certificate of completion of undergraduate studies. There are many people like myself who find themselves burdened with a heavy debt and unable to pay if off after years of studying, because no one accepts our qualifications.
>
> Is there no one there to tell these people that it would be better to raise their standards of education rather than opening new worthless Free Islamic universities in every street?[72]

Thus, despite the continued presence of the *Jahad*, the Islamification of universities had gradually come to an impasse. There was no way forward and no will to admit defeat; so the Islamic sector was allowed access to an inferior academic standard and denied the approval of academia. Once more the Islamists had miscalculated; the *maktabi* education, far from being free and open to all, had in practice proved expensive and useless – a failure that made the 'modern' Western-orientated old universities considerably more attractive than they had been before. The pre-revolutionary values had re-established their hold over education and the minds of the educated.

Yet, though the private sector's educational ventures had proved largely ineffective, both in terms of Islamic and educational success, the Plan Organisation remained intent on privatising universities. In the first five-year plan the Organisation proposed a gradual transfer to some of the educative and training responsibilities of the government to the private sector, to reduce the budget deficit. In December 1992 it proposed that all universities should be privatised,[73] and in January 1993 it suggested that students be provided with bank loans: 'The entire cost of education should be borne by each individual student'.[74] It also suggested that the state-funding of all research activities without an obvious practical use should be discontinued.[75]

The Plan Organisation's officials defended the policy by arguing that:

> The experience of Islamic and *Payameh Nour* universities had clearly demonstrated that Iranians were willing to purchase scientific and educational services, without imposing any charges on the national budget.[76]

Furthermore they announced that making students pay would give universities financial independence and enable them to spend their income as they wish. The Plan Organisation was of the view that, in addition to paying fees, students who failed in their exams should pay an additional 'levy', to discourage them from continuing, and to open the way for the more able students. So once more the revolutionary planners were aiming to reward the rich and bar the way to those without funds.

The Plan Organisation argued that publicly funded universities were too expensive and it was wasteful to spend public money to 'fund research for research's sake' and that research centres , 'like industrial and production units' should concentrate on profitable lines of enquiry.[77] Despite the continuing lip-service to the rhetorics of the revolution, the government's planning and financial sectors were already acting very much along Western monetarist lines.

## CENSORSHIP

For decades censorship had been part and parcel of intellectual life in Iran. Under the Shah all political criticism was banned and every newspaper had representatives of the secret service checking everything that was published. On occasion an article could well be cut halfway, if its conclusions were not deemed suitable.[78] Khomeini was part of the throng of opponents who condemned this process:

> It is illegal to curtail the media and information services... The media must be free to publish the whole truth about everything that is happening.[79]

But within months of his triumphant return, Khomeini had changed his views; the press had to be muzzled. The *volte face* on freedom of the press and liberty to write was anchored in Khomeini's fear of the press and intelligentsia – vociferous opponents who began condemning the Islamification measures early on. Khomeini could not abide criticism, since as the absolute theocrat, the *Faqih*, he considered himself supreme. No one was to question him. But he was all too aware that his people were not willing to follow submissively, as he had demanded. So he insisted on censorship to bar the way to alternative views and interpretations, to dim the 'lure' of immorality and above all to stifle political opposition:

> The media must mend their ways... They must not become traitors to Islam... they must not publish critical and harmful material... It is their duty to block anti-governmental plots, not to encourage trouble and strife.[80]

From the warning that the media could threaten the regime, to the decision that it must be prevented from doing so is but one step. By May 1979 the censors were returning to their old post with Khomeini's blessing. First he denounced the 'uncooperative' newspapers:

> A newspaper is involved in anti-governmental plots if it chooses to publish material that goes against the national interest or if it refuses to publish material which supports the government... [81]

Then he warned the press and set the Prosecutor-General on them to close down all those who refused to support the government:

> I advise newspaper editors to stop these false rumours and to stop telling lies just to get their sales up... they'd be wise not to make mountains of every molehill.[82] The Prosecutor-General must ensure that the press do not transgress; they must not undermine the national interest, and those who do so must be dealt with with the greatest severity... The media must align itself with the revolution... anyone who dares to write or publish anti-revolutionary materials deserves the severest punishment.[83]

Not only were most of the newspapers closed down, but those that remained open each had a 'representative of the *Imam*' who was entrusted with the task of ensuring the newspaper 'remained true to Islamic culture and its values and defended the revolution against the incursion of Western values'.[84] Such a premise made it easy to conclude that the pen and the intelligentsia that weilded it were the natural enemies of Islam:

We managed to overcome the bullets and the bayonets and now it is the pen that is working against us... Instead of the bayonets we have the nib and instead of bullets we have the articles by our adversaries. It is no longer the military and its arsenal, but the intellectuals and their pens who are holding us back, it is these people, who go on about liberty without ever understanding the true meaning of liberty, who are constraining our revolution.[85]

It was only if and when the 'wielders of pen' learned and understood about true Islam that they would be allowed to act freely. Otherwise 'national interest' demanded the maintenance of firm censorship:

They demanded that we allow freedom to publish, that we free the pen... but only those pens deserve to be free which serve our nation and are not in the service of the enemy poised to threaten our national interest. Only the pen and the publisher who is not actively seeking to pull down this revolution has the right to freedom of expression... This revolution has no room for the corrupting pen and corrupt ideas.[86] We will have to carry our desire for a free and independent country, with its free press to the grave unless or until these pitiless wielders of pen learn to use it to bar the way to harmful freedom and open the way to enlightening freedom.[87]

Censorship was codified by the 1985 Media Bill which listed ten major areas as out of bounds. In accordance with Islamic teachings which demand that Muslims do not slander or unjustly accuse any one, they banned the publication of anything that was in any way slanderous. But the Islamic Republic went further than the strict Islamic Scriptures and outlawed anything that could be construed as disrespectful to Islam, or to the religious leaders; or anything that amounted to speaking ill of the dead. The pre-revolutionary dead were clearly not included in this injunction, since it was customary for the press to allude to the members of the previous regime by all sorts of abusive names, whether they were dead or alive. In addition to a ban on publication of secret military materials and secret discussions of the *Majlis*, the press was instructed not to publish 'immoral' material and pictures, which meant that unveiled women were not to be shown at all. As a result heavy black lines were drawn across unveiled women in those Western magazines that were allowed in; so it was not unusual to find copies of *Times* magazine or the *Economist* with pictures of the unveiled heads of eminent women covered up, or whole pages pulled out!

Three years later, in August 1988, the High Council of Cultural Revolution *Shorayeh Aaliyeh Enqelab*, issued a further list of prohibitions. It reiterated the ban on the publication of any material that could be defined as anti-government or un-Islamic, or anything that denied religion or in any way supported irreligiosity or atheism; as well as any material that could be described as socially or politically divisive and likely to undermine the unity of the nation. In addition, any material supporting corrupt Western values, or hinting at any sort of superiority for the West, were also banned. Not surprisingly, anything advocating the views of guerrilla groups or the underground oppositional groups was strictly illegal, as was any attempt at ridiculing the government or undermining commitment to national goals. In addition anything that appeared to condone prostitution, in other words advocating sexual freedom or feminist activities, was also strictly banned. The High Council of Cultural Revolution appointed a committee of five persons to ensure that the media obeyed these rulings.

But despite all the insistence on censorship and the clamp-down on the media, the Islamic Republic has failed to impose its moralistic views on the mass of the population. A clear example of this was when an interviewer broadcasting live on Tehran radio asked an unsuspecting woman in the street about her ideal rôle model; it was the birthday of one of the Prophet's daughters and the expectation was that everyone would have her in mind. As it happened the interviewee mentioned the name of the heroine of a Japanese soap opera as her ideal rôle model and refused all prompts about changing her mind and choosing the Islamic saint.

Khomeini was irate. He wrote to the Head of Broadcasting, *Seda va Simayeh Enqelabeh Eslami*, Voice and Face of Islamic Republic, demanding that the reporter be hanged:

> It was with great sorrow that yesterday, 28 June 1989, I heard the Voice of Islamic Republic broadcast some material about female rôle models that I am ashamed to repeat. The person responsible for this must be castigated and most severely reprimanded. Should it be proven that the reporter was intent on dishonouring our religion then that reporter and all persons responsible for this transgression must be hanged. Should such a thing occur ever again then the entire top echelons of the broadcasting organisation will be apprehended and most severely punished.[88]

The episode had merely reinforced what Khomeini had always suspected; but for his vigilance and the government clamp-down the Iranian people would, like lambs to the slaughter, be led to their destruction by foreign influences. To ensure that such a thing would not occur ever again, Khomeini advised the *Shorayeh Baznegari*, Constitutional Revision Council, to appoint a seven-strong committee to supervise broadcasting; the committee with two representatives from each of the branches of Government, and one representative of the leader was to appoint a Controller. The Controller in turn was controlled by the committee who would ensure that there would be no transgression and that broadcasting remained answerable to the judiciary, the executive and the administrative branches of the government as well as to the leader.

Khomeini had come to the conclusion that censorship was there to stay. Even beyond the grave he maintained his strictures on this. His will and testament, which was intended to delineate the future path of the revolution, demanded that controls remain as firm as ever:

> My dying words to the *Majlis* and the Council of Guardians is to warn them never to permit the media, the news agencies and reporters, to waver from the revolutionary path and the defence of Islam... the Government must be unrelenting in its condemnation and punishment of anything that threatened

the public face of Islam... All such things must be firmly dealt with and eradicated... anyone who fails in this duty is responsible for the death and destruction of our revolution that would surely follow.[89]

Although there were severe restrictions on the media, the pro-revolution *bona fide* papers enjoyed a degree of freedom; they could publish complaints against minor officials and highlight failures of civic personalities and municipal civil servants whose room for manoeuvre was more restricted. In November 1989, there was a spate of controversy between the municipalities and *Kayhan* reporters. In the northern provinces of Khorassan, Torbateh Heidaryieh and Sarry, its reporters, were arrested and the kiosks selling the paper were closed down. The mayor of Shahre Kurd had arrested *Kayhan* reporter, Malek Mohamad Zamani, for the anti-revolutionary act of reporting the demands of the municipal workers for higher wages. The publishers were furious and *Kayhan* editorial poured out venomous criticisms of petty officialdom. A comment column asserted the paper's revolutionary credentials:

> We have a proud Populist tradition and our leader-writers and our managers come from the very core of the revolution and the masses and have always had the full support and absolute trust of our revolutionary people... But it appears that some of these supposedly responsible people hiding behind important titles of judiciary or municipal authorities are creating havoc and trying to gag our reporters... Some have handed down two-year prison sentences for our journalists, others have prescribed fifty lashes... These people are trying to stop the press from publishing their misdeeds. Such a behaviour is erroneous and could severely undermine public faith and support for the Islamic government... it will only create fear, and disbelief in the press and the government.[90]

The mayor had failed to realise that despite everything there was a particular concept of 'freedom of the press' operating in the country. The Minister of Guidance, *Hojatoleslam* Mohamad Khatami, had already defined it in 1986 when he declared:

> The media is free in the Islamic Republic and is willingly serving to educate and inform the Islamic society and facilitate its development.[91]

He then explained the particular sense of freedom that had become operative in the post-revolutionary state:

> People who talk of lack of freedom in this country have not understood the meaning of freedom. The press in this country is free to follow the general climate of popular opinion and to reflect the policies of the Islamic government.[92]

The press that Khatami had in mind consisted of the 183 official journals, newspapers and magazines that had been permitted to continue; these included children's and women's weekly, some statistical monthlies, with restricted distributions, as well as ten newspapers, mostly ardent Islam supporters and the two major dailies *Etelaat* and *Kayhan*.

After Khomeini's death there was some easing on imports of paper and printing materials and a slight relaxation of controls. This resulted in a rapid increase in the numbers of publications. Without the old *Faqih* at the helm, the Islamic government shed some its puritanism. Khatami proudly announced that the government had permitted a 47 per cent increase in the numbers of magazines and journals. As a result ninety-four new publications were launched between 1989 and 1991.[93] But the press was still firmly muzzled by the censorship regulations:

> Since the High Council of Revolution has stated the limits for publication of material and information, all publishers, who have secured the official permit to publish, must ensure that these legal limits are observed at all time. Otherwise their permits will be withdrawn and no one has the right to publish without an official permit.[94]

## LOVE, THE MEDIA AND THE COFFEE-DRINKING VIETCONGS

So long as Khomeini was alive, he insisted on the clamp-down on the media and control of publications and imposed a firm moral hold on the nation. But with his demise and the defeat in the war the grip of morality became less firm. In October 1991 the Minister of Guidance announced the removal of strict censorship on books. He declared that manuscripts were no longer to be submitted to the Ministry for inspection before publication, but he reiterated that any published material that went against the national interests, or the criteria set by the different laws on censorship, would be dealt with harshly and directly by the police and the judiciary – a view confirmed by the Director of the Department of Publication and Printing, Seyed Rasul Mussavi, who recalled the constitutional guarantees for a free press:

> According to article 21 of the constitution the press is free to publish every-thing, except that which goes against the interests of the nation or Islamic principles or is defined as impermissible by law.[95]

Hashemi Rafsanjani embarked on a path of gradual *rapprochement* with the West and the intellectuals began once more questioning, more or less openly, the government's oppressive rule.

Despite the warnings and the restrictions some of the journals began a tentative move towards analysing, rather than criticising, the achievements of the Islamic regime. Many of the erstwhile quietist magazines and some of the newer ones were also harking back to old-fashioned and pre-Khomeini concepts of freedom and democracy. *Salam* newspaper declared that:

> Human beings everywhere crave freedom. They want to be free of constraints imposed by duty and they wish to be allowed to think for themselves and speak openly and express their ideas.[96]

The literary weekly, *Adineh*, went even further quoting a statement by the Minister of Guidance to the effect that the Islamic government was prepared to listen to criticism, and 'welcomed freedom'. *Adineh* argued that the real aims of the revolution were to achieve freedom and the institution of a popular democracy:

> The aim of obtaining absolute freedom for the people had to be placed in abeyance during the war. Now that the war is over intellectuals and writers and the mass of the population have the right to demand that the revolutionary promises be fulfilled. Now it is time to close down the chapter on unquestioned rule and 'easy government' by the religious establishment and ask some hard questions about democracy and freedom.[97]

But the freedom-seekers and constitutionalists had to face the cacophony of Islamist protests by the pro-government press. Any questioning of policies of the government could be, and was, deemed anti-revolutionary. The criticism led to an open warfare between 'Islamic' and 'intellectual' publications. The revolutionarily correct *Kayhan* took up the *Imam's* cudgel against the libertines who were intentionally leading the Iranian youth astray. It published a massive condemnation of the quest for freedom, which in true Khomeini style it equated with moral laxity and foreign incursion into the country's 'pure' Islamic culture. *Kayhan* accused what it called 'the coffee-swigging Vietcongs', *Viet conghayeh cafe neshin*,[98] the revived pro-Western intellectuals, of denigrating Islam and its teachings. The newspaper blamed the Ministry of Guidance for being too trusting and too free and easy with its publication permits,[99] and went on to accuse Tehran's mayor and his newspaper, *Hamshahri*, of fuelling discontent.[100] The newspaper had dared to say that religious revolution aimed to resolve the tensions between three cultures; it sought to remove the contradictions between religion and modernity, modernity and arts and to create unity between the three cultures of Islam, humanity and nationality. *Hamshahri* had come to the conclusion that faith and religion were matters of personal and spiritual perspectives and could not and should not be imposed as a matter of government policy.[101]

*Kayhan* accused the intellectuals of unleashing pro-Western values and under the guise of journalism, philosophy, poetry and literature, of forming left-wing oppositional organisations. In particular it warned the government to be wary of the proposed Writers' Organisation, which, it assured its readers, was but a cover for the resurgence of the Marxists,[102] who were all set to 'awaken' and 'liberalise' 'our People':

> They have openly admitted this; they are giving interviews to the official organs of the Great Satan such as the *Voice of America*. These Marxists intellectuals, like Homa Nateq, the well-known opponent of our Islamic Republic, are sitting in the cafes on the Left Bank in Paris and using the Western media to tell us what to do. You get Ali Asqar Haj Seyed Javid who has the nerve to call on our authors and artists to continue their struggles towards enlightenment for our people.[103]

*Kayhan* poured scorn on these 'coffee-swigging layabouts' and accused the author, Abdollah Lahiji, of threatening the Republic by his statement that:

> Iran cannot go on systematically eliminating freedom and democracy and undermining human rights.[104]

But it was not only the exiled intelligentsia who were up in arms. Many were active in Iran itself and some revived the liberation Front, *Nehzateh Azadi*, and began publishing and broadcasting to the nation. Initially the government chose to disregard their activities. But the *hezbollahis* began mass protests and demonstrations. The revolutionary prosecutor, *Hojatoleslam* Rayissi, arrested fifteen members of the Liberation Front for engaging in anti-governmental activities and imprisoned eight of them.[105] They were accused of undermining public morality and faith in the revolution, of slandering the revolution and contravening the censorship laws. The Prosecutor-General condemned their activities as 'political', announcing that only those parties who had been given permission by the Ministry of interior to enter the political arena were entitled to do so. All other groups were, by definition, anti-revolutionary and illegal.[106]

In August 1991 a large mob gathered outside the offices of *Gardoun* magazine demanding that the Ministry of Guidance to exerts a closer supervision on these journals 'which are openly contesting our religious and national morality and values'. *Gardoun* had dared to welcome the relaxation of morality laws and the return of some of the Iranian intelligentsia.

As ever the laws of the streets prevailed. In July 1992 the long-standing Minister of Guidance, *Hojatoleslam* Mohamad Khatami, was again accused of encouraging laxity and he was finally forced to resign.[107]

Nevertheless, with the death of Khomeini there had been some relaxation of censorship and the Iranian leadership appeared to wish to project itself as liberal in the extreme. Khameneyi even declared that:

> No one could accuse the Islamic system of not granting complete freedom of the Press. You'd not find another country in the face of the earth where this many journals and newspapers are published and they write whatever they want... You'd not find a freer press anywhere in the world. Our system is oppressed by the freedom of the press.[108]

The only proviso, as far as the national leader was concerned, was that the Iranians barred the way to the 'cultural invasion' by the West. Should they fail to do so, or should they commit a crime, as defined by the law on publication, then they would be punished 'regardless of whom they may be'.

## FILMS

Film-makers, television programmes and even radio serials which portrayed dreams rather than realities, were assumed to be less threatening and were less constrained. They began by introducing unorthodox ideas such as love and freedom and even disillusionment with the war and the revolution into the public forum. The movie-makers were particularly daring. Mohsen Makhmalchian produced an award-winning film, *Nobateh Asheghi*, Time for Love, which showed, uncritically, a woman embarking on an extra-marital relationship. Massoud Kimyayi's famous film, *Gorouhban*, the Sergeant, depicted the terrible treatment that was handed out to war returnees – in this case a sergeant who could not get his land back. Makhmalchian's, *Arousyieh Khouban*, The Wedding of the Good People, one of the most popular films of 1991, was also about a war returnee, *basiji*, coming to terms with the many failures of the revolution. His *Shabhayeh Zayandeh Roud*, The Nights of Zayandeh Roud, transgressed on all counts. It showed the mother of a revolutionary soldier committing suicide and the soldier preferring to have an affair with a 'cheap' Western-style and not-totally-veiled woman. The theme of the disillusioned *basiji* was picked up again by Ebrahim Hatami Kia in his *Az Karkheh ta Rayin*. Once more the film was a powerful indictment of the failures of the state to honour its soldiers. Though highly acclaimed by *Adineh* and other art magazines, the film failed to get any awards at the 1993 film festival in Iran. *Kayhan* was quick to denounce the film as yet another example of failure of the cinema to mark the successes and glories of the war. The paper warned its readers about the new 'immoral' trend and noted that yet again the Ministry of Guidance and Culture was at fault; its cinema section had provided a $1million budget for the film.[109]

These 'immoral' films gave much cause for concern for the proponent of Islamic purity. Khomeini's daughter was furious. She complained that the media were portraying Muslim women as unattractive and applauding the behaviour of loose women:

> What we see on television and in the cinema is properly veiled actresses mis-behaving; they are portrayed as hussies, yelling and swearing and using foul language. But the badly veiled actresses speak with charm and poise and express poetic ideas. Instead of presenting the good Muslim women as rôle models, these films seem to praise the loose women. They seem to have for-gotten my dear father's saying that 'the television is a kind of university in its own right, and one that belongs to the majority of people'. They have forgotten that the majority support the revolution and the majority of women are veiled.[110]

This was a view echoed by an anonymous reader who complained about Mehdi Fakhimzadeh's film, *Shetabzadeh*, Precipitated,

> The only veiled woman in the film is projected as a hussy... it is not at all clear what her relationship with the boss is, whether she is his temporary wife or what?...Why is it that these films ridicule everything that is Islamic and at the same time by implication endorse all that is the symbol of cultural imperialism... Is it right that the veil, *chador*, which is the hallmark of pure Islam should be so publicly devalued... whenever they want to show an un-

educated impoverished person, they bring on a veiled woman, whereas all cultivated, intelligent people are wealthy and poorly veiled.[111]

It is worth noting that the journal's film critic, Mohsein Beigh Aqa, reviewing the film in the same issue said nothing at all about Islamic values or any disrespect to them.

Not surprisingly the media were unrepentant. In April 1992 the state-run national television ran a serial entitled *Taatilateh Norouzi*, New Year Holidays, about a factory owner who offered a flat, one of the scarcest resources of all in post-revolutionary Iran, as a reward for his best worker. Despite the presence of censorship committee, the series managed to show that the workers would go to any length to get their hands on the flat, even though this meant portraying them in the most un-Islamic light. Along the way, the serial ridiculed many of the traditional Islamic practices as being old-fashioned superstitions. Once more *Kayhan* newspaper was furious and its media critic was up in arms about the re-emergence of westoxification in Iran.

Undaunted some journalists and film-makers continued to struggle against repression. During the 1992 elections, *Salam* newspaper even demanded to know the candidate's political views, arguing that without expressing these views the election was going to be a 'pale shadow of democracy'. By implication it was contesting the *tohidi*, conformist, position of Khomeini who admitted no division amongst his supporters. *Salam* wanted to know whether the government was going to priorities Islam or republicanism?[112]

Eventually in April 1992 *Farad* magazine produced a caricature of Khomeini, thus breaking the most cardinal of the censorship rules. It showed him as a football player whose right arm was charred black and whose left arm was amputated. The caricature was about the fall of Islamification and the failure of the fundamentalist candidates from even getting their nomination accepted for the elections. Though a true picture of events, the disrespect shown to the *Imam* caused a rumpus. The militant clergy, *Basijeh Rohanioun*, demanded that the editor and the artist be hanged, several newspapers published condemnations of various kinds and the Ministry of Guidance immediately revoked *Farad*'s publication permit, invoking article 27 of the Media Law which declared disrespect to national and religious leaders to be a crime, but although the editor was imprisoned, he was not executed. *Farad*'s manager, Nasser Arabha, was the first journalist to be tried by a jury for a press violation. In September 1992 he was given a six-months jail sentence for insulting the religious leader, and 'acting against internal security'. The caricaturist, Karimzadeh, was tried by a revolutionary court and sentenced to one year in prison and 500 000 rials fine.

## WHENCE THE CULTURAL REVOLUTION?

Within a decade of its arrival the cultural revolution had had less impact than expected. The media were resisting some of the restrictions placed on them and the educational system was abandoning all faith and creaking under the ever-increasing demand. The war and the revolution had left the country much poorer and considerably less-well-educated. By the end of the decade nearly 40 per cent of the population was illiterate and despite government attempts at opening up the university system, only 0.5 per cent of the population gained access to any form of tertiary education.[113] The population was growing by leaps and bounds and the government had no resources to fund any kind of education for the ever-increasing number of pupils. Not surprisingly, on the basis that any teaching is better than none, the Islamic Republic chose to turn a blind eye to 'un-Islamic' activities of private schools. Many flaunted the segregation laws and, particularly in the case of girls' schools, employed qualified male teachers to teach mathematics and sciences. By the end of the decade, the revolution had not even radically changed the distribution of wealth. Only 10 per cent of the people owned 64 per cent of the wealth and enjoyed the privileges of private education and health-care services. They also had access to 'illegal' videos and 'immoral' films and music. Despite the teachings of Islam that proclaims the most virtuous to be the most noble, in Iran it was the most wealthy who were the most admired. It was this small upper-class minority who set the tone and adopted the 'immoral' Western values. All that Khomeini's son could do about this was to wring his hands and deplore the failure of the cultural revolution:

All these anti-religious films, videos and music, these un-Islamic ways of dressing and the these anti-Islamic books and magazines... they are leading our youths astray. If we are not careful the entire social culture will become anti-Islamic... Our unsuspecting youth is being lured away by the shiny tinsels of worldly materialism and self-centredness of careless living. The more we oppose these, the more they think it fashionable to adopt these ungodly ways. We have failed to produce anything like as attractive a material to woo our youths back. We are losing our Populist touch. With our dear leader dead, our new leaders no longer queue in the bus stops along with their people. The leadership is too busy amassing wealth and aping the West. We are in danger of losing our revolutions to Western values and ideas.[114]

# 9 Women and the Post-Revolutionary State

Women are amongst the most notable standard-bearers of the Islamic revolution and have continued to carry the burden of representing its public face to the world. Thus, though it is possible to argue that in terms of political impact the Islamic revolution has fallen far short of its own goals, the impact of the revolution on the lives of women in the country has been marked and catastrophic.

By 1979 Iranian women, after over 100 years of political struggle, had succeeded in obtaining improved legal, political and personal rights, and had gained access to much of the labour market. But since the revolution, in the name of Islam, they have been deprived of almost all those rights. With the exception of the right to vote, everything else has been lost. Yet the fact that women are allowed to vote indicates the government's confidence in their continuing support. This chapter will explore some of the reasons behind this conundrum.

Clearly many women across the country supported the revolution. They marched along with the men in the millions-strong demonstrations, the more radical ones fought shoulder to shoulder with men in the resistance groups and throughout the reign of the Islamic government many have remained faithful to the regime. Since women form half of the population of the country, and since it would be hard to argue that they have gained much by the revolution, it is important to look at the reasons they have offered for their opposition to the Pahlavis and their allegiance to the Islamic alternative. It is also important not to detract from what has been achieved for women, by women, through the post-revolutionary years, despite the Draconian laws enacted which gives them considerably less than half of men's legal rights and which circumvented their access to the public sector.

## ISLAM THE DREAM

The battle for freedom had enabled Iranian women to have equal access to education and the labour market in 1935, to the ballot box in 1962 and entitlement to child-care provisions in the work-place in 1974. They had also managed to reform the personal laws, to raise the age of marriage for girls to 18, to curtail the unilateral rights of men to divorce and polygamy and to make them subject to the decisions of family courts. By the late 1970s the road to freedom seemed paved with hope.

But at the same time Iranian women were faced with the problems that women the world over have to overcome. More opportunities did not free them of domestic labour and their duties as home-makers were merely added on to their employment obligations. For some wealthy women there was the option of employing domestic servants to carry much of this burden. With increasing employment opportunities across the board, in the 1970s Iran became one of the many Middle Eastern countries that resorted to importing cheap labour from South East Asia, for domestic employment. By 1975 the government passed the Domestic Labour Bill to protect home and immigrant workers.

But for the majority of women, waged employment was a necessary additional burden. Those working as cooks, cleaners or washer-women in the informal sector often had their wages negotiated and collected by their husbands, fathers or even sons. The 'moral economy of kin' could not be countered by legislation. For such women the Islamic promise, articulated repeatedly by Khomeini, that they were entitled to paid domesticity was a welcome prospect. To live at home and know that the male head of household had the Islamic obligation of paying for the household's needs was indeed a goal worth fighting for, particularly when the State and its constitution promised to shoulder the burden if necessary.

For the lower middle classes the rapid modernisation era had brought heightened aspirations and expectations, but the opportunities were not expanding as rapidly. For women the dilemma was one of conflicting values and traditions. Western-style compulsory schooling opened new possibilities. Many continued to secondary schools and trained as secretaries and clerks or worked as hairdressers, beauticians or shop assistants – almost all jobs that had dispensed with the veil and 'countered' traditional views of the feminine. Often these young women left their respectable homes downtown wearing a veil or a scarf, only to change halfway, removing the covers and emerging in the Western-style garments ready for work in the 'modern' sector. The clash of cultures was harder to negotiate in terms of the personal lives of these women. No longer suited to the arranged marriages of the traditionalists, they found it hard to break into the tight kinship networks of the upper classes who used marriages as a means of enhancing these connections. A return to Islam and traditional values offered an acceptable future of happy matrimony to the salaried, but unmarriageable, young women.

The female intelligentsia also was lured by Islam. Intellectuals were amongst the most ardent and articulate advocates of Islamification as a means of 'liberating' Iranian women from the trap of westoxification.

THE PROSPECT

Remarkable authors such as Zahra Rahnavard chose, in the 1970s, to change their mini-skirts for the veil. Rahnavard even changed her name from the modern 'Zohreh' to the Islamic 'Zahra' before launching into a thorough denunciation of Western-style feminism, capitalism and socialism. Using the Western feminist analysis and critique of the segmented labour market, Rahnavard argued that feminism had sought in vain to achieve equality for women. Furthermore she argued that in the helter-skelter pursuit of feminism, Western women have lost sight of their reproductive duties and have abandoned their honourable social positions as wives and mothers. As a direct result the young in the West are suffering from anomie, and alienation and the society has been destroyed by feminism.[1]

As to socialism, Rahnavard argued, the postulation of productive labour as the most important social factor had driven women out of their homes, packed their children into uncaring, unloving, nurseries, where they grow up disorientated and without any notion of morality. At the same time the unequal and unremitting burden of productive labour destroys women physically and mentally and makes them into 'old hags' long before their time. Too tired to be good workers and too exhausted to be good mothers and wives women failed on all counts in socialist societies.

According to Rahnavard, women did no better under capitalism. Discriminated against in the vertically and horizontally segregated labour market, women failed to succeed in the male-dominated work-places. The two roles allocated to women by capitalism were to be rapacious consumers, and to be sex objects, pointlessly straining to achieve the beauty myth. Capitalism placed women for ever on show, compelled them to buy their way to glamour, or draped their naked bodies around items that were proving too difficult to sell. The demands of the market-place reduced Western women and made them into mere painted dolls and sex objects.

This objectification of women's bodies created a universal standard of beauty, and a kind of sex appeal which was unattainable by most women. This in turn made women obsessed with their appearances and fuelled the ever-growing beauty industry. At the same time, the failure of women to become like the models paraded across the media, made most women insecure, undermined their self-respect and made them into ever-easier prey for the beauty trade.

The never-ending images of naked women also helped to enforce their objectification and make them vulnerable to ever-increasing cases of sexual assault. Rahnavard and many other Muslim women concluded that the West had failed women and feminism had merely exacerbated the plight of the sisterhood.[2]

Thus, women writers in Iran concluded, westoxification was severely detrimental to women the world over and the best solution for Iranian women was to return to Islam and the dignity that it bestowed on them. Rahnavard, Mahboubeh Rezayi and many more Iranian women joined the quest for the source, what the Westerners call fundamentalism and the Muslims see as the return to the glorious early days of Islam or revivalism. They pointed out that the first convert to Islam had been the prophet's wife, Khadija. A wealthy independent woman, considerably older than Mohamad, her erstwhile trade representative, Khadija had decided to marry the Prophet, and had protected him throughout her lifetime. Any religion that she espoused could not undermine women.

As a result Islam had not burdened women with the guilt of causing the downfall of man, as had Eve, or the downfall of humanity, as had Pandora. All women had to do was to return to the text of the *Quran*, accepted by all Muslims to be the actual words of God, and see for themselves. In the *Quran* it is Satan who is the source of all evil and not Eve (7:20, 7:22). Men's and women's devotions are valued for themselves, as are their transgressions; the wife of the Pharaoh is praised and the wife of Noah deprecated. Men and women are made of the same soul (4: 1), and soul is a feminine noun in Arabic. They are offered complementary parts in life. Men are made responsible for protecting women and securing their welfare. In return, on the basis of a marriage contract which pays women for their sexual services (4: 4, 4:24), women are to provide paid domestic care. A husband is in duty bound to maintain his wife in the style to which she has been accustomed (2:238, 4:34) and must pay her for suckling their babies (2:233). Nor is marriage a once and forever bind, it is a contract between consenting partners and could be terminated by divorce. Women could stipulate suitable terms to ensure that they did not lose out. Furthermore, for *Shias*, there is the institution of temporary marriages to accommodate momentary passions.[3] A return to Islamic values, the revivalists promised, would enable women to have an honoured role as wife and mother. They reminded the faithful that the Prophet had announced that heaven was at the feet of mothers. At the same time the Quranic demand that all Muslims, men and women, should be properly educated would, they said, keep open their access to knowledge and learning. They would be able to raise their children and then participate fully in the public sphere. Thus there was support for Islamification amongst a cross-section of women. The sceptics were mostly amongst the wealthy, 'westoxificated' upper classes, who remained committed to modernist views.

But Islamic protagonists such as Ali Shariati dismissed the women of the leisured classes as ignorant, corrupt and misguided:

The 'modern' woman is no more than the traditional woman dressed in fashionable garb... She has been freed of her traditional chains only to rush headlong toward corruption. Whereas the educated woman is freed... the modern woman is merely untramelled... the modern woman is the very same wealthy female who used to hide under the veil in the name of a religion that she did not study, now she is the unquestioning slave... of modernity, promiscuity and immorality; all attitudes prescribed for her by outsiders and adopted by her without consciousness or control.[4]

Thus, for different reasons, the poor uneducated women and the better-off and better-educated came to believe in the vision of a better life in the arms of Islamification and took to the streets to support the cause.[5]

## THE REALITIES

### The Laws and the Veil

The revolution has failed women, as it has failed all its supporters. But whereas in terms of politics, economics and social relations much of the pre-revolutionary practices have gradually percolated back, the official subordination of women has continued. This is because veiled women have become the symbols of the success of Islamification.

The subjugation of women has been paraded as the public endorsement and evidence of the continuing supremacy of Islamic law; laws that have no room for women. A month after his return to Iran, in March 1979, Khomeini sacked all female judges and ordered the compulsory veiling of all women. In May co-education was banned, in June married women were barred from attending school, and the government began to close down work-place nurseries. In July sea resorts were sexually segregated and women flogged in public for transgression of these rules. Morality codes were declared and for the first time women were executed on charges of prostitution and moral degradation.

By October the government was dismantling the checks placed on men by revising personal laws; men regained the right to polygamy, to unilateral divorce at will, and the right to prevent their wives from entering into paid employment. The official age of marriage for women was reduced from 18 to 13 and men regained the automatic custody of their children after divorce.

In July 1981, the *Majlis* ratified the Islamic *Qassas*, laws of retribution, demanding an eye for an eye and a life for a life. But these laws have made justice the prerogative of privileged wealthy men and have negated women's human rights to justice. Not only are two women's evidence equated with that of one man, as required by the *Quran* (2:82), but women's evidence, if uncorroborated by men, is not accepted by the courts. Women who insist on giving uncorroborated evidence are judged to be lying and subject to punishment for slander (article 92 of the *Qassas* laws).

Murder is punished by retribution; but the murderer can opt for the payment of *diyat*, blood money, to the descendants of the murdered, in lieu of punishment (Article 1 of *diyat* laws). Whereas killing a man is a capital offence, murdering a women is a lesser crime:

> Should a Muslim man wilfully murder a Muslim woman, he must be killed, *but* the murderer can be punished only after the woman's guardian has paid half of his *khounbaha* (blood money, or the sum that the man would be worth if he were to live a normal life; this is negotiated with and paid to the man's family) (article 5 of the *Qassas* laws).

By contrast, women murderers have no blood money and must be executed (article 6). Similarly violent attacks against women, resulting in maiming or severe injuries, can only be punished after payment of mutilation money to the male assailant before retribution can be administered. The reverse does not apply (article 60).

Men are now entitled to kill anyone who 'violates their harem', but women do not have such rights. Nor do they have the right of life and death over their children. But fathers who murder their children are 'excused' from punishment, provided they pay *diyat*, blood money, to the inheritors (article 16); however there is no specific blood money stipulated for children.

Of course women resisted both the imposition of the veil and the Draconian *Qassas* laws. They came out in mass demonstration on 8, 10 and 11 March 1979 and in October and November 1979. Over 20 000 women took to the streets, staged sit-ins, and rallies and protests. In July 1980 when the civil service imposed compulsory veiling on its female employees, again women took to the streets in protest, to no avail. The veil became and has remained the oppressive, public face of the Islamic Republic.

The imposition of the veil was very much the result of Khomeini's obsessive fear of women and their sexuality. He was convinced that women were the source of disorder and that their very presence in the public domain disempowered men and prevented them from functioning properly:

> In the name of providing gainful economic activity for half of the population of Iran [the women] that heartless ... man [Reza Shah] removed the veil. But instead of activating the female half of the population, he disempowered the other male half and halted their activities. By throwing these painted dolls into the streets and offices he managed to stop the ones who were working and to lure our youths towards corruption and moral turpitude.[6]

The official Muslim women's organisation, set up to support the regime of Islamification, presented the same idea in a more palatable way:

> The unveiling programme ... was a murderous and disgusting project... It was an inhuman plan ... to turn Muslim women into painted dolls ... all the books and the journals and the media colluded to corrupt women and erode the very foundations of the families.[7]

Since Islamification has failed in all other domains, the only obvious demonstration of its existence is the presence of veiled women on the streets. As the *Guardian* reporter Liz Thurgood has pointed out:

> Women are the barometers of Iranian politics. One look at how much ankle or calf is showing or how much hair can be seen beneath the veil and the colour of the headscarf tell a book about the regime's level of toleration.[8]

This view is shared, though expressed differently, by Shahla Habibi, President's advisor on women's issues:

> Women are the guarantors of culture and education in our country. The enemies of revolution seek to undermine us and rule us through the cultural subversion of our women. But our revolutionary women must retain their cultural identity [expressed by donning the veil][9] and must go to men for help. It would be a mistake to assume feminine self-reliance and superiority.[10]

This identity is one that is contested by many women. As early as July 1980 Azam Taleqani, daughter of the late Ayatollah Taleqani, and a member of the first *Majlis*, and Rahnavard and other Islamic activists including Shaheed Etezad Tabatabyi and Ansieh Mofid, contested what they saw as a one-sided interpretation of Islamic laws:

> Instead of tackling the root of the problem the over-zealous administrators have emphasised one side of the problem and forgotten about the other. They have concentrated on women's garments and insisted on imposing the veil on them. But they have forgotten that Islam demands that men too observe modest clothing and behaviour... Instead of imposing the veil on women, public decency – that is, modesty for all and absence of make-up – should be made compulsory for all.[11]

But it was the government and the *hezbollah*, who are more sensitive to women and the veil than to other political matters, who won the day. Time and again Iranian women chose to push back the veil, show a strand of hair here, a leg or an ankle there, and flaunt the imposed moralities of the regime. Every time there has been a severe reaction. In this the *hezbollahis* are even more ferocious than the government. In May 1982, for example, they took over the government-organised pro-morality protest marches. They demanded and obtained an assurance by the Public Prosecutor that taxis that allowed poorly veiled women to travel as passengers would be heavily fined and would lose their licences.

Ever since, whenever the government is suspected of failing in its duties towards Islam, women become the immediate target of attack. In July 1984, when pro-Islamic *maktabi* groups wished to demonstrate their allegiance to the God of Islam, they did so by protesting about falling moral standards, and by beating up women they considered to be poorly veiled and taking to the streets in disorganised rallies. Angry young men riding pillion on motor-bikes, yelling and shaking their fists, invaded the high streets of Tehran. Interviewed by the daily newspaper, *Kayhan*, one of them announced:

> After six years of revolution people are still indifferent to morality and women go about barely veiled. This is a clear indication of political failure.

The Department of Moral Guidance remonstrated with the rebels pointing out that true Islam conquered by reasoned discussion and through conviction rather than enforced imposition of moralities. But the men on the streets were not convinced; one of them told a *Kayhan* reporter:

> These Guidance men have no bottle! They are not up to the job. They are not really righteous. All they do is waste the large budget they have.[12]

The Department of Moral Guidance announced that such protests were illegal since they did not have the necessary, official, government permit. The demonstrators retaliated by saying that motor-bike parades were exempt from such ruling. So the *komiteh* guards ended up in the unusual situation of arresting some *hezbollahis*.

Nevertheless, as usual, the politics of the street had a marked impact on government policies. Not wishing to appear less moralistic than its followers, the government organised its own official anti-immorality demonstrations addressed by illuminaries such as *Majlis* representatives, Mrs Dabagh and Mrs Monireh Gorji. Within a week Tehran's Public Prosecutor announced that all public and private offices, institutions, companies, hotels, shops and utilities must bar the entry of poorly veiled women. Otherwise the owners or managers of such places would be prosecuted for flaunting the law. To ensure that women did not obtain immodest attires, in February 1985 the *komiteh* guards closed down 150 boutiques, for selling Western-style women's clothes.

But most years, as the summer approaches, women begin loosening their veil and the *hezbollahis* take to the street. There were three days of protests by bikers in April 1985 and in April 1987. Demonstrators attacked women and in some cases cut their hair off and threw acid in their faces. The Ministry of Interior declared the demonstration illegal and waited for the protests to subside. The *komiteh* publicly 'demanded' that women observe the full Islamic veil and the Minister of the Interior denounced 'international infiltrators' for leading Iranian women astray.

The effect was to legitimise the use of the anti-imperialist motto as an excuse for attacking women. A situation endorsed by Khameneyi who, as the leading religious light, in July 1992, commanded the *basijis*, the unemployed militia, to form a moral police and enforce Islamic values. What this did was to give them *carte blanche* to beat-up women; which they did. They joined force with the *hezbollahis*. As the daily paper, *Salam*, reported:

> A woman was attacked for being poorly veiled ... in Avenue Saadi in front of the shopkeepers and passers-by. The attack was so violent that she lost consciousness and had to be taken to hospital.[13]

It was not necessary to be unveiled for women to be beaten-up. A graphic example was reported in the weekly women's magazine, *Zaneh Rouz*.

> I was waiting for a taxi on Friday night at 7 p.m. when a bunch of bikers came by shouting and screaming ... Suddenly one of them came over to me and asked the bloke sitting pillion to beat me up, which he did. I was struck down and fell on the road... They were shouting 'death to the unveiled! Death to the poorly veiled!'... But I was fully veiled. I was wearing dark colours and was covered from head to foot ... The problem was that I was the only woman on the street and so they beat me up all the same.[14]

In May 1990 the revolutionary guards announced that they were going to

> check the hills and the mountains, the seaside and the parks, to stop cars with darkened window and make sure that no unveiled woman was ever seen in public.[15]

At the same time the more zealous *komiteh* men continued to administer the immediate penalty of 30 to 75 lashes to women they consider poorly veiled.[16]

Wealthier women can buy off this penalty by paying a 2000 tumans fine, a sum that amounts to the total monthly salary of lower echelon civil servants. But the poor have to suffer physically for any transgression. Government employees have the additional penalty of dismissal. It is estimated that over 100 000 women have been dismissed in the past twelve years for being poorly veiled.[17]

Women of course organise and protest. A rare glimpse was offered by the daily paper, *Kayhan*, in September 1991 when it published a heartfelt cry of protest from a young woman, Fatima Shafaq, who wished 'death to partriarchy'. 'Why are you so backward?' she asked:

> You must realise that no country can improve until and unless its women are treated like fully valued human beings and not like chattel forced to give up the veil one day, and forced to don it again another day. You should have been born a thousand years ago since your ideas fit that period and not this one.

She concluded defiantly 'I wish you death!'[18] Hers remains the only public protest to have been published by the staunchly Islamist paper, *Kayhan*, in Iran.[19]

Resistance to the veil found unexpected support from President Rafsanjani, when he was posturing as a liberal.[20] He called for less severity and announced that women did not need to wear the full veil, *chador*; an all-enveloping material shrouding women in dark colours. But his views were not reflected in the government directives that followed; it stipulated that female civil servants had to wear a veil and garments in black, navy blue and dark grey!

The brutal treatment meted out to women has disheartened even some of the most ardent supporters of Islamification. In a recent interview Zahra Rahnavard admitted to a feeling of desperation; she pointed out that these forms of brutality have undermined women's trust in the government and have turned women away from the veil and the commendable essence of Mohamadan Islam.

Many women have continued resisting the veil. Protests, sporadic riots, and spontaneous demonstrations against the veil have characterised the Iranian summers. But although sometimes the theocrats' counsel paternalist 'guidance', on the whole the regime is merciless. In December 1991 it arrested 300 women for 'rioting'. Nevertheless the resistance against the veil continues.

## Employment

The veil is a contested means of making women invisible and pointing out their exclusion from the public domain, but the task is not easy, given the vociferous opposition of Muslim women scholars who point out that the intention was neither to make women invisible nor to exclude them from the world.[21]

The government has retained an idealised view of women as silent, pliant and obedient home-based companions, or demure and dignified work-place under-lings. Even by the 1990s this vision had not changed. Gleefully the daily paper, *Kayhan*, translated an Algerian journalist's endorsement:

All Iranian women are veiled, calm and dignified... Since women's voices should not be heard speaking loudly, where men and women work together ... the women are serene and composed; you do not hear them laugh or shout ... this quietude is a form of social morality ... which protects women and allows them to be present everywhere [without distracting the men].[22]

But in terms of the stated ideology of the government women's quietism was more than a matter of modesty. It denoted the marked difference in their nature and the heavenly demands that they should be treated accordingly. *Hojatoleslam* Abdelmajid Moadikhah, the Minister of Guidance in 1992 pointed out the self-evident result:

Since Islam views men and women with two different perspectives, it accords specific roles to each and they develop in different ways.[23]

But Iranian women refuses to be follow such interpretations. Their protests have led to more sophisticated reiteration of the same arguments. For example, President Rafsanjani has had to alter the way he expressed his opinion. He began by asserting that women were not useful members of society:

Should the way be opened for women and they be driven to go beyond the limits of their natural talents ... the only result would be suffering and destruction for the women themselves and the society as a whole... You only have to look at Europe where an unbalanced world has been created. In the name of equality the industrial world has pushed human beings away from their own nature and natural gifts and talents. ... It has ensnared women in a miserable trap and led them away from the correct path. Their women have been deprived of the joy of healthy domesticity and family life and have been dragged to schools and work-places... Industrial society has placed a double burden on their shoulders. Some of their women have even been lured by immorality and have lost the deep and wonderful yearning of motherhood... This is why you find such extensive anomie and alienation amongst Westerners. They have become lifeless people who move but are unmoved by human love and familial passions.[24]

By the late 1980s his idyllic image of motherhood seemed to have receded and he was resorting to a different excuse. He saw women's subordination as being part of their destiny, arguing that the country's limited resources should not be squandered on them:

You do not have to have a legal requirement ... common sense tells you that ... if women study certain subjects then only a very small percentage would use their expertise to benefit society. Most women graduating at great expense and gaining great skills just become housewives and never serve the community ... this is what experience tells us and the law cannot change it ... In practice women graduates do not go and serve the society so the money spent on them is wasted; even when they do work they don't work well enough ... so the University should exercise their legal rights to train people who are going to be useful.[25]

It is interesting that inadvertently Rafsanjani indicates that in his view motherhood, that very bastion of women's strength and power, and matrimony and housework – the other domains that Muslims commend as havens for women – are not 'beneficial to society'.

Zahra Rahnavard argued energetically against such discrimination; naming no names she chose to denounce it on religious and political grounds:

> Our planners say 'we do not have the means to invest equally in men and women and must spend our limited resources on those who provide the highest return for our society. Therefore as women's natural obligations, in giving birth and raising their children, means that they work less, we cannot allocate too great a portion of our resources to them'. We respond that this is wrong since all Muslims are required to pursue knowledge regardless of their gender. It is of the essence, in terms of religious requirement and social well-being, that no barriers be put between women and their quest for knowledge.[26]

But, though she was married to the 1980s Prime Minister, Mir Hosein Mussavi, her views were not accepted. Women continued to be viewed parasitically; useless in the home and wasteful in the public domain. There were some theocrats who were not altogether of this view. People like *Hojatoleslam* Nateq Nuri, Minister of the Interior in 1985, supported the argument that it was un-Islamic to discriminate against women:

> Islam places no limitation whatever on the participation of women in the public, political and cultural domains.[27]

But they were a minority and in any case they were shifting the blame away from Islam; they had no objection to placing it on the nature of woman themselves. As Rafsanjani explained, it was 'natural' that women should engage:

> only in those gainful activities that were suited to them and permissible, namely in the health and education sectors.[28]

Accordingly the 1986 Budget introduced a clause blocking the funding for employment of women in any other sector.[29]

The head of the Public Sector's Personnel Office, Hushang Zamani, explained that efficiency and the national interest required such discrimination:

> If we do not pay attention to women's natural and physical and psychological characteristics when allocating jobs, then we fail to make good use of all our resources and fail managerially ... Men as managers should be aware that it is they who must shoulder the difficult and demanding responsibilities and take on the jobs that are complex and difficult. They should give women the sort of jobs that are best suited to their temperament.[30]

Women activists countered such opinions by going back to the historical roots; a favourite ploy for all revivalists who regard the rule of the Prophet as the Golden

Age of Islam. They argued that in the golden days of Islam during the reign of the Prophet women were very much in evidence in the public domain. They cited Mohamad's favourite wife, Ayesha, who even led a battle against the Shia *Imam*, Ali.[31]

The Iranian theocracy responded by defining the subordination of women in terms of progress:

> Women are half of our society and in our view they are complete human beings like the men ... Men and women are fully human and they complement each other ... Our society has a traditional division of labour and women naturally do the housework ... The days of the Prophet and the perfect rule of Islam were short-lived. It lasted only ten years and at the time society had not evolved to such a level and complexity ... Life was simple and the divisions between 'public' and 'private' minimal, so women had to take to the battlefields both as fighters and as nurses; of necessity they combined both roles and operated on both fronts ... But this is not to say that our women should become soldiers now. In our society the need for labour is smaller than the available pool of labour ... If and when we become fully operational then we would be silly not to use our womanpower ... but for the moment they are surplus to requirement ... When it comes to the presence of women in the public domain, where men are present, well, there are a number of niceties that must be followed. All that women need to do is not to be loose and immoral ... then we would have no women's problem.[32]

The situation is defined in terms of the unproblematised presence of men, it is women's duty not to invade this male space. Women, by their very nature are seen as unsuited to the public domain. This insistence on the supremacy of men in the work-place is echoed by the government-funded *Jamiyateh Zanaeh Jomhouriyeh Eslami*, Islamic Republic Women's Organisation:

> If women are not employed, it is not because they are women, but because the are less productive in that particular job. Nature and wisdom dictate that investors pay for the labour processes that bring the highest profit ... Sometimes that means that women are not employed.[33]

In reality the government is employing large numbers of women, not only because the segregated educational sector and rapidly growing population require more teachers, but also because many qualified men have long since left the country. So, of necessity, the qualified women who had stayed behind moved into their shoes. Interestingly, in the decade that followed the establishment of the theocracy in Iran, the only sector of female employment to grow was that of senior consultants and specialists.[34]

In fact there is no legal obstacle to female employment. As Azam Taleqani, founder-member of *Jame'yeh Zanaeh Enqelabeh Eslami*, the Women's Society of Islamic Revolution, explained:

> Article 28 of our constitution declares that anyone can choose any profession that they wish, provided they do not contravene Islam and public and social

interests. The government must provide equal opportunities for every one in every job according to social needs. The failure to implement this law properly has destroyed the trust of women in Islam and the government. When you ask a woman civil servant what do you think about Islam? The only answer is 'they have destroyed me! You only have to read the notices that are plastered all over the walls, you only have to see they way that they are treating me. They think of me as an easily exploitable being. They have reduced me to the level of beasts of burden; they have no respect for me, or what I do!' This is the heartfelt cry of working women and there is no one to hear them, they have destroyed the women workers, squeezed the working day, squeezed the very life out of them and destroyed their self-respect.[35]

This is a far cry from Rafsanjani's conclusions:

Without doubt nowhere in the world can women claim to have the benefits and honour that Iranian women have in their society ... Islam has delineated a balanced and rational path suited to the nature of women and the Islamic Republic is following that path.[36]

This view could not be shared by the wife of the previous Prime Minister, Zahra Rahnavard:

In our country there is a complex understanding about women ... which produces a culture of inequality ... this culture is very different and distant from the true Mohamadan Islam. Sadly, the result has been that although women had been active participants in the political process and are an integral part of this society at all levels, in the past decade they have not been able to participate fully in the economic and social reconstruction of our land.[37]

But there is a group of politically and economically active women who are determined to back the government all the way in its segregation and domestification policies. Soraya Maknoun, University Professor, head of the Research Group on Women and an influential member of High Council of Women's Social and Cultural Affairs, went so far as to denounce demands for equal opportunities as corruptive and pro-Western:

I am totally against the view that women's success depends on gaining access to equal opportunities in all sectors of the economy ... The truth is that our society does not have a women's problem and it is just pro-Western critics who have invented such a problem and imposed it on our lives.[38]

Not surprisingly the Employment Committee of the High Council of Women's Social and Cultural Affairs declared itself satisfied with the segregation of the labour market. It came to the conclusion that women were physically ill-suited to certain tasks. In a country where the staple food is rice – a grain which is almost entirely cultivated by women – Marzieh Mohamadianfar, Head of the High Council's employment committee demonstrated her blissful ignorance by announcing:

You see there are some activities which are based on physical strength and so are beyond women ... we cannot deny that men are physically stronger. So there are jobs like cultivation and agricultural work which women simply cannot do.[39]

Yet the reality was quite the opposite, as Azam Taleqani told the press:

Two thirds of women in this country live and work in the rural areas and carry a major burden of agricultural activity. Nevertheless we do not allow our women to study agricultural sciences at the University.[40]

But it was Mrs Mohamadianfar who had the ear of the government. She announced that the committee had come to the extraordinary conclusion that the existing rules and regulations did not discriminate against female employment:

Since the existing laws and regulations are not detrimental to the rights of working women we do not need to revise them. It is not the law that is deficient, it is its implementation ... It is the male employers who will not employ women. Of course women do cause their own problems. When they are giving birth or suckling their babies, they cannot work. That is why men prefer to employ men. So women graduates cannot hope to get the kinds of jobs that are offered to men and earn similar salaries even in the fields that are open to them to work in... We must also be aware that if we insist on welfare and special facilities for female employees, then the managers would simply refuse to employ women.[41]

With such friends in high places, Iranian women do not need any enemies! As a teacher told *Zaneh Rouz*:

Some of the women in positions of influence forget how they got there and in doing so not only do they fail all other women, but also they weaken the very fabric of our society.[42]

Despite the small increase in the numbers of employed female technocrats, the theocrats' 'rational' path has led to a dramatic fall in the overall levels of female employment (see Table 9.1). From 1976 to 1986 women's employment fell by 18.67 per cent. Whereas in 1976 women formed 14 per cent of the total labour force in Iran, by 1986 they formed only 9 per cent of the total.[43] Because of segregation of industrial jobs and elimination of women from certain sectors their industrial employment levels fell by 60 per cent.[44] In 1990 the level of active participation of Iranian women in the labour market ranked 108th in the International Labour Organisation's study of 110 countries. In Iran only 10 per cent of women in the relevant age group were deemed to be economically active.[45] An Iranian survey went even further, indicating that by 1991 95 per cent of females of 10 years or more had no visible means of income generation.[46]

The public sector provided 46 per cent of the total employment in the country, but only 12 per cent of its employees were women. Typically the women were considerably better educated than their male counterparts; only 6 per cent of male civil servants had tertiary qualifications, compared with 18 per cent of the females. But only 3 per cent of the women reached the higher echelons of the civil service.[47]

*Table* 9.1   Female employment

|  | *1976* | *1986* | *Percentage changes* |
|---|---|---|---|
| Experts | 187 856 | 346 111 | +84 |
| Managerial | 1348 | 1021 | −24 |
| Office Workers | 63 340 | 47 048 | −26 |
| Trade and saleswomen | 7659 | 10 097 | +31 |
| Service sector | 67 732 | 33 487 | −51 |
| Agriculture | 227 637 | 273 290 | +20 |
| Production and Transport | 640 560 | 226 197 | −65 |
| Others | 16 888 | 49 239 | +191 |

*Sources*: Based on data quoted by Nahid Yeganeh, *Nimeyeh Digar*, no. 12/13, Autumn/Winter, 1990/91; and *National Census of Population and Household*, Statistical Centre of Iran, 1976 and 1986.

As Table 9.1 clearly demonstrates, the government's policy of gender-segregation has marginalised women in public sector resulting in a dramatic fall in the number of women workers in offices, the service sectors and production and transport industries – this despite the Iran–Iraq war which had been raging and absorbing some of the male labour force at the fronts.

In 1987 the government extended the ban on new employment of women in all except the health sector,[48] a measure that was reflected in numerous government directives prohibiting female recruitment. A year later Hosein Ali Mussavi, Head of the Statistical Office and Human Resources Programme of the National Employment Bureau, indicated that the discrimination was to become a permanent feature of government policies:

> To create a balance between the domestic, social and employment duties of women we are planning to relocate women into jobs that are best suited to their physical and psychological needs and abilities... Accordingly posts in agriculture, engineering and technical sectors will be allocated to men and women will be moved from these sectors to the fields of health and education which have been deemed as suited to their nature.[49]

This view was expounded by the Ministry of Guidance and reported uncritically by the Ministry's female Cultural Under-secretary, Sabah Zangeneh:

> In recent years they have come to the conclusion that women can only be active as teachers or at most they should aspire to becoming nurses or maybe doctors.[50]

Thus, women, who form 32.3 per cent of the public-sector employees, can only work in the health and medical sectors. Their employment situation is indeed grim. In October 1989 *Zaneh Rouz* published a protest letter by a woman economist whose application to the Ministry of Petroleum was rejected because of the ban on female recruitment.[51] The situation was no better for factory workers; as a *Zaneh Rouz* report pointed out:

> When women are so devalued, they become not only the cheapest source of labour, but also dispensable. They are not educated, not trained, not valued; just used and sacked when they are too exhausted.[52]

The journal sited the case of factory workers at the *Etemadieh* textile factory in Bushehre. 70 per cent of the workers were young women and their average age was 13. The light was so poor that none of the photographs taken by the journalists had come out; there was no air conditioning, no first aid, no suitable facilities. A few weeks later *Zaneh Rouz* published an irate letter from the manager of *Etemadieh* textile declaring righteously that the factory did not employ any woman under the age of 12, and that he was doing them a favour by paying them a wage!

It is worth noting that, writing before the revolution, Zahra Rahnavard deplored communism for exploiting and destroying women in the same way:

> They exploit her labour in the fields and factories and offices so that in no time at all they turn her into an old hag, a broken woman who has nothing left... This is the disaster that has befallen the Russian women.[53]

Even by the lenient rod measures of its supporters, the revolution had clearly failed the Iranian women.

## The 1990s' Government Objectives on Female Employment

Yet direct discrimination was not only against the stated intentions of the post-revolutionary constitution, it was also eroding what little was left of women's support for the regime – a view repeatedly expressed by Zahra Rahnavard. By 1990 she had to admit that the government at least, if not the revolution had failed women:

> We have no strategy for including women in this country's destiny and in this respect we have fallen far short of our political aspiration[54]... In the five-year plan women are only mentioned once... despite all our protests we have

remained invisible. It is essential that women's role in the development process is clearly delineated.[55]

It was not only the government, but the bulk of the male population who had throttled the aspirations of pro-revolutionary Muslim women. Activists such as Rahnavard and Taleqani persevered and eventually found a foothold in the *Shorayeh A'aliyeh Engelabeh Farhangi*, the High Council of Cultural Revolution. There they managed to dilute some of the more Draconian measures and formulate an Islamic female employment policy. On 11 August 1992, 17 months after Zahra Rahnavard had joined the Council, it issued an official document, proposing a policy on female employment. Despite the President's directives to the Council 'to educate women about the correct ways of dealing with their husband and children',[56] the Council chose to educate the rulers about women's liberation. Its statement paid lip-service to the revolution:

Women in society who under the past regime had, in the name of freedom, suffered great oppression and lost many of their human and Islamic rights have had the opportunity to free themselves of the cheap Westoxificated voyeuristic societal gaze and find their real and pure Islamic status... Thus the Muslim Iranian woman is on the one hand faithfully fulfilling her pivotal social task in the familial context... and on the other hand according to need and availability of the right cultural conditions is active in the educational, social and economic domains.

The High Council accepted that women's first priority was to remain with the home and family.

*article 1*   Given the sanctity of motherhood and the importance of raising the next generation and home management... the material and spiritual value of women's role in the family must retain its paramount position.

The Council went on to note that not all women are mothers at all times. It requested that women's life-cycles be noted and 'suitable jobs' be provided. It excluded jobs like fire-fighting or even farming, as being too physically demanding. It also conceded that certain spheres, such as the entire legal domain, are unsuited to women. Dutifully the Council also accepted the theocracy's nature/nurture arguments, as annunciated by Ayatollah Guilani:

Given the nature and characteristics of women and the nature of law and its demands, undoubtedly being a male is the *sine qua non* for holding judicial posts... The requirement of virility, demanded unanimously of judges by the *Shia* theologians bars women's access to this post. This is the order of nature. It would be wrong to say that it denigrates women. On the contrary it elevates them and accords respect to them.[57]

But even the learned *ulema* were willing to allow some room for negotiation and they had agreed that:

Suitably qualified women who have attained the required levels of educational and legal training could be employed as advisors to family courts dealing with child care and protection of minors.[58]

Now the main problem is that women are no longer admitted to law schools. Even those who qualified before the revolution have to face the prejudices of dignitaries such as the Head of the Judiciary, Ayatollah Mohamad Yazdi, who simply cannot conceive of women as being suited to the law:

Women do not have the patience to follow all the complex arguments that are placed before the courts. I know, I have been there and seen the judges at work, it simply is not a task suited to women.[59]

Ayatollah Guilani is of the same view:

This job and what it demands does not suit women's tender hearts and gentle nature. ... It also detracts from their serenity and tarnishes their innocence and purity. Sitting in Courts and hearing all these squabbles demeans the exalted position of women and may even make them doubt the sanctity of marriage and the value and warmth of marital relationship and familial responsibilities. It would diminish them in every sense.[60]

The Council does not question these assertions, it simply attempts to carve out an acceptable space for female employment:

Employment which is desirable for women such as midwifery and similar medical posts as well as teaching (Article 5A).

Employment which best suits the nature and temperament of women such as laboratory work, electronic engineering, pharmacology, welfare work and translation work (Article 5B).

Employment where there is no superiority for men or women in performing the work such as simple workers in service and technical industries. In such cases experience and qualifications, rather than gender must be the determining factor for selection of the work-force (Article 5C).

Where the Council's resolution is of interest is in its demand that the familial duties of women be formally recognised. Hence the policy demands that in addition to equal pay for equal work, in the segment of the labour market allocated to women, the government should also allow women paid time off to enable them to fulfil their 'mothering obligations'. It states that they should be entitled to shorter working hours and an earlier retirement age – measures which would recognise women's double burden of unpaid domestic work and paid employment.

It is worth noting that in 1985 the government had passed a bill to facilitate half-time working for mothers of young children. Since the law required full-rate contributions towards their pension funds, and the State made no tax allowance for part-time workers, only 1 per cent of the female civil servants chose this option. Most women simply could not afford to give up half of their salary.

If, as the Council has suggested, the recognition of 'mothering duties' results in some flexibility in working hours, without cutbacks in pay, then women workers would indeed fare much better. At the moment, despite all the lip-service paid to complementarity in marriage and women's special qualities, Iranian women workers have to work as a 'manpower' in an inflexibly male labour market. For example, work and schools start at the same time, as do nurseries. There are few work-place nurseries and so most women have to travel considerable distances during rush hours depositing and collecting their children. As a result they are usually late for work. Most factories have two fortnight-long holidays, one for the Persian New Year in late March and one during the summer. The factories close for that period. Women are not allowed to use their paid holiday leave in small portions to deal with a sick child or do their 'mothering' duties; all such obligations have to be shouldered as unpaid leave. Furthermore anyone who accumulates more than four months unpaid leave in any working year can be sacked, even from tenured posts.

The High Council's declaration further states that working women should also have job security, unemployment benefits and welfare provisions (article 10). In addition women who are heads of household should be entitled to special retraining programmes to enable them to return to the labour market (article 11) and the government is urged to provide cooperative-type organisations to facilitate home working for women who wish to combine their paid and unpaid jobs (article 12).

Since only certain kinds of employment are deemed suited to women, so the Council advises women to pursue appropriate forms of education and urges the government to:

> Extend the proper choice and facilitate training and education in areas which will lead to suitable employment prospects for women (article 7 note 1).

Yet legally (a domain thought unsuited to women!) women are entitled to equal rights of access to the labour market in Iran and they had been promised a less discriminatory future at the inception of the revolution. In fact article 43 of the Constitution undertakes to provide employment opportunities for all and states that full employment is a fundamental aim of the revolution. Thus, even after the revolution, the Constitution, Labour Laws and the State Employment Laws make no distinction between men and women. Of course, in practice women do not benefit from equal pay for equal work provisions. Married women pay higher taxes on their incomes than do married men; and women pay higher child-insurance premiums than do men. It is the men who benefit from the married man's entitlement whereas it is usually women who end up paying for nursery care of their children. Men get larger bonuses, because it is assumed that they are the head of household, and they are entitled to cheap goods from the civil service cooperatives; their share increases with the numbers of their children. Not so for women, who do not even get a share for themselves.[61]

Besides the formal barriers, there are also the current practices which discriminate against women, as a reader told *Zaneh Rouz*:

> I am a university graduate working in a Ministry of Commerce's department in the north of Iran. I am employed on a temporary contract and paid on a daily basis... Recently they increased our male colleague's wages to 150 tumans per day, but the women's' wages were held at the previous level of 109 tumans per day on the pretext that women are not responsible for the household expenditure... As I am employed by the day, if I protest they'll sack me... yet I am the person who is wholly responsible for our household's expenditure, can you suggest a way out for me?[62]

*Zaneh Rouz* had no answer. In fact as a pro-woman journal it has had a stormy relation with the government itself: it has been accused of immorality, divisiveness and unrevolutionary attitudes; closed down, and reinstituted time and again. In January 1990 *Zaneh Rouz* had to defend itself against the accusation that it was creating a divisive mood in the nation by talking about women and seeing them as separate entities from men and the family. In a remarkable editorial it stated:

> It is not we who are creating a social cleavage, parting women from our society. It is the traditions and the history of exploitation and discriminatory practices of patriarchy that has long since separated women from society. She has been told that she has no intelligence and not even the physiological capacity in the brain to aspire to intelligence. She has been reduced to a mere reproductive tool. In some lands she is used merely as a sex object to further the interest of advertisers; in others she is instructed to hide herself and not even be seen by the fish in the pond. Used by men, she is discarded at their whim without entitlement to what she has produced in a life of shared domesticity, not material goods, not emotional ties and not even the very children that come from her womb. In our country it is meaningless to talk about integration of women into society.[63]

In the first decade after the revolution, women lost much ground, and most of their illusions about the Islamic government. As to their status in society, a clear illustration was provided by a series of interviews carried out for *Zaneh Rouz*. The interviewer, Forouq Kushsaz, asked a cross-section of men 'have you ever wanted to be a woman?' The universal response was 'Not to be man? How could you ever think of such a terrible fate, let alone choosing it?'[64]

## Women in Public and Politics

Not surprisingly, although they fought shoulder-to-shoulder with men, women were not given high office by the revolutionary government. It has never appointed a woman to a Ministerial post – a point made by Zahra Rahnavard when she complained:

Women have been and continue to be present, at times in larger numbers than men, in our public demonstrations, for the revolution and in its support. But when it comes to public appointments, they are pushed aside.[65]

Women like myself have continuously campaigned for better conditions. We have made our demands in the *Majlis*, in the press and in the public domain. But no one has taken any notice and our voices are not heard.[66]

What is remarkable is that despite constant pressures to confine women to 'suitable' social arenas, they have never been totally absent from 'unsuitable' domains, be they employment, education or politics. Throughout there has been a symbolic presence of women in *Majlis*, though for the first decade there were only three or four women representatives. But in the 1992 elections for the first time since the revolution, nine women were elected to the *Majlis*. Though few in number some, like Maryam Behrouzi and Azam Taleqani, who was not re-elected, have continuously campaigned for the cause of women.

But getting elected is only the first step, women members of *Majlis* are severely constrained by the ideological views that designate them as inferior, demand that they be modest, silent and invisible,[67] and define them as interlopers in the public domain. Maryam Behrouzi, a veteran representatives who had served a prison sentence before the revolution and whose 16-year-old son was 'martyred', still found herself firmly discriminated against in *Majlis*. She pointed out that women are never elected to high-powered committees. Nor did they become chair or officers of other parliamentary committees.[68] Azam Taleqani, the redoubtable daughter of Ayatollah Taleqani, gained a seat in the first post-revolutionary *Majlis*, but, she explained, women were expected to be 'naturally modest' and this prevented them from 'saying too much in the *Majlis*'.[69]

Sadly the few women who have gained high positions within the government structure, belong to the 'naturally modest' category.[70] A clear example is Shahla Habibi who, in 1991, was appointed to the newly created post of Presidential advisor on women's affair. Typically her previous post had been with the national Islamic propaganda organisation, *Sazemaneh Tabliqat*. The extent of her modesty was such that she would not even speak to the pro-government daily paper, *Kayhan*. The paper protested that Habibi was modest at home and brazen abroad, and that she was more willing to talk to the foreign media than to tell the national newspapers about her aims and ambitions.[71] In the event these proved to be rather modest. In an interview with *Kayhan* in January 1992, this pro-Islamic newspaper proved more woman-centred than the Presidential advisor. *Kayhan* asked about Mrs Habibi's priorities, demanded what she was going to do about the paucity of opportunities for women and the fact that there were so few women members of *Majlis* and that there were no women in the cabinet? Mrs Habibi declared that the women representatives were doing a splendid job, and that she was going to think about her priorities, in the meantime she asked *Kayhan* to remind the public about Khomeini's statement that women's place was in the home and that:

Women, whatever qualifications they may have or however learned they may be, must remain the pivotal core of the family and play their parts as exemplary housewives.[72]

In this she was fully supported by *Jamiyateh Zanaeh Jomhouriyeh Eslami* (the government-sponsored Women's Organisation). In December 1990 it had already declared:

As the *Imam* has repeatedly said good men are raised in the laps of good women. If we follow this example then we find our true station in life and recognise that motherhood is a sacred and holy duty of women.[73]

Once more it was Azam Taleqani who defended the cause of women:

Unfortunately after the revolution ... the government and the *Majlis* and even the religious institutions have not paid enough attention to women as full human beings. All their efforts has been concentrated on making women stay at home, at all costs; to make them accept self-sacrifice, oppression and to be submissive. Even if they go to court to get their due, I am not saying that the courts are totally patriarchal; but unfortunately there are these tendencies. So the problem is presented in a way that does not illuminate the truth.[74]

It was not Shahla Habibi who would help to shed any helpful light in these matters, quite the contrary. In April 1991 Maryam Behrouzi demanded that bills allowing an earlier retirement age for women, reform of some of the more Draconian divorce laws,[75] and provision of national insurance for women and children be put before the next session of the *Majlis*. Behrouzi also asked for the laws to be reformed to allow single women to travel abroad to continue their studies – a request that has not been endorsed by Habibi; she is of the view that such an act would devalue Iranian women and knock them off their perch of purity:

Since women are the public face of our society and the guardians of our honour, we must not intentionally dispatch them to a corrupt environment (i.e. the West).[76]

Behrouzi succeeded in pushing through a bill which allowed women to retire after 20 years of active service, while the men still had to serve 25 years. Her success was in part achieved because it permitted women to return to their proper sphere, that of domesticity, all the sooner.

For those who were actively campaigning for women, this bill was a remarkable success, since the path of women's liberation has been less than smooth. In 1991 *Shorayeh Farhangi va Ejtemayieh Zanan'* (the Women's Cultural–Social Council) appointed by the High Council of Cultural Revolution to coordinate government policies on women, submitted thirteen projects to the High Council of Cultural Revolution; but only one of these was considered and ratified by the Council. It was a proposal to eliminate the prejudicial treatment of women in higher education and in the selection for degree courses. This was no mean feat since there were discriminatory measures against women in 119 academic subject areas.[77]

Meantime, in February 1992, Shahla Habibi completed her lengthy deliberations and declared that her first priority was 'to present the best Islamic garments for women'.[78]

It was in quangos and organisations outside the direct control of the government that women activists were most successful in struggling for better economic and political opportunities. Although in the public domain success depended on espousing an Islamic stance, Islam itself is sufficiently flexible to allow a diversity of interpretation and much leeway for women. Azam Taleqani, for example, set up the *Jamiyateh Zananeh Enqelabeh Eslami'* Muslim Women's Society; a non-governmental activist group, whose members have included Zahra Rahnavard, Monireh Gorgi' a woman representative in the Assembly of Experts, and *Majlis* representative, Gohar Dastqeib.

Within the civil service it was women in the lower echelons of the governmental organisations who really fought for the cause. By 1992 the Minister of Interior had been prevailed upon to set up women's affairs committees to serve the social councils in all the provinces. Women working on these committees were much clearer about their aims than Mrs Habibi ever could be. Jaleh Shahrian Afshar, a member of Western Azarbaijan's women's committee, explained that first and foremost they wished to be independent, to have better opportunities and facilities and to embark on a wide-ranging family-planning programme.[79] They had taken their demands directly to *Majlis*. But the only one of their suggestions to meet with approval was the family planning one.

## Marriage and Motherhood

In the end it is the contradictory nature of the Islamic government's demands on women which will help the cause of liberation. For over a decade Iranian women have been encouraged to return to the home and hearth and become good mothers. As early as April 1982 a national-government-funded seminar on women in the Islamic perspective had come to the conclusion that:

> Although it is legitimate for women to seek to fulfil their duty towards society; those who are good Muslims would value their holy domestic obligations over and above all else. We advise our sisters to accord the highest priority to their family, and to raising their children as a matter of devotional duties. Only then, should they have any spare time left, and should they find the opportunity to do so, should they serve society by providing for its welfare.[80]

Marriage was advocated as the sole destiny of women. As men began dying in the war and it was feared that the percentage of women in the population might exceed that of men, the theocracy began advocating the delights of temporary marriages. Difficult as it was, many women did follow these directives, some by choice and most of necessity, since there were not many other options open to them. The unavoidable result was a massive population explosion. Even a decade of war and its millions of dead warriors did not break the pattern. Yet in November 1985 Hashemi Rafsanjani was blithely dismissing the problem. He confidently declared:

> We must remove the false paradigms and facilitate marriage. We view marriage as a natural right of all our citizens. We do not accept Malthus's theory. Basically we do not accept the hypothesis of population explosion and similar pessimistic forecasts.[81]

As far as Rafsanjani was concerned it was the duty of all men to marry and 'protect' the female population. He lamented the fact that one in every seven woman in the 20 to 50 years age group was single. 'What can we do with these women?' asked the *Hojatoleslam*. He provided the solution:

> First we must encourage everyone to marry... It is unfair for women not be married and we wish to undo this injustice. There is an Islamic solution which could ease this situation.[82]

Rafsanjani did not need to state that his solution was polygamy. He had made the same point eloquently in October of the same year:

> We have thousands of widows who need husbands and thousands of men who need a wife. We must not allow old traditions, which are not Islamic in any case, to prevent their marriage... We should not make marriage so difficult as to encourage our youths to hanker after corruptive Western-style sexual freedom.[83]

Women such as Azam Taleqani vigorously contested his views:

> There are 500 000 fewer women than men in our country ... Yet we are told that we must accept that our husbands have the right to remarry. I even went to some of our religious leaders and asked them whether they were backing the family or planning to destroy it? Since it is obvious that the moment a second wife steps in, effectively the first wife is discarded and her life is ruined ... But they are forcing women in this country to accept polygamy, if they do not then they are told that they have to quit and divorce the husband ... How can you have such a policy and still claim that women are respected and valued? What is there left for such a woman? How can she become a good mother and raise a healthy family?[84]

But it was Refsanjani's advice which appears to have been followed. By 1987 the Statistical Centre of Tehran was indicating that 96 per cent of the urban women of child-bearing age were married and only 1 per cent had never married. The non-literate women married at around 16 and literate ones at $17\frac{1}{2}$. But only 7 per cent of married women used any form of family planning. The average age for the first birth was 19, but it increased to 21 for women with secondary education. On average, mothers had four live births – rather more than their stated desired average which was two in urban areas, and three in rural areas. Interestingly over half of the women questioned did not mind whether they had a son or a daughter; 14 per cent actually preferred to have a daughter and only 31 per cent had a marked preference for a son.[85]

Thus by 1990 the Iranian population reached 59.5 million and was growing at an average annual rate of 3.9 per cent.[86] Yet though there was some disquiet, the devout were not panicking. Nevertheless both the high birth rates and temporary marriages came under new scrutiny.

The daily newspaper, *Kayhan*, warned that the country had only 12 million hectares of cultivable land which would feed 30 million people at the most.[87] But the *Majlis* deputy, Mrs Dastqeib, was unperturbed:

> If we had not had 50 million people in our country we would not have been able to oppose the ungodly. ... The enemy would have run us over in no time and we would have had no defences.[88]

It may be worth nothing that Iraq's population was 15 million and they won the war, but Mrs Dastqeib was not going to worry about minor factual details. She announced:

> The previous regime used to say 'fewer children a better life'. We do not say this... As the late Ayatollah Mottahari had repeatedly stated this 1 647 000 square kilometres of land in our country could feed 150 million people ... you only have to look around. There are lots of empty spaces in Sistan and Baluchistan [Eastern provinces bordering on the central desert].[89]

But already in 1988 the Islamic government had introduced a bill for population control and a year later a five-year programme was announced to curb the explosion.

By 1990 Ayatollah Yusef Saneyi was advocating birth control. He told the population control seminar in Isfahan that he had come to the conclusion that:

> None of the wise and learned people has ever said that it is good and desirable to have lots of children.[90]

His preferred solution was 'to tie up women's tubes and untie them whenever its necessary'! Even on the question of polygamy, the learned Ayatollah advised caution:

> Who says there are no barriers to polygamy in Islam? You should study Islamic law and then see whether you can make such a claim. The only thing that some men know about the *Quran* is the right to polygamy.[91]

The population crisis posed a severe dilemma for the Islamic government. It has long since outlawed the pre-revolutionary abortion law and dismantled the family planning clinics. Suddenly it found itself with families averaging five or more children and no clear policy for halting the momentum. In July 1991 the government decreed that for a fourth birth, working women were not entitled to their 3-months' paid maternity leave, nor could a fourth child be allowed any rations or a ration card. Any family that chose to have a fourth child would have to share out its resources and spread it more thinly, with no help from the state. At the same time the Minister of Health, Dr Reza Malekzadeh suggested to husbands that they should choose to have a vasectomy. A year later the courts decided to reconsider the abortion laws:

> It remains absolutely illegal to have an abortion or to carry out an abortion. Article 91 of the Criminal code imposes the death penalty, according to the Islamic *qassas* laws, for anyone murdering an unborn child 'if that child possess a soul'. But 'before the soul enters the body of a being' if a doctor is of the opinion that it is dangerous to continue with the pregnancy and issues a certificate to that effect; then the pregnancy can be terminated.[92]

At the same time the newspapers published the list of fifty hospitals in the country offering free vasectomy and female sterilisation.

By 1993 the Ministry of Health had its own population control bureau, with a 20 billion rials budget that was 300 per cent higher than that of the previous year. Assisted by an additional $30 million loan from the World Bank the Bureau it was about to launch a massive population control campaign offering free services at national, provincial and rural levels. The aim was to reduce population growth to 2.7 per cent annum.[93]

Suddenly marriage and motherhood have ceased to be alluring prospects for women; *Zaneh Rouz* even published a study indicating that later marriages were less likely to end in divorce and women with higher levels of education were likely to make better wives and mothers.[94]

In a remarkable move, women representatives also managed to change divorce laws to make it more expensive for men to leave their wives at will. The Islamic government had restored the male prerogative to easy divorce. Although by using the marriage contract, many Iranian women had resisted the move,[95] nevertheless on divorce they were not entitled to any of their husband's property. But in 1993, as a direct result of having a larger number of women representatives, the *Majlis* passed a bill demanding that men who 'unjustly' divorce their wives should pay 'wages' for the wife's domestic work during their marriage. The Council of Guardian refused its permission for the bill to become law, but *Majmayeh Tashkhisseh Maslleha*,[96] the Council for Arbitration, ratified the bill. The measure was hailed by women and the press as a great step forward.

Although the revolution has cost women dear in terms of social, political and economic advantages, Iranian women have continued their fight for liberation. Even within the establishment, although there are conservative women backing the government's line, there are numerous women, at all levels, actively resisting the iniquitous measures that have been imposed on them. Slowly but steadily they are gaining ground. They have managed to reverse the discriminatory policies on education, they are vociferously attacking the inequalities in the labour market and demanding better care and welfare provisions for working mothers. Although the road to liberty is one that is strewn with difficulties, Iranian women, as ever, have come out fighting and have proved indomitable, even by the current theocracy.

# 10 Islam for the People and Mammon for the Economy

Although in the early years of the revolution there was much discussion about what an Islamic economy would be like, theoretically and practically from its earliest days it was the conventional Western-style economists of the Plan Organisation who continued to dictate budgetary policies. While the intention of providing welfare for the people and protection of the poor and destitute was part of the daily propaganda handed out to the masses, the economists were advising cutbacks on government expenditure and attempting, more or less, to shadow the adjustment policies advocated by the major Western lending organisations. Social security, national health insurance and unemployment benefits were much discussed but slow in coming or altogether absent. The avoidance of welfare benefits helped the government to pay off more or less all of its foreign debts within the first five years of its inception. Despite the raging war and extensive under-development of the economy as a whole, the revolutionary government coped without substantial new loans until the 1990s.

The value of government's expenditure on social services and public goods was halved in the first decade of post-revolutionary government and has continued its downward spiral. The gap between the rich and poor, which had stopped widening for a brief period of growth, returned to its pre-revolutionary level by 1983. Yet even in 1991 the national leader, Ayatollah Khameneyi, was still mouthing promises for the poor:

> The most important obligation undertaken by this system is to remove deprivation and poverty and to protect the needy. This must form the most important priority in our policies and its success should be a measure for evaluating everything that we do.[1]

The eight years of war and the state's constant demands for soldiers and martyrs, combined with the marginalisation of women from the public domain and the withdrawal of family planning services, boosted the population growth in Iran and sent it spiralling up. The population increased from 33 million people in 1976 to 50 million in 1986, and has continued going up at over 4 per cent a year in the 1990s. At the same time many of the same factors halted the development process and eroded the existing health, education, and social services. The official rate of urban unemployment rose from 7.1 per cent in 1976 to 14.1 per cent in 1986.[2] The rapidly increasing population added 400 000 people each year to the rank of the unemployed. Yet, despite the profusion of commands, there was no official government sector that was responsible for either job creation or protection of the unemployed. By the end of the decade the Minister of Labour,

Seyed Hosein Kamali, announced his intention to 'monitor' the situation and said that he expected the Ministries of Economy and Industries to create jobs.[3]

But these Ministries could not deliver. For the decade that followed the revolution the Gross Domestic Product (GDP) continued to fall by an estimated annual average of 1.3 per cent and for the first five years the industrial production component of the GDP fell by about 7.2 per cent per annum.[4] The early nationalisation spree had placed some 14 per cent of the major industrial units under public control without producing a proportionate benefit. From the 1980s the war industries were the only growing industrial sector in the country. After the war the government decided to re-deploy 50 per cent of these industries for civilian use.[5] Attempts at enforcement of price controls, to curb inflation, meant that most manufacturing industries were unable to make any profits and most operated at less than half capacity.

In 1993 Dr Mohamad Hosein Adeli, the Director of the Central Bank, claimed that the recession was over and the Gross National Product (GNP) was going to grow to 6 per cent per annum.[6] But inflation showed no sign of retreat. It had climbed from its pre-revolutionary rate of 9.9 per cent per annum to 23.5 per cent in 1980, 19.1 per cent in 1982 and after dipping into single figures, 6.5 per cent in 1985, continued its upward trend to 28.9 per cent in 1988 [7] (see Table 10.1) and 21.6 per cent in 1992.[8] By 1993 most shops in middle-class districts had invested in money-counting machines, since the numbers of notes changing hands were far too great to be counted by the shop assistants. At the same time there was no evidence of any measurable income redistribution towards the

*Table* 10.1   Inflation rates and distribution of income, 1978–89

| Year | Inflation rate (%) | Income share of the poorest 10% of population | Income share of the richest 10% of population |
|------|------|------|------|
| 1978 | 9.9  | –    | –     |
| 1979 | 11.2 | 1.5  | 35    |
| 1980 | 23.5 | –    | 36    |
| 1981 | 23   | 1.29 | –     |
| 1982 | 19.1 | 1.15 | 31.6  |
| 1983 | 14.7 | 1.25 | 32.33 |
| 1984 | 10.2 | 1.30 | 22.9  |
| 1985 | 6.5  | –    | –     |
| 1986 | 23.6 | 1.15 | 34.25 |
| 1987 | 27.8 | 1.43 | 33.13 |
| 1988 | 28.9 | 1.45 | 32.18 |
| 1989 | 17.4 |      |       |

*Source*:   Based on *Mahnameyeh Baressihayeh Bazargani* (Monthly Trade Reports) no. 3, Summer 1991.

poorest section of the society. They obtained 1.5 per cent of the total national income in 1979 and 1.45 per cent in 1988 (see Table 10.1)

The government policies did little to alleviate the situation. Public sector salaries were held firmly down to prevent a wage-led inflationary spiral. But shortages, the war economy and clumsy exchange policies fuelled ever-greater demand for imported goods. To appease the destitute, who had formed its main constituent, the Islamic government subsidised imports of basic food and issued food and fuel rations. Although it was not always able to honour these rations, they formed the main lifeline for the poorest section of the society throughout the 1980s.

## FOOD SUBSIDIES AND RATIONING

Agriculture remains the largest single employer in Iran, and the government accorded one of its highest economic priorities to the rural sector. For example, the 1989 budget, despite having a 50 per cent deficit, still allocated 20 billion rials to the Agricultural Bank for provision of low-interest loan to cultivators. But the pre-revolutionary problems of low productivity and low returns, particularly on staple products, have proved difficult to surmount. On the whole, production in this sector has fallen steeply and what limited growth there has been, has taken place in the production of industrial crops such as sugar, cotton and tobacco and market gardens to the detriment of food grains.[9] As a result the government has been obliged to continue importing ever-larger amounts of food and it is estimated that some $2billion or more are spent annually to maintain the very austere rations allocated to feed people.[10]

At the same time the conscription of young able-bodied men from the rural areas has had a negative impact on the production of ploughlands and has contributed to the deterioration of food supplies. By 1983 the price of wheat was increasing twice as fast as that of other consumer prices and had increased by 500 per cent over the previous decade.[11]

In response the government has had a stated price policy, but a rather lax attitude towards black-market transactions, which were occasionally interrupted by short bouts of severity. In 1987, for example, Khomeini announced that the government was going to punish speculators and hoarders and would maintain its firm control on prices of essential goods. Some 12 000 civil servants were drafted to enforce this decree, to no effect.

The more consistent measure has been the issuing of rations, to enable households with low incomes and workers and civil servants to purchase basic goods at subsidised prices. There were a number of ways of obtaining rations. Initially mosques, work-places and influential religious leaders, distributed these rations. But eventually *Sazemaneh Taamineh Ejtemayi*, the Welfare organisation, and the *Setadeh Basij*, the Mobilisation Headquarters, were charged with the distribution of rations. The Welfare Organisation taxed all public-sector employees, and used these deductions to buy basic goods in bulk; these were then distributed at subsidised prices. The basij had its own share during the war, but its remit has been eroded since the ceasefire. By 1991 the Ministry of Trade had 106 organisations and economic units dealing with rations; these included thirteen centres of production and distribution.[12]

The government regularly announced that it had committed substantial sums of 15 000 billion rials or more to fund the subsidies but the results seemed meagre: 700gms of meat or chicken per head per three months; 450gms of ghee, 1200gms of sugar and a couple of kilos of rice and lentils a month. Officially, employers had been required by the government to contribute a cost-of-living levy to the workers' cooperatives, which in turn were supposed to provide subsidised goods for their members. In return workers were to have ration cards enabling them to prick up their share, free of charge. But delivery was always a problem. Far too often the cooperatives did not have the foodstuff, or if they had, it was of an extremely inferior quality. A letter to *Kayhan* illustrates the problem:

> From the beginning of the year till now – that is, for more than 8 months – the welfare organisation has deducted a percentage from the low wages of the workers and heads of households. This sum is extracted, without the possibility of opting out, from the bare subsistence wages that we are paid. These are extracted in the name of workers' rations, *bon*, but we have seen no sign of any sort of provision. Bearing in mind the numbers of workers and the fact that up to now each worker has had 54 000 rials deducted, God alone knows when we'll see any sign of the provisions. Besides if, and when, they ever get to the distribution centres we have to spend months and wear out iron boots to locate the place and catch sight of these provisions.[13]

A diarist for *Kayhan* summed up the situation in April 1990:

> First day of my yearly holidays I queued for meat, to no avail. The second day I spent queuing for medicated elastoplast, without any success. The third day was spent in the vain attempt to post a parcel abroad; you can only do this at the central post office, it is 10 kilometres from were I live and I got there too late, the queue was too long and the post office's time too short. The fourth day was spent in pursuit of a chicken; it is only possible to catch sight of one if you are prepared to pay double the price, and hand over your ration; even then I got there too late to qualify. The fifth day marked my failure to purchase a pencil for the children to take to school and the sixth day was marred by my arriving too late to get hold of the potatoes that the office was dishing out as the worker's share![14]

Frequently distribution of rationed goods stopped altogether. In January 1988 the Secretary to the *Basij* Headquarters, explained that the reason for the four-months stoppage of distribution of proteins was:

> We've stopped to enable people whose children were born after January 1979 to register their children's birth, to be able to get their ration cards.[15]

The government shop, *Qodse*, which had been singled out by critics for being always free of any subsidised consumer goods, protested to *Kayhan* reporters:

The production units in this country have failed to abide by their revolutionary duty to respect the government's distribution chains. They have chosen to deal with other free-market outlets and have allocated very small portions of their products to *Qodse*... Nor for that matter do the government's own production and distribution units respect the law, they choose not to deal with us, and keep this outlet empty, we cannot distribute that which we do not have.[16]

In fact many people have never been able to afford to buy goods even at the subsidised government prices and so they traded the ration cards. The ration-card black-market provided an informal job for the vendors and a (less than reliable) source of supply for the buyers. These were usually women employed as domestic servants or lower middle-class women who spent large parts of the day looking for supplies to feed the family. Although there was a five-years' prison sentence for illegal sale of rations, a combination of corruption and need kept the market going. As one black-marketeer explained:

Everyone thinks that trading in rations is a lucrative business. But it is not. In the past three months the officials pinched 7000 tumans from me without any receipts or anything. Now they deny ever having seen the money... If I do not do this who will support my wife and family? I asked the officials and they said 'I don't know, go thieving or smuggling or something!'[17]

Even for those people who managed to get hold of the rare subsidised products, the problems were not over:

A few days ago we got hold of 2 kilograms of chick peas as our workers' rations' share; for this I am grateful. It provided my household with some amusement and much work. We had to spend hours cleaning the chick peas. Eventually we extracted 250 grams of mud, stones and pebbles and useless material and left the rest of the cleaning for a rainy day.
My question is: how much am I really paying for these chick peas? Are the workers being charged the government subsidised rate or the free market rate? Basically the 200 tumans that I have had to pay one way or another is, it seems to me, worth a lot more than the load of rubbish that I got given.[18]

As for more mundane materials such as spare parts, the government was faced with even more critical blockages. The post-war economy, shortages and rations and the bureaucracy, halted distribution at every point. A consumer, Hamid Rabiyi Kangavari, told *Kayhan*:

I waited for 18 months for spare parts for my car to arrive. When they did, I had to have a formal list requesting the parts from my local mechanic. He duly produced the list. The cooperative's supervisor signed it, the regional headquarters stamped it and I had to take it to the regional trade Department, to be stamped yet again. Then I had to go to Tehran to the Trade Ministry's spare-part distribution point; not an easy task, since the Ministry refused to tell me where this department was situated. So I went from pillar to post and, finally, at the third attempt, located the Department. But then I was given the choice of purchasing a whole lot of items that the official in the Department had lobbed together, or nothing at all. So I was compelled to buy, not only the part that I needed, but also other items, that the department had decided I should have, whether I needed it or not.[19]

By 1991 the government decided to remove subsidies on 900 of the 960 items that it controlled and stipulate an official 'fair price' for trading these goods. The result was pandemonium, not least because official prices were openly flaunted and scarcities became even more serious. A consumer explained:

You should say to this government: OK Mister, when you announce that the free-market price of chickens will be 95 tumans, you should have the power to provide chicken at 95 tumans a kilo in the market... But what do we get in practice? You've announced your price and all over the town in the streets, on the side of the roads the chicken-sellers have put up notices as big as your head saying that they are selling it at 180 tumans a kilo.[20]

The relaxation of controls led to a rapid rise in food prices, 51 per cent for rice, 65 per cent for potatoes and 111 per cent for pulses. For most average-income-earners covering the cost of feeding the household became a major concern. As for pensioners, the dilemma had no solution:

If I cook just 1 kilogram of rice per day for our family of six it would cost me 100 tumans a day; that's just to buy the rice... Just to eat this rice, raw without using fuel, ghee or anything else I would have to pay 3000 tumans each month... Now add the 5000 tumans that I have to pay to rent the couple of rooms we live in and you've got 8000. But even when I was paid a full salary it was not this much. How much do you suppose a retired civil servants gets these days? I get 5000 tumans. So you just tell me how we are supposed to survive? What are we suppose to wear? How are we to keep warm? And who would pay the doctors's fee when we are sick?[21]

But the government has shown little concern for pensioners.


## MIGRATION, PRICES, INFLATION AND HEALTH AND HOUSING

The inflation and shortages have been exacerbated by the continuing influx of migrant to the cities. The failure to enact and implement land reforms, and the call-up of most of the able-bodied rural males over the first revolutionary decade, have contributed to the wave of migration from country to town, running at an average annual rate of about 5.4 per cent. That is an additional 1.2 million city-dwellers each year. By 1987 the proportion of urban dwellers rose to 54 per cent of the total population.

Medical care, as well as housing, is in critically short supply. Some cities, such as Ahvaz, have had to shoulder the additional burden of war migrants: at first refugees from Khoramshahre who had lost their houses during the initial invasion. Later, when Khoramshahre was recaptured more refugees went fleeing the larger cities which had been targeted for missile attacks. As a result its population increased by 300 per cent between 1980 and 1984 and continued to grow throughout the war. Meanwhile the provision of health care and services there remained almost static. The region has only 598 hospital beds and in some of the surrounding towns, such as Haftgel, the entire medical teams is foreign, many of the staff without a working knowledge of Persian.

At the same time food, goods, services, housing and health have all become more and more expensive and less and less accessible. By 1988 *Kayhan* was reporting that:

> Ordinary, low and middle-income urban-dwellers have long since had to abandon the thought of buying even secondhand electrical goods... Car prices have risen by 40 per cent in the past two weeks. Peykan (Iranian-assembled) was half a million tumans and is now 750 000 tumans. [The same car was worth 300 000 in 1984.]... Baby's powdered milk costs 200 tumans per box and normal delivery of baby in hospital costs 10 000 tumans.[22]

By 1993 the same Peykan, produced in Iran, was priced at 1.2 million tumans. Given that the average monthly salaries were 12 000 tumans per month, a Peykan was worth eight years' salaries.[23]

Shortages of infrastructural facilities in the provinces have made Tehran the most desirable city to live in. Tehran's population doubled in the decade, 1976–86, to 8 million and it has continued to increase. There is a low ratio of medical experts to population: nation-wide it is estimated to be about one physician for every 2500 people and one dentist for every 17 500 people. One third of medical experts live and practise in Tehran, with another third in regional centres and only one third in the more remote areas. The rural areas get less than 2 per cent of the total medical practitioners in the country.[24]

Absence of rural health care results in a continuing exodus towards the capital. As a harassed medical officer explained:

> We get patients from all over. Often cases that even a trainee specialist could deal with in the provinces, but there aren't any and so they bring them to the capital... Last night there was a patient with a burst appendicitis, he'd been to fifteen hospitals before arriving here and none admitted him. The only one that had even one empty bed was the Royal hospital and they'd asked for a down payment of 20 000 tumans, which the patient didn't have. We finally had to operate on him and put him in a bed in the corridor.[25]

There have been numerous campaigns conducted abroad to bring back the self-exiled physicians to Iran. But although a few did come back in the early days, about 300 in 1983 for example, pay and conditions were so appalling that most left again. As a physician told the press, in August 1984:

The salaries paid by the University's medical school are less than those earned by a mini-van driver. The salary of 2500 tumans per month barely pays the mortgage, but then who can afford to buy meat at 120 tumans per kg and ghee at 150 tumans per kg, let alone houses costing 25 000 tumans per square metre [floor space] and Peykan [Iranian-assembled car] at 300 000 tumans? Even so many of us are expected to wait years before getting a tenured post and we are prosecuted if we open private surgeries.[26]

So even Tehran, which has 35 per cent of all the country's hospitals and 16 per cent of its total population, suffers from critical shortages of beds, and medical care. Ordinary people find it almost impossible to get emergency admission to hospitals. Even access to medical expertise requires patience and perseverance:

I got here at 10 p.m. and have been given the fiftieth appointment for tomorrow. The man at the top of the queue was here at 2 p.m..[27]

There are also severe shortages of medicine and trained pharmacists and once more the provinces bear the brunt:

I went all over Kerman for this medicine with no success, so I had to come to Tehran... You should ask these people in charge why one has to travel 1100 kilometres to find one item of medicine for a heart patient?[28]

Similarly, Mohsein Taqvayi, from Arak complained:

I have had to come to Tehran several times. This time I waited five days to get the medicine. Now I am in trouble, because I am only entitled to four days' leave and heaven knows what will happen when I get back.[29]

Even in Tehran there is no guarantee of success:

I have been to fourteen pharmacies so far with no success... On the open market each of my tablets cost five tumans... As to the government pharmacies, you cannot even get in the queue because it is so long.[30]

During the war, the government was able to blame the shortages on the 'imposed war', *jangeh-tahmili*, the shortfall in foreign exchange and absence of home production for many of the medicines. Some government officials blame the doctors. Dr Marandi of the Health, Hygiene Treatment and Medical Training Headquarters announced:

Our doctors tend to overprescribe and people end up taking far too much medication. In fact most illnesses are cured without any medication and all medicines have harmful side-effects.[31]

It was the cumbersome bureaucracy and the profusion of commands which caused many of the problems. Six different government agencies have been in charge of distribution of medicines and policy coordination is non-existent.

Nor has the state been able to provide adequate water, gas or oil for urban dwellers; the electricity system regularly cuts off in Tehran; so much so that the press now carry daily timetables of electricity cuts. Petrol and paraffin queues often erupt into fights and disputes. It took nearly fourteen years to get gas pipes to the more prosperous northern district of Tehran. As early as 1983 the Water authorities in Tehran were warning the government that they could not meet the demands of the 6 million inhabitants and had no resources to cope with the increasing population.[32]

As for housing, immediately after the revolution, the government instituted a Revolutionary Housing Fund to house the homeless, with a five-year prerogative to override the Islamic sanctity of ownership rights. Within two years the organisation claimed to have distributed 125 000 plots of land. These measures in turn encouraged more out-migration from rural areas. A further 90 million square metres were distributed in the five years that followed the Urban Land Act of 1981. It is worth noting that the Urban land Organisation in charge of implementing the Act actually acquired 600 million square metres of land during this period.[33]

But housing shortages remain acute. By 1987 it was estimated that over 7 million urban housing units had to be built within a five-year period just to maintain the existing situation.[34] Shortages have led to a rocketing of rents, and the unrealistic rents, in turn, pressurise most people towards buying houses. In terms of proportion of average salaries rents increased from 60 per cent to 70 per cent in the first years of the revolution, and to 150 per cent to 200 per cent in subsequent years. Between 1974 and 1984 rents went up by 350 per cent.[35] As for purchase costs, by 1993 a single-bedroom flat in Tehran was priced at 3–4 million tumans, when average monthly income was at about 12 000 tumans for highly paid professionals. Nevertheless, by the end of the 1980s, 76.5 per cent of the total available housing stock was occupied by owner-occupiers, and only 4.2 per cent by tenants.[36] In Tehran some 700 000 families were tenants. The working class has done particularly badly. According to Ali Reza Mahjoub, the General Secretary of *Khaneyeh Kargar*, Worker's Centre, by 1991 49 per cent of the working population did not have adequate housing and 300 000 workers had no housing at all. 40 per cent of these were in Tehran.[37]

The government has made several attempts at providing subsidised housing. For example, *Bankeh Refaheh Kargary* Workers' Welfare Bank claimed that, in 1989, it had allocated 8 million rials for housing for university employees and a further 16.5 million rials for other workers. But the bulk of the Bank's resources had been spent on prestigious administrative buildings, such as an opulent headquarters in Shahroud which absorbed some 1500 million rials, leaving little for ordinary households.[38]

## FOREIGN EXCHANGE AND ADJUSTMENT POLICIES

The revolutionary government began by pretending to move towards some sort of Islamification of the economy. In practice this involved the nationalisation of those industries whose owners had fled, or been persecuted because they seemed to run a lucrative business. By 1986 14 per cent of the largest industrial units were under some form of public management. There was also much talk of nationalisation of trade. But the government more or less abandoned the implementation of its nationalisation of trade for fear of incurring the wrath of some of its staunchest allies, the *bazaar* merchants. The government's need to placate its various supporters, and the different factions within the burcaucracy, merely led to a profusion of commands, with several organisations in charge of trade and industry. In 1981, for example, the Ministry of Mines and Industries was disbanded, to be replaced by three new ministries each dealing separately with mines and natural resources, light industry, and heavy industries. At the same time the government managed to introduce eleven different official foreign exchange rates, as well as allowing a thriving black market in foreign exchange to operate. Even then, the state was not able to enforce its own regulations. The merchants, for example, generally refused to accept the unrealistic exchange rate set by the government for taxing their profits, and simply bribed their way out of the web of red tape.

Over the first decade of revolutionary government in Iran the economy gradually disintegrated; the nationalised sectors failed to make any gains and, with the exception of the war industries, internal production and productivity declined. By 1989 GDP had fallen by 10 per cent,[39] industrial production had gone down by an average annual rate of 7 per cent,[40] and the rate of capital investment reduced from 31 per cent of GDP to 10.9 per cent.[41] This was hardly surprising since, with inflation running at over 25 per cent and return on investments averaging at only 6 per cent,[42] the only successful investment was likely to be in trade, retailing and services. Money was made by deals. A product could be sold several times over in a day with each middle-man taking a cut on the way.[43] In fact many professionals used their office as a convenient place for making deals rather than treating patients, or seeing clients. This in turn fuelled further inflation and liquidity. Between 1974 and 1990 the liquidity levels had increased twenty-three times. By 1990 the Central Bank's claim on public sector had reached 87 per cent of the total asset. By 1988 the service industries accounted for 50 per cent of the GDP. At the same time foreign exchange earning had fallen from $25 billion rials to $7 billion.[44] The burgeoning bureaucracies, and revolutionary organs in the pay of the state, did nothing to help matters. They did not even manage to control production and distribution of consumer goods or price levels, which had been among the major aims of the war period. The government had resorted to printing money and was then faced with an ever-accelerating increase in money supply and liquidity.

Eventually, the chaotic economic situation, the uncontrolled inflation and rising unemployment led Rafsanjani towards the West. While it was deploring the corrupting effect of Westerners and their immorality, the government invited an IMF mission to visit Tehran in 1990 and informally agreed to follow a broadly based macroeconomic adjustment policy, cutting back the government's role and giving priority to the private sector. The public was warned that with the war ending the state was reducing its economic and welfare activities:

> The war had obliged our government to extend the bureaucracy and this has had a negative impact on the economy. Our first duty is to reduce this bureaucracy and reduce the people's expectations of the state and the government.[45]

This signalled the reversal of the 1989 decision to intervene and hold the rial. That had resulted in an overnight fall of 23 per cent in the price of the US dollar and an unrealistic lowering of import prices. Combined with relaxation of trade regulation, the measure had led to an influx of imports and a balance-of-trade crisis; the industrial sector could not compete. President Rafsanjani denounced the rampaging demand in Iran:

> In the country we are suffering from an excessive rate of consumption. In Iran we have not yet realised the need for equilibrium between supply and demand and this has created a serious problem for our economy.[46]

From 1991 the budgets were formulated with the stated intention of coming to grips with the balance-of-payment deficit, of absorbing the liquidity rate and reducing government indebtness. A three-tiered exchange rate was introduced. The official rate of exchange for the US dollar was supposed to be 70 rials, unchanged since 1979. In practice the government allowed favoured groups to buy the US dollar at 135 rials, the rate for consumer-goods imports was fixed at 350 rials and for exporters at 650 rials. At the time the unofficial open market rate was 1045 to 1500 rials per US dollar for individuals and the unofficial rate charged by banks to exporters was 975 rials.[47] But only 11 per cent of the total transactions in dollars were at the open market rates.[48]

It is worth noting that far from allowing supply and demand to meet at equilibrium levels, the government had been benefiting from rigging foreign exchange prices. From 1989 onward sale of foreign exchange at an inflated rate by the Central Bank made an important contribution to the government's income. Revenue from this source was 87 billion rials in 1987; it rose to 141.5 billion in 1988. The following year it increased by 6.5 per cent to 7443 billion; by 1990 the revenue was 22 568 billion and in 1991 it had increased yet again to 25 568 billion and in 1991 it had increased yet again to 25 107 billion. The sale of foreign exchange at an inflated rate by the government funded 30 per cent of the national budget.[49]

Nevertheless the government decided to shadow some of the IMF structural adjustment policies. It removed some of the subsidies and in August 1991 the government announced its decision to reduce the size of the public-sector employment and public-sector intervention in the education and training sectors by transferring some of these to the private sector.[50] It also stated its aim of reducing its assistance to bridge the loss gaps in the public-sector industries. At the same time it decided to raise the prices of government-provided products and services to increase the proportion of income from these sources in the GDP.

To increase revenues, the revolutionary government also decided to increase income tax and introduce a real estate and wealth tax.[51] The move was announced as a way of cutting Iran's dependence on foreigners, and curbing the liquidity spiral, which according to the Head of the Central Bank, Dr Seyed Mohamad Hosein Adeli, had gone up by 900 per cent over the previous twelve years.[52]

Finally, in 1993, shadowing IMF's restructuring policies, the government decided to float the rial; which in effect meant a severe devaluation of the currency. Article 29 of the 1993 budget stated:

> Rials' value in terms of other currencies will, from the beginning of 1372 (March 1993), be calculated on a daily basis by the Islamic Republic's Central Bank according to the markets' levels of supply and demand for foreign exchanges.[53]

Up to the 1990s the Iranian had virtually no major loans from IMF or the World Bank. But within months of the Cabinet decision to devalue the rial, Iran received a $165 million loan from the World Bank as part of a $213 million project to extend Qom's gas turbines and double its capacity for production of electricity to 200 megawatts.[54] With the exception of a $250 million earthquake emergency loan, and a $30 million population control loan, this was the second major World Bank loan to Iran since the revolution. The other was a $134 million loan obtained in May 1988; $77 million was to be spent on Tehran's drainage and sewerage system and $57 million on the rehabilitation of Sistan's river-bed.[55]

The devaluation of the rial was supposed to boost exports and curb imports. The move was hotly contested in the *Majlis*. Non-oil exports had never formed a substantial source of foreign exchange earnings. In the decade following the revolution they had accounted for 1.7 to 3.4 per cent of the total export earnings and had helped to pay for 2 to 10 per cent of the country's imports. The only exception had been in 1986, when the fall in oil prices meant that income from other exports formed 13.4 per cent of the total. In any case industrial product formed only 10 per cent of non-oil exports with agricultural products providing 50 per cent, and handicraft 14 per cent.[56] As *Majlis* representative, Mohamad Salamati, told the press, the industrial sector in Iran was not able to meet internal demand, let alone produce for export. In fact over the period 1978 to 1988 non-oil production had fallen from 0.8 per cent of GDP to 0.4 per cent. Salamati referred to a sampled survey of nationalised industries in Iran, conducted by the Finance Committee of the *Majlis* in 1986: of the eighty-three units consulted, fifty had said that they could not meet the home demand and had no surplus capacity for export. He argued that devaluation could do nothing to help matters.[57]

The failure of the nationalised industries had been attributed to its poor management structures and the government decided to sell them off. It was claimed that move was in the national interest rather than a blind following of the IMF dictate. Marashi, the Head of *Sanaye'eh Meli'eh Iran,* Iran Nationalised Industries, argued:

> privatisation is rooted in our faith in our people and in a free economy; it is to facilitate popular participation in a free economy.[58]

But when the industrial sector is heavily reliant on imported inputs, floating the currency would only result in much higher production prices.[59]

In fact, with the falling oil-prices, by 1992 Iran's negative balance of trade with the major industrial countries increased by 20 per cent, turning a 0.314 billion deficit in 1991 to 6.154 billion in 1992.[60] Nor could the deficit be helped. The government had been paying an annual average of 2 billion dollars to subsidise food imports and keep food prices manageable. With a free exchange rate these imports would cost 25 per cent more.[61]

Defending devaluation, the Plan Organisation experts argued that the supply side would benefit from free exchange rates; these would allow 'comparative advantages' to be correctly evaluated and would encourage producers to cut back on imported inputs and concentrate on products that were strongly based in local resources. Some *Majlis* deputies agreed, saying that it was essential to increase revenue from exports since oil merely paid for two or three months of government expenditure – the more optimistic rated the income to be enough for 60 per cent of government expenditure.[62] In either case the export sector had to come up with alternatives to pay for the deficit. The government also intended to use tariff and taxes to ensure that imports were brought in at their 'real prices' and importers were obliged to pay 'real taxes'.[63]

But the critics were right. Faced with the reality of exorbitant price rises, the government backtracked and decided to defer charging custom and excise duties at the floating exchange rate of 1655 rials per US dollar,[64] and used the 70 rials per dollar rate for 1993.[65] To meet the consumers' basic need, the Minister of Trade also announced that $1.25 billion was allocated to subsidise imports of rationed rice, sugar, ghee, meat and cheese for distribution by government agencies.[66]

It is doubtful that the estimated tariff and taxes will ever be realised. Large organisations such as the Oil, Petrochemical and related companies or the Communication Corporation or the Organisation of the Dispossessed have never paid any taxes and are not likely to start to do so in the in 1990s.[67] In 1989, for example, fixed income earners paid 69.7 billion rials in tax and the self-employed paid 86.4 billion rials; oil revenues accounted for only 30 billion rials.[68] So, albeit unwillingly, it has been those in employment that have funded the bulk of the government's revenue. Nevertheless Rafsanjani had had cause, more than once, to complain about the lack of a clear commitment on the part of the citizenry to their duty:

Unfortunately many people in our society do not consider the payment of taxes to be a religious and national duty. They do not realise that paying taxes is to pay one's debt to society. Taxes are a societal right and it is the duty of each and every citizen to respect this right.[69]

The Islamic government had gone a long way away from *Valayateh Faqih's* categorical rejection of secular taxes and Khomeini's assertion that no one needed to pay anything other than their religious dues.[70]

Given the tendency for non-payment of taxes, some of the *Majlis's* deputies were of the view that the Plan Organisation's optimistic forecasts about increasing revenue from future taxations were unrealistic. Tehran representative, Mohsein Yahyaee, noted that successive budget forecasts had overestimated the likely tax returns, and he saw no reason why income from taxation would change from 47 per cent of the total national income to 49.4 per cent. He pointed out the consistent failure of the Budget and Plan Organisation's economic forecasts, notably those predicting a fall in inflation to 8.9 per cent in 1993. He stressed that inflation had hovered around the 27 per cent mark for much of the decade. Similarly the liquidity rate had not fallen to 8.3 per cent as forecast by the Plan Organisation, but remained over 20 per cent. Given the shambolic state of economic forecasting, Yahyaee could not see why the expectations from floating exchange rate would prove any less misguided.[71]

Even President Rafsanjani had to admit that:

> floating exchange rates may in the short run be detrimental to the country as a whole.[72]

But he argued that in the long run, internal industrial and agricultural sectors stood to gain from these measures. The Minister of Agriculture, Dr Kalantari, promised that agricultural prices would be protected. There would be no maximum price imposed on dry pulses and market-garden products and cultivators would be offered easy long-term loans to bridge them over the difficult period. Nevertheless the expected negative results of devaluation were such that the government had to backtrack, then proceed slowly and provide a safety net of protective exchange rates for basic goods and medicine as well as military expenditure. The government began with the assumption that each US dollar was worth 1000 rials, and budgeted accordingly. But it agreed that should the exchange rate settle at a different level then the government would reimburse the importers and pay 66 per cent of the difference in rials.[73] The state also had to accept, at least provisionally, that the rise in prices had to be accompanied by some rise in incomes and the government would have to increase civil service salaries. The liquidity rate was unlikely to be reduced as a result of these policies.


CONCLUSION

The war has enabled the Iranian state to build up a cumbersome bureaucracy. Backed by the *komiteh* guards, and served by numerous mosques and religious centres and Islamic Associations in the factories, the clergy have created an alternative state machinery which has been running side-by-side with the dilapidated pre-revolutionary bureaucracy. So long as the war continued, these two systems continued to expand. For much of its life, the war provided a ready forum for channelling popular anger and frustration and for explaining away the shortages and hardships that people had to suffer.

The war also dealt with the problem of male unemployment by decimating much of the potential workforce. At the same time the war economy sparked off a small boom in the sectors serving the forces. For the first time the country began making some of its own military equipment.

Nevertheless it is ideological control that is the anchor of the regime and the entire propaganda machine, both formal and informal, is wielded to rationalise and defend its policies. To ease the process, the censorship laws permit a level of criticism to be carried out by the pro-government papers; they publish articles pointing out the shortcomings of various ministries and complain about shortages. There are even regular 'complaints' pages, where readers question Ministries and Municipalities about the absence of facilities. But any real opposition is firmly rooted out. The security forces actively repress all dissidents and critics.

Attempts to institute political controls enforced by the ubiquitous revolutionary guard *komitehs* became more blatant and less effective throughout the 1980s. Though present in factories, universities and work-places, the Islamists have not been able to stop wild-cat strikes, spontaneous demonstrations and sit-ins. At the same time the *komiteh* guards' strong-arm tactics are devaluing the righteous stance of the government and highlighting the failure of the revolution which has betrayed the very people who gave their lives in its service. But it is the failure of the post-war economy, the spiralling inflation, the acute shortages and rampant corruption which are effectively eroding what little has been left of the revolutionary ardour.

The first serious attempt at setting up an Islamic government in the twentieth century has proved to be an abysmal failure. In Iran all pretence of Islamification of the economy has been abandoned. Once more the country is turning to the West and attempting to borrow and perhaps spend its way out of its miseries. But the West's loans, at the end of the twentieth century, come tied with conditionalities which directly threaten the very group who took to the streets to bring about a revolution. There is no room for the poor, the dispossessed and the needy, in the agenda of conditionality; nor is there any respect for Islam or the *Foqaha*. It is too distressing to have to say that the Iranian experience of Islamification merely shows that *plus ça change plus c'est la même chose!*

# Notes

These notes inevitably contain some bibliographical references. The full publishing details of most of these can be found in the Bibliography. For those few books which are not included in the Bibliography, the publication details are given in the notes.

## Chapter 1

1. For an interesting insight see Mottahdedeh, Roy, *The Mantle of the Prophet, Religion and Politics in Iran* (New York: Pantheon Books, 1985).
2. For detailed discussions see Bakhash, Shaul *Iran: Monarchy, Bureaucracy and Reform under the Qajars.*
3. Abrahamian, Ervand, 'Oriental Despotism: The Case of Qajar Iran', p. 11.
4. Malkum Khan, *Majmuehyeh Asar*, ed. by Tabatabyi Mohamad Mohit, Tehran 1948–9 quoted by Bakhash, Shaoul, *Iran: Monarchy, Bureaucracy and Reform under the Qajars*, p. 106.
5. See for example, amongst many others, Madudi S. Abul Al'A, *First Principles of the Islamic State and Political Theory of Islam.*
6. Sura IV, verse 59
7. For further discussion see Afchar, Hassan, 'The Muslim Conception of law', pp. 84–155.
8. Akhavi, Shahrough, *Religion and Politics in Contemporary Iran*, p. 13.
9. See for example, Tabrizi, Nezam al Ulama, 'Hoquqeh Doval va Melal' in Adamiyat, Fereydoun and Nateq, Homa (eds) *Afkareh Ejtemayi va Siassi va Eqtessadi dar Aasareh Montasher Nashodeyeh Doreyeh Qajar*, pp. 68–70, quoted by Martin, Vanessa, *Islam and Modernism, The Iranian Revolution of 1906*, p. 29.
10. Enayat, Hamid, *Modern Islamic Political Thought.* For further discussion see Algar, Hamid, *Religion and State in Iran 1785–1906*; Eliash, Joseph, 'Some Misconceptions Concerning Shi'i Political Theory', and Lambton, A.K.S. '*Quis custodiet custodes?*', among others.
11. Algar, H., *Religion and State in Iran*, p. 2.
12. Ibid, p. 5.
13. Ibid, p. 5 and Mortimer, Edward, *Faith and Power: The Politics of Islam,* p. 35.
14. Corbin, Henry, 'Pour une Morphologie de la Spiritualism Shi'ite', *Eranos-Jahrbusch* (Zurich) XXIX (1960) p. 69. Quoted by Algar, *Religion and State*, p. 5.
15. Keddie, Nikki R, *Religion and Politics in Iran, Shiism from Quietism to Revolution* p. 7.
16. Fischer, M.M.J., *Iran from Religious Dispute to Revolution,* p. 30
17. Akhavi, Shahrough, *Religion and Politics in Contemporary Iran*, p. 11.
18. Hujjat-ul-Islam Muhammad Sangelagi, *Qaza' dar Islam* (Tehran: 1338), 1959–60, p. 14, quoted by Algar, H. *Religion and State*, p. 7.
19. Akhavi, Shahrough, *Religion and Politics in Contemporary Iran*, p. 11.
20. The Akbari school dominated until the early eighteenth century when Aqa Muhammad Baqer Behbahani (1705–1803) reorganised the more aggressive Usuli position. Fischer, M.M.J., *Iran From Religious Dispute to Revolution*, p. 30.
21. Ansari, Morteza, *Sirut an-Najat*, quoted by Cole in Cole and Keddie, *Shiism and Social Protests* (see next note).
22. Cole, R. and Keddie, N. (eds) *Shiism and Social Protests*, p. 9.
23. For further detail see Algar, H. *Religion and State in Iran*, p. 163, and Martin, V. *Islam and Modernism*, p. 57.

220

24. Tunukabuni, Muhammad B. Sulayman, *Qisas ul-Ulama* (Tehran: 1304), p. 64, quoted by Algar, H. in *Religion and State in Iran*, p. 24.
25. For further discussions, for example, Keddie, N.R., *Scholars, Saints and Sufis* p. 213; Algar, H., *Religion and State in Iran*, p. 19; Tabari, Azar, 'The Role of Clergy' in Keddie (ed.) *Religion and Politics*, p. 49.
26. In the 1960s Ali Shariati denounced this collaboration as a sign of corruption of the *ulema* and their failure to maintain their role as the defenders of the oppressed. For further discussions see Chapter 3.
27. For further detail see Keddie, N., *Scholars, Saints and Sufis*, pp. 212–26.
28. Tabari, A, 'The Role of Clergy in Modern Iranian Politics' in Keddie, N.R. (ed.) *Religion and Politics in Iran*, p. 55.
29. Lambton, A.K.S., 'The Persian Ulema and Constitutional Reform', ed. by Farhad, Tawfiq, *Le Shi'isme Imamite, Colloque de Strasbourg, 6–9 Mai 1969* (Paris: 1970).
30. Algar, H., *Religion and State*, p. 11.
31. The rate of exchange is based on the estimate of Homa Katouzian in *The Political Economy of Iran*, p. 38.
32. Durand, M., 'Memorandum on the Situation in Persia', 27 September 1895, part 1, section 6 FO 60/566, quoted by Martin, *Islam and Modernism*, p. 35.
33. Algar, H., *Religion and State in Iran*, p. 163.
34. Ibid, p. 60.
35. Akhavi, S. *Religion and Politics*, p. 211 footnote.
36. Tabari, Azar, 'The Role of Clergy in Modern Iranian Politics' in Keddie, Nikki R. (ed.) *Religion and Politics in Iran*, p. 49.
37. See, for example, Keddie, N.R., *Religion and Politics in Iran*, p. 9. Duran, M. Memorandum on the Situation in Persia, 27 September 1985, part 1, section 6, Foreign Office 60/566, quoted by Martin, Vanessa, *Islam and Modernism*, p. 38, estimates the government disbursement to the ulema at about 500 000 tumans.
38. For further details see Martin, V. *Islam and Modernism*, p. 38.
39. See, for example, Soudagar, Mohamad, *Nezameh Arbab Rayitai dar Iran*, p. 213.
40. Abrahamian, Ervand, 'The Crowd in Iranian Politics, 1905–53', p. 128.
41. Bakhash, Iran: *Monarchy, Bureaucracy and Reforms*, p. 291.
42. Enclosure in Wolff to Salisbury, no 24291250, Tehran, 3 November 1888, FO 539/40 quoted by Bakhash, *Monarchy, Bureaucracy and Reform*, p. 206. For further discussion see Lambton, A.K.S., 'Persia: The Breakdown of Society'.
43. Katouzian, Homa, *The Political Economy of Modern Iran*, p. 35.
44. For detailed discussion see Keddie, N.R. *Religion and Rebellion in Iran: The Tobacco Protest of 1891–1892* and Keddie, N.R., *Roots of Revolution*, pp. 40–62.
45. For further discussion see Keddie, N., 'The Origins of the Religious – Radical Alliance in Iran', Keddie, N., *Religion and Rebellion in Iran: The Tobacco Protest of 1891–92*.
46. For detailed discussions see Algar, H. *Religion and State in Iran*; Keddie, N.R. *Religion and Rebellion in Iran*.
47. For further discussion also see Fathi, Asghar, 'Preachers as Substitutes for Mass Media: The Case of Iran 1905–1909'.
48. Algar, *Religion and State*, p. 20.
49. Ibid, p. 241.
50. For further discussion see for example, Hairi, Abdul-Hadi, *Shiism and Constitutionalism in Iran*, p. 104.
51. Algar, H. *State and Religion*, p. 219.
52. See, for example, Martin, V., *Islam and Modernism*, p. 41.
53. Ibid, p. 56.
54. For further details see Abrahamian, E., 'The Crowd in Iranian Politics', p. 129.
55. Hairi, *Shiism and Constitutionalism*, pp. 104–5.

56. Algar, *State and Religion*, pp. 252–4.
57. Keddie, N.R. *Religion and Rebellion in Iran*, p. 15.
58. Adamiyat, F. *Ideologiyeh Nehzateh Mashroutiateh Iran*, p. 226, quoted by Tabari, A., 'The Role of Clergy', p. 57, footnote.
59. Mirza, Muhammad Hosein Naini, *Tanbih al-Ummah wa Tanzih al-Millah*, 1st edn, Baghdad 1909; 3rd edn, introduced and annotated by Sayyid Mahmud Taleqani, Tehran; 1955, pp. 44–7, quoted by Hairi, *Shiism and Constitutionalism*, p. 101.
60. Ibid, quoted by Algar, *Religion and State*, p. 239.
61. Hairi, *Shiism and Constitutionalism*, p. 192.
62. Ibid, p. 206.
63. Quoted in Adamiyat, Fereydun, *Ideologiyeh Nehzateh Mashruteyeh Iran*, p. 30.
64. Malkum, Khan, 'Persian Civilisation', *Contemporary Review*, February 1981, pp. 242–3.
65. Quoted by Keddie, Nikki R. *Religion and Rebellion In Iran*, pp. 28 –9.
66. Mansouri, Roshanak, '*Chehreyeh Zan dar Jarayedeh Mashroutiat*', p. 14.
67. For further discussion see Afshar, Haleh, 'The Emancipation Struggles in Iran: Past Experiences and Future Hopes', in Afshar, H. (ed.) *Women, Development and Survival in the Third World* (London: Longman, 1991) pp. 11–34.
68. Quoted in Adamiyat, Fereydun and Nateq, Homa, *Afkareh Ejtemayi va Siassi Eqtessadi as Assareh Montasher Nashodeh Doreh Qajar*, p. 260.
69. Kasravi, Ahmad, *Qanuneh Mashrutiat*.
70. Kasravi, Ahmad, *Tarikheh Mashrutiat*.
71. For detailed discussion see Keddie, N.R., *Roots of Revolution*, pp. 63–78.
72. For a detailed discussion see Hairi, Abdul–Hadi, *Shiism and Constitutionalism*.
73. Quoted by Akhavi, Shahrough, *Religion and Politics in Contemporary Iran*, p. 28.
74. Kasravi, A., *Tarikheh Mashrutiat*, p. 415.
75. Malik-Zadeh, Mehdi, *Tarikheh Engelabeh Mashrutiateh Iran*, p. 214, quoted by Hairi, Abdul-Hadi, *Shiism and Constitutionalism*, p. 220–1.
76. Fischer, M.M.J., *Iran from Religious Dispute to Revolution*, p. 149.
77. Arjomand, Said Amir, 'Traditionalism in twentieth-century Iran' pp. 199–202.
78. Balfour, J.M., *Recent Happenings in Persia*, p. 23.
79. For further discussion of the Jangali movement see Irfani, Suroosh, *Revolutionary Islam in Iran*; Mirfakhrani, E. Sardare Jangal.

## Chapter 2

1. For detailed discussions see Irfani, Suroosh, *Revolutionary Islam in Iran* and Mirfakhrani, E., *Sardare Jangal*.
2. Mostawfi, Abdol, *Shareh Zendeganiyeh Man*, quoted by Akhavi, *Religion and Politics*, p. 28.
3. For detailed discussion see Banani, Amin, *The Modernisation of Iran*, 1921–41; Katouzian, Homa, *The Political Economy of Modern Iran, 1926–1979* among many more.
4. For a detailed discussion see among others Banani, Amin, *The Modernisation of Iran*.
5. Fischer, M.M.J., *Iran: From Religious Dispute to Revolution*, p. 61.
6. For a detailed discussion see Algar, Hamid, *Religion and State in Iran 1785–19*.
7. Fischer, M.M.J., *Iran: From Religious Dispute to Revolution*, p. 91.
8. Akhavi, Shahrough, *Religion and Politics in Contemporary*, p. 72.
9. For further discussion see Afshar, Haleh, 'Women, Marriage and the State in Iran' in Afshar, H. (ed.) *Women, State and Ideology* (Macmillan, 1987) pp. 70–88 and Afshar, Haleh, 'Women and Reproduction in Iran' in Yuval-Davis, Nira and

Anthias, Floya (eds) *Women–Nation–State* (Basingstoke: Macmillan, 1989) pp. 110–25.

10. Kasravi, Ahmad, *Shiagari.*
11. Ibid, introduction.
12. Ibid, p. 33.
13. Ibid, p. 26.
14. Ibid, p. 43.
15. Ibid, p. 38.
16. Ibid, p. 99.
17. Ibid, p. 101.
18. Ibid, p. 117.
19. Khomeini, Rouhollah, *Kashf al Asrar.*
20. Ibid, pp. 292–5, quoted by Arjomand, Said Amir, 'Traditionalism in twentieth-century Iran, 206.
21. Khomeini, *Kashf al Asrar*, p. 214, quoted by Arjomand, Said Amir 'Traditionalism in Twentieth-century Iran', p. 207.
22. Ibid. Khomeini used very similar arguments in the 1980s in support of imposition of censorship on films and media, see Chapter 8.
23. Ibid, pp. 236 and 213, quoted by Arjomand, Said Amir 'Traditionalism in twentieth-century Iran', pp. 206 and 207.
24. Khomeini, *Kashf-al-Asrar*, p. 184.
25. Ibid, p. 189.
26. The *Fadayan's* manifesto, quoted by Arjomand, S.A. 'Traditionalism in twentieth-century Iran', p. 209.
27. Safavi, Navab, *Hokumateh Eslami*, p. 26.
28. Ibid, p. 24.
29. For detailed discussion see Rahnema, Ali, and Nomani, Farhad, *The Secular Miracle: Religion, Politics and Economic Policy in Iran*, pp. 73–96.
30. This view was subsequently put most forcefully by Ali Shariati; see Chapter 3.
31. Quoted by Arjomand S.A. 'Traditionalism in Twentieth century Iran', p. 208.
32. Kazemi, Farhad, 'The Fada'iyan-e Islam: Fanaticism, Politics and Terror' in Arjomand S.A. (ed.) *From Nationalism to Revolutionary Islam*, p. 169
33. For further discussion see Bill James A. and Louis, W.M. Roger (eds) *Musaddiq, Iranian Nationalism, and Oil* and Azimi, Fakhredin, *Iran the Crisis of Democracy 1941–1953.*
34. Homa Katouzian argues convincingly that such a charge has no foundation and that Razmara could not have been a traitor, *The Political Economy of Iran*, pp. 158–160.
35. Estimates vary, Farhad Kazemi states that they may have had as many as 25 000 members in Tehran and 12 000 in Mashad and other major cities. Kazemi, F., 'The Fada'iyan-e Islam: Fanaticism, Politics and Terror' in Arjomand, S.A. *From Nationalism to Revolutionary Islam*, p. 168.
36. Al Ahmad, Jalal, *Qarbzadegi.*
37. Senate Foreign Relation subcommittee on Multinational Corporations, 'The International Petroleum Cartel, the Iranian Consortium and US National Security', 21 February 1974, p. 68, quoted by Stork, Joe, *Middle East Oil and the Energy Crisis* pp. 54–5.
38. Fischer, M.M.J., *Iran: From Religious Dispute to Revolution*, p. 63.
39. Ibid, p. 77.
40. Nateq, Homa, '*Rohanyat va azadihayeh democratic*', p. 14.
41. Quoted by Fischer, *From Religious Disputes to Revolution*, p. 186.
42. Quoted by Irfani, Suroosh, *Revolutionary Islam in Iran*, p. 80.
43. Pesaran M.H., 'Economic Development and Revolutionary Upheavals in Iran', p. 22.

44. Katouzian, Homa, *The Political Economy of Modern Iran*, 1926–1979, p. 227.
45. Abrahamian, E., *Iran: Between Two Revolutions*, p. 473.
46. Quoted by Irfani, S., *Revolutionary Islam in Iran*, p. 81.
47. Badamchian and Bana'i *Hey'ateh Mootelefeyeh Eslami* Entesharateh Owj, p. 34, quoted by Rahnema, Ali and Nomani, Farhad, 'Competing Shi'i subsystems in Contemporary Iran'.
48. Fanon, Frantz, *Les damnés de la terre*.
49. For detailed discussions see Chapter 3.
50. For further discussion see Chapter 3.
51. Abrahamian, E. *Iran Between Two Revolutions*, pp. 216–18.
52. Ibid, p. 433.
53. Taleqani, Seyed Mahmud, Malekiat dar Islam in *Goftareh Mah*, 1, 1961.
54. Bazargan, Mehdi, 'Marz mianeh mazhab va omoureh ejtamaii', pp. 113–46.
55. For further discussion see Afshar, Haleh, 'The Army' in Afshar H. (ed.) *Iran: Revolution in Turmoil*, pp. 175–200.
56. Abrahamian, *Between Two Revolutions*, p. 354.
57. Ibid, p. 354.
58. Ibid, p. 445.
59. Census data, *Salnameh Amari* (Annual Statistics) (Iran Statistical Centre, 1363) 1984, p. 87.
60. Ibid.
61. Ibid, p. 91.
62. Ibid, p. 87.
63. Abrahamian, *Between Two Revolutions*, pp. 136, 439 and 430.
64. Quoted by Arjomand, S.A., 'Traditionalism in Twentieth-century Iran', p. 223.
65. Mansur, A.K., 'The Crisis in Iran', p. 28.
66. Abrahamian, E., *Iran: Between Two Revolutions*, p. 497.
67. Fischer estimates that there were some 300 000 foreigners working in Iran as skilled, semi-skilled and unskilled labourers, Iran: *From Religious Discourse to Revolution*, p. 189. Abrahamian estimates that there were 60 000 well-paid foreign technicians working in Iran, *Iran: Between Two Revolutions*, p. 497. According to the *US Military Sales to Iran, Staff Report*, (Washington: US Government Printing Office, 1976) there were 24 000 US citizens in Iran, a large percentage of whom were involved in military programmes, p. vii. Sullivan, William H, US Ambassador to Iran, notes that many of the American instructors proved to be a partially disruptive element in US–Iranian relations', *Mission to Iran*, p. 80.
68. Abrahamian, E., *Iran: Between Two Revolutions*, p. 497.
69. For detailed discussion see Abrahamian, E., *Iran: Between Two Revolutions*, pp. 427–97, and Afshar, Kamran, 'The Impact of Urban Income *per capita* on Agricultural Output: A Case Study of pre-1975 Iran' in Afshar H. (ed.) *Iran: A Revolution in Turmoil*, pp. 51–7.
70. There are wide disparities in the reported numbers of deaths and injured. The government figures always very low and those of the resistance very high, ranging from between 5 and 6 to 100 to 300, or more.
71. Abrahamian, E., *Iran: Between Two Revolutions*, p. 510.
72. This section has been based extensively on Abrahamian's excellent account in *Iran: Between Two Revolutions*, pp. 518–33; Fischer, *Iran: From Religious Dispute to Revolution*, pp. 123–313; and Bakhash, Shaoul, 'Sermons, Revolutionary

Pamphleteering and Mobilisation: Iran 1978' in Arjomand, S. (ed.) *From Nationalism to Revolutionary Islam.*

## Chapter 3

1. I am most grateful to AKSL for pointing out to me quite correctly that 'clergy' is not a correct translation for the word *rohaniat* or *alem*, since there is no sanctity in the office of religious leader.
2. Al Ahmad, Jalal, *Dar Khedmat va Khianat, Roshanfekran*, p. 181.
3. Ibid, vol. 2, p. 33.
4. Ibid, vol. 2, p. 13.
5. Ibid, vol. 2, p. 32.
6. Ibid, vol. 2, p. 34.
7. Ibid, vol. 2, p. 28.
8. Ibid, vol. 2, p. 13.
9. Shariati, Ali, *Tashiiyeh Alavi va Tashiiyeh Safavi*, pp. 1–3.
10. Ibid, p. 47.
11. Ibid, p. 149.
12. Ibid, p. 206.
13. Ibid, pp. 162–3.
14. Akhavi, S, *Religion and Politics in Contemporary Iran*, p. 88.
15. They were Ayatollah Mohamad Kazem Shariatmadari, Ayatollah Shahabedin Marashi-Najafi, and Ayatollah Mohamad Hadi Milani who were linked to wealthy *bazaaris*. Ayatollah Mohamad Reza Golpayegani related to small landlords and married into a family of shopkeepers. Ayatollah Rouhollah Mousavi Khomeini, Ayatollah Abolqassem Mousavi Khoyi and Ayatollah Ahmad Khonsari. Fischer M.M.J., *Iran: from Religious Dispute to Revolution*, pp. 8.9–93.
16. Abrahamian, E., *Iran: Between Two Revolutions*, p. 433.
17. Shariati, A., *Tashiiyeh Alavi*, p. 47.
18. Ibid, p. 213.
19. Al Ahmad, *Roshanfekran*, p. 181.
20. Quoted by Arjomand, S.A. 'Traditionalism in twentieth century...' p. 226.
21. Mottahari, Ayatollah Morteza, '*Moshkeleh assasi dar sazemaneh rohaniat*', p. 118
22. Shariati, A. *Tashiiyeh Alavi*, p. 213. As stated in Chapter 1 the Muslim clergy are not supposed to act as intermediaries between people and God. Nor are they expected to have a spiritual supremacy.
23. Shariati, A., *Tashiiyeh Alavi*, p. 71.
24. Ibid, p. 231.
25. Khomeini, Ayatollah Rouhollah, *Toziholmassael' massaleyeh*, problem numbers 434, 435 and 436. For further discussion see Afshar, Haleh, 'Khomeini's Teachings and the Implications for Iranian women' in Tabari, Azar and Yeganeh, Nahid (compilers) *In the Shadow of Islam* (London: Zed Press, 1982) pp. 75–90.
26. Shariati, Ali, *Tashiiyeh Alavi*, pp. 291–300. Also see Chapter 1, *Usuli* and *Akb* schools of thought.
27. Ibid, pp. 313–14.
28. Ibid, p. 230.
29. Ibid, p. 309.

30. Ibid. p. 300.
31. Shariati, Ali *Bazgasht beh Khishtan'* quoted by Abrahamian, *Radical Islam*, p. 119.
32. Abrahamian notes that this particular view was advocated by the Algeri author, Amar Ouzegwan, whose book *Le Meilleur Combat*, had been translated as *Bartaren Jehad* and was one of the basic readings used by the Mujahedin in their study groups in the early years. Lecture notes for paper delivered at Durham University Middle East Seminar series in 1985.
33. Abrahamian, E., 'The Ideology of Mujahedin', lecture delivered at Durham University as part of the Middle East seminar series, 1985.
34. *Mujahed*, May 1980, quoted by Irfani, *Revolutionary Islam*, p. 93.
35. Mujahedin Rezayi, Mehdi, *Zendeganinameh va Defayiat*, p. 18.
36. Mujahedin Pamphlet, *Chegouneh Quran Biamouzim*, vol. 1, p. 10. quoted by Abrahamian, *Radical Islam*, p. 95.
37. Rezayi, *Zendeqinameh*, p. 19.
38. Mujahedin pamphlet, *Cheqouneh Quran Biyamouzim*, p. 8.
39. The chapter on women, verse 74.
40. Mujahedin, *Zendeginameh*, p. 13.
41. Bazargan, *'Marz mianeh mazhab va omoureh ejtemayi'*, p. 119.
42. *Nehzateh Azadiyeh Iran*, 11 June 1961, quoted by Abrahamian, *Between Two Revolutions*, p. 460.
43. Mujahedin, April 1976 and April 1977 and *Etelaat*, 16 May 1979, quoted by Abrahamian, *Between Two Revolutions*, p. 460.
44. Bazargan, *Marzeh Mian*, p. 110 and 112.
45. Bazargan, Mehdi, *Mosalmaneh ejtemayi va jahani'*, p. 41.
46. Ibid, p. 41.
47. Ibid, p. 61.
48. See, for example, Madudi S. Abul Ala, *First Principles of the Islamic State*.
49. See, for example, Khomeini, Ayatollah Rouhollah, *Valayateh Faqih*.
50. Bani Sadre, Abol Hassan, *Eqtessadeh Tohidi*, quoted by Katouzian, Homa in 'Shiism and Islamic Economics, Sadr and Bani Sadr', p. 161.
51. Bani Sadre, Abol Hassan, *Bayaniyeh Jomhourieh Eslami*.
52. Addressee at the Faizieh seminary quoted by Irfani, *Revolutionary Islam*, p. 14.
53. For detail discussions see Irfani, Suroosh, *Revolutionary Islam in Iran*; and Dehqan S., *Taleqani va Tarikh*.
54. 18 January 1979, speech at Hedayat Mosque; Afrasiabi and Dehqan, *Taleqani*, pp. 371–3, quoted by Irfani, *Revolutionary Islam*, p. 144.
55. Speech at Baharestan square, 21 July 1979, quoted by Irfani, *Revolutionary Islam*, p. 145.
56. Excerpted from Ayatollah Taleqani's last Friday Prayer Sermon, Tehran, September 1979. Quoted in *Mardi as Tabareh Nour'* a man from the abode of light, Tehran: Anjomahen Tohidiyeh Resalat, 1979, pp. 10–18, quoted by Irfani *Revolutionary Islam*, p. ii.
57. Afrasiabi and Dehqan, *Taleqani*, p. 403.
58. Television address, 3 May 1979, quoted by *Yek Irani, Iran dar Chahar Raheh Sarnevesht*.
59. Quoted by Abrahamian, *Between Two Revolutions*, p. 506
60. *Tehran Times*, 2 June 1978, quoted by Abrahamian, *Between Two Revolutions*, p. 51.
61. Interview with Bamdad newspaper 20 September 1979, quoted by Yek Irani, *Ira dar Chahar Rah*, p. 160.
62. Quoted by Fischer, *From Religious Dispute*, p. 153.
63. Mottahari, Morteza, *Marx va Marxism*.
64. Ibid, vol. 2, pp. 76–80.

65. Ibid, vol. 2, pp. 103
66. Ibid, vol. 2, pp. 98–104.
67. Ibid, vol. 3, p. 90.
68. Mottahari, Ayatollah Morteza, *Barresiyeh Ejmali'i as Nehzateh Eslami dar Sad Saleh Akhir*, pp. 74 and 90–92.
69. The *Quran*, chapter on *zakhrof* (wealth and allurement) verse 32, quoted by Mottahari, Ayatollah Morteza, *Jahan Biniyeh Tohidi*, vol. 2, p. 100.
70. Mottahari, *Jahanbini*, pp. 99–100.
71. Mottahari, *Barresiyeh Ejmali*, pp. 76 and 70.
72. Ibid, pp. 82–3.
73. Ibid, p. 86.
74. Ibid, pp. 95–6.
75. Mottahari *Jahanbini*, pp. 103–4.
76. See Chapter 1.
77. Khomeini, Imam; *Islam and Revolution*, translated and annotated by Algar, H. Berkeley: Mizan press, 1981, pp. 78–79 and 96. There has been much debate about incorrect translations of *Marja Faqih* by supporters of Khomeini. Therefore this author has relied on the official translation as it appeared in the Tehran English language daily *Kayhan International* or the translation by Hamid Algar which has received the Islamic government's seal of approval. Occasionally when the Algar translation is found to have been unclear, the author has reverted to translating the text herself, but reference to Algar's translation is then given in the footnote.
78. Khomeini, *Islamic Government*, translated by Algar, p. 78.
79. Khomeini, *Islamic Government*, translated by Algar, p. 64.
80. Khomeini, Ayatollah Rouhollah, *Hokumateh Eslami* (Islamic Government), p. 49. Algar translates this as: 'If a worthy individual possessing these two qualities arises and establishes a government, he will possess the same authority as the Most Noble Messenger...', *Islamic government*, p. 62.
81. Khomeini, Ayatollah, Rouhollah, *Hokumateh Eslami*, p. 49, and Khomeini, *Islamic Government*, p. 63.
82. *Valayateh Faqih, Kayhan International*, 12 April 1981. Madudi makes the same point in his discussions on Islamic government.
83. Ayatollah Javadi Amoli, *Zan dar Ayineyeh Jalal va Jamal* (Women Reflected in the Mirror of Beauty and Worth) summarised in *Zaneh Rouz*, 29 August 1992, no. 1374.
84. Khomeini, *Islamic Government*, pp. 44–5.
85. *Valayateh Faqih, Kayhan International*, 12 April 1981.
86. Ibid, 12 April 1981.
87. Ibid, 1 March 1981.

## Chapter 4

1. For a detailed discussion see Vali, Abas and Zubaida, Sami, 'Factionalism: A Political Discourse in the Islamic Republic of Iran'.
2. See Bazargan, '*Marz mianeh din va omoureh ejtemayi*' (The Boundary Between Religion and Social Affairs), p. 145–46.
3. For further discussion see Vali, Abas and Zubaida, Sami, 'Factionalism and Political Discourse in the Islamic Republic of Iran', p. 139–73.
4. *The Economist*, 17 February 1979.
5. Bazargan, Mehdi, *Moshkelat va Massaeleh Avalin Saleh Enqelab*, p. 131.
6. *The Economist*, 20 October 1979.

7. See, for example, Madudi, *Islamic Government*, p. 53.
8. For detailed discussions see Afchar, Hassan, 'The Muslim Concept of Law', pp. 84–155.
9. A similar provision in the 1906 constitution was never enforced in the subsequent Parliamentary sessions.
10. For detailed discussion also see Madudi, S.A.A., *Political Theory of Islam*; and Khomeini's, *Kashfal Asrar*, p. 53.
11. See Chapter 1.
12. Ahmad Khomeini, quoted by Eric Rouleau writing for *Le Monde*, reprinted in the *Guardian Weekly*, 28 October 1979.
13. *The Economist*, 3 March 1979.
14. *The Observer*, 16 December 1979.
15. Nateq, '*Rohaniat va azadihayeh democratic*'.
16. *The Economist*, 10 March 1979.
17. For further details see Ervand Abrahamian's excellent book, *Radical Islam: The Iranian Mujahedin*.
18. Fanon, Frantz, *Les damnés de la terre*.
19. For further details see Chapter 1.
20. It is amusing to note that Khomeini did not share this disdain for *eau de cologne*; after his death his daughter proudly told the women's magazine, *zaneh rouz*, that her father drenched himself in *eau de cologne* at least seven times a day!
21. Quoted by David Hirst writing in *The Guardian*, 16 July 1981.
22. *The Guardian*, 16 July 1981.
23. Term coined by Liz Thurgood reporting for *The Guardian* from Tehran.
24. See Chapter 3.
25. Bakhash, Shaoul, *The Reign of the Ayatollahs*, p. 60.
26. Bazargan, *Moshkelat*, p. 93 and 131, quoted by Bakhash, *Reign of the Ayatollahs*, p. 57.
27. Bakhash, *The Reign of the Ayatollahs*, p. 102.
28. For further details see Afshar H. 'Khomeini's teachings and their implications for Iranian women' in Tabari A. and Yeganeh, N. (compilers) *In the Shadow of Islam*, pp. 75–90.
29. Qibla, Mufti Jafar Husain Sahib, *Nahj ul-Balagha*, pp. 116–17, quoted by Fischer, *Iran from Religious Dispute*, p. 162.
30. Quoted by Nateq, Home, '*Rohaniyat va azadihayeh democratic*'.
31. Address to Faizieh Seminary in Qom, 21 March 1963, quoted by Irfani, p. 81.
32. See Afshar, H. 'Khomeini's teachings', in Tabari and Yeganeh, *In the Shadow of Islam*.
33. Though initially vigorously enforced, the husband's right of custody has been gradually undermined by women. For further discussion see Afshar, H. 'Women, Marriage and State in Iran' in Afshar, H. (ed.) *Women, State and Ideology*, pp. 70–89; Haeri, S., 'Women, Law and Social Change in Iran', pp. 209–35; Haeri, S. *Law of Desire; Temporary Marriage in Iran*; and Mir-Hoseini, Ziba, 'Divorce in Islamic Law and Practice: The Case of Iran'; and Mir-Hoseini, Z., 'Women, Marriage and the Law in Post-Revolutionary Iran'.
34. For a detailed chronology of events see Tabari, A. and Yeganeh, N., *In the Shadow of Islam*, pp. 231–39.
35. Bahrier, J. *Economic Development in Iran*, 1981, p. 186.
36. Marshall, Phil, *Revolution and Counter-Revolution in Iran*, 1600, Bookmarks, 1988.
37. Bayat, Assef, *Workers and Revolution in Iran*, London: Zed Press, 1987.
38. For detailed discussion see Bayat, Assef, *Workers and Revolution in Iran*.
39. Ibid, p. 95.

40. Ibid, p. 108.
41. *Iran Liberation*, 19 April 1985.
42. Bayat, Assef, *Workers and Revolution*, p. 133.
43. Ibid, p. 133.
44. Ibid, p. 132.
45. For detailed discussion see Bayat, Assef, pp. 174–91.
46. *Kar* newspaper, 28 May 1980.
47. *Sunday Times*, 2 December 1979.
48. Bayat, Assef, *Workers and Revolution*, p. 178.
49. Reported by *Kar* the *Fadayan* newspaper, no. 60, 28 May 1980.
50. *Financial Times*, 2 July 1980.
51. *Iran Liberation*, 19 April 1985.
52. Bayat, Assef, *Workers and Revolution*, p. 178–9.
53. May Day speech, quoted by Bayat, p. 183.
54. Marshal, Phil, *Revolution and Counter Revolution*, p. 213.
55. Bakhash, *The Reign of the Ayatollahs*, p. 176.
56. Bazargan, *Massael va Moshkelat* p. 102, quoted by Bakhash, *The Reign of the Ayatollahs*, p. 176.
57. For detailed discussions see Katouzian, Homa, 'Shi'ism and Islamic Economics: Sadr and Bani Sadr' in Keddie, Nikki R. (ed.) *Religion and Politics in Iran: Shi'ism from Quietism to Revolution*, pp. 145–65. Also see Sadre, Musa, *Eqtesad dar maktabeh Eslam*; Sadre, Mohamad Baqer, *Eqtesadeh Ma*; Bani Sadre, Abol Hassan, *Eqtesadeh Tohidi*,; and Taheri, Ali, *Eqtesadeh Eslami*.
58. See Chapter 10
59. For detailed discussions see Bakhash, S. *The Reign of the Ayatollahs*, pp. 179–85.
60. For further details see Afshar, H. 'The Iranian Theocracy' in Afshar, H., *Iran: A Revolution in Turmoil*, pp. 232–3.

## Chapter 5

1. For further details see Chapter 1.
2. *Etelat*, 10 February 1980, quoted by Bakhash, *The Reign of the Ayatollahs*, p. 102.
3. *Dayereyh amre beh marouf va nahi as monker*, which literally translated means 'centres for prevention of wrongdoing and direction towards righteous deed'.
4. Ayatollah Javad Amoli, *Zan dar Ayineyeh Jalal va Jamal* 'Woman Reflected in the Mirror of Beauty and Honour', serialised by *Zaneh Rouz*, 24 August 1992, no. 1374.
5. Bani Sadre addressing the crowd at the Freedom Square, Meidaneh Azadi, reported by *Kayhan International*, 23 November 1980.
6. Bani Sadre commented on the large size of these losses in various articles in his paper, *Enqlabeh Eslami*, in May and June 1981.
7. *Kayhan*, 22 February 1982.
8. Bayat, *Workers and Revolution*, pp. 177–9.
9. Quoted by Bakhash, *The Reign of the Ayatollahs*, p. 102.
10. *Kar*, the newspaper of the *Fadayan*, 29 May 1980.
11. For further details see Afshar, H. 'An Assessment of Agricultural Development Policies in Iran', in Afshar, H. (ed.) *Iran: A Revolution in Turmoil*, Basingstoke: Macmillan, 1989.
12. See, for example, Bani Sadre's *Bayanieyeh Jomhourieh Eslami* (Manifesto of the Islamic Republic) published in Paris in 1971 and *Eqtessadeh Tohidi* (Unified Economy) published in Paris in 1974.
13. *Le Monde*, 18 November 1979.

14. Bani Sadre interviewed by *The Financial Times*, 28 January 1980.
15. Bani Sadre interviewed by Eric Rouleau for *Le Monde*, 18 November 1979.
16. *The Financial Times*, 10 January 1980.
17. See Abrahamian, E. 'The Crowd in Iranian Politics, 1905–53' in Afshar, H. (ed.) *Iran: A Revolution in Turmoil*, pp. 121–48.
18. Jonathan Randal writing in *The Washington Post*, reported in *The Guardian Weekly*, 18 November 1979.
19. *The Observer*, 11 November 1979.
20. Reported by *The Guardian*, 17 February 1980.
21. *Enqelabeh Eslami*, Bani Sadre's daily newspaper, 7 February 1980.
22. *Azadegan*, the official newspaper of the militant clergy, 17 February 1980.
23. *The Financial Times*, 2 February 1980.
24. Student spokesman interviewed by *The Economist*, 16 February 1980.
25. *Le Monde*, 2 February 1980.
26. Interview with Eric Rouleau, *Le Monde*, reported by the *Guardian Weekly*, 10 February 1980.
27. Ibid.
28. *Enqelabeh Eslami*, 14 May 1980.
29. *Kayhan*, 12 May 1980.
30. *Azadegan*, the militant newspaper printed by the revolutionary guards, 31 July 1980,
31. Ibid.
32. *The Financial Times*, 23 July 1980.
33. Bakhash, *The Reign of the Ayatollahs*, pp. 112–13.
34. *Mujahed*, October 1980.
35. *The Financial Times*, 11 June 1980.
36. *Bamdad* newspaper, 14 May 1980, quoted by Bakhash, *The Reign of the Ayatollahs*, p. 104.
37. *The Economist*, 16 June 1980.
38. Ibid.
39. *The Guardian*, 10 April 1980.
40. For detail analysis see Afshar, H. 'The Army' in Afshar, H. (ed.) *Iran: A Revolution in Turmoil*, and Salamatian, A. *Historique du Rôle Politique de l'Armée en Iran*.
41. Rose, Gregory F., 'The Post-Revolutionary Purge of Iran's Armed Forces: A Revisionist Assessment', in *Iranian Studies*, vol. xvii, nos 2–3, Spring–summer, 1984, pp. 160 and 172.
42. Ibid, p. 178.
43. *The Financial Times*, 18 February 1980.
44. Ibid, 11 June 1980.
45. Ibid, 23 July 1980.
46. *Enqelabeh Eslami*, 11 November 1980.
47. Central Bank governor, Nobari, explaining Bani Sadre's policies to the *Sunday Times* reporter, 31 January 1981.
48. *The Observer*, 22 February 1981.
49. *Sazemaneh etelaat va amniateh meli* only change was to alter the word *keshvar*, meaning country, in SAVAK, for *meli* meaning national in SAVAMA.
50. *The Sunday Times*, 1 February 1981.
51. Khomeini quoted by *Iran Times*, 27 February 1981.
52. *Iran Times*, 17 April 1981, quoted by Bakhash, *The Reign of the Ayatollahs*, p. 148.
53. Reported in *Kayhan International*, 23 November 1980.
54. Bakhash, *The Reign of the Ayatollahs*, p. 158.
55. The *Guardian*, 16 July 1981.
56. *The Sunday Times*, 28 June 1981.

57. In addition to the *Mujahedin*, foreign agents, royalists, army officers and others, have at different times been accused of planting this bomb. In Iran at least two sets of people in Tehran and Kermanshah have been executed on this charge. For further details see Abrahamian, *Between Two Revolutions*, p. 220.
58. Television broadcast in Tehran reported by *The Sunday Times*, 28 June 1981.
59. *The Sunday Times*, 28 June 1981.
60. *Iran Today*, communiqué no. 5.
61. *Iran Times*, 17 July 1981, quoted by Bakhash, *The Reign of the Ayatollahs*, p. 141.
62. Ibid.
63. *The Financial Times*, 23 August 1981.
64. Ibid.
65. *Kayhan*, 5 July 1981.
66. *Mujahedin's Communiqué* issued in England, 2 July 1981.
67. Ibid.
68. *Iran Today*, *Tudeh* party's newsletter, communiqué no. 3, 11 July 1981.
69. *The Times*, quoting *Jomhouriyeh Eslami*, 21 September 1981.
70. Quoted by *Mujahed*, 6 November 1981.
71. *The Times*, 21 September 1982.
72. Broadsheet published in London and Paris, 17 August 1981.
73. See Chapter 3.
74. For detailed discussions see Chapter 6, pp. 1–5, and Chapter 7.

## Chapter 6

1. Ayatollah Montazeri speaking in support of the Guards, *Kayhan*, 27 April 1982.
2. Morteza Rezayi, head of the Corps, interviewed by *Kayhan International*, 24 June 1981.
3. *Kayhan International*, 24 June 1981.
4. *Kayhan*, 10 February 1981.
5. *Kayhan*, 27 April 1982.
6. Ayatollah Mahdavi Kani, the Controller of the Revolutionary, *Komitehs*, *Kayhan*, 10 February 1982.
7. *Kayhan*, 16 December 1982.
8. *Kayhan*, 30 December 1982.
9. *Kayhan*, 13 February 1983.
10. *Kayhan*, 25 December 1982.
11. *Kayhan*, 25 December 1982.
12. *Kayhan*, 26 April 1984.
13. *Kayhan*, 26 April 1984.
14. Minister of Interior reporting to the Majlis, *Kayhan*, 13 September 1988.
15. *Kayhan*, 22 November 1988.
16. *Kayhan*, 22 November 1988.
17. *Kayhan*, 19 September 1988.
18. *Iran Liberation*, 2 October 1987.
19. *Kayhan*, 13 November 1988.
20. *Kayhan*, 27 June 1987.
21. *Kayhan*, 1 June 1988.
22. *Kayhan*, 25 November 1988.
23. For detailed discussions see Chapter 8.
24. *Kayhan*, 13 November 1988.
25. For detailed discussions see Abrahamian, E., 'The Crowd in Iranian Politics' in Afshar, H. (ed.) *Iran: A Revolution in Turmoil*.

26.	For detailed discussions see Chapter 9.
27.	Ayatollah Mussavi Ardabili reporting Khomeini's message, *Kayhan*, 17 December 1987.
28.	For detailed discussions see Afshar, H., 'The Army', in Afshar, H. *Iran: A Revolution in Turmoil*.
29.	*Kayhan*, 17 September 1988.
30.	*Kayhan*, 15 September 1988.
31.	Rezayi, *Kayhan International*, 24 June 1981.
32.	*Kayhan*, 21 May 1987 and 4 May 1988.
33.	Quoted by O'Ballance, Edgar, *The Gulf War*, p. 120.
34.	Reported in the *Guardian Weekly*, 30 November 1986.
35.	*The Observer*, 10 May 1987.
36.	*Kayhan*, 20 July 1986.
37.	Mohsen Rafiqdust, *Kayhan*, 27 April and 17 July 1986.
38.	Rafiqdust, *Kayhan*, 17 August 1987. For a more detailed study see Ehteshami, Anoushiravan, 'Iran's Domestic Arms Industry'.
39.	*Kayhan*, 5 September 1988.
40.	Mohsen Rezayi, Guards Commander-in-Chief, *Kayhan*, 13 April 1988.
41.	*Kayhan*, 19 September 1988.
42.	*Kayhan*, 24 November 1985.
43.	*Kayhan*, 10 November 1985 and 17 January 1987.
44.	*Kayhan*, 4 March 1987.
45.	*Kayhan*, 24 November 1985.
46.	*Kayhan*, 24 November 1985.
47	*Kayhan*, 17 July 1986.
48.	Mohsen Rafiqdust reporting on 1983 *basij* forces, in *Kayhan*, 4 March 1987 and 29 November 1988.
49.	*Kayhan*, 29 November 1988 and 1 December 1988.
50.	*Kayhan*, 29 November 1988.
51.	*Kayhan*, 2 June 1986.
52.	*Kayhan*, 17 August 1987.
53.	*Kayhan*, 22 November 1988.
54.	*Kayhan*, 29 September 1987.
55.	*Kayhan*, 22 September 1988.
56.	*Iran Liberation*, 20 October 1987.
57.	*Kayhan*, 5 November 1987.
58.	*Kayhan*, 7 November 1987.
59.	*Kayhan*, 16 November 1987.
60.	*Hojatoleslam* Seyed Mohamad Dezfully in an interview with *Kayhan*, 15 November 1988.
61.	*Kayhan*, 29 November 1988.
62.	*Kayhan*, 17 November 1988.
63.	For a discussion of the inception and early budgetary deficits of this organisation see Afshar, H. 'The Iranian Theocracy' in Afshar, H. (ed.) *Iran: A Revolution in Turmoil*.
64.	*Kayhan*, 17 and 19 November 1987, 14 December 1987 and 4 February 1988.
65.	*Kayhan*, 19 December 1987.
66.	*Kayhan*, 13 April 1987.
67.	*Kayhan*, 26 February 1987.
68.	Ali Khameneyi, *Kayhan*, 12 May 1985.
69	Rafsanjani, *Kayhan*, 25 April 1987
70.	Article 29 of the Armed Forces Act.
71.	Article 14.

72. For further details see Afshar, H. 'The Army', in Afshar, H. (ed.) *Iran: A Revolution in Turmoil.*
73. Article 16.
74. Article 16, note 1.
75. *Kayhan*, 16 November 1985.
76. *Iran Press Digest*, vol. 5, issue 1, p. 1, 13 January 1987.
77. *Kayhan*, 29 July 1987.
78. See Chapter 3.
79. Reported in *Kayhan*, 6 January 1982.
80. For detail discussions see Afshar, H. 'Khomeini's Teachings and Iranian Women', *Feminist Review*, no. 12, summer 1982, pp. 59–73.
81. President Khameneyi addressing the guards, *Kayhan*, 1 June 1988.
82. *Kayhan*, 30 August 1987.
83. *Kayhan*, 18 October 1987.
84. Rafiqdust speaking at the *Majlis*, reported in *Kayhan*, 13 September 1988.
85. *Kayhan*, 28 October, 5 and 19 November, 15 and 19 December 1987.
86. Khameneyi, *Kayhan*, 17 August 1988.
87. *Kayhan*, 29 September 1988.
88. *Kayhan*, 20 January 1988.
89. For more detailed discussions see Afshar, H. 'Khomeini's Teachings and their Impacts on the Lives of Women in Iran' in Tabari, A. and Yeganeh, N., *In the Shadow of Islam*, Afshar, H. 'Women in Iran', in *Third World Quarterly*, January 1987, and Afshar, H. 'Women and Poverty in Iran', in Afshar, H. and Agarwal, B. (eds) *Women, Ideology and Poverty in Asia*, Basingstoke, Macmillan, 1989.
90. See, for example, Nadia Hejab, *Womanpower*, Oxford University Press, 1988.
91. *Kayhan*, 30 October 1988.
92. Rafsanjani addressing the *Basij* forces marching before *Majlis*, *Kayhan*, 1 December 1988.
93. *Kayhan*, 22 November 1988.
94. *Hojatoleslam* Korubi, head of martyrs organisation, *Kayhan*, 31 October 1988.
95. Rafsanjani, *Kayhan*, 30 October 1988.
96. For further details see Afshar H., 'The Theocracy' in Afshar, H., (ed.) *Iran: A Revolution in Turmoil.*
97. *Kayhan*, 31 October 1988.
98. *Kayhan*, 28 November 1988.
99. See Chapter 8.
100. *Kayhan*, 24 January 1993.
101. *Kayhan*, 14 April 1993.

## Chapter 7

1. See Chapter 3.
2. R. Nima, *The Wrath of Allah*, p. 97.
3. Fischer, *Iran from Religious Dispute*, p. 283, footnote 27.
4. For detailed discussions see Afshar, H., 'Khomeini's Teachings and their Implication for Women' in Tabari, A. and Yeganeh, N. *In the Shadow of Islam*, London: Zed, 1982, pp. 79–90 and 'Legal and Socio-political Position of Women in Iran', in *The International Journal of Sociology of Law*, no. 13, February 1985, pp. 256–78, and Women in Iran in *Third World Quarterly*, vol. 2, no 2, April 1985, pp. 256–78, amongst others.
5. Article 10.
6. See Chapter 4.

7.  Article 91.
8.  Article 93.
9.  Articles 91 and 92.
10. See Mottahari; this volume Chapter 4.
11. Parliamentary proceedings reported in *Kayhan*, 28 May 1981.
12. Khomeini quoted by *Kayhan*, 28 May 1981.
13. Khomeini quoted in *Kayhan*, 28 May 1981.
14. *Kayhan*, 28 May 1981.
15. See Chapter 5.
16. See Chapters 1 and 3.
17. Article 24.
18. Article 26.
19. For detailed discussions see Chapter 5 and Abrahamaian, E., *Radical Islam*, p. 220.
20. For a detailed analysis see Vali, A. and Zubaida S. 'Factionalism and political discourse'.
21. Ibid, p. 159. Also see Chapters 1 and 3 in this volume.
22. Quoted by Vali and Zubaida, 'Factionalism and Political Discourse', p. 161.
23. The transient nature of this was referred to by Rafsanjani as an excuse for denying women the right of free participation in war and all other public domains that the wives of the Prophet had. See Chapter 9.
24. *Kayhan*, 26 October 1983.
25. Montazeri, interviewed by *Kayhan*, 15 November 1983.
26. *Kayhan*, 23 October 1983.
27. *Kayhan*, 4 August 1984.
28. *Kayhan*, 29 October 1983.
29. *Kayhan*, 4 August 1984.
30. The turn-out for the election was poor, but the electorate were sufficiently discriminating to deprive the hanging judge, Ayatollah Khalkhali, from gaining a seat at the Assembly. A year later when in the mid-term elections, Khalkhali was elected to the *Majlis*, as the representative of the holy city of Qom, a number of deputies, including Ahmad Kashani, questioned the validity of his credentials. It was only after a humiliating public exchange on the floor of the house and a subsequent review by Commission that the hanging judge managed to secure his seat.
31. Article 108.
32. Article 107.
33. See Chapter 6.
34. *Kayhan*, 9 November 1983
35. *Kayhan*, 15 November 1983.
36. Reported by *The Economist*, 15 January 1983.
37. *Kayhan*, 18 December 1982.
38. *Kayhan*, 18 December 1982.
39. See Chapter 6.
40. This is the literal translation of the interview. *Pasdar*, 25 May 1987.
41. *Pasdar*, 25 May 1987.
42. *Kayhan*, 20 April 1989.
43. See discussion about nationalisation of trade, Chapter 3.
44. *Kayhan*, 23 January 1988.
45. *Kayhan*, 31 May 1987.
46. *Kayhan*, 3 May 1987.
47. *Kayhan*, 1 June 1987.
48. *Kayhan*, 30 May 1987.
49. It was of course relevant that many religious leaders were owners or custodians of substantial rural properties. Khomeini had shown a similarly firm opposition to land reforms when he attacked the white revolution; see Chapter 2.

50. For detailed discussion see Mojtahed, A. and Esfahani, H.S. 'Agricultural Policies and Performance in Iran: The Post-Revolutionary Experience' in *World Development*, vol. 17, no. 6, pp. 840–59.
51. *Kayhan*, 28 January 1988.
52. *Kayhan*, 31 May 1987.
53. See Chapter 3.
54. See Chapter 3.
55. Abrahamian, *Radical Islam*, p. 72.
56. For detailed discussion see Afshar, H., 'The Iranian Theocracy' in Afshar, H. (ed.) *Iran: A Revolution in Turmoil.*
57. For further details see Chapter 1.
58. *Kayhan*, 9 July 1987.
59. *Kayhan*, 6 February 1988.
60. *Kayhan*, 23 February 1988.
61. *Kayhan*, 6 February 1988.
62. See Chapter 3.
63. For detailed discussion see Afchar, H 'The Muslim Concept of Law'.
64. See Chapter 1.
65. Reported in *Kayhan*, 31 May 1987.
66. *Kayhan*, 25 January 1988.
67. *Kayhan*, 11 January 1988.
68. *Kayhan*, 23 January 1988.
69. *Kayhan*, 23 January 1988.
70. Mohsen Armin, quoted by *Kayhan*, 17 January 1988.
71. *Kayhan*, 11 January 1988.
72. For detailed discussion see Chapter 1.
73. *Kayhan*, 14 January 1988.
74. *Kayhan*, 14 January 1988.
75. *Kayhan*, 24 January 1988.
76. Reported in *Kayhan*, 6 February 1988.
77. *Kayhan*, 23 January 1988.
78. *Kayhan*, 25 January 1988.
79. See Chapter 3.
80. See Chapter 1 for detailed discussion of the hierarchy in the *Shia* religious institutions.
81. See Chapter 6.
82. The letter was published in *Kayhan*, 9 April 1989.
83. See Chapter 4.
84. Article 107.
85. See Chapter 5.
86. Abrahamian, *Radical Islam*, p. 49.
87. A future Speaker of the *Majlis*, in 1991.
88. The daily paper, *Kayhan*, ran a series of articles based on Khomeini's *fatwas* to explain this point, 20–25 April 1989.
89. Article 113.
90. Article 57, 60, 64, 69, 70, 87, 88, 89 and 124, 126, 127, 130, 131.
91. Article 133, 135, 136.
92. Article 141.
93. Article 91.
94. Article 109.
95. Article 111.
96. *Kayhan*, 20 April 1989.
97. *Kayhan*, 20 April 1989.
98. *Kayhan*, 20 April 1989.

99.  Mousavi Khoyiniha speaking to *Kayhan*, 20 April 1989.
100. Article 91.
101. Interview in *Kayhan*, 20 April 1989.
102. For detailed discussions see Afchar, H., 'The Muslim concept of law'.
103. *Kayhan*, 20 April 1989.
104. *Kayhan*, 22 June 1989.
105. Article 157.
106. Article 160.
107. Article 162.
108. Article 99.
109. Article 112.

## Chapter 8

1.  For detailed discussion see Chapter 10 and p. 167.
2.  See Chapter 5.
3.  See Chapter 3.
4.  Eqbal, Alameh, *Az Didegaheh Zendeh Yadeh Dr Ali Shariati* (In Living Memory of Dr Shariati) *Kayhan*, 24 July 1991.
5.  Speech on 4 June 1979.
6.  For detailed discussion see Chapter 2.
7.  For detailed discussion see Chapter 3.
8.  For detailed discussion see Chapter 2.
9.  Khomeini, speaking on 6 June 1979.
10. Khomeini, speaking on 9 September 1979.
11. Khomeini, speaking on 24 August 1979.
12. Khomeini, speaking on 24 August 1979.
13. Khomeini, speaking on 9 September 1979.
14. For detailed discussion see Sabbah, F. *Women in the Muslim Unconscious*; Afshar, H., 'Women, State and Ideology in Iran', *Third World Quarterly*, vol. 7, no. 2, April 1985, pp. 256–78, and Chapter 9 in this volume.
15. Khomeini's last will and testament.
16. Khomeini, speaking on 24 August 1979.
17. For detailed discussion see Chapter 5.
18. Zia Katouzian, L., 'Education in Iran', Royal Institution Conference Proceeding, pp. 28–30.
19. For detailed discussion see Chapter 9.
20. *Kayhan*, 14 August 1990.
21. *Kayhan*, 19 September 1992.
22. See, for example, several reports in the daily papers, including *Kayhan*, 8 August 1985.
23. *Kayhan*, 16 October 1989.
24. *Kayhan*, 23 September 1989.
25. *Kayhan*, 7 September 1991.
26. *Zaneh Rouz*, 29 April 1989.
27. *Kayhan*, 27 September 1989.
28. Dr Najafi, Minister of Education, interviewed by *Kayhan*, 23 August 1990.
29. *Zaneh Rouz*, 29 April 1989.
30. *Zaneh Rouz*, 29 April 1989.
31. Mohamad Ali Najafi, Minister of Education, interviewed by *Kayhan*, 14, 21 and 23 August 1990.
32. *Kayhan*, 6 February 1990.
33. *Kayhan*, 19 September 1992.

34.  *Kayhan*, 19 September 1992.
35.  *Kayhan*, 24 January 1993.
36   *Kayhan*, 24 January 1993.
37.  *Kayhan*, 13 September 1989.
38.  *Kayhan*, 25 August 1991.
39.  *Zaneh Rouz*, 25 January 1992.
40.  *Kayhan*, 25 December 1991.
41.  *Kayhan*, 31 December 1991.
42.  *Kayhan*, 4 September 1990.
43.  *Zanan*, August 1992.
44.  *Kayhan*, 24 January 1993.
45.  Announcement published by *Kayhan* on the celebration of the anniversary of the cultural revolution, 5 August 1987.
46.  Bakhash, S., *The Reign of the Ayatollahs*, p. 122.
47.  *Financial Times*, 23 April 1980.
48.  *Kayhan*, 18 December 1982.
49.  Zia Katouzian, L., 'Education in Iran', p. 31.
50.  *Kayhan*, 26 August 1990.
51.  *Kayhan*, 11 September 1989.
52.  *Kayhan*, 26 August 1990.
53.  *Kayhan*, 19 September 1992.
54.  Plan organisation, outline for the second development plan of the Islamic Republic quoted in *Kayhan*, 18 January 1993.
55.  *Kayhan*, 27 September 1989.
56.  *Kayhan*, 14 October 1989.
57.  *Kayhan*, 5 August 1987.
58.  *Kayhan*, 13 July 1987.
59.  *Kayhan*, 17 August 1989.
60.  Behnam Sadeghi, electrical engineering student, and Banafsheh Sadeghi medical student, letter to *Zaneh Rouz*, 31 August 1991.
61.  *Kayhan*, 18 November 1989.
62.  Based on reports in *Kayhan*, 27 March and 20 October 1989.
63.  *Zaneh Rouz*, 24 August 1992.
64.  Letter to *Kayhan*, 27 March 1989, and to *Zaneh Rouz*, 10 October 1992.
65.  *Zaneh Rouz*, 2 May 1992.
66.  Dr Mustafa Moin, Minister of Education, quoted by *Kayhan*, 31 October 1989.
67.  *Kayhan*, 25 October 1989 and 28 April 1990.
68.  *Kayhan*, 14 October 1989.
69.  *Kayhan*, 19 September 1992.
70.  *Kayhan*, 10 September 1992.
71.  *Kayhan*, 31 October 1992.
72.  *Zaneh Rouz*, 6 March 1992.
73.  *Kayhan*, 31 December 1992.
74.  Article 12.2 of the plan organisation's response to the University teachers' protests, quoted by *Kayhan*, 18 January 1993.
75.  Article 12.2 of the plan organisation's response to the University teachers protests, quoted by *Kayhan*, 18 January 1993.
76.  *Kayhan*, 31 December 1992.
77.  *Kayhan*, 31 December 1992.
78.  In the summer of 1975 the author reported for the newspaper where she worked that meat prices in Tehran supermarkets were not pegged at government prices. The censors cut the article halfway and printed the beginning which discussed the government's price policies and left out the journalist's findings!
79.  Khomeini's speech, 2 December 1978.

80. 1 March 1979.
81. Extract from Khomeini's speech on 29 May 1979.
82. Speech, 27 July 1979.
83. Speech, 29 August 1979.
84. The duties of the representative of the *imam* were published on the appointment of the new representative to *Kayhan* on 24 September 1991.
85. Extract from Khomeini's speech on 29 May 1979.
86. Khomeini, speaking on 11 February 1985.
87. Khomeini, speaking on 8 September 1979.
88. Khomeini's open letter to the Head of Broadcasting published in *Kayhan*, 29 June 1989.
89. Khomeini's will, published in Tehran (1990).
90. *Kayhan*, editorial, 27 November 1989.
91. *Kayhan*, 30 August 1986.
92. *Kayhan*, 30 August 1986.
93. *Kayhan*, 26 February 1991.
94. Seyed Rasoul Musavi, quoted in *Kayhan*, 2 October 1991.
95. Reported in *Kayhan*, 2 October 1991.
96. *Salam*, 7 March 1992.
97. *Adineh*, issue no. 59, September 1991.
98. 5 May and 19 June 1991.
99. 12 April 1991.
100. *Jamaeyeh Dini dar negaheh Hamshahri*, (The Religious Society from the Perspective of Fellow-Citizen) *Kayhan*, 13–25 April 1993.
101. *Hamshahri*, 11 April 1993.
102. 5 May 1991.
103. *Kayhan*, 15 June 1991.
104. *Kayhan*, 15 June 1991.
105. They were Abdolali Bazargani, Ali Ardalan, Mohamad Reza Movahed, Mehdi Tavassoli, Hashem Sabaqian, Abolfazl Mir Shahshaini, Habib Davaran and Akbar Zarineh.
106. The trial was reported in *Kayhan*, 23 September 1991.
107. *The Observer*, 19 July 1992.
108. *Zaneh Rouz*, 22 August 1992.
109. *Kayhan*, 31 March 1993.
110. Dr Zahra Mostafavi, Khomeini's daughter, interviewed by *Zaneh Rouz*, 30 May 1990.
111. *Zaneh Rouz*, 25 July 1992.
112. *Salam*, 9 April 1992.
113. *Kayhan* reported that 558 in every 100 000 gained access to tertiary education and only 0.38 per cent were in recognised public educational institutions, 26 August 1990.
114. Ahmad Khomeini in interviewed by *Kayhan*, 3 September 1991.

## Chapter 9

1. Rahnavard, Z., *Toloueh Zaneh Mosalman* (The Dawn of the Islamic Woman).
2. For further discussion see: Rahnavard, Zahra, Toloueh Zaneh Mosalman; Rezayi, Mahboubeh, *Horiyat va Hoquqeh Zan dar Eslam* (Status and Rights of Woman in Islam); and Afshar, H. 'Fundamentalism and its Female Apologists' in Prendergast, R. and Singer, H.W. (eds) *Development Perspectives for the 1990s*, Basingstoke: Macmillan, 1991, pp. 303–318.

3. For detailed discussion see Afshar, H. 'Sex, Marriage and the Muslims', *The Sunday Correspondent*, 18 November 1990.
4. Eqbal, Alameh, '*Az didegah zendeh yadeh Dr Ali Shariati*' (In Living Memory of Dr Ali Shariati), *Kayhan*, 17 January 1991.
5. For detailed discussion see Tabari, Azar, 'Islam and the Struggle for Emancipation of Iranian Women'; and Yeganeh, Nahid, 'Women's Struggles in the Islamic Republic of Iran' in Tabari, A. and Yeganeh, N. *In the Shadow of Islam*.
6. *Kayhan*, 14 February 1983.
7. *Kayhan*, 11 April 1982.
8. The *Guardian*, 1 July 1989.
9. Author's addition.
10. *Kayhan*, 3 February 1992.
11. Resolution of the seminar held to discuss the implication of Khomeini's demand for purification published in *Etelaat* (Tehran daily paper) and reprinted in Tabari, A. and Yeganeh, N. *In the Shadow of Islam*, pp. 194–5.
12. *Kayhan*, 21 July 1984.
13. *Salam*, 28 June 1992.
14. *Zaneh Rouz*, 14 April 1990.
15. *Zaneh Rouz*, 12 May 1990.
16. Amnesty International report quoted by the communiqué of the World Organisation of Iranian Women Solidarity, Paris, 25 July 1992.
17. *Peyvandeh Azadi*, Paris, July 1992.
18. *Kayhan*, 2 September 1991.
19. *Kayhan's* weekly paper, *Kayhan Havayi*, published for Iranians abroad has published other controversial articles, notably one by Afsaneh Najmabadi warning the Iranians against complacency about incest and violence against women.
20. See Chapter 8.
21. See, for example, Mernissi, Fatima, *Women and Islam: A Historical Theological Enquiry*.
22. Report published in the Algerian paper, *Al Vahedeh*, and translated and published in *Kayhan*, 12 June 1991.
23. *Zaneh Rouz*, 19 April 1992.
24. *Zaneh Rouz*, 26 July 1984.
25. *Zaneh Rouz*, 6 February 1988.
26. *Zaneh Rouz*, 10 February 1990.
27. *Zaneh Rouz*, 14 March 1985.
28. *Zaneh Rouz*, 26 July 1984.
29. 1986 Budget, note 10.
30. *Zaneh Rouz*, 14 January 1989.
31. For detailed discussion see Abbot, Nadia, *Aisha, the Beloved of Mohammed*.
32. *Zaneh Rouz*, 14 July 1990.
33. *Zaneh Rouz*, 25 December 1990.
34. For detailed discussion see Afshar, H. 'Ideology and Work in Iran' in Afshar, H. and Dennis, C. (eds) *Women and Adjustment in the Third World*, Basingstoke, Macmillan, 1992.
35. *Zaneh Rouz*, 25 December 1990.
36. *Zaneh Rouz*, 26 December 1991.
37. *Zaneh Rouz*, 26 August 1989.
38. *Zaneh Rouz*, 27 January 1990.
39. *Zaneh Rouz*, 27 January 1990.
40. *Zaneh Rouz*, 25 December 1990.
41. *Zaneh Rouz*, 27 January 1990.
42. *Zaneh Rouz*, 27 January 1990.

43. Statistical Centre of Iran, *Census of Population and Housing*, November 1976 and October 1986.
44. Plan Organisation official, Marzieh Sadiqi, reporting on women's employment, *Zaneh Rouz*, 16 September 1989.
45. *Zaneh Rouz*, 15 June 1991.
46. Mitra Baqerian reporting on her research on Women's Employment in Iran, *Zanan*, vol. 1, no. 1, February–March 1992.
47. Firouzeh Sharify reporting in *Zanan*, February–March 1992.
48. Note 60 of 1987 budget.
49. *Zaneh Rouz*, 5 November 1988.
50. *Zaneh Rouz*, 27 January 1990.
51. 21 October 1989.
52. *Zaneh Rouz*, 19 January 1991.
53. Rahnavard, Z. *Toloueh Zaneh Mosalman* (The Dawn of the Muslim Woman), p. 80.
54. *Zaneh Rouz*, 10 February 1990.
55. *Zaneh Rouz*, 10 February 1990.
56. *Zaneh Rouz*, 26 December 1991.
57. Ayatollah Mohadi Guilani, 'Law in Islam', series of articles published in *Zaneh Rouz*, November 1982.
58. Note 5 of the Additional Notes for Selection of Judges, quoted by *Zaneh Rouz*, January 1990.
59. Interview reported in *Zaneh Rouz*, 20 January 1990.
60. *Zaneh Rouz*, 4 November 1982.
61. Jaleh Shahriar Afshar, feminist researcher interviewed by *Zaneh Rouz*, 29 August 1992.
62. 18 August 1990.
63. *Zaneh Rouz*, 20 January 1990.
64. *Zaneh Rouz*, 18 August 1990.
65. *Zaneh Rouz*, 10 February 1990.
66. *Zaneh Rouz*, 10 February 1990.
67. For a detailed analysis see Milani, Farzaneh, *Veils and Words, the Emerging Voices of Iranian Women Writers*.
68. *Zaneh Rouz*, 30 January 1988.
69. *Zaneh Rouz*, 20 January 1991.
70. For a detailed discussion see Moghissi, Haideh, 'Factionalism and Muslim Feminism in Iran'.
71. *Kayhan*, 2 December 1991.
72. *Kayhan*, 7 January 1992.
73. *Zaneh Rouz*, 25 December 1990.
74. *Zaneh Rouz*, 25 December 1990.
75. For a detailed analysis see Mir-Hosseini, Ziba, 'Women, Marriage and the Law in post-revolutionary Iran' in Afshar H (ed.) *Women in the Middle East*, pp. 59–84.
76. *Zaneh Rouz*, 29 October 1990.
77. *Zaneh Rouz*, 31 August 1991.
78. *Zaneh Rouz*, 1 February 1992.
79. *Zaneh Rouz*, 29 August 1992.
80. *Zaneh Rouz*, 20 April 1982.
81. *Zaneh Rouz*, 2 November 1985.
82. *Zaneh Rouz*, 2 November 1985.
83. *Kayhan*, 5 October 1985.
84. *Zaneh Rouz*, 25 December 1990.
85. 1978 sample survey of child-bearing women, carried out by the Statistical Centre and reported in *Kayhan*, 26 February 1987.

86. For discussion about the impact of this growth on the education sector see Chapter 8.
87. 18 September 1991.
88. *Zaneh Rouz*, 12 May 1990.
89. *Zaneh Rouz*, 12 May 1990.
90. *Zaneh Rouz*, 3 February 1990.
91. *Zaneh Rouz*, 3 February 1990.
92. *Kayhan*, 1 August 1992.
93. *Kayhan*, 18 April 1993.
94. 9 January 1993.
95. For detailed discussions see Mir-Hosseini, Ziba 'Women, Marriage and the Law', in Afshar, H. (ed.) *Women in the Middle East*, pp. 59–84.
96. For detailed discussions see Chapter 7.

## Chapter 10

1. King, Ralph *The Iran–Iraq War: The Political Implications*, p. 26.
2. *Kayhan*, 26 February 1991.
3. Hosein Amid writing in *Kayhan*, 8 December 1990.
4. *Enteqadhayeh khodemani'* (Friendly Criticisms) *Kayhan*, 26 April 1990.
5. Engineer Turkan, Minister of Defence in support of Armed forces, '*Defa va Pohstbani Nirouhayeh Mossalah', Kayhan*, 2 February 1993.
6. *Kayhan*, 29 April 1993.
7. *Kayhan*, 14 January 1988.
8. *Kayhan*, 28 April 1993.
9. Mujtahed, Ahmad and Tabatabaii, Allameh, 'Agricultural Policy and Performance in Iran', *World Development*, vol. 17, no. 6, 1989, pp. 840–59.
10. King, Ralph, *The Iran–Iraq War*, p. 26.
11. *Enteqadhayeh khodemani'* (Friendly Criticisms) *Kayhan*, 26 April 1990.
12. *Kayhan*, 26 February 1991.
13. Hosein Amid writing to *Kayhan*, 8 December 1990.
14. *Kayhan*, 20 April 1990.
15. *Kayhan*, 14 January 1988.
16. *Kayhan*, 23 August 1990.
17. *Kayhan*, 20 December 1988.
18. *Kayhan*, 23 October 1989.
19. *Kayhan*, 31 October 1989.
20. *Kayhan*, 24 August 1991.
21. *Kayhan*, 10 April 1991.
22. 11 January 1988.
23. *Kayhan*, 27 April 1993.
24. *Kayhan*, 16 June 1985.
25. Amir Alam hospital administrator speaking to *Kayhan* reporter, 7 July 1987.
26. Dr Mohamad Yeganeh, quoted by *Kayhan*, 5 August 1984.
27. *Kayhan*, 7 July 1988.
28. *Kayhan*, 16 April 1987.
29. 26 April 1993.
30. *Kayhan*, 16 April 1987.
31. *Kayhan*, 26 June 1986.
32. *Kayhan*, 13 July 1983.
33. For detailed discussions see Ghanbari, A.R. and Mandani Pour, A. 'A review of methods of public land ownership and allocation of housing in Iran'.

34. *Majlis* Representative for Abadan, Mohamad Rashidian, speaking on 22 April 1987.
35. *Kayhan*, 19 October 1987.
36. Central Bank's Cost of Living Index, 1989.
37. *Kayhan*, 29 September 1991.
38. *Kayhan*, 1 October 1989.
39. *Majlis* Representative, Mostafa Moazenzadeh, reporting to *Majlis*, 15 August 1991.
40. *Kayhan*, 13 April 1991.
41. *Majlis* Representative, Mostafa Moazenzadeh, reporting to *Majlis*, 15 August 1991.
42. *Kayhan*, 26 June 1991.
43. *Kayhan*, 13 November 1989.
44. *Majlis* Representative, Mostafa Moazenzadeh, reporting to *Majlis*, 15 August 1991.
45. *Majlis* Representative, Mostafa Moazenzadeh, reporting to *Majlis*, 15 August 1991.
46. *Kayhan*, 11 January 1992.
47. *Kayhan*, 23 January 1993.
48. *Kayhan*, 2 January 1993.
49. *Kayhan*, 26 April 1993.
50. For detailed discussions see Chapter 8.
51. *Kayhan*, 13 August 1991.
52. *Kayhan*, 4 September 1990.
53. *Kayhan*, 30 January 1993.
54. *Kayhan*, 31 March 1993.
55. Personal communication from Middle East Economic expert, V.P.
56. *Kayhan*, 3 April 1991.
57. *Kayhan*, 22 January 1991.
58. Mara'shi, quoted by *Kayhan*, 14 August 1991.
59. Dr Qolam Hosein Khorshidi, University lecturer, interviewed by *Kayhan*, 19 January 1993.
60. *Kayhan*, 30 March 1993.
61. *Kayhan*, 2 January 1993.
62. Reza Bahonar and Elias Hazrati, members of *Majlis*'s Economic and Finance committee, interviewed by *Kayhan*, 19 January 1993.
63. Reza Bahonar reporting to the *Majlis*'s Economic and Finance committee, 19 January 1993.
64. *Kayhan*, 18 April 1993.
65. *Kayhan*, 25 April 1993.
66. *Kayhan*, 30 March 1993.
67. Elias Hazrati, 19 January 1993.
68. *Kayhan*, 5 September 1991 and 24 January 1993.
69. *Kayhan*, 2 October 1991.
70. For detailed discussions see Chapter 3.
71. *Kayhan*, 24 January 1993.
72. *Kayhan*, 17 January 1993.
73. Mohamad Baqer Nobakht, *Majlis* Deputy explaining the policy, *Kayhan*, 24 January 1993.

# Bibliography

## Books

ABBOT, NADIA, *Aisha the Beloved of Mohammed* London: Al Saqi Books 1985

ABRAHAMIAN, ERVAND, 'The Crowd in Iranian Politics, 1905–53' in Afshar, H. (ed.) *Iran a Revolution in Turmoil*, Basingstoke: Macmillan, 1985.

ABRAHAMIAN, E., 'The Ideology of the Mujahedin', seminar paper delivered at the Middle East Centre, Durham 1985.

ABRAHAMIAN, E., *Iran Between Two Revolutions*, Princeton University Press, 1982.

ABRAHAMIAN, E., 'Oriental Despotism: The Case of Qajar Iran', *International Journal of Middle East Studies* vol. 5, 1974, pp. 3–31.

ABRAHAMIAN, E., *Radical Islam, the Iranian Mujahedin*, London: Tauris, 1989.

ADAMIYAT, FEREYDUN, *Ideologiyeh Nehzateh Mashruteyeh Iran* (Ideology of the Iranian Constitutional Movement) Tehran, n.p. 1976.

ADAMIYAT, FEREYDUN and NATEQ, HOMA *Afkareh Ejtemayi va Siassi va Eqtessadi dar assareh Montasher Nashodeh Doreh Qajar* (unpublished material on economic, social and political think of the Qajar period) Tehran: Navid Publication, 1989.

AFCHAR, HASSAN, 'The Muslim Concept of Law', The *International Encyclopaedia of Comparative Law*, Tubingen: J.C.B Mohr (Paul Siebeck), 1975.

AFRASIABI, B. and DEHQAN, S., *Taleqani va Tarikh* (Taleqani and History) Tehran: Naqsheh Jahan Press, 1981.

AFSHAR, HALEH (ed.) *Iran: A Revolution in Turmoil*, Basingstoke: Macmillan, 1985.

AKHAVI, SHAHROUGH, *Religion and Politics in Contemporary Iran*, State University of New York, 1980.

AL AHMAD, JALAL, *Dar Khedmat va Khianat, Roshanfekran* (Intellectuals as Providers of Service and as Traitors) Tehran: Kharazmi Publication, 1978.

AL AHMAD, JALAL, *Qarbzadegi*, Tehran: n.p, 1962.

ALGAR, HAMID, *Religion and State in Iran 1785–1906*, University of California Press, 1969.

AMIRAHMADI, HUSHANG, *Revolution and Economic Transition, the Iranian Experience*, State University of New York Press, 1990.

ANJOMAHEN THOHIDYEH RESALAT, *Mardi as Tabareh Nour*, (A Man from the Abode of Light), Tehran: n.p. 1979.

ARJOMAND, SAID AMIR, 'Traditionalism in Twentieth-Century Iran' in Arjomand, S.A. (ed.) *From Nationalism to Revolutionary Islam*, Basingstoke: Macmillan/ St Antony's Series, 1984.

AZIMI, FAKHREDIN, *Iran: The Crisis of Democracy 1941–1953*, London: Tauris, 1989.

BADAMCHIAN and BANA'I, *Hey'ateh Mootelefeyeh Eslami*, Tehran: Entesharateh Owj. 1362

BAKKER, ISABELLA (ed.) *Engendering Macro Economic Policy Reform in the Americas and Beyond*, forthcoming.

BAKHASH, SHAOUL, *Iran: Monarchy, Bureaucracy and Reform under the Qajars: 1858–1896*, The Middle East Centre St Antony's College Oxford; Ithaca Press, 1978.

BAKHASH, SHAOUL, *The Reign of the Ayatollahs, Iran and the Islamic Revolution*, London: Tauris, 1985.

BAKHASH, SHAOUL, 'Sermons, Revolutionary Pamphleteering and Mobilisation: Iran 1978' in Arjomand, S.A. (ed.) *From Nationalism to Revolutionary Islam*, Basingstoke: Macmillan/St Antony's Series, 1984.

BALFOUR, J.M., *Recent Happenings in Persia*, London: 16IJJ 1922.

BANANI, AMIN, *The Modernisation of Iran, 1921–41*, Stanford, University Press, 1961.

BANI SADRE, ABOL HASSAN, *Bayaniyeh Jomhourieh Eslami* (Manifesto of the Islamic Republic) Paris, n.p., n.d.

BANI SADRE, ABOL HASSAN, *Eqtessadeh Tohidi* (Unified Economy) Paris: n.p., 1974.

BANI SADRE, ABOL HASSAN, *Rabeteh Beyneh Madiyat va Maanaviyat* (Materialism and Spiritualism) published by the Palestinian Support Committee, October 1977.

BANI SADRE, ABOL HASSAN, *L'Espérance Trahie*, Paris: Papyrus, 1982.

BAZARGAN, MEHDI, '*Marz mianeh mazhab va omoureh ejtamayi*' (Boundary between Religion and Social Affairs) in *Mazhab dar Ourupa* (Religion in Europe) Tehran: n.p., 1965.

BAZARGAN, MEHDI, '*Mosalmaneh ejtemayi va jahani*' in *Masjed dar Ejtema va Mosalmaneh Ejtemayi va Jahani* (The Mosque in Society and Muslim in Society and the World Context) Nasser Khosro: Al Fath Publication, n.d.

BAZARGAN MEHDI, *Moshkelat va Massaleh Ovalin Saleh Enqelab* (Difficulties and Problems of the First Year of the Revolution) Tehran: Iran Freedom Movement, 1982.

BILL, JAMES A.Q. and LOUIS, W. ROGER (eds) *Musaddiq, Iranian Nationalism, and Oil*, London: Tauris, 1988.

CHUBIN, SHAHRAM, 'Iran and the War: From Stalemate to Ceasefire' in Karsh, E. (ed.) *The Iran–Iraq War; Impacts and Implications*, Basingstoke: Macmillan, 1989.

CHUBIN, SHAHRAM and TRIPP, CHARLES, *Iran and Iraq at War*, London: Tauris, 1988.

COLE, R. and KEDDIE, N. (eds) *Shiism and Social Protests*, Yale University Press, 1986.

DE GOBINEAU, *Les Religions et les Philosophies dans l'Asie Centrale*, Paris: n.p., 1866.

EHTESHAMI, ANOUSHIRAVAN, 'Iran's Domestic Arms Industry', paper presented at the conference on the Iranian revolution convened by the Royal Institute of International Affairs, the Middle East Institute, Washington, DC, and School of Advanced International Studies, John Hopkins University at Chatham House, London, January 1989.

ELIASH, JOSEPH, 'The *ithna ashari-shi'i* Justice Theory of Political and Legal Authority', *Studia Islamica*, 1969, vol. xxix pp. 2–30.

ELIASH, JOSEPH, 'Some Misconceptions Concerning Shi'i Political Theory', *International Journal Of Middle East Studies*, vol. ix, no, 1, February 1979 pp. 9–25.

ENAYAT, HAMID, *Modern Islamic Political Thought*, Basingstoke: Macmillan, 1982.

FANON, FRANTZ, *Les damnés de la terre*, Paris: François Maspero, 1961, translated into English and published under the title *The Wretched of the Earth* by Penguin, Harmondsworth, 1967.

FATHI, ASGHAR, 'Preachers as Substitutes for Mass Media: The Case of Iran' in Kedourie E. and Hain, S.G., *Towards a Modern Iran*, London: Frank Cass, 1980.

FISCHER, M.M.J, *Iran from Religious Dispute to Revolution*, Harvard University Press, 1980.

GHANBARI, A.R. and MANDANI POUR, A. 'A Review of Methods of Public Land Ownership and Allocation of Housing in Iran', *Planning outlook*, vol. 31, issue no. 2, pp. 110–16.

GITTINGS, JOHN (ed.) *Beyond the Gulf War: The Middle East and the New World Order*, CIIR, 1991.

HAERI, SHAHLA, 'Women Law and Social Change in Iran' in Smith, J.I. (ed). *Women in Contemporary Muslim Societies*, London: Associated University Press, 1980, pp. 209–35.

HAERI, SHAHLA, *Law of Desire, Temporary Marriage in Iran*, London: Tauris, 1989.

HAIRI, ABDUL-HADI, *Shiism and Constitutionalism in Iran*, Leiden: E.J. Brill, 1977.

HALLIDAY, F., *Iran: Dictatorship and Development*, Harmondsworth, Penguin, 1979.

HICKMAN, W.F., *Ravaged and Reborn: The Iranian Army 1982*, Washington, DC: Brooking Institution, 1982.

IRFANI, SUROOSH, *Revolutionary Islam in Iran*, London: Zed, 1983.

KAMRAVA, MEHRAN, *Revolution in Iran, the Roots of Turmoil*, London: Routledge, 1990.

KARSH, EFRAIM (ed.) *The Iran–Iraq War: Impacts and Implications*, Basingstoke: Macmillan, 1989.

KASRAVI, AHMAD, *Shiagari*, Noor publication, n.p, n.d.

KASRAVI, AHMAD, *Tarikheh Mashroutiateh Iran* (A History of the Iranian Constitution) Tehran n.p. 1951.

KATOUZIAN, HOMA, *The Political Economy of Modern Iran, 1926–1979*, Basingstoke: Macmillan, 1981.

KATOUZIAN, HOMA, 'Shiism and Islamic Economics, Sadr and Bani Sadr' in Keddie, N.R. (ed.) *Religion and Politics in Iran, Shiism from Quietism to Revolution*, Yale University Press 1983.

KEDDIE, NIKKI R., 'The Origins of the Religious–Radical Alliance in Iran', *Past and Present*, no. 34, July 1966, pp. 70–80

KEDDIE, NIKKI R., *Religion and Rebellion in Iran: The Tobacco Protest of 1891–92*, London: Frank Cass, 1966.

KEDDIE NIKKI R. (ed.) *Scholars, Saints and Sufis: Muslim Religious Institutions in the Middle East since 1500*, University of California Press, 1972.

KEDDIE, NIKKI R., *Religion and Politics in Iran: Shiism from Quietism to Revolution*, Yale University Press, 1983.

KEDDIE, NIKKI R., *Roots of Revolution*, Yale University Press, 1981.

KHOMEINI, AYATOLLAH ROUHOLLAH, *Hokumateh Eslami* (Islamic Government), Bozorg Bookshop, 1981.

KHOMEINI, AYATOLLAH ROUHOLLAH, *Kashf al Assar* (Secrets Revealed) Tehran: n.p. 1944.

KHOMEINI, AYATOLLAH ROUHOLLAH, *Toziholmassael* (explanation of problems) Hozeyeh Elmieyeh Qom, n.d.

KHOMEINI, IMAM, *Islam and Revolution*, translated and annotated by Algar, H., Berkeley: Mizan Press, 1981

KING, RALPH, *The Iran Iraq War: The Political Implications*, London: International Institute of Strategic Studies, paper 219, Spring 1987.

LAMBTON A.K.S., 'A reconsideration of the Position of the *marja' al-taqlid* and the Religious Institution', *Studia Islamica*, vol. xx, 1960, pp. 115–35.

LAMBTON A.K.S., 'Persia: The Breakdown of Society' in Holt *et al. The Cambridge History of Islam*, Cambridge University Press, 1970, vol. 1, pp. 430–67.

LAMBTON A.K.S., 'Quis custodiet custodes?' *Studia Islamica*, vol. 5, 1956.

LAMBTON A.K.S., 'Secret Societies and the Persian revolution', London: *St. Antony's Papers*, 1958, vol. iv, pp. 43–60.

LAMBTON A.K.S., 'The Persian *ulema* and Constitutional Reform', ed. by Fahad, Tawfiq, *Le Shi'isme Imamite*, Colloque de Strasbourg, 6–9 Mai 1969, Paris: 1970.

MADUDI S. ABUL AL'A, *First Principles of the Islamic State*, Lahore: Islamic Publications, 1960.

MADUDI S. ABUL AL'A, *Political Theory of Islam*, Lahore: Islamic Publications, Pakistan 1960.

MALIK-ZADEH, MEHDI, *Tarikheh Enqelabeh Mashrutiateh Iran* (History of the Iranian Constitutional Revolution) 7 volumes, Tehran: n.p. 1949.

MALKUM KHAN, 'Persian Civilisation', *Contemporary Review*, February 1981.

MANSOURI, ROSHANAK, 'Chehreyeh zan dar jarayedeh mashrutiat' (Women as Represented by the Constitutional Publications) *Nimeyeh Digar* 1, year 1 (Spring 1984).

MANSUR, ABUL KASIM, 'The Crisis in Iran: Why the US Ignored a Quarter Century of Warning', *Armed Forces Journal International*, January 1979.

MARTIN, VANESSA, *Islam and Modernism: The Iranian Revolution of 1906* London: Tauris, 1989.

MENARSHI, DAVID, 'Iran, Doctrine and Reality', in Karsh, E. (ed.) *The Iran–Iraq War: Impacts and Implications*, Basingstoke: Macmillan, 1989.

MERNISSI, FATIMA, *Women and Islam: A Historical Theological Enquiry*, Oxford: Blackwell, 1991.

MILANI, FARZANEH, *Veils and Words: The Emerging Voices of Iranian Women Writers*, London: Tauris, 1992.

MIRFAKHRANI, E., *Sardare Jangal*, Tehran: Javedan Publication, 1978.

MIR-HOSSEINI ZIBA, 'Divorce in Islamic Law and Practice: The Case of Iran', *Cambridge Anthropology*, vol. 11, no 1, pp. 41–69.

MIR-HOSSEINI, ZIBA, 'Women, Marriage, and the Law in Post-Revolutionary Iran', in Afshar, H. (ed.) *Women in the Middle East*, Basingstoke: Macmillan, 1993, pp. 59–84.

MOGHADAM, VAL, 'Women, Work and Ideology in the Islamic Republic', *International Journal of Middle East Studies*, vol. 20, May 1988, pp. 221–42.

MOGHISSI, HAIDEH, 'Factionalism and Muslim Feminism in Iran' in Rahnama, S. (ed.) *Contemporary Iran*, London: Tauris, forthcoming.

MUJAHEDIN, *Chegouneh Qoran Biamouzim*, vol. 1, Long Beach, California: Muslim Student Association Press, 1980.

MUJAHEDIN, Rezayi, Mehdi, *Zendeganinameh va Defayiateh Mehdi Rezayi*, (Life Story and Defence Speech of Mehdi Rezayi), n.d., n.p.

MOJTAHED, A and ESFAHANI, H.S., 'Agricultural Policy and Performance in Iran: The Post-Revolutionary Experience' in *World Development*, vol. 17, no. 6, 1989, pp. 840–59.

MORTIMER, EDWARD, *Faith and Power: The Politics of Islam*, London: Faber & Faber, 1982.

MOSTAWFI, ABDOL, *Shahreh Zendeganiyeh Man* (The Story of My Life) Tehran: Sadar Bookshop,1964, 2nd edn, vol. iii.

MOTTAHARI, AYATOLLAH MORTEZA, *Barresiyeh Ejmali'i as Nehzateh Eslami dar Sad Saleh Akhir* (A Short Survey of Islamic Movements in the Past Century) Qom: Sadre Publication, 1978.

MOTTAHARI, AYATOLLAH MORTEZA, *Jahan Biniyeh Tohidi* (The Unified World View) 2 volumes, Qom: Sadre Publication, n.d.

MOTTAHARI, AYATOLLAH MORTEZA, *Marx va Marxism* (Marx and Marxism) 3 volumes, n.d., n.p.

MOTTAHARI, AYATOLLAH MORTEZA, '*Moshkeleh assasi dar sazemaneh rohaniat*', in *Bahsi dar Bareyeh Marjaiyat va Rohaniat*, Tehran: 1962.

NATEQ, HOMA, 'Rohaniyat va azadihayeh democratic' (The Clergy and Democratic Freedoms) *Jahan*, 13 April 1982.

O'BALLANCE, EDGAR, *The Gulf War*, London: Brassey's Defence Publications, 1988.

PESARAN M.H., 'Economic Development and Revolutionary Upheavals in Iran', in Afshar H. (ed.) *Iran: A Revolution in Turmoil*, Basingstoke: Macmillan, 1985.

POYA, M. 'Murder, Corruption, Crisis', *Socialist Review*, November 1982.

QIBLA, MUFTI JAFAR HOSAIN SAHIB, *Nahj ul-Balagha*, Karachi: n.p., 1972.

RAHNAVARD, ZAHRA, *Toloueheh Zaneh Mosalman* (The Dawn of the Muslim Woman) Tehran: Mahboubeh Publication, n.d.

RAHNEMA, ALI and NOMANI, FARHAD, *The Secular Miracle: Religion, Politics and Economic Policy in Iran*, London: Zed Books, 1990.

RAHNEMA, ALI and NOMANI, FARHAD, 'Competing Shi'i Subsystems in Contemporary Iran', in Rahnema, Saeed (ed.) *Contemporary Iran*, London: Tauris, forthcoming.

RAHNEMA, SAEED (ed.) *Contemporary Iran*, London: Tauris, forthcoming.

REZAYI, MAHBOUBEH, *Horiyat va Hoquqeh Zan dar Eslam* (Status and Rights of Woman in Islam) Milad Publication, 3rd reprint 1979 (Sharivar, 1358).

SABBAH, FETNA, *Women in the Muslim Unconscious*, Oxford: Pergamon Press, 1983.

SADRE, MUSA, *Eqtesad dar Maktabeh Eslam* (Islamic School of Economics) translated from Arabic by Kermani, Hojat, Tehran Entesharat Press 1971.

SADRE, MOHAMAD BAQER, *Eqtesadeh Ma* (Our Economics) vol. 1, translated from Arabic by Musavi, Mohamad Kazem; vol. 2 translated from Arabic by Espahbodi, Abdol Ali, Tehran: Borhan Press 1987.

SAFAVI, NAVAB, *Hokumateh Eslami* (Islamic Government) reprinted, Tehran: n.p., 1992.

SALAMATIAN, A., *Historique du Rôle Politique de l'Armée en Iran*, thesis, Paris University, 1970.

SANGELAGI, HOJATOLESLAM MUHAMMAD, *Qaza' dar Islam*, Tehran: n.p., 1338 (1959–60).

SHARIATI, ALI, *Bazgasht beh Khishtan* (Return to Self) Hoseinieyeh Ershad, n.d.

SHARIATI, ALI, *Masuliateh Shia Budan* (The Responsibilities of Being a Shiia) Ketabkhaneh Melli, 1352, 1974.

SHARIATI, ALI, *Tashiiyeh Alavi va Tashiiyeh Safavi* (Alavi and Safavid Forms of Shiism) Hoseinieyeh Ershad Publication, n.d.

SOUDAGAR, MUHAMMAD, *Nezameh Arbab Rayitai dar Iran* (The Landlord and Peasant System in Iran) Tehran: Moassesseyeh Tahqiqateh Eqtessadi va Ejtamayi Pazand, 1359.

STORK, JOE, *Middle East Oil and the Energy Crisis*, Monthly Review Press, 1975.

SULLIVAN, WILLIAM H. *Mission to Iran*, New York: W.M. Norton & Co, 1981.

TABARI, AZAR, 'The Role of Clergy in Modern Iranian politics', in Keddie (ed.) *Religion and Politics in Iran*, New Haven: Yale University Press, 1983.

TABARI, AZAR, 'Islam and the Struggle for Emancipation of Iranian Women', in Tabari, A. and Yeganeh, N. (compilers) *In the Shadow of Islam*.

TABARI, AZAR, 'Hazards of Modernity and Morality: Women, State and Ideology in Contemporary Iran', in Kandiyoti, Denize (ed.) *Women, Islam and the State*, Basingstoke: Macmillan, 1991.

TADARI, A. and YEGANEH, N. (compilers) *In the Shadow of Islam: The Women's Movement in Islam*, London: Zed, 1982.

TAHERI, ALI, *Eqtesadeh Eslami*, Mashad: Khorasan Press, 1974.

TALEQANI, AYATOLLAH MAHMUD, *Malekiat dar Islam* in *Goftareh Mah*, 1, 1961.

*US Military Sales to Iran Staff Report*, Washington: US Government Printing Office, 1976.

VALI, ABBAS and ZUBAIDA, SAMI, 'Factionalism: A Political Discourse in the Islamic Republic of Iran: The Case of the *Hujjatieyeh* Society', *Economy and Science*, vol. 14, no. 2, May 1985, pp. 139–173.

YEGANEH, NAHID, 'Women's Struggles in the Islamic Republic of Iran', in Tabari, A. and Yeganeh, N. (compilers) *In the Shadow of Islam: The Women's Movement in Iran*, London: Zed, 1982.

YEK IRANI, *Iran Dar Chahar Raheh Sarnevesht* (Iran at the Cross-roads of Destiny) selection of articles from the Pardis weekly, Tehran: n.p., 1980.

ZABIH, SEPEHRE, *The Iranian Military in Revolution and War*, London: Routledge, 1988.

ZIA KATOUZIAN, LILA, 'Education in Iran since the 1979 Revolution', Proceedings of the conference on The Iranian Revolution Ten years Later, Royal Institution of International Affairs, Chatham House, London 1989, pp. 27–34.

ZONIS, MARVIN, *The Political Elite of Iran*, Princeton University Press, 1971.

ZUBAIDA, S., 'The Ideological Conditions for Khomeini's doctrine of Government', *Economy and Society*, vol. 11, no. 2, 1982.

## Newspapers and Periodicals

*Adineh*
*Al Vahedeh*
*Ayandegan*
*Azadegan*
*Bamdad*
*Etelaat*
*Enqelabeh Eslami*
*Farad*
*Gardoun*
*Goftareh Mah*
*Hamshahri*
*Jahan*
*Kar*
*Kayhan*
*Kayhaneh Havayi*
*Le Monde*
*Mizan*
*Mujahed*
*Nimeyeh Digar*
*Panjerah*

*Pardis*
*Pasdar*
*Payvandeh Azadi*
*Salam*
*Zaneh Irani*
*Zaneh Rouz*
*Zanan*
*Kayhan International*
*Socialist Review*
*The Economist*
*The Financial Times*
*The Guardian*
*The Guardian Weekly*
*The Iran Times*
*The Middle East Economic Digest*
*The Observer*
*The Sunday Times*
*The Sunday Correspondent*
*The Times*
*The Washington Post*

# Glossary

| | |
|---|---|
| *alem* | religious leader, singular of *ulema* |
| *alyhasalam* | may peace be upon him |
| *aql* | the use of interpretive reason |
| *anjoman* | political society |
| *ashura* | a day of religious mourning |
| *ayatollah* | sign of God, title accorded to leading clergy |
| *ayatollah ozma* | greatest sign of God; title accorded to the highest ranking of clergy |
| *azadi* | freedom |
| | |
| *Baha'i* | a religious group |
| *barandazi* | overthrow |
| *basij* | small-scale neighbourhood defence units, militia |
| *bast* | sanctuary; a symbol of the function fulfilled by the *ulema* mediating between the state and the people. It enabled those who were persecuted by the illegitimate tyranny of the state to take refuge |
| *bazaar* | The traditional financial and trade centre in Iran |
| *beytolmal* | public wealth |
| | |
| *chador* | full veil |
| *caliph* | Muslim chief civil and religious ruler |
| | |
| *dasteh* | public mourning demonstrations by flagellants |
| *dayeh* | blood-money payable by murderer to family of the victim |
| | |
| *ebadat* | devotion |
| *edaltkhaneh* | house of justice |
| *ejtehad* | the teaching of religious leader, *mujtahed* |
| *eideh fetre* | the feast day marking the end of a month of fasting, *Ramazan* |
| *ejazeh* | formal signed permission granted by an ayatollah to indicate that a pupil is fully trained and permitted to embark on *ejtehad* |
| *emam Jomeh* | the Friday *imam*, the city's public prayer leader |
| *estebdadeh rohani* | despotism of the clergy |
| | |
| *faqih* | learned religious leader |
| *fatwa* | a decree issued by a religious leader which has to be obeyed by the *Shia* believers |
| *foqaha* | religious jurisconsults |
| *fru'* | the specific provisions of religious law |
| *feqh* | Islamic law |
| | |
| *hejab* | veil |
| *heyateh gozinesh* | appointment committees set up to purge civil service |
| *hezbolah* | the party of God; hence *hezbolahi*, member of party of God |

249

| | |
|---|---|
| *hojat el eslam* | proof of Islam; title accorded to middle-ranking clergy |
| *id'a* | innovation |
| *imam* | male descendants of Ali who became saintly religious leaders; also used as a title by Khomeini and Friday prayer leaders, hence *imam jomeh*, i.e. Friday prayer leader |
| *ijma* | consensus (of Islamic community) |
| *jahel* | ignorant |
| *jaheliat* | ignorance |
| *jam'* | public |
| *javanmardi* | manly valour |
| *jehad* | holy war |
| *kargar* | worker; bearer of labour |
| *karpazir* | capable of accepting work |
| *khaneyeh kar* | the employment houses, workers' centres |
| *khavarej* | early followers of Ali (Mohamad's son-in-law and successor) who deserted him |
| *khoms* | one-fifth of the yearly income, surplus to expenditure, paid to the *mujtahed* as religious dues. |
| *khoshneshinan* | landless rural workers |
| *kola sharii* | religious cover |
| *komiteh* | committee |
| *la mazhab* | irreligious |
| *lutis* | the *ulema*'s private armies; devout followers who benefited from the alms that the *ulema* could disburse, or exchanged their strong arms for the religious establishment's protection in times of need |
| *maddaress* | seminaries, plural of *maddresseh* |
| *maddresseh* | singular of *maddaress*; higher institute of religious learning, usually found in centres such as Qom, Isfahan or Najaf |
| *Majales* | Parliaments, plural of *Majlis* |
| *Majlis* | Parliament |
| *maktab* | Islamic school |
| *maktabi* | basic Islamic style of teaching |
| *manbar* | pulpit |
| *marajeh* | plural of *marja* |
| *marja 'taqlid* | highest-ranking religious leader; source of emulation |
| *maslehat* | personal or public interest |
| *ma'soum* | protected from sin |
| *ma'soumiat* | freedom from sin |
| *mazhabeh tohidi* | monotheistic religion |
| *Moharam* | a month of religious mourning |
| *mohre* | a prayer stone |
| *moqaled* | imitator |
| *mostaazafin* | the dispossessed |

| | |
|---|---|
| *mujahedin* | Islamic fundamentalist freedom fighter |
| *mulla* | a derogatory term meaning uneducated religious preacher |
| *mullayen* | plural of *mulla* |
| *nahadhayeh enqelabi* | revolutionary organisations |
| *nahi as monker* | demanding people to avoid wrong doing, an obligatory duty of all Muslims |
| *naql* | transmission of knowledge |
| *nezame tohidi* | classless society; literally, a united order |
| *oqaf* | plural of *vaqf,* religious endowment |
| *ojrat* | rent |
| *paksazi* | cleaning up programme, purging the civil service of un-Islamic elements |
| *qarbzadegi* | "Westoxification"; poisoning or intoxication with Western ideas |
| *qassas* | Islamic laws of retribution |
| *Quran* | Koran |
| *rahayi* | liberty |
| *rohaniat* | clergy |
| *rozeh* | religious recitals, mourning the dead martyrs of Karbala |
| *rozeh khani* | reciting tales to mourn the martyrs of Karbala |
| *sazemanhayeh khodkhoroushideh* | self-propelling organisations, derogatory name given to the revolutionary organisations |
| *sazemane oqaf* | the endowment organisation |
| *seyed* | descendants of the prophet of Islam |
| *shar, sharia* | religious law(s); the correct Islamic path for Muslims to follow |
| *Shia* | the Muslim sect which recognises Mohamat's son-in-law Ali as his successor |
| *Shiagari* | the Shia tendency |
| *shivan* | moans and wailing (in mourning ceremonies) |
| *shora* | workers' committees formed in factories and work places soon after the revolution |
| *Sunna* | the customs and practices of the Prophet |
| *sepaheh din* | religion corps |
| *taazieh* | passion play, acted during the ceremonies for mourning the dead martyrs of Karbala |
| *takiyeh* | religious hall |
| *talabeh* | student of religion, (singular of *tolab*) |
| *taqlid* | following the example set by *marja' eh taqlid* |
| *tarheh labik* | unity project |
| *taqut* | an absolute and arbitrary holder of the reins of power |
| *tarheh golak* | money-box project |
| *tohidi* | united monotheistic |

| | |
|---|---|
| *tolab* | students of religious leader |
| *tuman* | unit of currency |
| *tuyuldar* | fief-holder; entitled to collect taxes in a given area, or entitled to the revenue from a post or crown lands |
| | |
| *ulema* | religious leaders |
| *umma, ummat* | society of Muslim people |
| *urf* | common law, normally dealt with by the state |
| *usul* | principles of religious law |
| *usuli* | a Shia school which gained importance in the nineteenth century |
| | |
| *vaqf* | singular of *oqaf*, private and religious endowments |
| *valayat* | the supervisorship of the *ulema* |
| *Valayateh faqih* | Government by religious leader |
| | |
| *zakat* | alms, religious dues (one quarter of surplus material goods) |
| *zolm* | injustice (which must not be tolerated by Muslims) |

# Index

253